ORATIONS

ABRAHAM LINCOLN

Orations—Volume fifteen

ORATIONS

FROM HOMER TO
WILLIAM McKINLEY

EDITED BY

MAYO W. HAZELTINE, A.M.

ILLUSTRATED
IN TWENTY-FIVE VOLUMES
VOL. XV

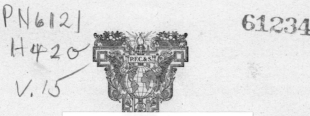

NEW YORK
P. F. COLLIER AND SON
MCMII

CONTENTS

VOLUME FIFTEEN

ORATIONS

FIELD

DAVID DUDLEY FIELD, one of the greatest lawyers that America has produced, was the son of the Rev. D. D. Field, a Congregational clergyman of Stockbridge, Massachusetts, and was born at Haddam, Connecticut, February 13, 1805. He was educated at Williams College, and after studying law and being admitted to the bar in 1828, began the practice of his profession in New York city, where he soon gained for himself a foremost place in the legal ranks. He early took an interest in the subject of law reform, and being appointed in 1847 one of a commission to reform legal practice in New York State, at once began the preparation of a civil and a criminal code of procedure. The civil code, when completed, was adopted in the main not only by his own State, but by nearly thirty other States, and it now forms the basis of practice in several English colonies. In 1857 he was placed at the head of a commission to codify the whole law of his State, and in 1865 this commission reported civil, penal, and political codes, which were almost wholly the work of Field, and these five codes of his cover the entire practice of common and statute law in the United States. At the meeting of the British Association in Manchester, England, in 1866, Field brought forth a proposition to frame an international code. Six years later, in 1873, he published " Outlines of an International Code," which has been widely circulated and has been translated into French and Italian. In 1877 Field was a representative in Congress, and in 1890 he presided over a peace convention in London. His death occurred in New York city April 13, 1894. His writings include " What Shall be Done with the Practice of the Courts " (1847); " The Electoral Votes of New York " (1870); " Speeches, Arguments, and Miscellaneous Papers " (1890).

AN INTERNATIONAL CODE OF ARBITRATION

AN ADDRESS BEFORE THE BRITISH SOCIAL SCIENCE ASSOCIATION, AT MANCHESTER, OCTOBER 5, 1866

MR. PRESIDENT AND GENTLEMEN,—Standing for the first time before the members of this association I must begin by making my acknowledgments for the honor which you conferred upon me some years ago by electing me a corresponding member. Though I have not been able to take part in your meetings I have felt scarcely less interest in them than if I were present and even take to myself a share of the self-congratulation which the actual participators must have felt. If I have not contributed to your transactions I have been a humble sharer in the fame which the contributions of others have won.

The distinction which your association has earned is, however, the least of its honors. The good which it has done in stimulating inquiry, concentrating opinion and combining efforts toward the improvement of the law and the education and health of the people would be a sufficient reward for all your labors even if no distinction had been obtained.

The scope of your labors is not confined to your own country; it extends to every part of Christendom. So intimate is now the connection between all Christian nations that the social progress of one is sure to be felt more or less in the others. More especially is this true of your country and mine. We are bound together by so many ties that, forgetting for the present all things else, I will only think of the good we may do each other and the spirit of kindliness we may both promote.

The particular subject to which I am to bespeak your attention is international law. In discoursing of it my purpose will be to answer, so far as I may be able, these questions: 1. What is that which is called international law? 2. Who made it? 3. Who enforce it? 4. Are any changes in it desirable? 5. If so, how can they be effected?

Law is a rule of property and of conduct prescribed by sovereign power. In strictness, therefore, there is no such thing as a human law binding the nations, since they have no human superior. They may however, as they have in part done, agree among themselves upon certain rules, both of property and of conduct, by which they will pledge themselves to regulate their own conduct toward each other and the conduct of their citizens respectively. These rules form what is called sometimes international law and sometimes the law of nations.

Neither expression is precisely accurate. There is a body, of rules more or less distinctly stated by which nations profess to comport themselves in their relations with each other; but they are not laws nor are they imposed upon nations nor yet are they international. They are laws only in each state so far as they are promulgated by the sovereign power of that state and they serve international purposes.

Take for example a treaty concluded between the United States and Great Britain; when ratified and promulgated by the treaty-making power in the two nations it becomes a rule for both by virtue of their compact, and a rule in each nation for its own citizens by virtue of the promulgation by its own sovereign authority.

For want however of a better designation and adopting the suggestion of Bentham, publicists and statesmen now generally refer to this body of rules as international law. If the word law is to be retained I should have thought the expression public law or the public law of the world a better one.

Who made these rules, or this international law if you so call it, is explained by the definition which I have given. It was made by the nations themselves either through express compact with each other or through general practice; that is to say by treaty or by usage. Publicists I know, looking beyond the rules so made or sanctioned, have sought, in those moral precepts by which nations not less than individuals ought to be governed in their intercourse with each other, for guides in other circumstances; and statesmen and diplomatists have often fortified their arguments by reference to such opinions and it has thus frequently happened that those precepts have been gradually adopted into the usage of nations.

These views of the publicists are however to be regarded rather as suggestions of what ought to be the conduct of nations in particular circumstances than as a statement of established rules. They are entitled to the same weight in the decision of a national dispute as a treatise on natural law is entitled to in the decision of a case by the courts of America or England.

Some writers are in the habit of treating the law of nations as if it were something above the nations and having an authority superior to their will. In our late civil war, for example, it became the practice of certain persons to speak of the law of nations as a guide or warrant for the Executive in the conduct of the war, beyond the constitution, and paramount to acts of Congress. This, I apprehend, was a mistaken view. The law of nations is only such because each individual nation adopts it, and so far only as it is thus adopted. It is legally, I do not say morally, or without just complaint from other nations, competent for any nation to reject the whole or any part of it as far as its own citizens are concerned. The Parliament of England might enact, if it would, that no English court should decide and no English subject act in a particular manner, even though that manner were enjoined by the law of nations as understood by the whole body of Christendom.

Who enforce the rules thus made or sanctioned and known as international law? The nations themselves, first by applying them as occasion requires to litigants in the national tribunals; and, secondly, by punishing the nation which infringes them in such manner as nations may punish each other; that is to say, by non-intercourse, or by force.

The controversies respecting captures by land or sea and the questions concerning the responsibility of individuals for the violation of private rights are of course determined by the courts, and where the municipal law is silent international usage is the rule of decision.   When a question arises between nations it is debated and arranged between themselves, or submitted to arbiters, or decided by force.

The next question will lead us into a large discussion.   Are any changes desirable in these rules of international obligation?   The slightest acquaintance with the disputes which have arisen and do so constantly arise between nations will convince us that the rules themselves are full of uncertainty and in many respects defective.   If we make for ourselves an examination, even incomplete, of the subjects which fall within the scope of international law we perceive at once how many of them are uncertain or require revision.   Within it are embraced all the rules which should govern the relations of states with each other in peace and in war.   All of them spring from the intercourse of nations.

If a people shut themselves up from others, as the Chinese attempted to do, building a wall between themselves and their neighbors, there can be no international law as there can be no international relations.   That condition, however, is unnatural and irrational.

Man is a social being and his nature impels him to intercourse with all the family of man.   Whether this intercourse is demandable as a right, and if so when and by whom and upon what conditions and how it should be carried on, are the first questions which present themselves.   From intercourse as from a source spring the rights and duties of those who carry it on, making it necessary to determine how far they who pass from one country to another retain their own nationality and to what extent they subject themselves to the jurisdiction of the country which they enter.   Hence arise the questions respecting the right of foreigners to liberty of religion, residence, and trade; their obligations to civil or military service; the liability of their property to taxation or other imposition, and its devolution when they die.

Traffic brings with it contracts. These are to be expounded and enforced in different nations and between the citizens of all. Thence comes that department of jurisprudence which, under the general title of the conflict of laws has engaged so many minds and led to such profound investigations.

The intercourse of nations is public or private. The former is carried on by embassies, legations, and consulates. Here is required a large body of rules declaring the rights and duties of public ministers and consuls, with their attendants, their reception, residence, functions, and immunities.

When private persons pass from one country to another they go either for transient purposes or for permanent residence. In the latter case there arise two opposite claims; on one hand that of expatriation and on the other that of perpetual allegiance. Fugitives from one country into another have certain privileges; hence the practice of extradition, as modified by that right of asylum which, older than Christianity, has been exalted by its spirit and precepts and which it is the honorable boast of your country and mine never to have violated or rejected.

The instruments of intercourse by sea; ships and those who navigate them; and they who pass and repass with them, and that which they carry; the control of them on the ocean and in port—all these are to be regulated by that body of rules of which I am speaking. Next are those rights of property which, acquired in one country, should be recognized and respected in another; the title to personal chattels and the title, quite as good, in my opinion, to the products of the mind; inventions for which patents are commonly issued; and writings, for which the law of copyright provides, or should provide, a sanction and a guarantee. Then there are the subjects of weights, measures, money, and postal service, which fall within the scope of international regulation. Passing from direct intercourse between nations to their rights, exclusive or concurrent, to things outside of themselves, we come to the subjects of the free navigation of the ocean, the fisheries, the discovery and colonization of islands and continents, and the right of one nation to an outlet for itself through the close seas or rivers of another.

After these various topics regarding the relations of nations in a state of peace we come to those of a state of hostility. Force or constraint is applied in three ways—one by non-intercourse, another by reprisal, and a third by war. I will speak only of the relations in war. First, in respect to intestine or civil war: when and how far may other nations interfere, and when may interference go so far as to recognize a new nation out of the fragments of a broken one, and what is the effect of the separation upon the citizen of the different parts of the divided nation and upon the citizen of other states.

Then in respect to foreign war, when it is justifiable, what must be done to avoid it, and what formalities must precede it. And when it comes what must be the conduct first of the belligerents and then of neutral nations; and in respect to the former who may attack, who and what may be attacked, and in what manner may the attacks be made. Those questions being answered embrace the whole subject of belligerent rights. But into what an infinitude of subdivisions do these topics divide themselves; explaining to what extent it may be truly said that upon the breaking out of a war all the citizens of one belligerent state become the enemies of all the citizens of the other; what may be done by one side to the citizens and property of the other, including the seizure and confiscation of debts or other property; how the persons and property of the enemy found in a country in the beginning of a war may be treated; whether private citizens, without commission from the government, may assail the enemy; whether it be lawful to take or destroy private property on land or sea; whether all kinds of public property may be taken or destroyed; how public buildings and monuments of art are to be treated; what is the effect of war upon pending contracts; and what future traffic may be carried on between the citizens of the belligerent nations.

Then, when we proceed to consider the conduct of armies toward each other, what are the rules of honorable warfare, what stratagems are allowable, the proper treatment of prisoners, the disposition of spies, the flag of truce, the armistice, and the exchange of prisoners of war—all these are subjects of international regulation.

Turning from belligerents to neutrals we come to consider what are the rights and what the obligations of the latter; what are the conditions of a true neutrality; what is a just blockade, and the effect of it; what things are contraband of war; and to what extent a belligerent may be supplied from neutral territory. When a state departs from its neutrality and becomes an ally, the rights which then attach to her and arise against her form another department of the rules which determine the relations and the rights of states.

This rapid and imperfect enumeration of the principal subjects embraced within the scope of international law will suggest to those who are conversant with them the uncertainty which hangs about many of them and the need of numerous amendments. Let us refer to some by way of example.

Take the case of recapture at sea. America has one rule, England has another, while France, Spain, Portugal, Holland, Denmark, and Sweden have each a rule different from either and different from each other. It was in reference to such a case that Sir William Scott, the great admiralty judge, whose judgments command respect for their ability, even when they do not win assent to their conclusions, was obliged thus to speak:

" When I say the true rule I mean only the rule to which civilized nations according to just principles ought to adhere, for the moment you admit, as admitted it must be, that the practice of nations is various, you admit that there is no rule operating with the proper force and authority of a general law."

Take the question respecting the effect of a declaration of war upon the persons and property of an enemy found in the country at the time. How important that it should be settled beforehand by a uniform rule! And yet the practice of nations is various, more various even than the nations themselves; for in the same nation the practice has varied with the interest or caprice of rulers.

You had a controversy with the Great Frederick about the confiscation of the Silesian loan. The seizure of French ships in your ports, upon the rupture of the Peace of Amiens, and the detention by Napoleon of English subjects found in France, produced an immense amount of suffering, which might have been in great part avoided by the establishment beforehand of a proper rule. What articles are contraband of war ought to be settled and everywhere known. But you do not agree with us respecting them; you do not agree with most of the continental nations.

There must, however, be some rule founded upon just principles to which intelligent and impartial publicists and statesmen would give their assent, could they but approach the subject in a time of peace undisturbed by passions and enmities.

The vexed questions respecting the right of neutrals to send goods by the ships of a belligerent, or to carry the goods of a belligerent in their own neutral ships—questions illustrated by the formulas, "free ships, free goods," and "enemies' ships, enemies' goods"—are matters in which the trade of the whole civilized world is interested, and yet how unsettled! The obligations of a true neutrality, what are they? Do they permit the supply to a belligerent of ships and munitions of war? Do they require a neutral to prevent the fitting out and sailing of ships? Do they require a neutral to disarm and arrest bands of professed travellers or emigrants who are seeking to pass the border, with the real intent of making a hostile incursion?

Take the case of the "Alabama," to which I refer for no other purpose than illustration. Here is an instance where the people of my country think that you are responsible for all the damage done by that vessel. Your own people, I am told, are of a contrary opinion. Ought such a question to be in doubt; or, rather, ought there to be any such question at all? The security of property and the peace of nations require that there should be none such hereafter. Then there are grave questions respecting the doctrines of expatriation and allegiance, which have given rise to some misunderstanding already and which may give rise to greater misunderstanding hereafter.

It is time that the conflicting claims of ancient monarchies on the one hand and of young republics on the other were, if possible, reconciled.   You have in the list of topics for discussion on this occasion that of the extradition of criminals as affected by the right of asylum.   This is a subject which requires you to assert the right of society to protect itself against crime and the right of humanity to an asylum from oppression.   You have also in the list the subject of copyright.   This is a question properly to be left to international regulation.   We need a uniform rule binding upon all Christian countries and affecting not only the subject of copyright, but that of patents for inventions, money, weights, and measures.

I might continue this list to a much greater length.   There is the question of the right of search, which has already given rise to angry disputes not yet quite settled; there is the question of the right of nations inhabiting the upper banks of rivers or the shores of inland seas to an outlet to the ocean; both of them greatly needing a just and ready settlement.

What might not be done for the prevention or mitigation of the greatest scourge of the human race, war?   First, by way of prevention.   Let us suppose that the governments of England and America were to commission their wisest men to confer together and discuss a treaty for the express purpose of preventing war between them.   Can there be a doubt that if these representatives should come together, animated solely by a love of justice and peace, they would agree upon a series of mutual stipulations which, without compromising the dignity or independence of either country, would make it extremely difficult to fall into open war without putting one party or the other so completely in the wrong as to subject it to dishonor?

Whatever those stipulations might be, whether providing for an arbitration before an appeal to arms or for some other means of adjustment, the same stipulations which would be inserted in a treaty between our two countries could be inserted also in treaties between them and others. Is it too much to hope that by this means the time may come when it would be held impious for a nation to rush into war without first resorting to remonstrance, negotiation, and offer of mediation?

Supposing, however, war to become inevitable and two nations at last engaging in actual hostilities, how much may be done in favor of humanity and civilization by adding to the rules which the usages of nations have established for mitigating the ferocity and distress of war!

Could not private war and war upon private property be forever abolished? Could not more be done in the same direction as that taken by the late conference at Geneva, which produced such excellent effect during the last contest in Germany in exempting surgeons and nurses from capture? Could not the sack of a captured city or the bombardment of a defenceless town be forever prohibited? Might not such transactions as the storming of Magdeburg and San Sebastian and the bombardment of Valparaiso be made violations of the laws of war? Could there not be a great improvement upon the rules which provide for the proper treatment and exchange of prisoners? What indeed might not be effected if an earnest effort were made to lessen to the utmost its evils before the passions become aroused by the actual conflict of arms? Discarding at once the theory that it is lawful to do everything which may harass your enemy, with a view of making the war as short as possible—a theory worthy only of savages and carried out to its logical conclusion leading to indiscriminate fire and slaughter, even of women and children—the aim should be, while not diminishing the efficiency of armies against each other, to ward off their blows as much as possible from all others than the actual combatants.

How can these changes so desirable in themselves be effected? I answer, by the adoption of an international code. Every consideration which serves to show the practicability and expediency of reducing to a code the laws of a single nation applies with equal force to a code of those international rules which govern the intercourse of nations. And there are many grave considerations in addition. The only substitute for a code of national law—an imperfect substitute, as I think it—is judiciary or judge-made law. This is tolerable, as we know from having endured it so long, where there is but one body of magistrates having authority to make it.

But when the judges of each nation, having no common source of power and not acting in concert, make the laws they will inevitably fall into different paths and establish different rules. And when they do there is no common legislature to reconcile their discrepancies or rectify their rules. Indeed, if there is ever to be a uniform system of international regulations made known beforehand for the guidance of men it must be by a means of an international code.

How can such a code be made and adopted? Two methods present themselves as possible: one a conference of diplomatists to negotiate and sign a series of treaties forming the titles and chapters of a code; the other the preparation by a committee of publicists of a code which shall embody the matured judgment of the best thinkers and most accomplished jurists, and then procuring the sanction of the different nations. The latter method appears to me the more feasible.

The difficulties in the way will arise, not in the labor of

preparation but in procuring the assent; yet, great as are these difficulties, and I do not underrate them, I believe they would be found not insurmountable, and that the obstacles and delays which the rivalries of parties and the jealousies of nations might interpose would finally give way before the matured judgment of reflecting and impartial men.

The importance of the work is so great, and the benefits that will result from it in promoting beneficial intercourse, protecting individual rights, settling disputes, and lessening the chances of war are so manifest, that when once a uniform system of rules desirable in themselves is reduced to form and spread before the eye it will commend itself to favor and the governments, which after all are but the agents of the public will, must at last give it their sanction.

Let us suppose this association to make the beginning. There is no agency more appropriate and no time more fitting. You might appoint at first a committee of the association to prepare the outlines of such a code to be submitted at the next annual meeting. At that time subject this outline to a careful examination, invite afterwards a conference of committees from other bodies—from the French Institute, the professors of universities, the most renowned publicists— to revise and perfect that which had been thus prepared. The work would then be as perfect as the ablest jurists and scholars of our time could make it. Thus prepared and recommended it would of itself command respect and would inevitably win its way. It would carry with it all the authority which the names of those concerned in its formation could give. It would stand above the treatise of any single publicist; nay, above all the treatises of all the publicists that have ever written.

Is it a vain thing to suppose that such a work would finally win the assent one by one of those nations which now stand in the front rank of the world, and which of course are more than others under the influence of intelligent and educated men? The times are favorable; more favorable indeed than any which have occurred since the beginning of the Christian era. Intercourse has increased beyond all precedent and the tendency of intercourse is to produce assimilation. When they who were separated come to see each other more and know each other better they compare conditions and opinions; each takes from each and differences gradually lessen.

Thus it has happened in respect to the arts and in respect to laws, manners, and language. In a rude state of society when men are divided into many tribes each tribe has a language of its own; but as time melts them into one a common language takes the place of the many. Your own island furnishes a familiar example of the influence of intercourse in blending together different elements and forming a united whole.

This tendency to assimilation was never before so strong as it is now, and it will be found a great help toward forming a uniform international code. The tendency toward a unity of races is another element of immense importance. Germany will hereafter act as a unit. Italy will do likewise. In America no man will hereafter dream of one public law for northern and another for southern States. Even the asperity which always follows a rupture between a colony and the mother country will give way before the influence of race, language, and manners, so far as to allow a large conformity of disposition and purpose, however impossible may be a reunion of governments. The relations between America and England are or were till lately softening under this influence; and if Spain is ever governed by wiser counsels she will make friends of her ancient colonies instead of continuing to treat them as enemies, and will confer on them benefits rather than wage war against them.

Would it not be a signal honor for this association, rich in illustrious names and distinguished for its beneficent acts, to take the initiative in so noble an undertaking? Would it not be a crowning glory for your country to take it up and carry it on? Wearing the honors of a thousand years, and standing at the head of the civilization of Europe, England would add still more to her renown, and establish a new title to the respect of future ages, if she would perform this crowning act of beneficence.

The young Republic of the West, standing at the head of the civilization of America, vigorous in her youth and far-reaching in her desires, would walk side by side with you and exert herself in equal measures for so grand a consummation. She has been studying during all her existence how to keep great States at peace and make them work for a common object, while she leaves to them all necessary independence for their own peculiar government.

She does this it is true by means of a federated system which she finds best for herself, and which she has cemented by thousands of millions in treasure and hundreds of thousands in precious lives. How far this system may be carried is yet unknown. It may not be possible to extend it to distinct nationalities or to heterogeneous races.

But there is another bond less strict yet capable of binding all nations and all races. This is a uniform system of rules for the guidance of nations and their citizens in their intercourse with each other, framed by the concurring wisdom of each and adopted by the free consent of all. Such an international code, the public law of Christendom, will prove a gentle but all-constraining bond of nations, self-imposed, and binding them together to abstain from war except in the last extremity, and in peace to help each other, making the weak strong and the strong just, encouraging the intellectual culture, the moral growth, and the industrious pursuits of each, and promoting in all that which is the true end of government, the freedom and happiness of the individual man.

MARTINEAU

JAMES MARTINEAU, a distinguished English theologian and philosopher, of Huguenot descent, was born at Norwich, Norfolk, April 21, 1805. He was educated at the grammar school in the cathedral close and at Manchester New College (then at York), and in pursuance of early formed desires studied for the ministry, and in 1828 was ordained junior pastor of Eustace Street Presbyterian (more properly Unitarian) Church in Dublin. In 1832 he was called to Paradise Chapel in Liverpool, where he soon became known as the most brilliant Unitarian preacher in England, remaining there nearly twenty-five years. In 1840 he was appointed professor of mental and moral philosophy at Manchester New College, a post which he retained until 1885. While his congregation were building a new chapel in Hope Street, Liverpool, 1848-49, Martineau spent some fifteen months in Germany, in which period he gave himself up to the most careful examination and study of the German philosophy of that day, the result of which was what he described as "a new intellectual birth." In 1859 he was called to the pastorate of Little Portland Street Chapel in London, remaining its minister until 1870. During this latter period the chapel was visited by English and American statesmen and men of letters, attracted thither by his lofty eloquence and his wide range of thought. As old age came on, the sphere of his influence continually widened until he came to be recognized as the foremost theologian and philosopher in Great Britain. On his eighty-third birthday he was presented with an address signed by nearly seven hundred men, representing the foremost thinkers and men of letters of Europe and America, testifying to their appreciation of his work. He continued his labors up to the very close of his life, writing and studying as industriously after he had entered his ninth decade as he had done for the seventy years preceding. He died in London January 11, 1900. In figure he was tall and spare, and even in his latest years exhibited few signs of physical infirmity. His principal writings include "The Rationale of Religious Inquiry" (1836); "Endeavors After the Christian Life" (1843-47); "Miscellanies" (1852); "Studies of Christianity" (1858); "Essays—Theological and Philosophical" (1866-68); "Religion and Modern Materialism" (1874); "Hours of Thought" (1876); "A Study of Spinoza" (1882); "Types of Ethical Theory" (1885); "The Study of Religion, Its Sources and Contents" (1888), by some critics considered his greatest work; "The Seal of Authority in Religion" (1890); "Essays, Reviews, and Addresses" (1890-91); "Faith the Beginning, Self-Surrender the Fulfilment of the Spiritual Life" (1897).

SERMON: THE GOD OF REVELATION HIS OWN INTERPRETER

DELIVERED AT HOPE STREET CHURCH, LIVERPOOL, JUNE 15, 1851

" But we have this treasure in earthen vessels, that the excellency of the power may be of God, and not of us."—2 Corinthians iv, 7.

THE old adage, " Man proposes, but God disposes," receives its proper illustration, not from individual life, but from the long courses of history. If men do but limit their aims to that which is proportioned to their power and opportunity, their " proposals " will receive little contradiction from God's "disposal;" and the expectation of success, however qualified by the quiet sense of dependence, is little less than a faith in the divine constancy. We can perhaps conceive of a world, where every one should form his plans so wisely and so modestly as to encounter no disappointment, and where the all-ruling hand should endorse all his drafts upon the morrow.

But even in such a world it would soon become apparent that the human will, though always acting and never failing, was not the only power. If not against it yet without it and beyond it, ends would be accomplished which it never contemplated; which take it altogether by surprise; which eclipse all its personal intentions; and before which it stands and says, " This is no thought of mine."

The first party of painted savages that raised a few huts upon the Thames did not dream of the London they were creating, or know that in lighting the fire on their hearth they were kindling one of the great foci of time. When the Athenians refused earth and water to the Persian king, they were intent only on repelling the insolence of foreign ambition and did not foresee that they were opening for the genius of their nation a channel of perpetual influence that should ever widen as the ages advance. The Puritans who could not tolerate a surplice or bend their necks to bow at the bidding of a rubric or a priest, spent their zeal upon the merits of a gesture or a form; and were little aware that they were educating a national character and creating a practical liberty which should be the pride and hope of two worlds. All the grand agencies which the progress of mankind evolves are formed in the same unconscious way. They are the aggregate results of countless single wills, each of which, thinking merely of its own end and perhaps fully gaining it, is at the same time enlisted by Providence in the secret service of the world.

Thus it is that out of separate acts, directed, it may be, on something quite distinct, politics, literature, religions, arise; the very influences which acquire in the end an ascendency over all individual life and become the school of nations. Nothing is more startling than to see, as we compare the biography of persons with these great powers of history, how the latter absorb and appropriate the former; how private purpose often drops into insignificance and vanishes in higher ends that use it up; how gigantic schemes of action, making perhaps the turmoil and the torture of an age, die away like thunder on the summer air; while a silent thought or aimless deed emerges from obscurity and speaks with royal voice through many a century.

To lose sight of this principle in estimating Christianity, and to insist on judging it not by its matured character in Christendom, not by the unconscious spirit of its founders, but by their personal views and purposes, is to overlook the divine in it in order to fasten on the human; to seek the winged creature of the air in the throbbing chrysalis; and is like judging the place of the Hebrews in history by the court and the proverbs of Solomon, or the value of Puritanism by the sermon of a hill-preacher before the civil war. The primitive Christianity was certainly different from that of other ages; but there is no reason for believing that it was better. The representation often made of the early church as having only truth, and feeling only love, and living in simple sanctity, is contradicted by every page of the Christian records. The Epistles are entirely occupied in driving back guilt and passion or in correcting errors of belief; nor is it always possible to approve of the temper in which they perform the one task, or to assent to the methods by which they attempt the other. Principles and affections were, indeed, secreted in the heart of the first disciples which were to have a great future and to become the highest truth of the world.

But it was precisely of these that they rarely thought at all. The apostles themselves speak slightingly of them as baby's food; and the great faith in God, the need of repentant purity of heart, with the trust in immortality, the very doctrines which we should name as the permanent essence of Christian faith, are expressly declared by them to be the childish rudiments of belief, on which the attention of the grown Christian will disdain to dwell. And what did they prefer to these sublime truths as the nutriment of their life and the pride of their wisdom? Allegories about Isaac and Ishmael, parallels between Christ and Melchisedec, new readings of history and prophecy to suit the events in Palestine, and a constant outlook for the end of all things.

These were the grand topics on which their minds eagerly

worked and on which they labored to construct a consistent theory. These give the form to their doctrine, the matter to their spirit. These are what you will get if you go indiscriminately to their writings for a creed; and these are no more Christianity than the pretensions of Hildebrand or the visions of Swedenborg.

The true religion lies elsewhere, just in the things that were ever present with them but never esteemed. Just as your friend may spend his anxiety on his station, his usefulness, his appearance and repute, and fear lest he should show nothing deserving your regard, while all the time you love him for the pure graces, the native wild flowers of his heart— so do the choicest servants of God ever think one thing of themselves, while they are dear to him and revered by us for quite another. "The weak things" in the church not less than in " the world, hath he chosen to confound the mighty; the simple, to strike dumb the wise; and things that are not, to supersede the things that are."

The life of Christ in Palestine was a brief phenomenon, justly regarded by every disciple as the point of divinest brilliancy in the course of providential affairs. At the time and when it was in recent remembrance little notice was taken of its intrinsic character and real peculiarities; its moral perfectness and spiritual beauty is handed down to us by those who perceived it very imperfectly; and had he perceived it himself the reality would have vanished in the preception. From that gracious life itself all eyes were turned away in order to join it on to the past which it finished and to the future which it began. " How did it come out of the ages which it closed? What did it augur in those which it led on?" These were the two questions with which the first disciples, with the power of his soul sleeping silently at heart, consciously and exclusively concerned themselves and neither of these, as time has shown, were they able to answer right. They connected him with the past by regarding him as the foretold of prophets and the descendant of kings—as the crowning gift for which alone the ages had prepared the way, and whose step of approach pressed its visible trace on the soil of ancient history.

Yet is it now confessed that, when he came, he was not such an one as Isaiah saw or Daniel ever dreamed; that no prediction had spoken of him, no type suggested him; and that it is only his shadow, cast by the fond light of retrospective love, that lies upon the old Hebrew centuries. They connected him with the future, by carrying forward to his account in years to come the visions which his stay, as they supposed, was too short to realize; by assigning to him a a quick return to finish what yet was unfulfilled. The suffering, the scorn, the rejection of men, the crown of thorns, were over and gone; the diadem, the clarion, the flash of glory, the troop of angels, were ready to burst upon the world, and might be looked for at midnight or at noon.

Yet, though a sentinel gazed wherever a Christian prayed, all the watchmen died without the sight; the storm swept down the horizon of time, and for many a century the sky has now been clear. The whole Messianic doctrine, by which the apostles found their master's providential place, was in its very essence the fabric of a dream; a landscape traced upon the clouds by the creative eye of faith and disappointment. To discuss whether Jesus was the Messiah is even more unmeaning than the question whether John the Baptist were Elijah; for Elijah was at least a person, but Messiah was only a conception.

It was from trying Jesus by this conception, and endeavoring to force him into its realization, that Judas was tempted to betray him. And it is by perversely applying the same test, and coercing his spirit into the Hebrew framework—by compelling him to belong to a system, instead of permitting him to be what he is in himself, that divines, with kiss of reverence scarcely less fatal, have delivered him bound, to be defaced by priests and compared with rulers. Seeking Christianity in the creed of the first age, we have necessarily fallen in with this notion, that " Jesus is the Messiah;" and have thus set up the chief Judaic error as the chief Christian verity.

Among his countrymen this conception was natural and inevitable; it was the human condition on which alone they could recognize in him what was divine: it was the only key with which their culture supplied them for interpreting the mysterious impression which he made upon their hearts: it was their ideal formula for perfect life, and when he was before them the real and the ideal presence could not but coalesce.

It must be obvious however to every thoughtful reader, how much the story and portraiture of Christ have been deformed by the tyranny of this haunting idea. It is plain that he himself dwelt little, if at all, upon his official claims; it was to be kept a secret what he was—a precaution which could never be reported of him if he had notoriously held and proclaimed himself to be the Messiah and framed his course in conformity with that conception.

The deficiency seems to have been felt by the evangelists, and it is over-compensated by their zeal. Their principle of selection, in the biographical fragments they have left, appears to have been to take what would best identify Jesus with the Messiah; and so his inward struggles of soul are turned into an official victory over Satan; demons are brought upon the stage to give preternatural witness to his dignity; miracles of blessed healing are spoiled by thoughts and arguments of exorcism; and counterfeit meanings are put on the old poets and prophets to fit the unexpected shape of new events. A Messianic goal is evidently set up in the disciples' mind, and Jesus is exhibited to us as living towards it and nearing it.

Yet beneath this artificial disguise, quite a different life gleams through; a life rather of shrinking and recoil from the very end he is set to reach; a life not upon system at all; shaping itself forth by the efflorescence of an inward beauty rather than the solicitations of an outward aim; a life of the Spirit that bloweth where it listeth, wandering with the breath of sweet affections over the verdure of good hearts, and carrying the south wind of pity to soften the fallow and bring blossoms from the clod.

That divine life without a plan, that free movement from the determination of love and thought within, that inspired soliloquy in action, is the real soul of the entire religion; and it reaches us, alas! only in refracted lights, or through unintended openings in the crust of Messianic doctrine. Observe, too, the effect of this Judaic medium upon the titles of honor which disciples apply to Christ—a matter of no small moment, for as the relation is described such will the relative affection tend to be. We are taught, with a tenacity forbidding alteration now, to call Jesus " our Lord;" and the apostles expressly call themselves his slaves. To them these words were natural; exactly describing the relation present to their minds. Their faith was as much political as religious.

As God himself was chiefly conceived of under the image

of absolute sovereignity so was Messiah to them the appointed satrap of this world. When he came, he would come to reign, bearing with him the united powers of administrator, judge, and king. And according to the Oriental type, whatever he ruled that would he possess; and all that his subjects had would be received as favors from his hand and held as fiefs by his investiture.

Under the solemn expectation of the world's immediate end the kingdom of Christ was to take the place of the kingdoms of the earth, and the disciples in looking for this revelation felt themselves citizens of a supernatural state and subjects of a resistless lord. In rude ages and amid feudal customs it has perhaps been no unhappy thing that this image of servitude has been transmitted into the conceptionsof faith; it may have touched with some sanctity an inevitable submission and mingled a sentiment of loyalty with religion.

But the external relation of serf and lord is no type of the internal relation of spirit to spirit which alone constitutes religion to us. To God himself, with all his infinitude, we are not slaves; we are not his property, but his children; he regards us not as things but as persons; he does not so much command us as appeal to us; and in our obedience it is not his bidding that we serve, but that divine law of right of which he makes us conscious as the rule of his nature only more perfectly than of ours.

To obey him as slaves in fear, and with an eye upon his power, is, with all our punctuality and anxiety, simply and entirely to disobey him; nor is anything precious in his sight except the free consent of heart with which we seize what is holy to his thought and embrace what is in harmony with his perfection.

Still less can we be slaves to Christ, who is no autocrat to us, but our freely followed leader towards God; the guide of our pilgrim troop in quest of a holy land; who gives us no law from the mandates of his will, but only interprets for us, and makes burn within us, in characters of fire, the law of our own hearts; who has no power over us, except through the affections he awakens and the aspirations he sets upon the watch.

We have emerged from the religion of law, whose only sentiment is that of obedience to sovereignty; we have passed from the religion of salvation, whose life consists in gratitude to a deliverer; and we are capable only of a religion of reverence, which bows before the authority of goodness. And in the infinite ranks of excellence, from the highest to the lowest, there are no lords and slaves; the dependence is ever that of internal charm, not of external bond; the authority represented and impersonated in another and a better soul has its living seat within our own; and in this true and elevating worship the more we are disposed of by another the more do we feel that we are our own.

This is a relation which the political terms of the expected theocracy are ill adapted to express; and if we have required many centuries to grope our way to this clearest glory of religion, to disengage it from the impure admixture of servile fear and revolting presumption; if it has taken long for us to melt away in our imagination the image of thrones and tribunals, of prize-givings and prisons, of a police and assizes of the universe; if only at the eleventh hour of our faith the cloud has passed away and shown us the true angel-ladder that springs from earth to heaven, the pure climax of souls whereon each below looks up and rises, yet each above bends down and helps, the discovery which brings such peace and freedom to the heart has been delayed by the mistaken identi-

fication of the entire creed of the first age with the essence
of Christianity.

Now that God has shown us so much more, has tried the
divine seed of the gospel on so various a soil of history, and
enabled us to distinguish its fairest blossoms and its choicest
fruits, a much larger meaning than was possible at first must
be given to the purpose of his revelation.

Even to Paul, Christ was mainly the great representative
of a theocratic idea; and was in no other sense an object of
spiritual belief than that he was not on earth and mortal, but
in heaven and immortal. That faith in Christ, which then
prominently denoted belief in his appointed return and allegiance to him as God's viceroy in this world, is now transformed into quite a different thing. It is altogether a moral
and affectionate sentiment; an acknowledgment of him as
the highest impersonation of divine excellence and inspired
insight yet given to the world; a trust in him as the only
realized type of perfection that can mediate for us between
ourselves and God; a faithfulness to him, as making us conscious of what we are and what God and our conscience
would have us to be.

It is vain to pretend that revelation is a fixed and stereotyped gift. It was born, as the divinest things must be,
among human conditions; and into it ever since human conditions have perpetually flowed. The elements of Hebrew
thought surrounded the sacred centre at first, and have been
erroneously identified with it by all Unitarian churches in
every age. The Hellenic intellect afterwards streamed towards the fresh point of life and faith, and gathered around
it the metaphysical system of Trinitarian dogma, in which
orthodox communions of all times have, with parallel error,
sought the essence of the Gospel.

The true principle of the religion has been secreted in both, and consisted in neither; it has lain unnoticed in the midst, in the silent chamber of the heart, around which the clamor of the disputatious intellect whirls without entrance. The agency of Christ's mind as the expression of God's moral nature and providence, and as the realized ideal of beauty and excellence,—this is the power of God and the wisdom of God, which has made vain the counsels of the world and baffled the foolishness of the church.

This is the Gospel's centre of stability,—" Jesus Christ, the same yesterday, to-day, and forever."

2

GARRISON

WILLIAM LLOYD GARRISON, a famous American Abolitionist, was born in Newburyport, Massachusetts, December 12, 1805, and began his career as a printer in the "Herald" office of his native town. He frequently contributed political articles to that and other journals, and in 1829 joined with Benjamin Lundy, a philanthropic Quaker, in editing at Baltimore "The Genius of Universal Emancipation." Here his bold speaking in regard to slavery resulted in his being imprisoned for libel, but after a few months his fine was paid by Mr. Tappan, a New York merchant, and Garrison was set free. On January 1, 1831, he issued at Boston the first number of "The Liberator," a paper which he continued to edit for thirty-five years, until the close of the civil war. It at once aroused great opposition, and the Georgia legislature in December of that year offered five thousand dollars to any person who should arrest and prosecute its editor or publisher according to the laws of Georgia. The New England Anti-Slavery Society was founded in January, 1832, as a direct result of "The Liberator's" influence, and in 1843 Garrison founded the American Anti-Slavery Society, and was its president until 1865. In 1832 he published "Thoughts on African Colonization," in which he affirmed the colonization scheme to be an ally of slavery. In October, 1835, the "Liberator" office was broken into by a mob and its editor was dragged through the streets with a rope about his neck. His life was saved only by his being placed in jail for temporary protection. Garrison visited England several times in the interests of the abolition movement, and received a warm welcome from the English anti-slavery leaders. He died in New York city May 24, 1879. His "Sonnets and Poems" were issued in 1843 and "Selections from Writings and Speeches" in 1852.

WORDS OF ENCOURAGEMENT TO OPPRESSED

I NEVER rise to address a colored audience without feeling ashamed of my own color; ashamed of being identified with a race of men who have done you so much injustice and who yet retain so large a portion of your brethren in servile chains. To make atonement in part for this conduct I have solemnly dedicated my health and strength and life to your service. I love to plan and to work for your social, intellectual, and spiritual advancement. My happiness is augmented with yours; in your sufferings I participate.

Henceforth I am ready, on all days, on all convenient occasions, in all suitable places, before any sect or party, at whatever peril to my person, character or interest, to plead the cause of my colored countrymen in particular, or of human rights in general. For this purpose, there is no day too holy, no place improper, no body of men too inconsiderable to address. For this purpose I ask no church to grant me authority to speak—I require no ordination—I am not careful to consult Martin Luther, or John Calvin, or His Holiness the Pope. It is a duty which, as a lover of justice, I am bound to discharge; as a lover of my fellow men I ought not to shun; as a lover of Jesus Christ, and of his equalizing, republican and benevolent precepts, I rejoice to perform.

Your condition, as a people, has long attracted my attention, secured my efforts, and awakened in my breast a flame of sympathy which neither the winds nor waves of opposition can ever extinguish. It is the lowness of your estate, in the estimation of the world, which exalts you in my eyes. It is the distance that separates you from the blessings and privileges of society which brings you so closely to my affections. It is the unmerited scorn, reproach, and persecution of your persons by those whose complexion is colored like my own which command for you my sympathy and respect. It is the fewness of your friends—the multitude of your enemies—that induces me to stand forth in your defence.

Countrymen and friends! I wish to gladden your hearts and to invigorate your hopes. Be assured your cause is going onward, right onward. The signs of the times do indeed show forth great and glorious and sudden changes in the condition of the oppressed. The whole firmament is

tremulous with an excess of light; the earth is moved out of
its place; the wave of revolution is dashing in pieces ancient
and mighty empires; the hearts of tyrants are beginning to
fail them for fear, and for looking forward to those things
which are to come upon the earth.   There is—

> " A voice on every wave,
>   A sound on every sea!
>   The watchword of the brave,
>   The anthem of the free!
>   Where'er a wind is rushing,
>   Where'er a stream is gushing,
>   The swelling sounds are heard,
>   Of man to freeman calling,
>   Of broken fetters falling—
> And, like the carol of a cageless bird,
> The bursting shout of freedom's rallying word! "

Let this be an occasion of joy.   Why should it not be so?
Is not the heaven over your heads, which has so long been
clothed in sackcloth, beginning to disclose its starry principalities and illumine your pathway?   Do you not see the
pitiless storm which has so long been pouring its rage upon
you breaking away, and a bow of promise as glorious as that
which succeeded the ancient deluge spanning the sky,—a
token that to the end of time the billows of prejudice and
oppression shall no more cover the earth to the destruction
of your race; but seedtime and harvest shall never fail, and
the laborer shall eat the fruit of his hands?   Is not your
cause developing like the spring?   Yours has been a long
and rigorous winter.   The chill of contempt, the frost of
adversity, the blast of persecution, the storm of oppression—
all have been yours.   There was no substance to be found—
no prospect to delight the eye or inspire the drooping heart—
no golden ray to dissipate the gloom.   The waves of derision
were stayed by no barrier, but made a clear breach over you.
But now—thanks be to God! that dreary winter is rapidly
hastening away.   The sun of humanity is going steadily up

from the horizon to its zenith, growing larger and brighter, and melting the frozen earth beneath its powerful rays. The genial showers of repentance are softly falling upon the barren plain; the wilderness is budding like the rose; the voice of joy succeeds the notes of woe; and hope, like the lark, is soaring upwards and warbling hymns at the gate of heaven.

And this is but the outbursting of spring. What, think you, shall be the summer and autumn?

> " Then shall the trembling mourner come,
> And bind his sheaves, and bear them home;
> The voice, long broke with sighs, shall sing,
> And heaven with hallelujahs ring! "

This is but " the twilight, the dim dawn " of day. What, then, shall be the brightness of the day itself? These are but a few drops of mercy. What shall be the full shower, the rolling tide? These are but crumbs of comfort to prevent you wholly from perishing. What shall be the bountiful table?

Why should this not be an occasion of joy instead of sorrow? Listen to those trumpet tones which come swelling on the winds of the Atlantic, and which shall bring an echo from every harp in heaven! If there is joy in that blissful abode over one sinner that repenteth, how mighty and thrilling must it be over a repentant nation! And Great Britain is that nation. Her people are humbling themselves before God, and before those whom they have so long held in bondage. Their voices are breaking in peals of thunder upon the ear of Parliament, demanding the immediate and utter overthrow of slavery in all the colonies; and in obedience to their will the mandate is about being issued by Parliament which shall sever at a blow the chains of eight hundred thousand slaves.

What heart can conceive, what pen or tongue describe, the

happiness which must flow from the consummation of this
act? That cruel lash which has torn so many tender bodies
and is dripping with innocent blood; that lash which has
driven so many human victims, like beasts, to their unre-
quited toil; that lash whose sounds are heard from the rising
of the sun to its decline, mingled with the shrieks of bleeding
sufferers; that lash is soon to be cast away, never again to
wound the flesh or degrade those who are made in the image
of God.

And those fetters of iron which have bound so many in
ignominious servitude, and wasted their bodies, and borne
them down to an untimely grave, shall be shivered in pieces,
as the lightning rends the pine, and the victims of tyranny
leap forth, " redeemed, regenerated, and disenthralled by the
irresistible genius of universal emancipation." And that
darkness, which has for so many generations shrouded the
minds of the slaves—making them like the brutes that perish
—shall give way to the light of freedom and religion. O,
how transforming the change! In contemplating it, my imagination overpowers the serenity of my soul and makes
language seem poor and despicable.

Cheers for Great Britain! cheers for her noble men and
women! cheers for the bright example which they are setting
to the world! cheers for their generous sympathy in the cause
of the oppressed in our own country!

Why should we not rejoice this evening, brethren? Find
we nothing at home to raise our drooping spirits, to invigorate
our hopes, and to engage our efforts? Have we made no
progress, either in self-improvement, or in the cause of bleeding humanity? Are there no cheering signs of the times, in
our moral sky, upon which we may fix our joyful gaze?

Look, in the first place, at the abolition-standard—more

gorgeous and spirit-stirring than the star-spangled banner—floating high in the air! Fresh is the breeze that meets it! bright are the sunny rays which adorn it! Around it thousands are gathering, with high and holy courage, to contend, not with carnal but spiritual weapons, against the powers of darkness. Oh, the loftiness of that spirit which animates them! It towers above the Alps; it pierces beyond the clouds.

Oh, the intensity of that flame of brotherly love which burns within their breasts! It never can burn out—nor can many waters extinguish it.

Oh, the stability of that faith which sustains them under all their toils and trials! It is firmer than the foundations of the earth—it is strong as the throne of God.

Oh, the generous daring of that moral principle which inspires their hearts and governs their actions! Neither reproach nor persecution, neither wealth nor power, neither bolts nor bars, neither the gibbet nor the stake, shall be able to subdue it.

Yes, my colored countrymen, these are the men—ay, and the women, too, who have espoused your cause. And they will stand by it until life be extinct. They will not fail in strength, or faith, or courage, or zeal, or action. Loud as the tempest of oppression may rage around them, above it shall their rallying cry be heard in the thunder-tone of heaven. Dark as their pathway may be, it shall blaze with the light of truth in their possession. Numberless as may be the enemies who surround them, they will not retreat from the field; for he who is mightier than legions of men and devils is the captain of their salvation and will give them the victory.

I know your advocates well—I know the spirit which actuates them. Whether they reside in the east or west or north, they have but one object—their hearts are stirred with the same pulsation; their eye is single, their motives are pure. Tell me not of the bravery and devotedness of those whose life-blood reddened the plains of Marathon, poured out in defence of liberty. Tell me not of the Spartan band, with Leonidas at their head, who defended the pass of Thermopylæ against a Persian host. I award to them the meed of animal courage; but the heroism of blood and carnage is as much below the patient endurance of wrong and the cheerful forgiveness of injury as the earth is below the sky—it is as often displayed by brute animals as by men.

With infinitely higher satisfaction, with a warmer glow of emulation, with more intense admiration, do I contemplate the Abolition phalanx in the United States who are maintaining your cause unflinchingly through evil report—for the good report is yet to come—and at the imminent peril of their lives; and, what is dearer than life, the sacrifice of their reputation.

If ever there was a cause which established the disinterestedness and integrity of its supporters yours is that cause. They who are contending for the immediate abolition of slavery, the destruction of its ally, the American Colonization Society, and the bestowal of equal rights and privileges upon the whole colored population, well knew what would be the consequences of their advocacy to themselves. They knew that slander would blacken their characters with infamy; that their pleadings would be received with ridicule and reproach; that persecution would assail them on the right hand and on the left; that the dungeon would yawn for their bodies; that the dagger of the assassin would gleam behind them; that the arm of power would be raised to crush them to the earth; that they would be branded as disturbers of the

peace, as fanatics, madmen, and incendiaries; that the heel
of friendship would be lifted against them and love be turned
into hatred and confidence into suspicion and respect into
derision; that their worldly interests would be jeoparded
and the honor and emoluments of office would be withheld
from their enjoyment.

Knowing all this, still they dare all things in order to save
their country by seeking its purification from blood. Will
the base and the servile accuse them of being actuated by a
hope of reward? Reward! It is the reward which calumny
gives to virtue—the reward which selfishness bestows upon
benevolence; but nothing of worldly applause or fame or pro-
motion. Yet they have a reward—and who will blame them
for coveting it? It is the gratitude of the suffering and the
oppressed—the approbation of a good conscience—the blessing of the Most High.

> " Tempt them with bribes, you tempt in vain;
> Try them with fire, you'll find them true."

To deter such souls from their purposes or vanquish them
in combat is as impossible as to stop the rush of the ocean
when the spirit of the storm rides upon its mountain billows.
They are hourly increasing in number and strength and going
on from conquering to conquer. Convert after convert,
press after press, pulpit after pulpit, is subdued and enlisted
on the side of justice and freedom.

A grave charge is brought against me, that I am exciting
your rage against the whites and filling your minds with
revengeful feelings. Is this true? Have not all my addresses and appeals to you had just the contrary effect upon
your minds? Have they not been calculated to make you
bear all your trials and difficulties in the spirit of Christian
resignation and to induce you to return good for evil? Where

is the calumniator who dares to affirm that you have been
turbulent and quarrelsome since I began my labors
in your behalf? Where is the man who is so ignorant as not to know or perceive that, as a people,
you are constantly improving in knowledge and virtue?
No, brethren; you will bear me a unanimous testimony that I have not implanted in your minds any malice
toward your persecutors but on the contrary forgiveness of
injuries. And I can as truly aver that in all my intercourse
with you as a people I have not seen or heard anything of a
malignant or revengeful spirit. No, yours has been eminently a spirit of resignation and faith under the most aggra-
vating circumstances.

I will notice but one other charge which the enemies of
our cause have brought against me. It is that I am unduly
exciting your hopes and holding out to your view prospects
of future happiness and respectability which can never be
realized in this country. Pitiful complaint! Because I have
planted a solitary rose, as it were, in the wilderness of suffering in which your race has so long wandered, to cheer
your drooping hearts, I am sharply reproved for giving even
this little token of good things to come—by those too who
make loud professions of friendship for you, that is if you
will go to Liberia, but who are constantly strewing in your
path briars and thorns and digging pits into which you may
stumble to rise no more. These querulous complainants
who begrudge every drop of comfort which falls upon your
thirsty lips as a miser mourns the loss of a penny seem to
forget or discard the promise of Jehovah, that " the wilderness shall bud and blossom like the rose." I have faith to
believe that this promise will ultimately be fulfilled even in
this land of republicanism and Christianity. Surely I may

be pardoned when so many are endeavoring to break down all your rising hopes and noble aspirations if I urge you not to despair, for the day of redemption will assuredly come. Nay, I may still be forgiven if I transcend the limits of probability and suffer my imagination to paint in too glowing colors the recompense which is to be yours; since, strive as I may, I can scarcely hope to equalize the heart-crushing discouragements and assaults made by your enemies.

All things considered, you have certainly done well as a body. There are many colored men whom I am proud to rank among my friends; whose native vigor of mind is remarkable; whose morals are unexceptionable; whose homes are the abode of contentment, plenty, and refinement. For my own part, when I reflect upon the peculiarities of your situation; what indignities have been heaped upon your heads; in what utter dislike you are generally held even by those who profess to be the ministers and disciples of Christ; and how difficult has been your chance to arrive at respectability and affluence, I marvel greatly, not that you are no more enlightened and virtuous, but that you are not like wild beasts of the forests. I fully coincide with the sentiment of Mr. Jefferson, that the men must be prodigies who can retain their manners and morals under such circumstances. Surely you have a right to demand an equal position among mankind.

Oh, if those whose prejudices against color are deeply rooted—if the asserters of the natural inferiority of the people of color would but even casually associate with the victims of their injustice and be candid enough to give merit its due, they could not long feel and act as they now do. Their prejudices would melt like frost-work before the blazing sun; their unbelief would vanish away, their contempt be turned into admiration, their indifference be roused to benevolent activity, and their dislike give place to friendship Keeping aloof from your society, ignorant of the progress which you are making in virtue, knowledge, and competence, and believing all the aspersions of malice which are cast upon your character, they at length persuade themselves that you are utterly worthless and nearly akin to the brute creation. Cruel men! cruel women! thus hastily and blindly to pass condemnation upon those who deserve your compassion and are worthy of your respect!

Be this your encouragement in view of our separation. Although absent from you in body I shall still be with you in spirit. I go away, not to escape from toil, but to labor more abundantly in your cause. If I may do something for your good at home I hope to do more abroad. In the meantime, I beseech you fail not, on your part, to lead quiet and orderly lives. Let there be no ground whatever for the charge which is brought against you by your enemies, that you are turbulent and rude. Let all quarrelling, all dramdrinking, all profanity, all violence, all division, be confined to the white people. Imitate them in nothing but what is clearly good and carefully shun even the appearance of evil. Let them, if they will, follow the devices and perform the drudgery of the devil; but be ye perfect, even as your heavenly Father is perfect. Conquer their aversion by moral excellence; their proud spirit by love; their evil acts by acts of goodness; their animosity by forgiveness. Keep in your hearts the fear of God and rejoice even in tribulation; for the promise is sure that all things shall work together for good to those who love his name.

As for myself, whatever may be my fate—whether I fall in the springtime of manhood by the hand of the assassin, or be immured in a Georgia cell, or be permitted to live to a ripe old age—I know that the success of your cause is not dependent upon my existence. I am but as a drop in the ocean, which if it be separated cannot be missed.

My own faith is strong—my vision clear—my consolation great. " Who art thou, O great mountain? Before Zerubbabel thou shalt become a plain; and he shall bring forth the headstone thereof with shoutings, crying, Grace, grace unto it." Let us confidently hope that the day is at hand when we shall be enabled to celebrate not merely the abolition of the slave trade by law but in fact, and the liberation of every descendant of Africa, wherever one exists in bondage under the whole heavens.

SPEECH IN LONDON

DELIVERED AT PUBLIC BREAKFAST HELD IN HIS HONOR, JUNE 29, 1867

M R. CHAIRMAN, LADIES, AND GENTLEMEN,— For this marked expression of your personal respect and appreciation of my labors in the cause of human freedom, and of your esteem and friendship for the land of my nativity, I offer you, one and all, my grateful acknowledgments. But I am so profoundly impressed by the formidable array of rank, genius, intellect, scholarship, and moral and religious worth which I see before me, that I fear I shall not be able to address you except with a fluttering pulse and a stammering tongue. For me this is indeed an anomalous position! Assuredly this is treatment with which I have not been familiar! For more than thirty years I had to look the fierce and unrelenting hostility of my countrymen in the face with few to cheer me onward. In all the South I was an outlaw and could not have gone there, though an American citizen guiltless of wrong, and though that flag [here the speaker pointed to the United States ensign] had been over my head, except at the peril of my life; nay, with the certainty of finding a bloody grave. In all the North I was looked upon with hatred and contempt. The whole nation, subjugated to the awful power of slavery, rose up in mobocratic tumult against any and every effort to liberate the millions held in bondage on its soil. And yet I demanded nothing that was not perfectly just and reasonable,—in exact accordance with the Declaration of American Independence and the Golden Rule. I was not the enemy of any man living. I cherish no personal enmities; I know nothing of them in my heart. Even whilst the Southern slaveholders were seeking my destruction, I never for a moment entertained any other feeling toward them than an earnest desire, under God, to deliver them from a deadly curse and an awful sin. It was neither a sectional nor a personal matter at all. It had exclusive reference to the eternal law of justice between man and man, and the rights of human nature itself.

Sir, I always found in America that a shower of brickbats had a remarkably tonic effect, materially strengthening to the backbone. But, sir, the shower of compliments and applause which has greeted me on this occasion would assuredly cause my heart to fail me were it not that this generous reception is only incidentally personal to myself. You, ladies and gentlemen, are here mainly to celebrate the triumph of humanity over its most brutal foes; to rejoice that universal emancipation has at last been proclaimed throughout the United States, and to express, as you have already done through the mouths of the eloquent speakers who have preceded me, sentiments of peace and of good will toward the

American Republic.   Sure I am that these sentiments will be heartily reciprocated by my countrymen.

I must here disclaim, with all sincerity of soul, any special praise for anything that I have done.   I have simply tried to maintain the integrity of my soul before God and to do my duty.   I have refused to go with the multitude to do evil.   I have endeavored to save my country from ruin.   I have sought to liberate such as were held captive in the house of bondage.   But all this I ought to have done.

And now, rejoicing here with you at the marvellous change which has taken place across the Atlantic, I am unable to express the satisfaction I feel in believing that henceforth my country will be a mighty power for good in the world.   While she held a seventh portion of her vast population in a state of chattelism it was in vain that she boasted of her democratic principles and her free institutions; ostentatiously holding her Declaration of Independence in one hand and brutally wielding her slave-driving lash in the other!   Marvellous inconsistency and unparalleled assurance!   But now, God be praised, she is free—free to advance the cause of liberty throughout the world!

Sir, this is not the first time I have been in England.   I have been here three times before on anti-slavery missions, and wherever I travelled I was always exultingly told, " Slaves cannot breathe in England! "   Now at last I am at liberty to say, and I came over with the purpose to say it, " Slaves cannot breathe in America! "   And so England and America stand side by side in the cause of negro emancipation; and side by side may they stand in all that is just and noble and good, leading the way gloriously in the world's redemption.

I came to this country for the first time in 1833 to un-

deceive Wilberforce, Clarkson, and other eminent philanthropists in regard to the real character, tendency, and object
of the American Colonization Society. I am happy to say
that I quickly succeeded in doing so. Before leaving I had
the pleasure of receiving a protest against that society as an
obstruction to the cause of freedom throughout the world, and
consequently as undeserving of British confidence and patron-
age,—signed by William Wilberforce, Thomas Fowell Buxton, Zachary Macaulay, and other illustrious philanthropists.
On arriving in London I received a polite invitation by letter
from Mr. Buxton to take breakfast with him. Presenting
myself at the appointed time, when my name was announced,
instead of coming forward promptly to take me by the hand
he scrutinized me from head to foot, and then inquired, somewhat dubiously, " Have I the pleasure of addressing Mr. Garrison, of Boston, in the United States ? " " Yes, sir," I replied, " I am he; and I am here in accordance with your invitation." Lifting up his hands he exclaimed, " Why, my
dear sir, I thought you were a black man! And I have consequently invited this company of ladies and gentlemen to be
present to welcome Mr. Garrison, the black advocate of
emancipation from the United States of America!" I have
often said, sir, that that is the only compliment I have ever
had paid to me that I care to remember or to tell of! For Mr.
Buxton had somehow or other supposed that no white American could plead for those in bondage as I had done, and therefore I must be black!

It is indeed true, sir, that I have had no other rule by which
to be guided than this. I never cared to know precisely how
many stripes were inflicted on the slaves. I never deemed it
necessary to go down into the southern States, if I could have
gone, for the purpose of taking the exact dimensions of the

slave system. I made it from the start and always my own case—thus: Did I want to be a slave? No. Did God make me to be a slave? No. But I am only a man—only one of the human race, and if not created to be a slave, then no other human being was made for that purpose. My wife and children—dearer to me than my heart's blood—were they made for the auction-block? Never! And so it was all very easily settled here (pointing to his breast). I could not help being an uncompromising Abolitionist!

Here allow me to pay a brief tribute to the American Abolitionists. Putting myself entirely out of the question, I believe that in no land, at any time, was there ever a more devoted, self-sacrificing, and uncompromising band of men and women. Nothing can be said to their credit which they do not deserve. With apostolic zeal they counted nothing dear to them for the sake of the slave and him dehumanized. But whatever has been achieved through them is all of God, to whom alone is the glory due. Thankful are we all that we have been permitted to live to see this day, for our country's sake, and for the sake of mankind. Of course we are glad that our reproach is at last taken away, for it is ever desirable, if possible, to have the good opinions of our fellow men; but if, to secure these we must sell our manhood and sully our souls, then their bad opinions of us are to be coveted instead.

Sir, my specialty in this great struggle was in first unfurling the banner of immediate and unconditional emancipation, and attempting to make a common rally under it. This I did, not in a free State, but in the city of Baltimore, in the slave-holding State of Maryland. It was not long before I was arrested, tried, condemned by a packed jury, and incarcerated in prison for my anti-slavery sentiments. This was in 1830. In 1864 I went to Baltimore for the first time since my imprisonment. I do not think that I could have gone at an earlier period except at the peril of my life, and then only because the American government was there in force, holding the rebel elements in subserviency. I was naturally curious to see the old prison again, and if possible to get into my old cell, but when I went to the spot, behold! the prison had vanished and so I was greatly disappointed. On going to Washington I mentioned to President Lincoln the disappointment I had met with. With a smiling countenance and a ready wit he replied, " So, Mr. Garrison, the difference between 1830 and 1864 appears to be this: in 1830 you could not get out and in 1864 you could not get in!" This was not only wittily said, but it truthfully indicated the wonderful revolution that had taken place in Maryland, for she had adopted the very doctrine for which she imprisoned me, and given immediate and unconditional emancipation to her eighty thousand slaves.

I commenced the publication of the " Liberator " in Boston on the 1st of January, 1831. At that time I was very little known, without allies, without means, without subscribers; yet no sooner did that little sheet make its appearance than the South was thrown into convulsions, as if it had suddenly been invaded by an army with banners! Notwithstanding the whole country was on the side of the slave power—the Church, the State, all parties, all denominations, ready to do its bidding! O the potency of truth, and the inherent weakness and conscious insecurity of great wrong! Immediately a reward of five thousand dollars was offered for my apprehension by the State of Georgia. When General Sherman was making his victorious march through that State it occurred to me, but too late, that I ought to have accompanied him and in person claimed the reward, but I remembered that had I done so I should have had to take my pay in Confederate currency and therefore it would not have paid travelling expenses. Where is Southern slavery now? Henceforth, through all coming time, advocates of justice and friends of reform be not discouraged, for you will and you must succeed if you have a righteous cause. No matter at the outset how few may be disposed to rally round the standard you have raised—if you battle unflinchingly and without compromise—if yours be a faith that cannot be shaken because it is linked to the Eternal Throne—it is only a question of time when victory shall come to reward your toils. Seemingly no system of iniquity was ever more strongly intrenched, or more sure and absolute in its sway, than that of American slavery; yet it has perished.

> " In the earthquake God has spoken:
> He has smitten with his thunder
> The iron walls asunder,
> And the gates of brass are broken."

So it has been, so it is, so it ever will be throughout the earth, in every conflict for the right.

In 1840 I came to England to attend the world's Anti-Slavery Convention in London. The American Anti-Slavery Society chose me among its delegates, some of whom were women, noble women, who were pre-eminent in their self-sacrifice and devotion to the cause of the enslaved. I may name one of them at least—Lucretia Mott. On the score of intelligence, moral worth, and philanthropic consecration, the glory of their sex, they came over with me duly accredited; but they were not allowed to sit in the convention because they were women! As they could not get in I would not consent to enter. I said, " I will not dishonor them; I will not dishonor the society which has given them the same credentials as myself by creeping into a convention from which they are excluded." Since that time a very consider-

able change has taken place in public sentiment on both sides
of the Atlantic in regard to the proper sphere of woman. I
rejoice that there is a growing interest in her cause; for, rely
upon it, whether as respects Church or State, laws or institutions, the better will these be in proportion to the extent of
brains and hearts represented, and of responsibilities imposed, duties required, and rights enjoyed without regard to
sex. I am glad to see on this platform one eminently distinguished for his intellectual powers and philosophical acute-
ness of mind [alluding to Mr. John Stuart Mill], who has
recently stood up in his place in the House of Commons, and
with masterly ability advocated the rights of woman—rights
which pertain to all the human race, the exclusive possession
of which cannot be safely entrusted to those who are for class
interests and who reject the doctrine of human equality.

One of the most gratifying incidents of my life was to
have been invited by the United States government with my
eloquent coadjutor George Thompson to accompany Major-
General Anderson and his party on board of the "Arago,"
in April, 1865, to see the star spangled banner once more unfurled on the walls of Fort Sumter. The time was when I
refused to have that banner wave over my head because it
was stained and gory with the blood of the slave. But now
as a symbol of universal emancipation I am proud of it. On
entering Charleston, a public procession over a mile long was
quickly extemporized by the freedmen, old and young, and
with a band of music we and our associates were escorted
through the principal streets of that proud but deeply abased
city, the vast throng singing—

    " John Brown's body lies moldering in the grave,
    But his soul is marching on "—

and giving cheer after cheer for Abraham Lincoln and others

of their Northern friends. On our leaving Charleston they came down *en masse* to the Battery to give us the parting hand and the heartfelt benediction. Ladies and gentlemen, I began my advocacy of the anti-slavery cause at the North in the midst of brickbats and rotten eggs. I ended it on the soil of South Carolina almost literally buried beneath the wreaths and flowers which were heaped upon me by her liberated bondmen!

I have alluded to my friend George Thompson. Let me say here that he has no small share in hastening the downfall of American slavery. He was first, as you know, mightily instrumental in this country in bringing West India slavery to an end. I happened to be here just as the Emancipation Act was passing through Parliament in 1833—an Act with the success of which Earl Russell who was I believe at that time in the cabinet, had something to do—and I said to Mr. Thompson, "Now that your anti-slavery work is here accomplished will you go to the United States and plead the cause of the millions there in bondage?" I had nothing to offer him—no money—no reward of any kind except that which ever comes from well-doing. I supposed he would meet with a good deal of opposition, but I did not invite him to martyrdom. I did not imagine that he would be subjected to such diabolical treatment as was afterwards shown to him. I only felt sure that if he could but obtain a fair hearing it would ere long be all over with slavery. I was confident that no audience would be able to withstand the power of his eloquence and the force of his arguments. But they would not hear him. Denounced as " a British emissary who had come to the United States with his pockets lined with British gold for the purpose of destroying our glorious Union," he was hunted for his life. But he never flinched and was willing to

confront danger and death in every direction until his abolition friends and associates compelled him to leave the country, after laboring for more than a year as best he could
under such circumstances, doing a mighty work in agitating
the nation from end to end; for they would not have the
garments of their infatuated countrymen stained with his
blood.   What an astonishing change he too has lived to
witness in America!   He has been received with high honors
at Washington and a regenerated people hold him in admiration and recognize in him a disinterested friend and a
noble benefactor.   He deserves to have his name honor-
ably remembered on both sides of the Atlantic to the
latest posterity.

Let me say a single word in regard to my own country.
And first, as respects the late war, I may say, as one who stood
by the side of the government on the issue raised by the Confederate States that never was there a more causeless war in
the world.   The government of the United States had never
at any time done anything in the way of injustice to the
slaveholding States; and the people of the North had never
dreamt of doing any injustice whatever to them.   On the
contrary even after secession took place such was the infatua-
tion of the North that it was willing to enter into fresh compromises for the sake of keeping the Union together; and up
to the time of the election of President Lincoln the slave
power had always ruled our country and shaped our destiny.
Even when he was chosen President he had only the House
of Representatives on his side.   The Senate and the Supreme
Court of the United States were against him, and on the
side of the South.   There was therefore no justification for
the rebellion whatever.   The American government was
wholly in the right, the South was wholly in the wrong.

How then could I doubt where I should take my position?
Yet there never was a war that came more necessarily and
unavoidably, on moral considerations. It was not because of
this thing or of the other thing specially; it was not because
of the Abolitionists simply; for if the South had not had
slavery there would have been no Abolitionists; but it was
because of this—" Ye have not proclaimed liberty, every
man to his brother, and every man to his neighbor; therefore
I proclaim a liberty to you, saith the Lord, to the sword, to the
pestilence, and to the famine;" and that is the whole story.
We had slavery and there followed rebellion and war, for
we deserved to be visited with chastisement; and I am profoundly impressed with the justice of God as meted out to
our whole country. There was always this difference between the South and the North. The South wanted slavery
and was willing to sacrifice everything in the world for it; and
while the North did not want it at all, it wanted union
and peace at any price. And so the slave power all the
while was threatening—"If you do not yield to my demands
then the Union shall be dissolved "—and the North all the
while was yielding to the threat. The North ought not to
have yielded whatever might have become of the Union.
It was a Union which at that time deserved to be broken in
pieces; for it was a covenant with death and an agreement
with hell because of its pro-slavery compromises; because it
provided for a slave representation in Congress in order to
uphold the power of the slaveholder; because it provided for
the seizure of fugitive slaves; and because it provided also
for the suppression of any insurrection on the part of the
slaves, should they think of imitating the example of those
who on Bunker Hill rose up to achieve their independence.
Thank God, that slaveholding Union has gone. The cove-

nant with death has been annulled — the agreement with
hell no longer stands; and now, instead of providing for the
suppression of slave insurrections, the catching of slaves, and
a slave representative Congress, it provides that no human
being in the United States of America shall ever be held in
bondage.

Before I sit down I desire to return my thanks to those on
this side of the Atlantic, who, in the midst of our terrible
struggle, were able to understand its nature and to give a
clear and unequivocal testimony in behalf of the right. I
may perhaps be permitted to name one or two for a noble
example. The Duke of Argyll, a peer of the realm, who, I
think, all will now confess, was, in point of clearness of vision, soundness of understanding, and accuracy of opinion
relative to the real merits of the American struggle, without
a peer. Then there is our respected and honored chairman.
We always felt greatly encouraged and strengthened when
we got hold of his telling speeches. They were exactly to
our mind. I cannot of course enumerate all who stood up
firmly in behalf of President Lincoln and his administration—a Mill, a Foster, a Stansfeld, a Hughes, a Potter, a Taylor, and a Monckton Milnes, now the Right Hon. Lord
Houghton—but, without meaning to be invidious, I offer my
thanks to those I have named. [A voice: "And Cobden."]
Yes, the lamented Cobden of course—who, if he had had been
living now, doubtless would have been here on this occasion.[1]
Then there are Professors Goldwin Smith, Cairns, Newman,
and Huxley. Amongst the newspapers, I must name the

---

[1] Mr. Cobden put his opinion on record thirty-three years ago, when he
predicted that "the indelible stain" of negro slavery would serve to teach
mankind "that no deed of guilt or oppression can be perpetrated with im-
punity, even by the most powerful," and "that early or late the invincible
cause of truth will triumph against any assault of violence or injustice."
—Cobden's Political Writings, Vol. I, p. 96.

" Daily News," the " Morning Star," the " Spectator," and the "Nonconformists." If my memory be not utterly at fault I believe the " Times " was rather inclined to bring discredit upon the American government, but only succeeded in bringing discredit upon itself. However let us hope for better times to come.

I cannot tell you with what pleasure I listened to the ingenuous speech of Earl Russell. I know there was at one time a good deal of feeling in our country in regard to some sentiments which had fallen from his lips and which seemed to me if not hostile to, at least equivocal about our position. I do not wonder that there was a good deal of misconception and misapprehension on the subject at so great a distance. It was a very mixed up question for a long time, until President Lincoln sent forth his immortal proclamation of emancipation—and then the pulse of England beat to the music of that jubilee bell. Earl Russell cannot exalt himself more than he has done this day by making a manly confession of his mistake. I am sure that he who in his place in the cabinet, agitated the question of emancipation for the West Indies never could have entertained a sentiment of hostility to the emancipation of the slaves in America. Russell and Reform—the words are synonymous—and having championed the old Reform through Parliament with great courage and fidelity, I expect to see him soon with another Reform bill furthering still more the work on behalf of the rights of men and the glory and prosperity of England.

Now, in parting, thanking you again for this marked ovation, let me say, we must not allow ourselves to be divided— England from America, America from England. By every consideration under heaven let us resolve to keep the peace. If we have old grudges let them be thrown to the winds.

Let there be peace—a true and just peace—peace by forbearance—peace by generous concession—for the sake of the cause of mankind, and that together England and America may lead the nations of the world to freedom and glory. There is your country's flag, there is mine.　　Let them be blended.

> "Then let us haste these bonds to knit,
> And in the work be handy,
> That we may blend ' God Save the Queen '
> With ' Yankee Doodle Dandy.' " [1]

[1]A verse from a song written by Mr. George Thompson.

HALE

JOHN PARKER HALE, an American statesman, was born in Rochester, New Hampshire, March 31, 1806, and was educated at Dartmouth College. After studying law and being admitted to the bar in 1830, he entered the legislature of his native State in 1832. He was United States district attorney for New Hampshire, 1834-41, and a Democratic representative in Congress 1843-45. He was nominated for re-election, but having announced that he should not vote for the annexation of Texas his name was dropped. A coalition of Whigs and Independent Democrats subsequently made him speaker of the House, and in 1847 he was chosen senator. He was an earnest opponent of slavery extension and was for that reason the presidential candidate of the Free-Soil party in 1852. Leaving the Senate in 1853, he returned to it in 1855 and was as conspicuous as formerly in his opposition to the slave power, a theme upon which he often spoke. He possessed a pleasing voice and cordial manners, and his speeches exhibited both wit and pathos. He remained in the Senate until 1865, when he received the appointment of minister to Spain. He was recalled in 1869, and died at Dover, New Hampshire, November 19, 1873.

SPEECH ON SECESSION

DELIVERED IN THE UNITED STATES SENATE, DECEMBER 5, 1860

MR. PRESIDENT,—I was very much in hopes, when the message was presented, that it would be a document which would commend itself cordially to somebody. I was not so sanguine about its pleasing myself, but I was in hopes that it would be one thing or another. I was in hopes that the President would have looked in the face the crisis in which he says the country is, and that his message would be either one thing or another. But, sir, I have read it somewhat carefully. I listened to it as it was read at the desk, and if I understand it, and I think I do, it is this: South Carolina has just cause for seceding from the Union; that is the first proposition. The second is that she has no right to secede. The third is that we have no right to prevent her from seceding. That is the President's message, substantially. He goes on to represent this as a great and powerful country, and that no State has a right to secede from it; but the power of the country, if I understand the President, consists in what Dickens makes the English constitution to be— a power to do nothing at all.

Now, sir, I think it was incumbent upon the President of the United States to point out definitely and recommend to Congress some rule of action, and to tell us what he recommended us to do. But, in my judgment, he has entirely avoided it. He has failed to look the thing in the face. He has acted like the ostrich, which hides her head and thereby thinks to escape danger.

Sir, the only way to escape danger is to look it in the face. I think the country did expect from the President some exposition of a decided policy, and I confess that, for one, I was rather indifferent as to what that policy was that he recommended, but I hoped that it would be something; that it would be decisive. He has utterly failed in that respect.

I think we may as well look this matter right clearly in the face, and I am not going to be long about doing it. I think that this state of affairs looks to one of two things; it looks to absolute submission, not on the part of our Southern friends and the southern States, but of the North, to the abandonment of their position,—it looks to a surrender of that popular sentiment which has been uttered through the constituted forms of the ballot-box, or it looks to open war.

We need not shut our eyes to the fact. It means war, and it means nothing else; and the State which has put herself in the attitude of secession so looks upon it. She has asked no council, she has considered it as a settled question, and she has armed herself. As I understand the aspect of affairs, it looks to that, and it looks to nothing else except unconditional submission on the part of the majority.

I did not read the paper—I do not read many papers—but I understand that there was a remedy suggested in a paper printed, I think in this city, and it was that the President and the Vice-President should be inaugurated (that would be a great concession!) and then, being inaugurated, they should quietly resign! Well, sir, I am not entirely certain that that would settle the question. I think that after the President and Vice-President-elect had resigned there would be as much difficulty in settling who was to take their places as there was in settling it before.

I do not wish, sir, to say a word that shall increase any irritation, that shall add any feeling of bitterness to the state of things which really exists in the country, and I would bear and forbear before I would say anything which would add to this bitterness. But I tell you, sir, the plain, true way is to look this thing in the face—see where we are. And I avow here—I do not know whether or not I shall be sustained by those who usually act with me—if the issue which is presented is that the constitutional will of the public opinion of this country, expressed through the forms of the constitution, will not be submitted to, and war is the alternative, let it come in any form or in any shape.

The Union is dissolved and it cannot be held together as a Union if that is the alternative upon which we go into an election. If it is pre-announced and determined that the voice of the majority, expressed through the regular and constituted forms of the constitution, will not be submitted to, then, sir, this is not a Union of equals; it is a Union of a dictatorial oligarchy on one side and a herd of slaves and cowards on the other. That is it, sir, nothing more, nothing less.

If this discussion is proceeded with I shall take occasion, by the indulgence of the Senate, once more to address myself to that phase of this controversy which is so constantly, so perseveringly, so continuously held up—that the northern States of the Union are the aggressors in producing this unhappy state of things. The northern States of the Union are the aggressors in one sense; we have a set of presses and a set of politicians among us traitorous to the public voice and the public interests, ministering to a diseased appetite, that lend their energies to the dissemination of aspersions and slanders upon the people among whom they live and upon whom they feed, and I very much fear that our friends upon the other side have listened too much to their aspersions of their fellow citizens, rather than to their own convictions of what the truth is.

I desire, if this discussion proceeds, to show up what I conceive to be the true character of this position of things so far as relates to the alleged aggressions of the northern States, but I do not pretend to speak for the northern States; I have no right to do so; they did not send me here; I was not elected by the northern States; I am only here to speak for one, and let me say, sir, that I have no fear, not the slightest, no doubt, not the minutest, let the result of this unhappy controversy be what it may; let it be settled in any form it may; drenched in blood, if it may—I have no fear—no doubt, that that little State which I have the honor in part to represent on this floor, will stand acquit—not before posterity; I do not care so much about that—but will stand acquit before the tribunal of the civilized world; will stand acquit before the verdict of Christendom of to-day; will stand acquit before the impartial and independent judgment of the men of to-day.

I have no such distrust of the position that State occupies, that I wish to appeal from the present to the future. No, sir. I say that the State which I have the honor in part to represent here, upon the constitution, upon the record, and upon the truth of history, will stand to-day and forever fully acquitted of every charge that can be brought against her of looking to the infraction, on her part, of the constitution or any of its provisions, be they onerous or otherwise.

Let me say further, sir, that if there are gentlemen who look to the settlement of this controversy by further concessions from the North, I think they miscalculate and mistake. I believe the difficulty has been that we have conceded too much; we have compromised too much, and we have got to that position of things that whenever any fault is found the ever-recurring remedy to the minds of patriots and statesmen is still further concessions from the North.

I agree—I have said it here, I have said it to my own people at home, I am willing to repeat it here—I agree that under the constitution of the United States you are entitled to demand and to have an honest and a fair discharge of that obligation which is imposed on all the States in regard to the rendition of fugitive slaves, and I am willing, perfectly willing, that there shall be an honest, fair, and faithful performance of that pledge.

I listened to the senator from North Carolina yesterday and I agree in very much that he said—more in what he said as general truths than in the particular application that he wished to make; but I can tell that honorable senator if he will sum up every case of injury, of suffering, of aggression by the whole of the free States upon the right that they have to recapture fugitive slaves and put it all down in its darkest colors; draw the image as hideous as truth and fancy can make it; when the sum is all told I can show him aggressions upon the rights of citizens of the free States—upon the constitutional right which is conferred on the citizens of each State in every State—I can show cases of aggression against that right that will infinitely outweigh and outnumber everything that can be brought in the way of aggression by the free States upon the rights of the South in regard to the recapture of their slaves.

Sir, we are trying an experiment. I believe we are in its crisis. I have never been of that number who have been disposed to sympathize with 4th of July orators, who have been in the habit, for the last half or three quarters of a century, of glorifying this country and telling what great things she had done. I have uniformly said, when I have had occasion to address the public on the subject, " We have done nothing; we are but at the beginning of a great experiment."

We talk of our republic! Why, sir, it has not yet outlived the ages of the soldiers who fought its battles and won its victories; but yet we are boasting of our victory. Sir, I think Rome existed as a republic for six hundred years, and they might well boast of something that they had done; but that republic passed away. We have not yet survived the lifetime of the men who fought the battles of liberty, or of the patriots and sages who formed our constitution of government. What we have obtained we have obtained by a great effort and a great price. It was not the mere price of the American Revolution; it was not the mere price of the patriot blood that was shed, or of the patriot counsels that formed the constitution; but away back, centuries upon centuries in English history, where power and principle contended against each other with alternate success and defeat— in all those centuries there had been going on the contest which is culminating in our experiment here; and no patriot blood that was poured out on the battle fields in the civil wars of England has been insignificant in relation to this conflict.

Now, sir, I have said nearly all that I propose to say, unless I am provoked by and by to say more, which I hope I shall not be; but, sir, I will add this; we shall present a most humiliating spectacle to the world if at this time, when by the acknowledgment of the President of the United States the blessings of heaven have descended upon this people in all the channels of their efforts and their business to an unexampled degree; when the bounties of heaven have been showered down upon us with no niggard hand; at a time, too, when by the confession of a senator from Georgia, not now in his seat [Mr. Toombs], made last year on the floor of the senate—I cannot quote his very words, but I can his sentiment—this general government was faithfully performing all its functions in relation to the slave States, and in relation to every State, never more faithfully than at the present time; I say, if under such circumstances, with a faithful government, and, I will add, a subservient judiciary, with the blessings of Providence coming down upon us as they are, if at such a time this confederacy should burst, this glorious fraternity of States be dissevered, and we try by the doubtful contingencies of separate State action to carry out the great experiment of human liberty, we shall present a most humiliating spectacle.

Why, sir, the very day, the very hour, that we are coming to such a result and thus developing our experiment, the States of Italy that for centuries have gone through the baptism of fire and blood, groaning beneath the iron heel of despotism, one under this and another under that, are throwing off the yoke and uniting together—I say that at such a
3 time when the classic States of Italy, taught by the bitter ex-

perience of centuries, are seeking by a consolidated constitutional government to come together and unite their energies for liberty, for independence, and for progress, if we, untaught by all the past, reckless of the present and blind to the future, should madly dash ourselves upon this dark ocean whose shores no eye of prophecy or of faith can discern, we shall present a sad spectacle to the world.

Sir, I do not know what is to be the future; but I do hope that if we cannot settle this difficulty in the spirit in which it ought to be settled, we shall at least have the courage and the manhood to look it straight in the face and understand what it is.

I know nothing, sir, about the policy of the incoming administration. I have never passed a word by mouth or by letter with the President-elect since he has been nominated for the high office to which the people have elected him. It has been my fortune since I have had a seat upon this floor to find myself uniformly, constantly, and perseveringly in the opposition to the administration. I am far from certain that I have not got to take the same position in regard to the incoming administration—very far. One thing is certain; if that administration shall quail in the performance of its duty, if its head shall hestitate, as Mr. Buchanan has done, to look the thing clearly in the face and mark out a policy consistent with honor and patriotism, he certainly will not find me among the number of his supporters.

MILL

JOHN STUART MILL, an eminent English philosopher, political economist, and statesman, was born in London, May 20, 1806. His father, James Mill, the philosopher and historian, gave him a strenuous training; at three he began Greek, and before he was fourteen he had read widely in Greek, Latin, and English, and made considerable progress in mathematics and philosophy. In 1820 he visited France, where he took a keen interest in French politics and social conditions. On his return, after working diligently at history and law, he obtained an appointment in the India Office under his father, who was assistant examiner with charge of the revenue department, and afterwards, in 1832, in control of all the departments of Indian administration. The same year (1823) he joined a small society which met at the house of Jeremy Bentham and adopted the name Utilitarian. Before he was twenty he was the acknowledged leader of the Utilitarians and a frequent contributor to the "Westminster Review." In 1826 he had begun to change his views in regard to human happiness and the importance of external circumstances in training the mind. This reaction from his inherited creed was largely modified by his acquaintance with Mrs. John Taylor, whom he married, after a long friendship, in 1851. In 1843 he published his "System of Logic," which in its treatment of inductive science has never been superseded. He published his "Principles of Political Economy" in 1848; in this valuable treatise, while mainly following Ricardo's abstract theory, he clearly recognized its hypothetical character and discussed the application of economic conditions to social questions. He retired from the India Office in 1858, the head of his department. In 1865 he was elected member of Parliament for Westminster, and during the four years that he sat he voted with the advanced Radical party and advocated female suffrage. He died at Avignon May 8, 1873. Among his other publications may be mentioned his essay on "Liberty" (1859); "Examination of Sir William Hamilton's Philosophy" (1865); "Comte and Positivism" (1865); "England and Ireland" (1868); "The Subjection of Women." His "Autobiography" was published the year of his death; the following year "Three Essays on Religion." His occasional writings were collected in four volumes, and a new volume of essays was published in 1897.

TRIBUTE TO GARRISON

MR. CHAIRMAN, LADIES, AND GENTLEMEN,— The speakers who have preceded me have, with an eloquence far beyond anything which I can command, laid before our honored guest the homage of admiration and gratitude which we all feel due to his heroic life. Instead of idly expatiating upon things which have been far better said than I could say them, I would rather endeavor to recall one or two lessons applicable to ourselves, which may be drawn from his career. A noble work nobly done always contains in itself not one but many lessons; and in the case of him whose character and deeds we are here to commemorate two may be singled out specially deserving to be laid to heart by all who would wish to leave the world better than they found it.

The first lesson is,—Aim at something great; aim at things which are difficult; and there is no great thing which is not difficult. Do not pare down your undertaking to what you can hope to see successful in the next few years, or in the years of your own life. Fear not the reproach of Quixotism or of fanaticism; but after you have well weighed what you undertake, if you see your way clearly, and are convinced that you are right, go forward, even though you, like Mr. Garrison, do it at the risk of being torn to pieces by the very men through whose changed hearts your purpose will one day be accomplished. Fight on with all your strength against whatever odds and with however small a band of supporters. If you are right, the time will come when that small band will swell into a multitude; you will at least lay the foundations of something memorable, and you may, like Mr. Garrison — though you ought not to need or expect so great a reward— be spared to see that work completed which, when you began it, you only hoped it might be given to you to help forward a few stages on its way.

The other lesson which it appears to me important to en- force, amongst the many that may be drawn from our friend's life, is this: if you aim at something noble and suc- ceed in it, you will generally find that you have succeeded 'not in that alone. A hundred other good and noble things which you never dreamed of will have been accomplished by the way, and the more certainly, the sharper and more agonizing has been the struggle which preceded the victory. The heart and mind of a nation are never stirred from their foundations without manifold good fruits. In the case of the great American contest these fruits have been already great, and are daily becoming greater. The prejudices which beset every form of society—and of which there was a plentiful crop in America—are rapidly melting away. The chains of prescription have been broken; it is not only the slave who has been freed—the mind of America has been emancipated The whole intellect of the country has been set thinking about the fundamental questions of society and government; and the new problems which have to be solved and the new difficulties which have to be encountered are calling forth new activity of thought, and that great nation is saved, probably for a long time to come, from the most formidable danger of a completely settled state of society and opinion—intellectual and moral stagnation. This, then, is an additional item of the debt which America and mankind owe to Mr. Garrison and his noble associates; and it is well calculated to deepen our sense of the truth which his whole career most strikingly illustrates—that though our best directed efforts may often seem wasted and lost, nothing coming of them that can be pointed to and distinctly identified as a definite gain to humanity, though this may happen ninety-nine times in every hundred, the hundredth time the result may be so great and dazzling that we had never dared to hope for it, and should have regarded him who had predicted it to us as sanguine beyond the bounds of mental sanity. So has it been with Mr. Garrison.

GARIBALDI

GIUSEPPE MARIA GARIBALDI, a famous Italian soldier and patriot, was born at Nice, July 4, 1807. He was a sailor in the earlier part of his career, but for taking part in the Young Italy movement in 1833-34 was exiled. For a time he served in the French navy, and then going to South America in 1836 he offered his services to the struggling republic of Rio Grande. He fought in many battles in her cause, and because of conspicuous bravery displayed by him at the battle of San Antonio in 1846 received the title of " The Hero of Montevideo." In 1848 he returned to Italy and fought in the defence of Rome against French intervention in 1849. After the fall of Rome he, with many of his followers, sought refuge in San Marino, but being surrounded by the Austrian troops he was compelled to disband his forces. Escaping thence to Chiaviri in Liguria he was offered the choice of exile or captivity by the Sardinian government, and thereupon sailing to Tunis he was prevented from landing through French influence. After some little interval he went to New York, but returned to Italy in 1854 and purchased a part of the small island of Caprera near the Sardinian coast. Here he lived till 1859, when he made himself prominent in the Lombard campaign, and after the peace of Villa Franca he formed the design of liberating Rome. In this matter he was prevented by the Sardinian government; but in his expedition in 1860 against Sicily he was aided as far as possible by Cavour. After the battle of Reggio and the flight of King Francis to Gaeta, Garibaldi was proclaimed at Naples the dictator of the Two Sicilies. In 1862, 1866, and 1867 he engaged in other expeditions for the liberation of Italy, and in the year last named was for some time a prisoner in the fortress of Varignano. With his sons he went in 1870 to the aid of the French Republic against the Germans. In 1875 he became a member of the Italian Parliament, but his legislative career was not a particularly wise one. His later years were spent almost entirely at Caprera. He died June 1, 1882.

LAST SPEECH AS A MEMBER OF THE CHAMBER

DELIVERED IN PARLIAMENT, APRIL 12, 1860

GENTLEMEN,—The fifth article of the constitution says: Such treaties as involve any variation in the territory of the State shall have no effect until after the assent of the Chambers shall have been obtained. The consequence of this article of the fundamental law is that any attempt to put into execution a diminution of the state, before such diminution shall have had the sanction of Parliament, is contrary to the constitution. That one section of the state should vote for a separation before the Chambers should have decided that such a separation ought to take place, before they should have decided whether or how there should be any voting at all for the bare principle of putting into execution that very separation—is an unconstitutional act.

This, gentlemen, is the question of Nice, as regarded from a constitutional point of view, and which I submit to the sagacious judgment of Parliament. Now I will speak a few words upon the question of my country considered politically.

The people of Nice after the submission of 1388 to the house of Savoy, established on the 19th of November, 1391, that the Count of Savoy could never alienate the city in favor of any other prince whatsoever, and that if he should do so the inhabitants should have the right to resist *vi et armis* and to choose for themselves another sovereign according to their own pleasure, without rendering themselves guilty of rebellion. Therefore in the year 1388 Nice united herself to the dynasty of Savoy upon condition of not being alienated to any foreign power. Now the government, by its treaty of March 24th, has ceded Nice to Napoleon. Such a concession is contrary to the rights of nations. It will be said that Nice has been exchanged for two more important provinces. Nevertheless every traffic in people is repugnant to the universal sense of civilized nations and ought to be abolished, because it establishes a dangerous precedent, which might easily diminish that faith that a country has a just right to place in its own future.

The government justifies its proceeding by the popular vote

which is to take place on the 15th and 16th of the current month.

In Savoy this has been appointed for the 22d, but there is more of a hurry about Nice. The pressure under which the people of Nice finds itself crushed, the presence of numerous police officials, the limitless flatteries and threats exercised upon those poor people, the stress which the government is employing to help on the union to France—as results from the proclamation of the governor, Labonis—the absence from Nice of very many of our citizens, fairly compelled by such means to leave the city, the precipitation and constrained manner in which the vote of the population is demanded—all these circumstances take from what should be universal suffrage its true characteristic of liberty.

I and my colleagues are confident that the Chamber and the ministry will be disposed to provide immediately and energetically to the end that this supreme vote of my native country may be free from every pressure, and pronounced with that surety and legal regularity with which the Chamber will desire to safeguard, demanding in the meantime the suspension of any vote at Nice.

[Special translation.]

SPEECH TO HIS SOLDIERS

[Delivered in the royal palace at Naples, on the occasion of the presentation of the returns of the popular vote to Victor Emmanuel, November 9, 1860.]

MY COMPANIONS IN ARMS,—At this, the penultimate break in our march of resurrection, it is our duty to reflect upon the period which is just coming to an end and then to prepare ourselves to terminate splendidly the admirable work performed by the elect of twenty generations; the entire accomplishment of which has been assigned by Providence to our fortunate generation.

Yes, young men, Italy owes to you the enterprise which merits the plaudits of all the world.

You have conquered, and you will continue to conquer, because you are from now to henceforth trained to those tactics which decide the fate of battles. You have in no wise degenerated from the virtues of those who penetrated to the profoundest centre of the Macedonian phalanxes and humbled the proud victor of Asia.

To this astonishing page of our country's history there will succeed one yet more marvellous, when the slave shall at last show to his free brother the sharpened steel which he has drawn and forged from the links of his own chain.

To arms, then, all, all! And the oppressors and tyrants shall vanish away like the dust of the streets.

May women repel far from them all cowards. Daughters of a land of battles, they can only desire heroic and generous descendants. Let the timid and the doctrinaires depart, to trail along elsewhere their servility and their shame.

The Italian people is now its own master. It would indeed be as a brother to the other peoples, but holding ever its forehead high; and it would neither crawl along begging for its liberty, nor suffer itself to be towed on by anybody. No, no; a hundred times, no!

Providence has bestowed on Italy the gift of Victor Emmanuel. All men should attach themselves to him and gather round him. Before the *Re Galant'uomo* all rivalry should cease, every rancor disappear. So once more I repeat my cry, " To arms, to arms, all! "

If the month of March, 1861, does not find a million Italians on foot—alas for poor liberty, for the poor Italian existence!

But far be from me such a thought, which is as deadly for me as poison! But surely next March—and even if need be next February—will find each man at his post.

Italians of Catalfini, Palermo, the Volturno, Ancona, Castelfidardo, and Iservica; and with us every inhabitant of this land, who is not cowardly or senile, crowd around the glorious soldier of Palestro, and we will bring the last shock, will deal the last blow against the crumbling and tottering dynasty.

Receive now, young volunteers, ye who in honor remain of those who won ten battles, my farewell words. I address them to you from my deepest soul. I must withdraw from you to-day, but only for a few days. The hour of battle will find me beside you—beside you, the warriors of Italian liberty.

Let such only return to their homes as imperious domestic duties demand, and those who, having been gloriously wounded, have a right to the gratitude of the common fatherland. They can still serve her at their own firesides by their advice and by the display of the noble scars which adorn their brows of twenty years. With these exceptions let all remain under the glorious banners!

We shall soon meet again to march together to the rescue of those brothers who are still enslaved. We shall soon find ourselves again united to march on together unto new triumphs! [And to those who stood nearest him.] *A rivederci sulta via di Roma.*—To our meeting again, then, on the road to Rome!

[Special translation.]

ADAMS

CHARLES FRANCIS ADAMS, a distinguished American diplomatist and writer, was the son of John Quincy Adams, sixth President of the United States, and was born in Boston, Massachusetts, August 18, 1807, and died there, November 21, 1886. When two years old he was taken by his father to St. Petersburg, where, during his father's diplomatic mission, he learned French, German, and Russian. At the age of ten he returned to America. He was educated at Harvard University, studied law, and in 1828 was admitted to the Suffolk bar. He sat in the Massachusetts House of Representatives as a Whig member, 1831-36, but afterward adopted the views of the Free-Soil party and was its candidate for vice-president in 1848. From 1858-61 he was a representative in Congress; and from 1861-68 minister to England, rendering extremely valuable service to his country in his diplomatic capacity during a very critical period. In 1872 he served on the Geneva Board of Arbitration. Adams was a man of great firmness of character, but he was never popular with the people in general on account of the cold, unsympathetic manner he had inherited from his father. He wrote a " Life of John Quincy Adams," and a number of his addresses have been published singly.

ON THE STATES AND THE UNION

FROM SPEECH DELIVERED IN THE HOUSE OF REPRESENTATIVES, JANUARY 31, 1861

MR. SPEAKER,—In this hour of inexpressible import to the fate of unborn millions I would that I could clear from my eyes the film of all human passions, to see the truth and the right in their naked, living reality, and with their aid to rise to the grandeur of the opportunity to do good to my fellow men. There have been occasions when the fitting words uttered in the true place have helped to right the scale when wavering towards the ruin of a nation. At no time have they been more necessary than now. At no place more requisite than here.

The most magnificent example of self-government known to history is in imminent danger of suffering an abrupt mutilation by reason of the precipitate violence of a few desperate men. I purpose to discuss briefly and I trust with proper calmness the cause and the effect of this proceeding as well as the duty that it entails upon us.

On the 6th of November the people of the United States were called for the nineteenth time to give in their votes for the election of the highest officers known to the constitution. Nothing marked the proceeding with any unusual features. No reluctance had been manifested in any quarter to fulfil the duty, the proof of which is that no more full expression of opinion was ever made.

No complaint of unfairness or fraud was heard. No contested question sprang up. With the single exception of the State of Virginia not a doubt was entertained of the true reflection of the popular sense in designating the electors whose province it is to complete the process. Not a soul has been bold enough to deny the fact, that, from the origin of the government, not a single election which had been disputed at all was ever more fairly conducted or more unequivocally determined.

The sublime spectacle viewed thus far by foreign nations with a degree of amazement, proportioned to the ever-expanding nature of the operation of so many millions of people spread over so many thousands of miles of a continent stretching from sea to sea, peacefully in a single day selecting their chief rulers for the next four years was once more presented to all outward appearance, as successfully executed as in any preceding and more contracted stage of the republic.

Yet, no sooner was the result positively ascertained than the people of one of the States, even whilst engaged in performing the common duty as faithfully as all the rest and without the intervention of a single new disturbing cause, suddenly broke out into violent remonstrance and dashed into immediate efforts to annul all their obligations to the constitution. Such a step had never before been taken in any quarter. The same spirit directly manifested itself in the region round about, and it has continued ever since to spread until it has more or less affected the loyalty of ten or twelve of the States. At the precise period of this occurrence no new provocation had been given, unless it were to be found in the single fact that the successful candidates were persons for whom those States had not voted.

A similar instance had never occurred. There have been several cases of popular resistance to federal laws. South Carolina had herself furnished a memorable one. But here was an example of resistance to a constitutional election of men. The former may be conducted without necessarily shaking the very foundations of the social system. But the latter at once denies the validity of the only process by which the organic law can be executed at all. To refuse to acknowledge the constituted authorities of a nation when successfully carried out is revolution; and it is called rebellion when it fails under every code of laws known over the globe.

It is an appeal to physical force, which depends for its justification before God and man only upon the clear establishment of proof of intolerable tyranny and oppression. It is sometimes the last resource of patriots who feel themselves impelled to overthrow a despotism, but oftener the contrivance of desperate adventurers, who seek for their own private ends to establish one.

Had the present outbreak seemed to me the consequence of mature deliberation and deep-settled convictions among the people, I should at once have despaired of the republic. But apart from the merely outward indications of haste and of passion that attended it I had other reasons for believing differently. During the previous summer the representative candidate of the most extreme party in the slaveholding States had labored more than once to declare himself a devoted friend of the Union. Whilst on the other hand the distrust in him inspired by the character of his principal advocates, had had the effect of alienating from him numbers even in his own State, who preferred the security offered to them by the friends of another candidate brought forward exclusively as the upholder of " the Union, the constitution, and the enforcement of the laws."

The slaveholding States were thus divided between these two influences, neither of them venturing before the people to whisper the theory of disunion. A very large minority of the aggregated voters sustained the most thoroughly pledged candidate whilst Tennessee and Kentucky gave him their electoral votes and even the Old Dominion, never known before to waver in the course marked out by her acknowledged and ancient leaders, was seen to transfer her votes to the more loyal side.

All these events were not the natural forerunners of premeditated disaffection to the constitutional government. They can only be accounted for by presuming a fund of honest attachment to it at bottom. And the inference which I draw is, that the feelings of a majority of well-disposed persons have been suddenly carried away by sympathy with their warmer and more violent friends in South Carolina, so that they have not stopped calmly to weigh the probable consequences of their own precipitation.

If I were to need more evidence to prove to me the absence of deliberate intent, outside of South Carolina, to set aside an election regularly made, I think I could find it in the earnestness with which other causes have been set up in justification of resistance. It has been alleged that various grievances have been suffered, much oppression has been endured, and certain outrages have been committed upon the people of the slaveholding States, which render their longer stay in the Union impossible, unless confidence can be inspired that some remedies may be applied to stop the evils for the future. They aver that their rights are no longer secure in remaining with us, and that the alternative left is to withdraw themselves before acquiescence shall have prepared them for ultimate subjugation. They come to us and demand that these complaints shall be listened to and these apprehensions allayed before they can consent to farther abide under the authority of a common head.

And here some of my friends on the right reply, with equal warmth and not less reason, that they are unconscious of having done wrong in electing a President according to the constitution; that they are not aware of any real grievances that demand redress; and that they feel disinclined to enter upon any experiment to quiet apprehensions which are in their opinion either artificial or imaginary; that they appeal to the constitution as it is—and if obedience to its requisitions be not voluntarily rendered in any quarter the only proper remedy is coercion.

I should perhaps be disposed to concur in this view were this a case of deliberate and wilful conspiracy to subvert the government. I am not sure that I would not apply the doctrine to the people of South Carolina, who have long been known to be generally disaffected. They neither demand nor expect any redress, or even a consideration of their grievances. They declare themselves only to be executing a treasonable project that they have been meditating for twenty years. They have therefore put themselves without the pale of negotiation. There is not even a minority of the citizens who remonstrate. The case is otherwise with the other States. There is evident hesitation and reluctance in adopting the irrevocable policy of disunion. There is a lingering desire to receive assurances that this step is not absolutely needed. Now I, for one, am not ready yet to take the responsibility of absolutely closing the door to reconciliation.

I cannot permit myself to forget the warnings that have descended to us from many of the wisest and best statesmen and patriots of all time, against this rigid and haughty mode of treating great discontents. I cannot overlook the fact that in the days of our fathers the imperious spirit of Chatham did not feel itself as sacrificing any of his proud dignity by proposing to listen to their grievances, and even to concede to every reasonable demand, long after they had placed themselves in armed resistance to all the power of Great Britain.

Had George III listened to his words of wisdom he might have saved the brightest jewel of his crown. He took the opposite course. He denied the existence of grievances. He rejected the olive branch. He insisted upon coercion. And what was the result? History records its verdict in favor of Chatham and against his king. And who is there in the mother country at this day who does not regret the blunder, if he does not condemn the motive of the monarch? When the great grandson of that same king, on his late visit to this capital, so handsomely made his pilgrimage to the tomb of the arch-rebel of that time, do you imagine that his countrymen and future subjects would have applauded the act if they still believed that the stiff-backed old king had been right in shutting the door of reconciliation?

For my part, Mr. Speaker, I am more inclined to accord with that philosophical statesman, Edmund Burke, who during the same struggle was not afraid to bring forward his plan of conciliation with America. And in the elaborate speech which he made in its defence he used the following language—not entirely inappropriate to these times:

" Now, in such unfortunate quarrels among the component parts of a great political union of communities, I can scarcely conceive anything more completely improvident than for the head of the empire to insist that, if any privilege is pleaded against his will or his acts, his whole authority is denied, instantly to proclaim rebellion, to beat to arms, and to put the offending provinces under the ban. Will not this, sir, very soon teach the provinces to make no distinctions on their part? Will it not teach them that the government, against which a claim of liberty is tantamount to high treason, is a government in which submission is equivalent to slavery? "

Mr. Speaker, it is not my custom to lean much upon authority. As a general thing it appears to me to pass for more than it is worth. But there are persons who are always more or less influenced by the source from which anything comes, and who are better disposed to believe in the testimony of a witness two centuries old than if the same reasoning were issued from the lips of the best of living contemporaries. To such I will commend a passage drawn from the most profound of British statesmen and philosophers, Francis Bacon:

" Concerning the materials of seditions it is a thing well to be considered; for the surest way to prevent seditions (if the times do bear it) is to take away the matter of them; for if there be fuel prepared it is hard to tell whence the spark shall come that shall set it on fire. . . .

"As for discontentments, they are in the politic body, like to humors in the natural, which are apt to gather a preternatural heat and to inflame; and let no prince measure the danger of them by this, whether they be just or unjust; for that were to imagine people to be too reasonable, who do often spurn at their own good; nor yet by this, whether the griefs whereupon they rise be, in fact, great or small; for they are the most dangerous discontentments where the fear is greater than the feeling. *Dolendi modus, timendi non item;* besides, in great oppressions the same things that provoke the patience, do withal mete the courage; but, in fears, it is not so. Neither let any prince or state be secure concerning discontentments, because they have been often, or have been long, and yet no peril hath ensued; for, as it is true, that every vapor or fume doth not turn into a storm, so it is nevertheless true, that storms, though they blow over divers times, yet may fall at last; and, as the Spanish proverb noteth well, ' The cord breaketh at last by the weakest pull.' "

Such deep sagacity as this convinces me, if I ever doubted, that the way to peace in times of disorder is not always found by refusing to listen to complaints. I differ, then, with some of my rigid friends on this point. I prefer to consider grievances, were it but to be sure that they have no just foundation; much more if they prove to merit attention for their reasonableness. My notion of the duty of a public man is to watch the growth of offences and not to neglect, still less to despise them. I have therefore faithfully labored in my humble way to comprehend the nature of the discontents actually prevailing and to judge of the extent to which they justify the resort to so violent a mode of relief as the overthrow of a government. After a full hearing of all that has been said in committee and elsewhere I easily embrace the topics of complaint under three heads, to wit:

1. The passage of laws in some of the free States operating to discourage the recovery of fugitive slaves.

2. The denial of equal rights in the Territories

3. The apprehension of such an increase of political power in the free States as to tempt an invasion, under new forms of the constitution, of the right of the slave States to manage their domestic affairs.

After a full and calm examination of the grounds furnished to sustain these complaints I am ready to declare that if these are all that endanger the continuance of the present common bond of association between the States, in my opinion no similar sacrifice to mere abstractions was ever before made among reasoning men. . . .

For the sake of these three causes of complaint, all of them utterly without practical result, the slaveholding States, unquestionably the weakest section of this great confederacy, are voluntarily and precipitately surrendering the realities of solid power woven into the very texture of a government that now keeps nineteen millions of freemen willing to tolerate, and in one sense to shelter, institutions which but for that would meet with no more sympathy among them than they now do in the remainder of the civilized world!

For my own part I must declare that, even supposing these alleged grievances to be more real than I represent them, I think the measures of the committee dispose of them effectually and forever. They contribute directly all that can be legitimately done by Congress, and they recommend it to the legislatures of the States to accomplish the remainder. Why then is it that harmony is not restored? The answer is, that you are not satisfied with this settlement, however complete. You must have more guarantees in the constitution. You must make the protection and extension of slavery in the Territories now existing and hereafter to be acquired a cardinal doctrine of our great charter. Without that you are determined to dissolve the Union. How stands the case then?

We offer to settle the question finally in all of the present territory that you claim by giving you every chance of establishing slavery that you have any right to require of us. You decline to take the offer because you fear it will do you no good. Slavery will not go there. But if that be true what is the use of asking for the protection anyhow, much less in the constitution?

Why require protection where you will have nothing to protect? All you appear to desire it for is New Mexico. Nothing else is left. Yet you will not accept New Mexico at once, because ten years of experience has proved to you that protection has been of no use thus far. But if so how can you expect that it will be of so much more use hereafter as to make it worth dissolving the Union about?

But if we pass to the other condition is it any more reasonable? Are we going to fight because we cannot agree upon the mode of disposing of our neighbor's lands? Are we to break up the union of these States, cemented by so many years of common sufferings and resplendent with so many years of common glory, because it is insisted that we should incorporate into what we regard as the charter of our freedom a proclamation to the civilized world that we intend to grasp the territory of other nations whenever we can do it, for the purpose of putting into it certain institutions which some of us disapprove, and that, too, whether the people inhabiting that territory themselves approve of it or not?

I am almost inclined to believe that they who first contrived this demand must have done so for the sake of presenting a condition which they knew beforehand must be rejected or which if accepted must humiliate us in the dust forever. In point of fact this proposal covers no question of immediate moment which may not be settled by another and less obnoxious one. Why is it then persevered in and the other rejected? The answer is obvious. You want the Union dissolved. You want to make it impossible for honorable men to become reconciled.

If it be indeed so then on you and you alone shall rest the responsibility of what may follow. If the Union be broken up the reason why it happened shall remain on record forever. It was because you rejected one form of settling a question which might be offered and accepted with honor in order to insist upon another which you knew we could not accept without disgrace. I answer for myself only when I say that, if the alternative to the salvation of the Union be only that the people of the United States shall before the Christian nations of the earth print in broad letters upon the front of their charter of republican government the dogma of slave propagandism over the remainder of the countries of the world, I will not consent to brand myself with what I deem such disgrace, let the consequences be what they may.

But it is said that this answer closes the door of reconciliation. The slaveholding States will secede, and what then?

This brings me to the last point which I desire to touch to-day, the proper course for the government to pursue in the face of these difficulties. Some of the friends with whom I act have not hesitated to express themselves in favor of coercion, and they have drawn very gloomy pictures of the fatal consequences to the prosperity and security of the whole Union that must ensue. For my own sake I am glad that I do not partake so largely in these fears. I see no obstacle to the regular continuance of the government, in not less than twenty States and perhaps more, the inhabitants of which have not in a moment been deprived of that peculiar practical wisdom in the management of their affairs, which is the secret of their past success.

Several new States will before long be ready to take their places with us and make good in part the loss of the old ones. The mission of furnishing a great example of free government to the nations of the earth will still be in our hands, impaired I admit but not destroyed; and I doubt not our power to accomplish it yet in spite of the temporary drawback. Even the problem of coercion will go on to solve itself without our aid.

For if the sentiment of disunion become so far universal and permanent in the dissatisfied States as to show no prospect of good from resistance, and there be no acts of aggression attempted on their part, I will not say that I may not favor the idea of some arrangement of a peaceful character, though I do not now see the authority under which it can be originated. The new confederacy can scarcely be other than a secondary power. It can never be a maritime State. It will begin with the necessity of keeping eight millions of its population to watch four millions and with the duty of guarding against the egress of the latter, several thousand miles of an exposed border, beyond which there will be no right of reclamation. Of the ultimate result of a similar experiment, I cannot in my own mind have a moment's doubt. At the last session I ventured to place on record in this House a prediction by which I must abide, let the effect of the future on my sagacity be what it may. I have not yet seen any reason to doubt its accuracy. I now repeat it. The experiment will ignominiously fail.

But there are exceptions to the adoption of this peaceful policy which it will not be wise to overlook. If there be violent and wanton attacks upon the persons or the property of the citizens of the United States or of their government, I see not how demands for immediate redress can be avoided. If any interruptions should be attempted of the regular channels of trade on the great watercourses or on the ocean, they cannot long be permitted. And if any considerable minorities of citizens should be persecuted or proscribed on account of their attachment to the Union and should call for protection, I cannot deny the obligation of this government to afford it. There are persons in many of the States whose patriotic declarations and honorable pledges of support of the Union may bring down upon them more than the ill will of their infatuated fellow citizens.

It would be impossible for the people of the United States to look upon any proscription of them with indifference. These are times which should bring together all men by whatever party name they may have been heretofore distinguished upon common ground. When I heard the gentlemen from Virginia the other day so bravely and so forcibly urging their manly arguments in support of the Union, the constitution, and the enforcement of the laws, my heart involuntarily bounded towards them as brethren sacredly engaged in a common cause. Let them, said I to myself, accept the offered settlement of the differences that remain between us on some fair basis like that proposed by the committee, and then what is to prevent us all who yet believe that the Union must be preserved from joining heart and hand our common forces to effect it?

When the cry goes out that the ship is in danger of sinking the first duty of every man on board, no matter what his particular vocation, is to lend all the strength he has to the work of keeping her afloat. What! shall it be said that we waver in the view of those who begin by trying to expunge the sacred memory of the Fourth of July? Shall we help them to obliterate the associations that cluster around the glorious struggle for independence or stultify the labors of the patriots who erected this magnificent political edifice upon the adamantine base of human liberty? Shall we surrender the fame of Washington and Laurens, of Gadsden and the Lees, of Jefferson and Madison, and of the myriads of heroes whose names are imperishably connected with the memory of a united people? Never, never.

For myself I can only interpose against what seems to me like the madness of the moon, the barrier of a single feeble remonstrance. But in any event it shall never be said of my share in the action of this hour of danger, that it has been guided by vindictive passions or narrow considerations of personal or party advantage. I well know what I hazard among many whose good opinion has ever been part of the sunlight of my existence, in following what I hold to be a higher duty. Whilst at any and at all times I shall labor to uphold the great principles of liberty, without which this grand system of our fathers would seem to be a mockery and a show, I shall equally strive to give no just ground to enemies and traitors to expand the circle of mischief they may do.

Although not very frequently indulging in the profession of a devotion to the Union which has heretofore been too often associated with a public policy I deemed most dangerous to its safety, I will venture to add that no man over the boundless extent of our dominion has more reasons for inextinguishable attachment to it than myself. It is inwoven in my affections with the faithful labors in its support of two generations of my race. It is blended with a not inconsiderable personal stake in its continuity. It is mingled with my earnest prayers for the welfare of those who are treading after me. And more than all these, it colors all my visions of the beneficent spread of Republican institutions as well in America as over the rest of the civilized world.

If, then, so great a calamity as a division be about to befall us it shall be hastened by no act of mine. It shall come from the wilful passions of infatuated men, who demand it of us to destroy the great principles for which our fathers struggle in life and in death to stain our standard with the symbol of human oppression and to degrade us in the very hour of our victory, before our countrymen, before all the nations of the civilized world, and before God. Rather than this let the heavens fall. My duty is performed.

DAVIS

JEFFERSON DAVIS was born in Christian County, Kentucky, in 1808. He received a classical education at Translyvania University, graduated at West Point in 1828, and served as Lieutenant of Infantry and of Dragoons until 1835, when he engaged in cotton planting in Mississippi. He was a Presidential elector on the Polk and Dallas ticket in 1844; served in Congress from December, 1845, to June, 1846, when he resigned to command a regiment in the Mexican War, wherein he distinguished himself at Monterey and Buena Vista. He declined the appointment of Brigadier-General in the regular army in May, 1847, was sent in the same year from Mississippi to the United States Senate, and kept his seat there until 1851. In the year last named he was defeated for Governor of Mississippi, but two years later became Secretary of War under President Pierce. In 1857 he was again chosen United States Senator, and served until January 21, 1861. He was inaugurated President of the Confederate States on February 18 of the year just named, and remained at the head of the Confederacy until the close of the Rebellion. Captured by Federal troops in Georgia, in May, 1865, he was imprisoned for two years at Fortress Monroe, and then released on $100,000 bail. Though indicted for treason in May, 1866, he was never brought to trial. The last years of his life were spent on a plantation at Beauvoir, Mississippi, and he died in New Orleans in 1889.

ON WITHDRAWAL FROM THE UNION; SECESSIONIST OPINION

UNITED STATES SENATE, JANUARY 21, 1861

I RISE, Mr. President, for the purpose of announcing to the Senate that I have satisfactory evidence that the State of Mississippi, by a solemn ordinance of her people in convention assembled, has declared her separation from the United States. Under these circumstances, of course my functions are terminated here. It has seemed to me proper, however, that I should appear in the Senate to announce that fact to my associates, and I will say but very little more. The occasion does not invite me to go into argument, and my physical condition would not permit me to do so if it were otherwise; and yet it seems to become me to say something on the part of the State I here represent, on an occasion so solemn as this.

It is known to Senators who have served with me here, that I have for many years advocated, as an essential attribute of State sovereignty, the right of a State to secede from the Union. Therefore, if I had not believed there was justifiable cause; if I had thought that Mississippi was acting without sufficient provocation, or without an existing necessity, I should still, under my theory of the government, because of my allegiance to the State of which I am a citizen, have been bound by her action. I, however, may be permitted to say that I do think that she has justifiable cause, and I approve of her act. I conferred with her people before that act was taken, counselled them then that if the state of things which they apprehended should exist when the convention met, they should take the action which they have now adopted.

I hope none who hear me will confound this expression of mine with the advocacy of the right of a State to remain in the Union, and to disregard its constitutional obligations by the nullification of the law. Such is not my theory. Nullification and secession, so often confounded, are indeed antagonistic principles. Nullification is a remedy which it is sought to apply within the Union, and against the agent of the States. It is only to be justified when the agent has violated his constitutional obligation, and a State, assuming to judge for itself, denies the right of the agent thus to act, and appeals to the other States of the Union for a decision; but when the States themselves, and when the people of the States, have so acted as to convince us that they will not regard our constitutional rights, then, and then for the first time, arises the doctrine of secession in its practical application.

A great man who now reposes with his fathers, and who has been often arraigned for a want of fealty to the Union, advocated the doctrine of nullification, because it preserved the Union. It was because of his deep-seated attachment to the Union, his determination to find some remedy for existing ills short of a severance of the ties which bound South Carolina to the other States, that Mr. Calhoun advocated the doctrine of nullification, which he proclaimed to be peaceful, to be within the limits of State power, not to disturb the Union, but only to be a means of bringing the agent before the tribunal of the States for their judgment.

Secession belongs to a different class of remedies. It is to be justified upon the basis that the States are sovereign. There was a time when none denied it. I hope the time may come again, when a better comprehension of the theory of our government, and the inalienable rights of the people of the States, will prevent any one from denying that each State is a sovereign, and thus may reclaim the grants which it has made to any agent whomsoever.

I therefore say I concur in the action of the people of Mississippi, believing it to be necessary and proper, and should have been bound by their action if my belief had been otherwise; and this brings me to the important point which I wish on this last occasion to present to the Senate. It is by this confounding of nullification and secession that the name of the great man, whose ashes now mingle with his mother earth, has been invoked to justify coercion against a seceded State. The phrase "to execute the laws" was an expression which General Jackson applied to the case of a State refusing to obey the laws while yet a member of the Union. That is not the case which is now presented. The laws are to be executed over the United States, and upon the people of the United States. They have no relation to any foreign country. It is a perversion of terms, at least it is a great misapprehension of the case, which cites that expression for application to a State which has withdrawn from the Union. You may make war on a foreign State. If it be the purpose of gentlemen, they may make war against a State which has withdrawn from the Union; but there are no laws of the United States to be executed within the limits of a seceded State. A State finding herself in the condition in which Mississippi has judged she is, in which her safety requires that she should provide for the mainte- nance of her rights out of the Union, surrenders all the benefits (and they are known to be many), deprives herself of the advantages (they are known to be great), severs all the ties of affection (and they are close and enduring), which have bound her to the Union; and thus divesting herself of every benefit, taking upon herself every burden, she claims to be exempt from any power to execute the laws of the United States within her limits.

I well remember an occasion when Massachusetts was arraigned before the bar of the Senate, and when then the doctrine of coercion was rife and to be applied against her because of the rescue of a fugitive slave in Boston. My opinion then was the same that it is now. Not in a spirit of egotism, but to show that I am not influenced in my opinion because the case is my own, I refer to that time and that occasion as containing the opinion which I then entertained, and on which my present conduct is based. I then said, if Massachusetts, following her through a stated line of conduct, chooses to take the last step which separates her from the Union, it is her right to go, and I will neither vote one dollar nor one man to coerce her back; but will say to her, God speed, in memory of the kind associations which once existed between her and the other States.

It has been a conviction of pressing necessity, it has been a belief that we are to be deprived in the Union of the rights which our fathers bequeathed to us, which has brought Mississippi into her present decision. She has heard proclaimed the theory that all men are created free and equal, and this made the basis of an attack upon her social institutions; and the sacred Declaration of Independence has been invoked to maintain the position of the equality of the races. That Declaration of Independence is to be construed by the circumstances and purposes for which it was made. The communities were declaring their independence; the people of those communities were asserting that no man was born—to use the language of Mr. Jefferson—booted and spurred to ride over the rest of mankind; that men were created equal—meaning the men of the political community; that there was no divine right to rule; that no man inherited the right to govern; that there were no classes by which power and place descended to families, but that all stations were equally within the grasp of each member of the body politic. These were the great principles they announced; these were the purposes for which they made their declaration; these were the ends to which their enunciation was directed. They have no reference to the slave; else, how happened it that among the items of arraignment made against George III. was that he endeavored to do just what the North had been endeavoring of late to do—to stir up insurrection among our slaves? Had the Declaration announced that the negroes were free and equal, how was the prince to be arraigned for stirring up insurrection among them? And how was this to be enumerated among the high crimes which caused the Colonies to sever their connection with the mother country? When our Constitution was formed, the same idea was rendered more palpable, for there we find provision made for that very class of persons as property; they were not put upon the footing of equality with white men—not even upon that of paupers and convicts; but, so far as representation was concerned, were discriminated against as a lower caste, only to be represented in the numerical proportion of three-fifths.

Then, Senators, we recur to the compact which binds us together; we recur to the principles upon which our government was founded; and when you deny them, and when you deny to us the right to withdraw from a government which, thus perverted, threatens to be destructive of our rights, we but tread in the path of our fathers when we proclaim our independence, and take the hazard. This is done not in hostility to others, not to injure any section of the country, nor even for our own pecuniary benefit; but from the high and solemn motive of defending and protecting the rights we inherited, and which it is our sacred duty to transmit unshorn to our children.

I find in myself, perhaps, a type of the general feeling of my constituents toward yours. I am sure I feel no hostility to you, Senators from the North. I am sure there is not one of you, whatever sharp discussion there may have been between us, to whom I cannot now say, in the presence of my God, I wish you well; and such, I am sure, is the feeling of the people whom I represent toward those whom you represent. I therefore feel that I but express their desire when I say I hope, and they hope, for peaceful relations with you, though we must part. They may be mutually beneficial to us in the future, as they have been in the past, if you so will it. The reverse may bring disaster on every portion of the country; and if you will have it thus, we will invoke the God of our fathers, who delivered them from the power of the lion, to protect us from the ravages of the bear; and thus, putting our trust in God, and in our own firm hearts and strong arms, we will vindicate the right as best we may.

In the course of my service here, associated at different times with a great variety of Senators, I see now around me some with whom I have served long; there have been points of collision; but whatever of offence there has been to me, I leave here; I carry with me no hostile remembrance. Whatever offence I have given which has not been redressed, or for which satisfaction has not been demanded, I have, Senators, in this hour of our parting, to offer you my apology for any pain which, in heat of discussion, I have inflicted. I go hence unencumbered of the remembrance of any injury received, and having discharged the duty of making the only reparation in my power for any injury offered.

Mr. President, and Senators, having made the announcement which the occasion seemed to me to require, it only remains for me to bid you a final adieu.

INAUGURAL ADDRESS

MONTGOMERY, ALABAMA, FEBRUARY 18, 1861

Gentlemen of the Congress of the Confederate States of America, Friends and Fellow Citizens:

OUR present condition, achieved in a manner unprece-dented in the history of nations, illustrates the American idea that governments rest upon the con-sent of the governed, and that it is the right of the people to alter and abolish governments whenever they become destructive to the ends for which they were established. The declared compact of the Union from which we have withdrawn was to establish justice, insure domestic tran-quillity, provide for the common defence, promote the gen-eral welfare, and secure the blessings of liberty to ourselves and our posterity; and when in the judgment of the sover-eign States now composing this Confederacy it has been perverted from the purposes for which it was ordained, and ceased to answer the ends for which it was established, a peaceful appeal to the ballot-box declared that, so far as they were concerned, the government created by that com-pact should cease to exist. In this they merely asserted the right which the Declaration of Independence of 1776 defined to be inalienable. Of the time and occasion of this exercise they as sovereigns were the final judges, each for himself. The impartial, enlightened verdict of mankind will vindicate the rectitude of our conduct; and He who knows the hearts of men will judge of the sincerity with which we labored to preserve the government of our fathers in its spirit.

4

The right solemnly proclaimed at the birth of the States, and which has been affirmed and reaffirmed in the bills of rights of the States subsequently admitted into the Union of 1789, undeniably recognizes in the people the power to resume the authority delegated for the purposes of government. Thus the sovereign States here represented proceeded to form this Confederacy; and it is by the abuse of language that their act has been denominated revolution. They formed a new alliance, but within each State its government has remained. The rights of person and property have not been disturbed. The agent through whom they communicated with foreign nations is changed, but this does not necessarily interrupt their international relations. Sustained by the consciousness that the transition from the former Union to the present Confederacy has not proceeded from a disregard on our part of our just obligations or any failure to perform every constitutional duty, moved by no interest or passion to invade the rights of others, anxious to cultivate peace and commerce with all nations, if we may not hope to avoid war, we may at least expect that posterity will acquit us of having needlessly engaged in it. Doubly justified by the absence of wrong on our part, and by wanton aggression on the part of others, there can be no use to doubt the courage and patriotism of the people of the Confederate States will be found equal to any measure of defence which soon their security may require.

An agricultural people, whose chief interest is the export of a commodity required in every manufacturing country, our true policy is peace and the freest trade which our necessities will permit. It is alike our interest and that of all those to whom we would sell and from whom we would buy, that there should be the fewest practicable restrictions upon the interchange of commodities. There can be but little rivalry between ours and any manufacturing or navigating community, such as the northeastern States of the American Union. It must follow, therefore, that mutual interest would invite good-will and kind offices. If, however, passion or lust of dominion should cloud the judgment or inflame the ambition of those States, we must prepare to meet the emergency, and maintain by the final arbitrament of the sword the position which we have assumed among the nations of the earth.

We have entered upon a career of independence, and it must be inflexibly pursued through many years of controversy with our late associates of the Northern States. We have vainly endeavored to secure tranquillity and obtain respect for the rights to which we were entitled. As a necessity, not a choice, we have resorted to the remedy of separation, and henceforth our energies must be directed to the conduct of our own affairs, and the perpetuity of the Confederacy which we have formed. If a just perception of mutual interest shall permit us peaceably to pursue our separate political career, my most earnest desire will have been fulfilled. But if this be denied us, and the integrity of our territory and jurisdiction be assailed, it will but remain for us with firm resolve to appeal to arms and invoke the blessing of Providence on a just cause. . . .

Actuated solely by a desire to preserve our own rights, and to promote our own welfare, the separation of the Confederate States has been marked by no aggression upon others, and followed by no domestic convulsion. Our industrial pursuits have received no check, the cultivation of our fields progresses as heretofore, and even should we be involved in war, there would be no considerable diminution in the production of the staples which have constituted our exports, in which the commercial world has an interest scarcely less than our own. This common interest of producer and consumer can only be intercepted by an exterior force which should obstruct its transmission to foreign markets, a course of conduct which would be detrimental to manufacturing and commercial interests abroad.

Should reason guide the action of the government from which we have separated, a policy so detrimental to the civilized world, the Northern States included, could not be dictated by even a stronger desire to inflict injury upon us; but if it be otherwise, a terrible responsibility will rest upon it, and the suffering of millions will bear testimony to the folly and wickedness of our aggressors. In the meantime there will remain to us, besides the ordinary remedies before suggested, the well-known resources for retaliation upon the commerce of an enemy. . . . We have changed the constituent parts but not the system of our government. The Constitution formed by our fathers is that of these Confederate States. In their exposition of it, and in the judicial construction it has received, we have a light which reveals its true meaning. Thus instructed as to the just interpretation of that instrument, and ever remembering that all offices are but trusts held for the people, and that delegated powers are to be strictly construed, I will hope by due diligence in the performance of my duties, though I may disappoint your expectation, yet to retain, when retiring, something of the good-will and confidence which will welcome my entrance into office.

It is joyous in the midst of perilous times to look around upon a people united in heart, when one purpose of high resolve animates and actuates the whole, where the sacrifices to be made are not weighed in the balance, against honor, right, liberty, and equality. Obstacles may retard, but they cannot long prevent, the progress of a movement sanctioned by its justice and sustained by a virtuous people. Reverently let us invoke the God of our fathers to guide and protect us in our efforts to perpetuate the principles which by his blessing they were able to vindicate, establish, and transmit to their posterity; and with a continuance of his favor, ever gratefully acknowledged, we may hopefully look forward to success, to peace, to prosperity.

NO DIVIDED FLAG

FROM REPLY TO SENATOR DOUGLAS, UNITED STATES SENATE,
MAY 1860

WE believed then, as I believe now, that this Union, as a compact entered into between the States, was to be preserved by good faith and by a close observance of the terms on which we were united. We believed then, as I believe now, that the party which rested upon the basis of truth; promulgated its opinions, and had them tested in the alembic of public opinion, adopted the only path of safety. I cannot respect such a doctrine as that which says " you may construe the constitution your way and I will construe it mine; we will waive the merit of these two constructions and harmonize together until the courts decide the question between us." A man is bound to have an opinion upon any political subject upon which he is called to act; it is skulking his responsibility for a citizen to say " let us express no opinion, I will agree that you may have yours, and I will have mine; we will co-operate politically together, we will beat the opposition, divide the spoils, and leave it to the courts to decide the question of creed between us."

I do not believe that this is the path of safety; I am sure it is not the way of honor. I believe it devolves on us, who are principally sufferers from the danger to which this policy has exposed us, to affirm the truth boldly and let the people decide after the promulgation of our opinions. Our government, resting as it does upon public opinion and popular consent, was not formed to deceive the people nor does it regard the men in office as a governing class. We, the functionaries, should derive our opinions from the people. To know what their opinion is it is necessary that we should pronounce, in unmistakable language, what we ourselves mean.

My position is that there is no portion of our country where the people are not sufficiently intelligent to discriminate between right and wrong, and no portion where the sense of justice does not predominate. I therefore have been always willing to unfurl our flag to its innermost fold, to nail it to the mast with all our principles plainly inscribed upon it. Believing that we ask nothing but what the constitution was intended to confer; nothing but that which, as equals, we are entitled to receive; I am willing that our case should be plainly stated to those who have to decide it, and await, for good or for evil, their verdict. . . .

Mr. President, after having for forty years been engaged in bitter controversy over a question relating to common property of the States we have reached the point where the issue is presented in a form in which it becomes us to meet it according to existing facts; where it has ceased to be a question to be decided on the footing of authority and by reference to history. We have decided that too long had this question been disturbing the peace and endangering the Union, and it was resolved to provide for its settlement by treating it as a judicial question. Now, will it be said, after Congress provided for the adjustment of this question by the courts, and after the courts had a case brought before them and expressed an opinion covering the controversy, that no additional latitude is to be given to the application of the decision of the court, though Congress had referred specially to them; that it is to be treated simply and technically as a question of *meum et tuum*, such as might have arisen if there had been no such legislation by Congress? Surely it does not become those who have pointed us to that provision as the peace offering, as the means for final adjustment, now to say that it meant nothing more than that the courts would go on hereafter, as heretofore, to try questions of property.

The courts have decided the question so far as they could decide any political question. A case arose in relation to property in a slave held within a Territory where a law of Congress declared that such property should not be held. The whole case was before them; everything except the mere technical point that the law was not enacted by a Territorial legislature. Why, then, if we are to abide by the decision of the supreme court in any future case, do they maintain this controversy on the mere technical point which now divides, disturbs, distracts, destroys the efficiency and the power of the Democratic party? To the senator, I know, as a question of property, it is a matter of no consequence. I should do him injustice if I left any one to infer that I treated his argument as one made by a man prejudiced against the character of property involved in the question. That is not his position; but I assert that he is pursuing an *ignis fatuus*—not

a light caught from the constitution—but a vapor which has
arisen from the corrupting cesspools of sectional strife, of faction and individual rivalry. Measured by any standard of
common sense, its magnitude would be too small to disturb
the adjustment of the balance of our country. There can be
no appeal to humanity made upon this basis. Least of all
could it be made to one who like the senator and myself has
seen this species of property in its sparse condition on the
northwestern frontier, and seen it go out without disturbing
the tranquillity of the community, as it had previously existed
without injury to any one, if not to the benefit of the individual who held it. He has no apprehension, he can have
none, that it is to retard the political prosperity of the future
States—now the Territories. He can have no apprehension
that in that country to which they never would be carried except for domestic purposes, they could ever so accumulate as
to constitute a great political element. He knows and every
man who has had experience and judgment must admit that
the few who may be so carried there have nothing to fear but
the climate, and that living in that close connection which belongs to one or half a dozen of them in a family, the kind-
est relations which it is possible to exist between master
and dependent, exist between these domestics and their
owners.

There is a relation belonging to this species of property,
unlike that of the apprentice or the hired man, which awakens
whatever there is of kindness or of nobility of soul in the
heart of him who owns it; this can only be alienated, obscured,
or destroyed by collecting this species of property into such
masses that the owner is not personally acquainted with the
individuals who compose it. In the relation, however, which
can exist in the Northwestern Territories, the mere domestic

connection of one, two, or at most half a dozen servants in a family, associating with the children as they grow up, attending upon age as it declines, there can be nothing against which either philanthropy or humanity can make an appeal. Not even the emancipationist could raise his voice for this is the high road and the open gate to the condition in which the masters would from interest in a few years desire the emancipation of every one who may thus be taken to the northwestern frontier.

Mr. President, I briefly and reluctantly referred, because the subject had been introduced, to the attitude of Mississippi on a former occasion. I will now as briefly say that in 1851 and in 1860 Mississippi was and is ready to make every concession which it becomes her to make to the welfare and the safety of the Union. If on a former occasion she hoped too much from fraternity, the responsibility for her disappointment rests upon those who fail to fulfil her expectations. She still clings to the government as our fathers formed it. She is ready to-day and to-morrow, as in her past and though brief yet brilliant history, to maintain that government in all its power, and to vindicate its honor with all the means she possesses. I say brilliant history; for it was in the very morning of her existence that her sons on the plains of New Orleans were announced in general orders to have been the admiration of one army and the wonder of the other. That we had a division in relation to the measures enacted in 1850 is true; that the Southern rights men became the minority in the election which resulted is true; but no figure of speech could warrant the senator in speaking of them as subdued; as coming to him or anybody else for quarter. I deemed it offensive when it was uttered, and the scorn with which I repelled it at the instant, time has only softened to contempt. Our flag was never borne from the field. We had carried it in the face of defeat with a knowledge that defeat awaited it; but scarcely had the smoke of the battle passed away which proclaimed another victor, before the general voice admitted that the field again was ours; I have not seen a sagacious reflecting man, who was cognizant of the events as they transpired at the time, who does not say that within two weeks after the election our party was in a majority; and the next election which occurred showed that we possessed the State beyond controversy. How we have wielded that power it is not for me to say. I trust others may see forbearance in our conduct—that with a determination to insist upon our constitutional rights then and now there is an unwavering desire to maintain the government and to uphold the Democratic party.

We believe now as we have asserted on former occasions that the best hope for the perpetuity of our institutions depends upon the co-operation, the harmony, the zealous action of the Democratic party. We cling to that party from conviction, that its principles and its aims are those of truth and the country, as we cling to the Union for the fulfilment of the purposes for which it was formed. Whenever we shall be taught that the Democratic party is recreant to its principles; whenever we shall learn that it cannot be relied upon to maintain the great measures which constitute its vitality, I for one shall be ready to leave it. And so, when we declare our tenacious adherence to the Union it is the Union of the constitution. If the compact between the States is to be trampled into the dust; if anarchy is to be substituted for the usurpation and consolidation which threatened the government at an earlier period; if the Union is to become powerless for the purposes for which it was established, and we are vainly to appeal to it for protection, then, sir, conscious of the rectitude of our course, the justice of our cause, self-reliant, yet humbly, confidingly trusting in the arm that guided and protected our fathers, we look beyond the confines of the Union for the maintenance of our rights. A habitual reverence and cherished affection for the government will bind us to it longer than our interests would suggest or require; but he is a poor student of the world's history who does not understand that communities at last must yield to the dictates of their interests. That the affection, the mutual desire for the mutual good which existed among our fathers may be weakened in succeeding generations by the denial of right and hostile demonstration, until the equality guaranteed but not secured within the Union may be sought for without it, must be evident to even a careless observer of our race. It is time to be up and doing. There is yet time to remove the causes of dissension and alienation which are now distracting and have for years past divided the country.

If the senator correctly described me as having in a former period against my own preferences and opinions acquiesced in the decision of my party; if when I had youth, when physical vigor gave promise of many days and the future was painted in the colors of hope, I could thus surrender my own convictions, my own prejudices, and co-operate with my political friends, according to their views as to the best method of promoting the public good; now, when the years of my future cannot be many, and experience has sobered the hopeful tints of youth's gilding; when approaching the evening of life, the shadows are reversed and the mind turns retrospectively, it is not to be supposed that I would abandon lightly or idly put on trial the party to which I have steadily adhered. It

is rather to be assumed that conservatism which belongs to
the timidity or caution of increasing years would lead me to
cling to; to be supported by rather than to cast off the organization with which I have been so long connected. If I
am driven to consider the necessity of separating myself from
those old and dear relations, of discarding the accustomed support, under circumstances such as I have described, might not
my friends who differ from me pause and inquire whether
there is not something involved in it which calls for their
careful revision?

I desire no divided flag for the Democratic party, seek not
to depreciate the power of the senator or take from him anything of that confidence he feels in the large army which follows his standard. I prefer that his banner should lie in its
silken folds to feed the moth; but if it unrestrainedly rustles
impatient to be unfurled, we who have not invited the conflict
shrink not from the trial; we will plant our flag on every hill
and plain; it shall overlook the Atlantic and welcome the sun
as he rises from its dancing waters; it shall wave its adieu as
he sinks to repose in the quiet Pacific.

Our principles are national; they belong to every State of
the Union; and though elections may be lost by their assertion, they constitute the only foundation on which we can
maintain power on which we can again rise to the dignity the
Democracy once possessed. Does not the senator from Illinois see in the sectional character of the vote he received that
his opinions are not acceptable to every portion of the
country? Is not the fact that the resolutions adopted by
seventeen States on which the greatest reliance must be placed
for Democratic support are in opposition to the dogma to
which he still clings, a warning that if he persists and succeeds
in forcing his theory upon the Democratic party its days are

numbered? We ask only for the constitution. We ask of the Democracy only from time to time to declare as current exigencies may indicate what the constitution was intended to secure and provide. Our flag bears no new device. Upon its folds our principles are written in living light; all proclaiming the constitutional Union, justice, equality, and fraternity of our ocean-bound domain for a limitless future.

CHASE

SALMON PORTLAND CHASE, an American statesman and jurist of distinction, was born in Cornish, New Hampshire, January 13, 1808, and received his education at Dartmouth College. He subsequently studied law with William Wirt, and was admitted to the bar in 1829, and the next year began practice at Cincinnati. An edition by him of the statutes of Ohio brought him into notice soon after, and in 1834 he was appointed solicitor for the United States Bank in Cincinnati. He engaged in the anti-slavery movement in 1837 as counsel for a fugitive slave, and in 1842 defended Van Zandt, the original of Van Tromp in "Uncle Tom's Cabin," who was indicted for aiding slaves to escape. The case was carried up to the supreme court of the United States and there argued by Seward and Chase in 1848. His connection with this famous case brought Chase into great prominence as an anti-slavery champion, and in 1849 he was elected to the United States Senate. In 1855 he was chosen governor of Ohio and re-elected to that office in 1857. In 1861 he entered Lincoln's cabinet as secretary of state and continued to occupy that responsible position until appointed chief justice of the United States in 1864. As chief justice he presided at the impeachment trial of President Johnson. He died in New York city, May 7, 1873. Chase was a man of unusual abilities in more than one direction, and during the Civil War period was of the utmost service to the government. His legal opinions are noted for the excellence of their literary style.

SPEECH ON THE KANSAS-NEBRASKA BILL

DELIVERED IN THE UNITED STATES SENATE, FEBRUARY 3, 1854

[The bill for the organization of the Territories of Nebraska and Kansas being under consideration, Mr. Chase submitted the following amendment: "Strike out from section 14 the words ' was superseded by the principles of the legislation of 1850, commonly called the compromise measures, and;' so that the clause will read: ' That the constitution and all laws of the United States which are not locally inapplicable shall have the same force and effect within the said Territory of Nebraska as elsewere within the United States, except the eighth section of the act preparatory to the admission of Missouri into the Union, approved March 6, 1820, which is hereby declared inoperative,' " and proceeded to say:]

MR. PRESIDENT,—I had occasion a few days ago to expose the utter groundlessness of the personal charges made by the senator from Illinois [Mr. Douglas] against myself and the other signers of the Independent Democratic Appeal. I now move to strike from this bill a statement which I will to-day demonstrate to be without any foundation in fact or history. I intend afterward to move to strike out the whole clause annulling the Missouri prohibition.

I enter into this debate, Mr. President, in no spirit of personal unkindness. The issue is too grave and too momentous for the indulgence of such feelings. I see the great question before me and that question only.

Sir, these crowded galleries, these thronged lobbies, this full attendance of the Senate, prove the deep, transcendent interest of the theme.

A few days only have elapsed since the Congress of the United States assembled in this Capitol. Then no agitation seemed to disturb the political elements. Two of the great political parties of the country in their national conventions had announced that slavery agitation was at an end, and that henceforth that subject was not to be discussed in Congress or out of Congress. The President in his annual message had referred to this state of opinion and had declared his fixed purpose to maintain, as far as any responsibility attached to him, the quiet of the country. Let me read a brief extract from that message:

"It is no part of my purpose to give prominence to any subject which may properly be regarded as set at rest by the deliberate judgment of the people. But while the present is bright with promise, and the future full of demand and inducement for the exercise of active intelligence, the past can never be without useful lessons of admonition and instruction. If its dangers serve not as beacons, they will evidently fail to fulfil the object of a wise design.

" When the grave shall have closed over all those who are now endeavoring to meet the obligations of duty, the year 1850 will be recurred to as a period filled with anxious apprehension. A successful war had just terminated. Peace

brought with it a vast augmentation of territory. Disturbing questions arose bearing upon the domestic institutions of
one portion of the confederacy, and involving the constitutional rights of the States. But, notwithstanding differences
of opinion and sentiment which then existed in relation to
details and specific provisions, the acquiescence of distinguished citizens, whose devotion to the Union can never
be doubted, had given renewed vigor to our institutions and
restored a sense of repose and security to the public mind
throughout the confederacy. That this repose is to suffer
no shock during my official term, if I have power to avert it,
those who placed me here may be assured."

The agreement of the two old political parties thus referred to by the chief magistrate of the country was complete, and a large majority of the American people seemed
to acquiesce in the legislation of which he spoke.

A few of us indeed doubted the accuracy of these statements and the permanency of this repose. We never believed that the acts of 1850 would prove to be a permanent
adjustment of the slavery question. We believed no permanent adjustment of that question possible except by a return to that original policy of the fathers of the Republic, by
which slavery was restricted within State limits, and freedom without exception or limitation was intended to be secured to every person outside of State limits and under the
exclusive jurisdiction of the general government.

But, sir, we only represented a small though vigorous
and growing party in the country. Our number was small
in Congress. By some we were regarded as visionaries—by
some as factionists; while almost all agreed in pronouncing
us mistaken.

And so, sir, the country was at peace. As the eye swept
the entire circumference of the horizon and upward to mid-
heaven not a cloud appeared; to common observation there
was no mist or stain upon the clearness of the sky.

WENDELL PHILLIPS

Orations—Volume fifteen

But suddenly all is changed. Rattling thunder breaks from the cloudless firmament. The storm bursts forth in fury. Warring winds rush into conflict:

" Eurus, Notusque ruunt, creberque procellis Africus."

Yes, sir, " *creber procellis Africus* "—the South wind thick with storm. And now we find ourselves in the midst of an agitation the end and issue of which no man can foresee.

Now, sir, who is responsible for this renewal of strife and controversy? Not we, for we have introduced no question of territorial slavery into Congress—not we who are denounced as agitators and factionists. No, sir; the quietists and the finalists have become agitators; they who told us that all agitation was quieted, and that the resolutions of the political conventions put a final period to the discussion of slavery.

This will not escape the observation of the country. It is slavery that renews the strife. It is slavery that again wants room. It is slavery, with its insatiate demands for more slave territory and more slave States.

And what does slavery ask for now? Why, sir, it demands that a time-honored and sacred compact shall be rescinded—a compact which has endured through a whole generation—a compact which has been universally regarded as inviolable, North and South—a compact, the constitutionality of which few have doubted and by which all have consented to abide.

It will not answer to violate such a compact without a pretext. Some plausible ground must be discovered or invented for such an act; and such a ground is supposed to be found in the doctrine which was advanced the other day by the senator from Illinois, that the compromise acts of 1850

" superseded " the prohibition of slavery north of 36 degrees 30 minutes, in the act preparatory for the admission of Missouri. Aye, sir, " superseded " is the phrase—" superseded by the principles of the legislation of 1850, commonly called the compromise measures."

It is against this statement, untrue in fact and without foundation in history, that the amendment which I have proposed is directed.

Sir, this is a novel idea. At the time when these measures were before Congress in 1850, when the questions involved in them were discussed from day to day, from week to week, and from month to month, in this Senate chamber, who ever heard that the Missouri prohibition was to be superseded ? What man, at what time, in what speech, ever suggested the idea that the acts of that year were to affect the Missouri compromise ?

The senator from Illinois the other day invoked the authority of Henry Clay—that departed statesman in respect to whom whatever may be the differences of political opinion none question that among the great men of this country he stood proudly eminent. Did he in the report made by him as the chairman of the Committee of Thirteen, or in any speech in support of the compromise acts, or in any conversation in the committee or out of the committee, ever even hint at this doctrine of supersedure ? Did any supporter or any opponent of the compromise acts ever vindicate or condemn them on the ground that the Missouri prohibition would be affected by them ? Well, sir, the compromise acts were passed. They were denounced North, and they were denounced South. Did any defender of them at the South ever justify his support of them upon the ground that the South had obtained through them the repeal of the Missouri prohibition? Did any objector to them at the North ever even suggest as a ground of condemnation that that prohibition was swept away by them? No, sir! No man, North or South, during the whole of the discussion of those acts here, or in that other discussion which followed their enactment throughout the country ever intimated any such opinion.

Now, sir, let us come to the last session of Congress. A Nebraska bill passed the House and came to the Senate and was reported from the committee on Territories by the senator from Illinois as its chairman. Was there any provision in it which even squinted toward this notion of repeal by supersedure? Why, sir, Southern gentlemen opposed it on the very ground that it left the Territory under the operation of the Missouri prohibition. The senator from Illinois made a speech in defence of it. Did he invoke Southern support upon the ground that it superseded the Missouri prohibition? Not at all. Was it opposed or vindicated by anybody on any such ground? Every senator knows the contrary. The senator from Missouri [Mr. Atchison], now the president of this body, made a speech upon the bill in which he distinctly declared that the Missouri prohibition was not repealed and could not be repealed.

I will send this speech to the secretary and ask him to read the paragraphs marked.

The secretary read as follows:

" I will now state to the Senate the views which induced me to oppose this proposition in the early part of this session.

" I had two objections to it. One was that the Indian title in that Territory had not been extinguished, or at least a very small portion of it had been. Another was the Missouri compromise, or as it is commonly called, the slavery restriction. It was my opinion at that time—and I am not now very clear on that subject—that the law of Congress when the State of

Missouri was admitted into the Union excluding slavery from the Territory of Louisiana north of 36 degrees 30 minutes, would be enforced in that Territory unless it was specially rescinded, and whether that law was in accordance with the constitution of the United States or not, it would do its work, and that work would be to preclude slaveholders from going into that Territory. But when I came to look into that question I found that there was no prospect, no hope, of a repeal of the Missouri compromise excluding slavery from that Territory.

" Now, sir, I am free to admit that at this moment, at this hour, and for all time to come, I should oppose the organization or the settlement of that Territory unless my constituents and the constituents of the whole South—of the slave States of the Union,—could go into it upon the same footing, with equal rights and equal privileges, carrying that species of property with them as other people of this Union. Yes, sir, I acknowledged that that would have governed me, but I have no hope that the restriction will ever be repealed.

" I have always been of opinion that the first great error committed in the political history of this country was the Ordinance of 1787, rendering the Northwest Territory free territory. The next great error was the Missouri compromise. But they are both irremediable. There is no remedy for them. We must submit to them. I am prepared to do it. It is evident that the Missouri compromise cannot be repealed. So far as that question is concerned we might as well agree to the admission of this Territory now as next year or five or ten years hence."[1]

That, sir, is the speech of the senator from Missouri [Mr. Atchison] whose authority I think must go for something upon this question. What does he say ? " When I came to look into that question "—of the possible repeal of the Missouri prohibition—that was the question he was looking into— " I found that there was no prospect, no hope of a repeal of the Missouri compromise excluding slavery from that Territory." And yet, sir, at that very moment, according to this

---

[1] " Congressional Globe," Second Session, 32d Cong., vol. xxvi, p. 1113.

new doctrine of the senator from Illinois, it had been repealed three years!

Well, the senator from Missouri said further that if he thought it possible to oppose this restriction successfully he never would consent to the organization of the Territory until it was rescinded. " But," said he, " I acknowledge that I have no hope that the restriction will ever be repealed." Then he made some complaint, as other Southern gentlemen have frequently done, of the Ordinance of 1787, and the Missouri prohibition; but went on to say: " They are both irremediable; there is no remedy for them; we must submit to them; I am prepared to do it, it is evident that the Missouri compromise cannot be repealed."

Now, sir, when was this said? It was on the morning of the 4th of March, just before the close of the last session, when that Nebraska bill, reported by the senator from Illinois, which proposed no repeal and suggested no supersedure, was under discussion. I think, sir, that all this shows pretty clearly that up to the very close of the last session of Congress nobody had ever thought of a repeal by supersedure. Then, what took place at the commencement of the present session? The senator from Iowa early in December introduced a bill for the organization of the Territory of Nebraska. I believe it was the same bill which was under discussion here at the last session, line for line, word for word. If I am wrong the senator will correct me.

Did the senator from Iowa then entertain the idea that the Missouri prohibition had been superseded? No, sir, neither he nor any other man here, so far as could be judged from any discussion or statement or remark had received this notion.

Well, on the 4th day of January the Committee on Territories, through their chairman, the senator from Illinois, made a report on the Territorial organization of Nebraska; and that report was accompanied by a bill. Now, sir, on that 4th day of January, just thirty days ago, did the Committee on Territories entertain the opinion that the compromise acts of 1850 superseded the Missouri prohibition? If they did they were very careful to keep it to themselves. We will judge the committee by their own report. What do they say in that? In the first place they describe the character of the controversy in respect to the Territories acquired from Mexico.

They say that some believed that a Mexican law prohibiting slavery was in force there, while others claimed that the Mexican law became inoperative at the moment of acquisition and that slaveholders could take their slaves into the Territory and hold them there under the provisions of the constitution. The Territorial compromise acts, as the committee tell us, steered clear of these questions. They simply provided that the States organized out of these Territories might come in with or without slavery, as they should elect, but did not affect the question whether slaves could or could not be introduced before the organization of State governments. That question was left entirely to judicial decision.

Well, sir, what did the committee propose to do with the Nebraska Territory? In respect to that, as in respect to the Mexican Territory, differences of opinion exist in relation to the introduction of slaves. There are Southern gentlemen who contend that notwithstanding the Missouri prohibition they can take their slaves into the territory covered by it and hold them there by virtue of the constitution. On the other hand the great majority of the American people North and South believe the Missouri prohibition to be constitutional and effectual. Now, what did the committee propose?

Did they propose to repeal the prohibition? Did they suggest that it had been superseded? Did they advance any idea of that kind? No, sir; this is their language:

" Under this section, as in the case of the Mexican law in New Mexico and Utah, it is a disputed point whether slavery is prohibited in the Nebraska country by valid enactment. The decision of this question involves the constitutional power of Congress to pass laws prescribing and regulating the domestic institutions of the various Territories of the Union. In the opinion of those eminent statesmen who hold that Congress is invested with no rightful authority to legislate upon the subject of slavery in the Territories, the eighth section of the act preparatory to the admission of Missouri is null and void, while the prevailing sentiment in a large portion of the Union sustains the doctrine that the constitution of the United States secures to every citizen an inalienable right to move into any of the Territories with his property, of whatever kind and description, and to hold and enjoy the same under the sanction of law. Your committee do not feel themselves called upon to enter into the discussion of these controverted questions. They involve the same grave issues which produced the agitation, the sectional strife, and the fearful struggle of 1850."

This language will bear repetition:

" Your committee do not feel themselves called upon to enter into the discussion of these controverted questions. They involve the same grave issues which produced the agitation, the sectional strife, and the fearful struggle of 1850."

And they go on to say:

"" Congress deemed it wise and prudent to refrain from deciding the matters in controversy then, either by affirming or repealing the Mexican laws or by an act declaratory of the true intent of the constitution and the extent of the protection afforded by it to slave property in the Territories; so your committee are not prepared now to recommend a departure from the course pursued on that memorable occasion, either by affirming or repealing the eighth section

of the Missouri act or by any act declaratory of the meaning
of the constitution in respect to the legal points in dispute."

Mr. President, here are very remarkable facts. The committee on Territories declared that it was not wise, that it
was not prudent, that it was not right to renew the old controversy and to arouse agitation. They declared that they
would abstain from any recommendation of a repeal of the
prohibition or of any provision declaratory of the construction of the constitution in respect to the legal points in dispute.

Mr. President, I am not one of those who suppose that the
question between Mexican law and the slaveholding claims
was avoided in the Utah and New Mexico act; nor do I think
that the introduction into the Nebraska bill of the provisions
of those acts in respect to slavery would leave the question
between the Missouri prohibition and the same slaveholding
claims entirely unaffected. I am of a very different opinion.
But I am dealing now with the report of the senator from
Illinois, as chairman of the committee, and I show beyond
all controversy that that report gave no countenance whatever to the doctrine of repeal by supersedure.

Well, sir, the bill reported by the committee was printed
in the "Washington Sentinel" on Saturday, January 7th. It
contained twenty sections, no more, no less. It contained no
provisions in respect to slavery except those in the Utah and
New Mexico bills. It left those provisions to speak for themselves. This was in harmony with the report of the committee.   On the 10th of January—on Tuesday—the act appeared again in the " Sentinel;" but it had grown longer
during the interval. It appeared now with twenty-one sections. There was a statement in the paper that the twenty-
first section had been omitted by a clerical error.

But, sir, it is a singular fact that this twenty-first section is entirely out of harmony with the committee's report. It undertakes to determine the effect of the provision in the Utah and New Mexico bills. It declares among other things that all questions pertaining to slavery in the Territories and in the new States to be formed therefrom are to be left to the decision of the people residing therein through their appropriate representatives. This provision in effect repealed the Missouri prohibition, which the committee in their report declared ought not to be done. Is it possible, sir, that this was a mere clerical error? May it not be that this twenty-first section was the fruit of some Sunday work between Saturday the 7th and Tuesday the 10th?

But, sir, the addition of this section it seems did not help the bill. It did not I suppose meet the approbation of Southern gentlemen, who contended that they have a right to take their slaves into the Territories notwithstanding any prohibition either by Congress or by a Territorial legislature. I dare say it was found that the votes of these gentlemen could not be had for the bill with that clause in it. It was not enough that the committee had abandoned their report and added this twenty-first section, in direct contravention of its reasonings and principles. The twenty-first section itself must be abandoned and the repeal of the Missouri prohibition placed in a shape which would not deny the slaveholding claim.

The senator from Kentucky [Mr. Dixon], on the 16th of January, submitted an amendment which came square up to repeal and to the claim. That amendment probably produced some fluttering and some consultation. It met the views of Southern senators and probably determined the shape which the bill has finally assumed. Of the various mutations which it has undergone I can hardly be mistaken in attributing the last to the amendment of the senator from Kentucky. That there is no effect without a cause is among our earliest lessons in physical philosophy, and I know of no causes which will account for the remarkable changes which the bill underwent after the 16th of January, other than that amendment and the determination of Southern senators to support it, and to vote against any provision recognizing the right of any Territorial legislature to prohibit the introduction of slavery.

It was just seven days, Mr President, after the senator from Kentucky had offered his amendment that a fresh amendment was reported from the committee on Territories, in the shape of a new bill enlarged to forty sections. This new bill cuts off from the proposed Territory half a degree of latitude on the south and divides the residue into two Territories—the southern Territory of Kansas and the northern Territory of Nebraska. It applies to each all the provisions of the Utah and New Mexico bills; it rejects entirely the twenty-first clerical-error section and abrogates the Missouri prohibition by the very singular provision which I will read:

" The constitution and all laws of the United States which are not locally inapplicable shall have the same force and effect within the said Territory of Nebraska as elsewhere within the United States, except the eighth section of the act preparatory to the admission of Missouri into the Union, approved March 6, 1820, which was superseded by the principles of the legislation of 1850, commonly called the compromise measures, and is therefore declared inoperative."

Doubtless, Mr. President, this provision operates as a repeal of the prohibition. The senator from Kentucky was right when he said it was in effect the equivalent of his amendment. Those who are willing to break up and destroy the old compact of 1820 can vote for this bill with full assurance that such will be its effect. But I appeal to them not to vote for this supersedure clause. I ask them not to incorporate into the legislation of the country a declaration which every one knows to be wholly untrue. I have said that this doctrine of supersedure is new. I have now proved that it is a plant of but ten days' growth. It was never seen or heard of until the 23d day of January, 1854. It was upon that day that this tree of Upas was planted; we already see its poison fruits.

The provision I have quoted abrogates the Missouri prohibition. It asserts no right in the Territorial legislature to prohibit slavery. . . .

The truth is that the compromise acts of 1850 were no' intended to introduce any principles of Territorial organiza tion applicable to any other Territory except that covered by them. The professed object of the friends of the compromise acts was to compose the whole slavery agitation. There were various matters of complaint. The non-surrender of fugitives from service was one. The existence of slavery and the slave-trade here in this District and elsewhere, under the exclusive jurisdiction of Congress, was another. The apprehended introduction of slavery into the Territories furnished other grounds of controversy. The slave States complained of the free States and the free States complained of the slave States. It was supposed by some that this whole agitation might be stayed and finally put at rest by skilfully adjusted legislation. So, sir, we had the Omnibus Bill and its appendages, the Fugitive-Slave Bill and the District Slave-Trade Suppression Bill. To please the North—to please the free States—California was to be ad-

mitted and the slave depots here in the district were to be
broken up. To please the slave States a stringent fugitive-
slave act was to be passed and slavery was to have a chance
to get into the new Territories. The support of the senators
and representatives from Texas was to be gained by a liberal
adjustment of boundary and by the assumption of a large
portion of their State debt.

The general result contemplated was a complete and final
adjustment of all questions relating to slavery.

The acts passed. A number of the friends of the acts
signed a compact pledging themselves to support no man for
any office who would in any way renew the agitation. The
country was required to acquiesce in the settlement as an absolute finality. No man concerned in carrying those measures through Congress, and least of all the distinguished man
whose efforts mainly contributed to their success, ever imagined that in the Territorial acts, which formed a part of the
series, they were planting the germs of a new agitation. Indeed, I have proved that one of these acts contained an express stipulation which precludes the revival of the agitation
in the form in which it is now thrust upon the country, without manifest disregard of the provisions of those acts themselves.

I have thus proved beyond controversy that the averment
of the bill which my amendment proposes to strike out is
untrue. Senators, will you unite in a statement which you
know to be contradicted by the history of the country? Will
you incorporate into a public statute an affirmation which is
contradicted by every event which attended or followed the
adoption of the compromise acts? Will you here, acting
under your high responsibility as senators of the States, assert as a fact, by a solemn vote, that which the personal

recollection of every senator who was here during the discussion of those compromise acts disproves?

I will not believe it until I see it. If you wish to break up the time-honored compact embodied in the Missouri compromise, transferred into the joint resolution for the annexation of Texas, preserved and affirmed by these compromise acts themselves, do it openly—do it boldly. Repeal the Missouri prohibition. Repeal it by a direct vote. Do not repeal it by indirection. Do not " declare " it " inoperative," " because superseded by the principles of the legislation of 1850."

Mr. President, three great eras have marked the history of this country in respect to slavery. The first may be characterized as the " Era of Enfranchisement." It commenced with the earliest struggles for national independence. The spirit which inspired it animated the hearts and prompted the efforts of Washington, of Jefferson, of Patrick Henry, of Wythe, of Adams, of Jay, of Hamilton, of Morris—in short, of all the great men of our early history.

All these hoped for, all these labored for, all these believed in, the final deliverance of the country from the curse of slavery. That spirit burned in the Declaration of Independence and inspired the provisions of the constitution and the Ordinance of 1787.

Under its influence, when in full vigor, State after State provided for the emancipation of the slaves within their limits prior to the adoption of the constitution. Under its feebler influence at a later period, and during the administration of Mr. Jefferson, the importation of slaves was prohibited into Mississippi and Louisiana in the faint hope that those Territories might finally become free States. Gradually that spirit ceased to influence our public councils and lost its control over the American heart and the American policy.

Another era succeeded, but by such imperceptible gradations that the lines which separate the two cannot be traced with absolute precision. The facts of the two eras meet and mingle as the currents of confluent streams mix so imperceptibly that the observer cannot fix the spot where the meeting waters blend.

This second era was the "Era of Conservatism." Its great maxim was to preserve the existing condition. Men said: Let things remain as they are; let slavery stand where it is; exclude it where it is not; refrain from disturbing the public quiet by agitation; adjust all difficulties that arise, not by the application of principles, but by compromises.

It was during this period that the senator tells us that slavery was maintained in Illinois, both while a Territory and after it became a State, in despite of the provisions of the Ordinance. It is true, sir, that the slaves held in the Illinois country under the French law were not regarded as absolutely emancipated by the provisions of the ordinance. But full effect was given to the Ordinance in excluding the introduction of slaves, and thus the Territory was preserved from eventually becoming a slave State. The few slaveholders in the Territory of Indiana, which then included Illinois, succeeded in obtaining such an ascendency in its affairs that repeated applications were made, not merely by conventions of delegates, but by the Territorial legislature itself, for a suspension of the clause in the Ordinance prohibiting slavery. These applications were reported upon by John Randolph of Virginia in the House and by Mr. Franklin in the Senate. Both the reports were against suspension. The grounds stated by Randolph are specially worthy of being considered now. They are thus stated in the report:

"That the committee deem it highly dangerous and inexpedient to impair a provision wisely calculated to promote the happiness and prosperity of the northwestern country and to give strength and security to that extensive frontier. In the salutary operation of this sagacious and benevolent restraint it is believed that the inhabitants of Indiana will at no very distant day find ample remuneration for a temporary privation of labor and of emigration."

Sir, these reports made in 1803 and 1807, and the action of Congress upon them in conformity with their recommendation saved Illinois and perhaps Indiana from becoming slave States. When the people of Illinois formed their State constitution they incorporated into it a section providing that neither slavery nor involuntary servitude shall hereafter be introduced into this State. The constitution made provision for the continued service of the few persons who were originally held as slaves and then bound to service under the Territorial laws and for the freedom of their children and thus secured the final extinction of slavery. The senator thinks that this result is not attributable to the Ordinance. I differ from him. But for the ordinance I have no doubt slavery would have been introduced into Indiana, Illinois, and Ohio. It is something to the credit of the " Era of Conservatism," uniting its influences with those of the expiring " Era of Enfranchisement," that it maintained the Ordinance of 1787 in the northwest.

The " Era of Conservatism " passed, also by imperceptible gradations, into the " Era of Slavery Propagandism." Under the influences of this new spirit we opened the whole territory acquired from Mexico, except California, to the ingress of slavery. Every foot of it was covered by a Mexican prohibition; and yet by the legislation of 1850 we consented to expose it to the introduction of slaves. Some, I believe, have actually been carried into Utah and New Mexico. They may be few, perhaps, but a few are enough to affect materially the probable character of their future governments. Under the evil influences of the same spirit we are now called upon to reverse the original policy of the republic, to support even a solemn compact of the conservative period, and open Nebraska to slavery.

Sir, I believe that we are upon the verge of another era. That era will be the " Era of Reaction." The introduction of this question here and its discussion will greatly hasten its advent. We who insist upon the denationalization of slavery and upon the absolute divorce of the general government from all connection with it will stand with the men who favored the compromise acts and who yet wish to adhere to them in their letter and in their spirit against the repeal of the Missouri prohibition. But you may pass it here. You may send it to the other House. It may become a law.

But its effect will be to satisfy all thinking men that no compromises with slavery will endure except so long as they serve the interests of slavery; and that there is no safe and honorable ground for non-slaveholders to stand upon, except that of restricting slavery within State limits and excluding it absolutely from the whole sphere of federal jurisdiction. The old questions between political parties are at rest. No great question so thoroughly possesses the public mind as this of slavery. This discussion will hasten the inevitable reorganization of parties upon the new issues which our circumstances suggest. It will light up a fire in the country which may perhaps consume those who kindle it.

I cannot believe that the people of this country have so far lost sight of the maxims and principles of the Revolution, or are so insensible to the obligations which those maxims and principles impose, as to acquiesce in the violation of this

NAPOLEON III

C HARLES LOUIS NAPOLEON BONAPARTE, President and Emperor of France, was born at Paris, April 20, 1808. He was the reputed third son of Louis Napoleon, king of Holland, and Hortense, step-daughter of Napoleon I. At his birth he was regarded as the second heir of the empire, and Napoleon took great interest in his education even after the birth of the King of Rome. After the battle of Waterloo, his mother having been exiled from France, he was brought up at Geneva, Augsburg, his mother's residence at Arenenberg, and at Rome. He began his military studies and exercises at Constance and made good progress in artillery, engineering, history, physics, and chemistry. In 1831 he went with his elder brother, Louis, to assist the Romagna in its revolt against the Pope. The death of Louis in this expedition, followed by that of the Duke of Reichstadt in 1832, made him the head of the Napoleonic dynasty. He returned to Paris with his mother, but, owing to a demonstration made by the people on the anniversary of the death of Napoleon, Louis Philippe insisted on their departure and they went to England. In 1832 he accepted the mission of leading the Polish insurrection and actually started for the border, but the fall of Warsaw, September 7, changed his plans. He returned to Switzerland and employed his leisure in the composition of various works. His " Reveries Politiques " had for its fundamental principle the idea of universal suffrage. In recognition of his work on Switzerland, published in 1833, he was proclaimed a citizen of the Swiss republic. In 1835 he completed a " Manual of Artillery " which brought him into favorable notice in the military circles of Europe. During the five years that followed he made two melodramatic and abortive attempts to gain the throne of France. Condemned to perpetual imprisonment he managed to escape in May, 1846, and returned to England. In 1848 he was elected deputy for Paris and three other departments and in September he was made President of the anomalous republic. In December, 1851, he dissolved the constitution and was re-elected President for ten years. He almost immediately threw off the mask and assumed the title of Emperor. Among the important events of his reign were the annexation of Savoy and Nice, the Hausmannization of Paris, the great Paris exposition, and the Crimean war. He wrote his " Life of Cæsar " as a veiled defence of his political measures. In 1870 he declared war against Prussia, but, though he assumed the chief command, he failed to cross the Rhine, and after a disastrous campaign he was obliged to surrender, September 2, 1870. In March, 1871, he was allowed to join the Empress Eugenie, his wife, at Chiselhurst, England, where he resided till his death, January 9, 1873.

(6245)

SPEECH IN THE NATIONAL ASSEMBLY

OF my sentiments or of my opinions I shall not speak; I have already set them before you, and no one as yet has had reason to doubt my word. As to my parliamentary conduct, I will say that as I never permit myself the liberty of bringing any of my colleagues to an account for the course which he thinks proper to pursue, so, in like manner, I never recognize in him the right to call me to an account for mine; this account I owe only to my constituents.

Of what am I accused? Of accepting from the popular sentiment a nomination after which I have not sought. Well! I accept this nomination that does me so much honor; I accept it, because three successive elections and the unanimous decree of the National Assembly, reversing the proscriptions against my family, authorize me to believe that France regards the name I bear to be serviceable for the consolidation of society, now shaken to its foundations,—and for the establishment and prosperity of the Republic.

How little do those who charge me with ambition know my heart! If an imperative duty did not keep me here, if the sympathy of my fellow citizens did not console me for the violence of the attacks of some, and even for the impetuosity of the defences of others, long since would I have regretted my exile.

I am reproached for my silence! Few persons here are gifted with the faculty of eloquent speech, obedient to just and sound ideas. But is there only one way to serve our country? What she wants most of all is acts; what she wants is a government, firm, intelligent, and wise, more desirous to heal the evils of society than to avenge them—a government that would openly set itself at the head of just ideas, and thus repel a thousand times more effectually than with bayonets those theories which are not founded on experience and reason.

I know that parties intend to set my path with pits and snares; but I shall not fall into them. I shall always follow in my own way the course which I have traced out, without troubling myself or stopping to see who is pleased. Nothing shall interrupt my tranquillity, nothing shall induce me to forget my duty. I have but one aim; it is to merit the esteem of the Assembly, and with this esteem, that of all good men, and the confidence of that magnanimous people that was made so light of here yesterday.

I declare, then, to those who may be willing to organize a system of provocation against me that henceforward I shall reply to no questioning, to no species of attack, to none who would have me speak when I prefer to be silent. Strong in the approval of my conscience, I shall remain immovable amidst all attacks, impassable towards all calumnies.

FIRST INAUGURAL ADDRESS AS PRESIDENT

CITIZEN REPRESENTATIVES,—The suffrages of the nation and the oath which I have taken command my future conduct. My duty is marked out; I shall fulfil it as a man of honor.

I shall treat as enemies of the country all those who may attempt to change, by illegal means, what entire France has established.

Between you and me, citizen representatives, no real dissensions should exist; our wills, our desires are the same.

I wish, like you, to place society on its bases, to strengthen democratic institutions, and to try every means to relieve the sufferings of the generous and intelligent people that has just given me such a splendid mark of confidence.

The majority which I have obtained not only fills me with gratitude, but it shall impart to the new government the moral force without which there is no authority.

With the re-establishment of peace and order our country can arise, heal her wounds, collect her stray children, and calm her passions.

Animated with this conciliatory spirit, I have called around me men of honesty, talent, and patriotism, fully assured that, notwithstanding the differences of their political origin, they are determined to co-operate harmoniously with you in applying the constitution to the perfection of the laws, to the glory of the Republic.

The new administration in entering on business must thank its predecessor for its efforts to transmit the power intact, and to maintain public tranquillity.

The conduct of the honorable General Cavaignac has been worthy of the loyalty of his character and of that sentiment of duty which is the first qualification of the head of a State.

We have, citizen representatives, a great mission to fulfil; it is to found a republic for the interest of all, and a government just, firm, and animated with a sincere love of progress without being either reactionary or Utopian.

Let us be men of the country, not men of a party, and with the assistance of God we shall accomplish useful if not great things.

ANNUAL MESSAGE TO THE ASSEMBLY, NOVEMBER, 1850

O UR arms have overthrown that turbulent demagogism which has compromised the cause of real liberty throughout the Italian peninsula, and our brave soldiers have had the signal honor of restoring Pius IX to the throne of St. Peter. Party spirit shall never obscure this fact, which will always form a glorious page in the history of France. The constant aim of our exertions has been to encourage the liberal and philanthropic dispositions of the Holy Father. The pontifical power continues to realize the promises contained in the "Motu Proprio" of September, 1849.

Touching questions that most deeply engaged the minds of all, the message spoke with reserve, though the meaning of several passages was clear enough. Towards the end it said:

Notwithstanding the difficulty of circumstances, law and authority have so far recovered their empire that now no one dreams of the success of violent measures. But, on the other hand, the more fears diminish regarding the present, the more they increase regarding the future. France first of all wants repose. She is hardly yet recovered from the dangers that threatened society, and remains indifferent to quarrels between parties or individuals in the presence of the great interests that are at stake. . . .

As first magistrate of the Republic, I have been obliged to put myself in communication with the clergy, the magistracy, the agriculturists, the manufacturers, the people, in short, and the army; and I have taken care to seize every opportunity to show them my gratitude for the support they have given me.

If my name and my efforts have succeeded in arousing the spirit of the army, of which I alone, according to the terms of the constitution, have the power to dispose, it is a service, I venture to say, which I have rendered the country, for I have always directed my personal influence to the advantage of order.

It is now permitted to every one except myself to desire the speedy revision of our fundamental law. If the constitution contains vices and dangers, you are at liberty to hold them up before the gaze of the country. I alone, bound down by my oath, circumscribe myself within its strictly drawn limits.

The councils general have in great numbers expressed a wish for its revision. This wish is addressed to the legislative power. As for me, the elect of the people, amenable but to the people, I shall always conform to the wishes of the people legally expressed.

If in this session you vote the revision of the constitution, our fundamental laws shall be reformed, and the system of the executive authority regulated; if you do not vote it, the people in 1852 will solemnly manifest the expression of their new wishes. But whatever may be the solutions of the future, let us understand each other so that it may never be left to passion, or surprise, or violence, to decide the fate of a great nation. Let us inspire the people with a love of repose, by introducing calmness into our deliberations; let us inspire them with a love of rectitude, by never forgetting its dictates ourselves; then, rely upon it, the progress made in our political morals will compensate for the danger of institutions created in days of suspicions and uncertainties.

What occupies me especially is, not to know who shall govern France in 1852, but to employ the time at my disposal in such a manner that the transition, whatever it may be, may take place without trouble or agitation.

The employment which is noblest and worthiest of a generous soul is, not to seek when one is in power by what expedients he can retain himself there, but to seek incessantly for the means of consolidating, for the benefit of all, those principles of authority and morality which are continually struggling with the passions of men and the instability of the laws.

I have loyally opened my heart to you; you will correspond to my frankness by your confidence, to my good intentions by your co-operation, and God will do the rest.

SECOND ANNUAL MESSAGE AS PRESIDENT

A VAST demagogical conspiracy is now organizing in France and Europe. Secret societies are endeavoring to extend their ramifications even into the smallest communes. Without being able to agree on men or things, they have agreed to bring all the madness, the violence, and the obduracy of parties to a focus in 1852, not to construct, but to overthrow.

Your patriotism and your courage, with which I will endeavor to keep pace, will, I am sure, save France from the dangers with which she is threatened. But to conquer these dangers we must look at them without fear and without exaggeration; and whilst convinced, thanks to the strength of the administration, to the enlightened zeal of the magistrates, and to the devotion of the army, that France cannot perish, let us unite our efforts to deprive the spirit of evil even of the hope of a momentary success.

The best means to attain this end has always appeared to me the application of that system which consists, on the one hand, in satisfying the legitimate interests; and, on the other, in stifling at the moment of their appearance the slightest symptoms of an attack against religion, morality, or society.

Thus, to procure labor by granting to companies our great lines of railway, and with the money which the State will procure from these projects to give a strong impulse to the other works in all the departments; to encourage the institutions destined to develop agricultural or commercial credit, to come, by the establishment of charitable institutions, to the assistance of poverty—such has been and such still must be our first care; and it is by following this course that it will be easier to recur to means of repression when their necessity shall have become felt.

[After describing the state of the country he comes to the grand feature of the message—the restoration of universal suffrage. He uses every argument to urge them to an adoption of the measure, and he says:]

The state of general uneasiness is increasing every day. Employment grows slack, poverty spreads, the interests become more apprehensive, and expectations hostile to society become more exulting as the almost exhausted public authorities approach their term.

In such a state of things my duty is the same to-day as it was yesterday. It consists in maintaining order and in removing every occasion of disturbance, so that the resolutions which are to decide our fate may be conceived in tranquillity and adopted in peace.

These resolutions can emanate only from a decisive act of the national sovereignty, since they have popular election for a basis. Well! I have asked myself whether, in the presence of the delirium of passions, of the confusion of doctrines, of the division of parties, when everything is combined to attack morality, justice, and authority, we ought to leave shaken and incomplete the only principle which in the middle of the general chaos Providence has kept standing to rally us around it.

Since universal suffrage has reconstructed the social edifice by substituting a right for a revolutionary fact, is it wise in us to narrow its basis any longer? Finally, I have asked myself if, when new powers shall preside over the destinies of the country, it would not be compromising their stability beforehand to leave behind us a pretext for questioning their origin or for misrepresenting their legitimacy?

No doubt on the subject was possible; and without wishing to swerve for a single instant from the policy of order which I have always followed out, I have been obliged, much to my regret, to separate from a cabinet which possessed all my confidence, in order to choose another, which, equally composed of honorable men, publicly known for their conservative sentiments, has moreover consented to admit the necessity of re-establishing universal suffrage on the broadest possible basis.

You will therefore have presented to you the draft of a law which restores the principle in all its fulness.

The project has no features which can offend this Assembly; for if I think it expedient to ask to-day for the withdrawal of the law of the 31st of May I do not mean to deny the approbation which I gave at that time to the cabinet which claimed from the chief of the majority, whose work it was, the honor of presenting it.

If we remember the circumstances under which this law was presented we shall not, I believe, refuse to allow that it was an act of policy rather than an electoral law, that it was really and truly a measure to ensure the public tranquillity. Whenever the majority shall propose to me energetic measures for the safety of the country it may rely on my loyal and disinterested support. But even the best of such measures have but a limited time.

The law of the 31st of May has in its application even gone beyond the object intended to be attained. No one foresaw the suppression of three millions of electors, two thirds of whom are peaceful inhabitants of the country. What has been the result? Why, that this exclusion has served as a pretext to the anarchist party, who cloak their detestable designs by appearing to conquer back a right of which they had been despoiled. Too weak in numbers to take possession of society by their votes, they hope under favor of the general emotion and the decline of the powers of the State to kindle at several points of France, instantaneously, troubles which would be quelled, no doubt, but which should inevitably throw us into fresh complications.

Another serious objection is this: The constitution requires for the validity of the election of a president by the people at least two millions of suffrages; and if this number is not made up the right of election is conferred on the Assembly. The Constituent Assembly had therefore decided that out of ten million voters inscribed on the lists one fifth was sufficient to render the election valid.

At the present time, the number of electors being reduced to seven millions, to require two millions is to invert the proportion; that is to say, it is to demand one third instead of one fifth, and thus in a certain eventuality to take the election out of the hands of the people and give it to the Assembly. It is therefore positively changing the condition of the eligibility of the president of the Republic.

Lastly, I call your particular attention to another reason, which perhaps may prove decisive.

The re-establishment of universal suffrage on its principal basis furnishes an additional chance of obtaining the revision of the constitution. You have not forgotten why the adversaries of this revision refused last session to vote for it. They used this argument, which they knew how to render specious: "The constitution," said they, "which is the work of an Assembly taking its rise in universal suffrage, cannot be modified by an Assembly issuing from a restricted suffrage." Whether this be a real motive or only a pretext it is expedient to set it aside and be able to say to those who would bind the country down to an immutable constitution, "Behold universal suffrage re-established. The majority of the Assembly, supported by two millions of petitioners, by the greater number of the councils of arrondissement, and almost unanimously by the councils general, demands the revision of the fundamental compact. Have you less confidence than we in the expression of the popular will?"

The question therefore may be thus stated to all those who desire a pacific solution of the difficulties of the day: "The law of the 31st of May has its imperfections; but even were it perfect, should it not nevertheless be repealed if it resists the revision of the constitution, that manifest wish of the country?"

It is objected, I am aware, that on my part these proposals are inspired by personal interest. My conduct for the last three years ought to repel such an allegation. The welfare of the country, I repeat, will always be the sole moving spring of my conduct. I believe it my duty to propose every means of conciliation and to use every effort to bring about a pacific, regular, legal solution, whatever may be its issue.

Thus then, gentlemen, the proposal I make to you is neither a piece of party tactics nor an egotistical calculation, nor a sudden resolution; it is the result of serious meditation and of profound conviction. I do not pretend that this measure will banish all the difficulties of the situation. But to each day its own task.

To-day to re-establish universal suffrage is to deprive civil war of its flag, the opposition of its last argument. It is to furnish France with the possibility of giving itself institutions which may ensure its tranquillity. It is to give the future powers of the State that moral force which can only exist so long as it reposes on a consecrated principle and on an incontestable authority.

FAMOUS SPEECH AT DIJON

I WISH that such persons as entertain apprehensions regarding the future had accompanied me through the populations of the Yonne and the Côte d'Or. They would have had their minds set at rest by being able to judge for themselves of the real state of public feeling. They would have seen that neither intrigue, nor attacks, nor passionate discussions of parties are in harmony with the sentiments and the situation of the country.

France does not wish either the return of the ancient régime—no matter under what form it may be disguised—or the trial of evil and impracticable Utopias. It is because I am the most natural adversary of the one and the other that she has placed her confidence in me. If it be not so, how else can be explained this touching sympathy entertained by the people toward me, which, whilst it repels the most ruinous controversies, absolves me from being the cause of their sufferings?

In fact, if my government has not realized all the ameliorations which it has had in view, the blame lies in the manœuvres of factions which paralyze the good dispositions of Assemblies as well as those of governments the most devoted to the public good. For the last three years it could be remarked that I was always seconded whenever the question was to subdue disorder by coercive enactments. And whenever I wished to do good, to establish the landed influence, or to ameliorate the condition of the poorer classes, I met with nothing but inertness. It is because you have shared those convictions that I have found in patriotic Burgundy such a reception as is at once for me both approbation and encouragement.

I take advantage of this banquet as if it were a public tribune, to open to my fellow citizens the bottom of my heart. A new phase of our political life is commencing. From one end of France to the other petitions are being signed in favor of the revision of the constitution; I await with confidence the manifestation of the country and the decision of the Assembly, which can only be actuated by the sole thought of the public good. If France feels that she must not be disposed of against her will, France has but to say so; she shall not be without my courage and my energy.

Since I came into power I have proved how much, in the presence of the grave interests of society, I disregarded whatever affected myself personally. The most unjust and the most violent attacks have failed to affect my attitude of calmness. Whatever duties the country may impose she shall find me resolute to execute her will. And believe me, gentlemen, France shall not perish in my hands.

ADDRESS TO THE FRENCH LEGISLATURE

DELIVERED JANUARY 18, 1858

I HAVE not accepted the honors of the nation with the aim of acquiring an ephemeral popularity, but in hope of deserving the approbation of posterity as the founder of established order. And I declare to you to-day, notwithstanding all that has been said on the contrary, that the future perils of your country will not arise from the excessive prerogatives of the throne, but from the absence of repressive laws. Thus the last elections, despite their satisfactory results, offered in some districts a sad spectacle. Hostile parties availed themselves of that opportunity to create disturbances; and some men even avowed themselves as the enemies of our national institutions, deceived the electors by false promises, and after gaining their suffrages, rejected them with disdain. You will never allow such a scandal to occur again; and you will hereafter compel all the eligible to take the oath to the constitution before presenting themselves as candidates for office.

The tranquillizing of the public mind has been the aim of our constant efforts, and you will aid me in seeking means for reducing the factious opposition to-silence. Is it not painful to witness, in a country peaceful and prosperous at home, and respected abroad, one party decrying the government to which it is indebted for the security it enjoys, while another exerts its political liberty to undermine the existing institutions?

I offer a hearty welcome to all those who recognize the national will, and I do not inquire into their antecedents.

As for those who have originated disturbances and organized the conspiracies, let them know that their time has gone by!

I cannot close without mentioning that criminal attempt which has been recently made. I thank heaven for the visible protection which it has granted to the Empress and myself; and I deeply deplore that a plan for destroying one life should have ended in the loss of so many. Yet this thwarted scheme can teach us some useful lessons. The recourse to such desperate means is but a proof of the feebleness and impotence of the conspirators. And again, there never was an assassination which served the interests of the men who armed the murderer. Neither the party that struck Cæsar, nor that which slew Henry IV, profited by their overthrow. God sometimes permits the death of the just, but he never allows the triumph of the evil agent. Thus these attempts neither disturb my security in the present nor my trust in the future. If I live, the Empire lives with me; if I fall, the Empire will be strengthened by my death, for the indignation of the people and of the army will be a new support for the throne of my son.

Let us face the future with confidence, and calmly devote ourselves to the welfare and to the honor of our country. *Dieu protège la France!*

MANNING

CARDINAL HENRY EDWARD MANNING, a distinguished English Roman Catholic prelate and pulpit orator, the son of a London merchant, was born at Totteridge, Hertfordshire, July 15, 1808. He was educated at Harrow, and at Balliol College, Oxford, and in his university course showed himself to be a ready and effective speaker. His first intention was to enter political life, but he soon decided to go into the church, and after studying theology he took orders in the Established Church in 1832. The next year he became rector of Woolavington-cum-Graffham, Sussex, and remained there seventeen years, receiving the preferment of the archdeaconry of Chichester meanwhile, in 1840. After Ward and Newman had entered the Roman communion, Manning was regarded as one of the leaders of the High Church party, but the decision in the famous " Gorham Case " determined him to leave the Anglican Church, and on April 6, 1851, he was received into the Roman Catholic Church. After several years' residence in Rome he was appointed rector of St. Mary's, Bayswater, London, and on the death of Cardinal Wiseman in 1865 became archbishop of Westminster. He was created cardinal in 1875, and died in London, January 14, 1892. Manning was a preacher of much eloquence, a learned theologian, and a most acute and skilful controversialist. For the last twenty years of his life he was active in the cause of Christian socialism and a strong believer in total abstinence, writing and lecturing much in its behalf. He was untiring in philanthropic labors, and was conspicuous in educational affairs as well as in all movements for social reform. In spite of the uncritical character of his mind, he exercised a broad charity in religious matters. His mode of life was extremely simple, and the asceticism of his later years made his tall spare figure seem even emaciated. His principal writings include " The Unity of the Church " (1842); " Thoughts for Those that Mourn " (1843); " Sermons at Oxford " (1844); " Sermons on Ecclesiastical Subjects " (1863); " The Temporal Mission of the Holy Ghost " (1865-75); " England and Christendom " (1867); " The Infallible Church " (1875); " The Vatican Decrees in their Bearing on Civil Allegiance " (1875); " Four Great Evils of the Day; " " The Eternal Priesthood " (1883).

THE TRIUMPH OF THE CHURCH

" We give thanks unto God, who maketh us always to triumph in Christ Jesus, and manifesteth the odor of the knowledge of Him by us in every place. For we are a good odor of Christ unto God, both in them that are saved and in them that perish; in the one indeed an odor of life, in the other an odor of death unto death."— 2 Cor. ii, 14-16.

(6260)

DUKE OF WELLINGTON

SUCH was the confidence of the Apostle in the face of all that was most hostile, mighty, and triumphant in the judgment of this world. He was confident that through God his mission in the world was being accomplished, that the word of God was triumphing over all the power of men. They may well have said to him, "What is this triumph you speak of? If this be triumph, what is defeat? You were stoned the other day at Lystra; you were imprisoned at Philippi; you were scourged at Jerusalem; you were saved out of the hands of the people only by Roman soldiers; you were confounded by the philosophers at Athens; and you were refuted out of the holy Scriptures by the Jews of Berea. If this is triumph, you are welcome to it." Such, no doubt, was the lordly and confident language of men in the face of the apostles of Jesus Christ then, and such is the language of confidence with which the world looks on the Catholic Church at this hour. It counts it to be a comedy played out, a stale mediæval superstition, and a name that is trampled in the earth. In every age the Church has been militant and in warfare. It is under the same law of suffering which crucified its Divine Head. His throne was a cross, and his crown was of thorns. Nevertheless he triumphed, and he triumphs still, and shall triumph to the end. And so at this moment, in this nineteenth century, in the century of modern civilization, of light, of progress, of scientific affectation, the Catholic Church is derided. They say to us, "Look at the Catholic Church in Germany; look at it in Italy; the head of the Church dethroned; and not a spot on earth for the incarnation to set its foot upon. If this be triumph you are welcome to it." Our answer is: "Yes, even now we triumph always and in every place. The Catholic Church is triumphing now in America, and in Ireland, and in the colonies of the British empire; aye, and in the midst of the confusions in Spain, and in France through revolution after revolution, and in the furnace of infidelity; aye, and in Germany, in the midst of all that the might of man can do against it; and in Italy too, where the head of the Church is morally a prisoner, it is triumphing even now."

But how can I verify this assertion? It would be enough indeed to quote the words of the Apostle, but I hope to do more. The world esteems the triumph of the Church to be in wealth, power, glory, honor, public sway over empires and nations. There was a time indeed when the world laid these things at the feet of the apostles of Jesus Christ. There was a time when the Catholic Church and the Christian world knew how to sanctify the society of men; but there is this difference—the world then believed, and the world now is apostate. Nevertheless, there is a triumph in the Christian world and there is a triumph in the anti-Christian world; and what is it? It is that the Church in every age and in every condition, and in the midst of all antagonists, fulfils its mission and accomplishes its work, and no power of man can hinder it. Men may, as we shall see hereafter, to their own destruction, resist the mission of the Church, but its work will be accomplished nevertheless, and accomplished even in them; and its work will be a good odor of Christ unto God both in those that are saved and in those that perish. The world has neither tests nor measures by which to understand what the mission and the work of the Church are; but they who see by the light of faith have both. Let us examine, then, what is its mission, what is its work, and how it is fulfilled.

1. First of all, the mission of the Church among men is this—to be a witness for God, and for the incarnation of God in the face of the world. Our Divine Lord said of himself:

" For this was I born, and for this came I into the world, that I should give testimony unto the truth." As it was with him, so it is with his Church; and therefore he said to his apostles: " You shall be witnesses unto me," and St. John said: " That which was from the beginning, which we have heard, which we have seen with our eyes, which we have looked upon, and our hands handled, of the word of life; for the life was manifested, and we have seen it, and do bear witness, and declare unto you, the life eternal which was with the Father, and hath appeared unto us; that is to say, the manifestation of God in the flesh, the incarnation of the Son of God." The Church was the witness of this divine fact to the world, and it is witness to this hour. I may say it is an eye-witness. It was eye-witness of what it declares. It was an ear-witness of what it affirms. I may say in truth that the Church of God, which testifies at this hour, saw the Son of God, and heard his words, and was witness of his miracles. So St. Peter expressly declares, speaking of his transfiguration: " We have not, by artificial fables, made known to you the power and presence of our Lord Jesus Christ; but we were eye-witnesses of his greatness. For he received from God the Father honor and glory, this voice coming down to him from the excellent glory: This is my beloved Son, in whom I am well pleased; hear ye him. And this voice we heard brought from heaven, when we were with him in the holy mount." More than this: it was a witness of the day of Pentecost, and upon it the Holy Ghost descended. It heard the sound of the mighty wind and it saw the tongues of fire. The Church there-fore testifies at this day as an ear-witness and an eye-witness of the divine facts which it declares. And how can this be said? Because that which the apostles saw and heard they delivered to others who believed in them upon a full test and knowledge of their truth, and those who received their testimony held it as a sacred trust and declared it to those who came after. From age to age the testimony of the apostles has descended unbroken. The intrinsic certainty of their witness, resting on their own eye-witness and ear-witness of the facts, has not diminished by a shade, jot, or tittle in the lapse of time, and the external evidence of that fact has multiplied and extended throughout all time and throughout the world. Therefore the testimony of the apostles to these divine realities and truths is as living and fresh at this day as it was in the beginning. Then twelve men testified; now the nations of the world, united in one body by faith and by baptism, take up and perpetuate that testimony. And part of that testimony is this—that when the Son of God ascended into heaven, as they saw him ascend, he fulfilled his promise that he would send the Spirit of Truth, the Holy Ghost, to abide with them forever; that when one Divine Teacher had gone up to his Father's throne, another should come in his stead; that the world should never be without a divine person and a divine teacher in the midst of it; and that the Spirit of Truth by which they were united to their Divine Head in heaven should unite them also to each other as his members in one mystical body, and should form to himself a dwelling-place in which to abide forever. As the soul abides in the body of the man, so the Holy Ghost abides in the body of the Church. It is the sanctuary in which he dwells; the organ by which he speaks, so that the words of our Divine Lord are fulfilled to the very letter— "He that heareth you heareth me"; for the voice of the head and that of the body, as St. Augustine says, are one and the same voice. As they make one moral person, so their voice is identical, and the assistance of the Holy Spirit keeps the voice of the Church always in perfect harmony with the voice of its Divine Head, fulfilling the promise of the Lord by his prophet: "My spirit which is upon thee and my word which I put in thy mouth, shall never depart out of thy mouth, nor out of the mouth of thy seed, nor out of the mouth of thy seed's seed from this time and forever." Thus, then, the mission of the Church is fulfilled always; whether the world believe or disbelieve, whether it gainsay or assent, it matters not; the testimony of the Church forever triumphs in every place.

2. Another part of the mission of the Church is this—to teach the doctrines of Jesus Christ in the midst of all the controversies and contradictions of men. In the face of all the errors and heresies of men there is one Divine Teacher perpetually declaring the same immutable truth. In the clamor and confusion of the human voices of philosophers and human guides, of the scribes and pharisees of the new laws, there is one Divine Voice—articulate, clear, and piercing —which cleaves through all the confusion, and is to be heard above the clamor of men and of nations—the voice of that one holy, Catholic, and Roman Church, spreading from the sunrise to the sunset, immutable in its doctrine, teaching the same truths identically in every place, and abiding always the same unchanging teacher in every age. This is a fact legible in human history. I need not offer proof of it from histories written by ourselves; it is proved by histories and controversies of those who are most opposed to us. There is an accusation which is repeated from age to age against the Catholic and Roman Church; and what is it? That it always persists in its old errors. I accept the accusation. Its persistence proves its immutability, and that which they account

error we know to be the doctrine of Jesus Christ; because, as I have already shown from the word of God, neither can the Catholic Church ever err in believing, nor can the Catholic Church err in teaching. These are two impossibilities, and they descend from one and the same divine truth. God, the Holy Ghost, abiding forever in the mystical body of Christ, illuminates the whole body of the faithful from the time of their baptism. From the time that the graces of faith, hope, and charity are infused into their souls, they are illuminated with the light of faith as the world is illuminated by the splendor of the sun at noonday; and the faithful throughout the world continue passively in their persistence in that one baptismal faith wherewith they were enlightened from their earliest consciousness. And further, they can never err in believing, because the Church which teaches them can never err in teaching. The episcopate throughout the world, which is the college of the apostles multiplied and expanded among all nations, has always the assistance of the Spirit of Truth to guide and preserve it, so that the errors of men and infirmities of our intellect never prevail over the light of faith by which the whole Episcopate of the Church is sustained in the revelation of the day of Pentecost. And more than this: nineteen general councils, from the first which declared the coequality and consubstantiality of the Son with the Father and the Holy Ghost, down to the last which declared the infallibility of the vicar of Jesus Christ,—those nineteen councils have been the organ of the Holy Ghost, preserving the truth in all ages; and the pontiffs, two hundred and fifty-seven in number, have also been guided and assisted by the same Spirit of Truth; so that no doctrine of faith and morals from their hand and from their lips has been out of harmony with the revelation of Jesus Christ. For these reasons the Church is fulfilling its mission, always and in every place, and it can say in every age, with a divine certainty of knowledge and with a divine authority of teaching: " It seemed good to the Holy Ghost and to us."

3. Once more, and lastly: there is another part of the mission of the Church which never fails, and is never baffled— and that is, that the Church judges between the truth of God and the errors of men, and gives decision with divine certainty what is truth, what is falsehood, what is light, and what is darkness. Here again the world, in the confusion of its discordant witnesses, bears testimony to our truth. The world disclaims altogether the presence of any divine teacher in the midst of us. It derides the very notion. There is not a sect or a communion, or a so-called church, which lays claim to this divine guidance. They say infallibility exists nowhere but in God. As the Pharisees said: " Who can forgive sins but God only?" thereby acknowledging the divinity of him who forgave the palsied man. And while they say: " We have no infallibility in us; we do not claim it; we deny its existence on the face of the earth," the one Teacher, who never varies in his voice, says: " He that heareth me heareth him that sent me. It seemed good to the Holy Ghost and unto us that we should claim that infallibility, and we cite you before the tribunal of God to answer for your denial of that truth." We say further that no man knows that any revelation was ever made to man except through our testimony. You never saw the Word made flesh, you nor your forefathers; and you have no unbroken succession of witnesses who trace upward these eighteen hundred years to the day when the Holy Ghost descended with wind and fire; you are not in contact with the original revelation of God. How can you rise up and say: " This was revealed upwards of

eighteen hundred years ago," when you have no proof to give, except that which you borrow from me, that the Son of God ever came into the world? You take my witness for the fact of Christianity, and you then contradict me when I teach you what the doctrines of Christianity are. And if men appeal to the Scriptures, our answer is the same. How do you know the Scriptures were ever written? How can you prove that there ever was a book called the Word of God? You had it from me; you snatched it out of my hand, and you then read it and interpret it in contradiction to my teaching. How do you know that there were four greater prophets and twelve less in the Old Testament; that there are four evangelists and fourteen epistles of St. Paul in the New? Who told you all these things? You had them all from me—from me alone, to whom these Scriptures were committed in custody and in guardianship; from me, who preserved and handed them on to this day. You, who are denying the inspiration of this book and of that, of this text and of that text, and who are gnawing away, as a moth fretteth a garment, the whole written word of God, you rise up and tell us: " This is the meaning of the holy Scriptures," and you reject the holy Catholic faith.

Dear brethren, it needs great patience to hear these things; nevertheless the judge is always calm and patient while he is fulfilling his work among men, and that because it is a grave thing to be the odor of life unto life and of death unto death to the eternal souls of men. And when men appeal to antiquity and tell us that " this is not the primitive tradition," the Church answers: Were you ever in antiquity, or any one that belongs to you? I was there, and as a perpetual witness antiquity is to me nothing but my early days. Antiquity exists in my consciousness to this hour, as men grown to riper years remember their childhood.   Men of the world know that the cotemporaneous interpretation of a law is the most authentic and certain interpretation.   But I have the cotemporaneous interpretation of holy Scripture; and more than this, men who practise before human tribunals know that the continuous usage of a country is the interpretation of its laws written and unwritten.   But I have the cotemperaneous and the continuous usage of the Church of God.   The seven sacraments are institutions of Jesus Christ and every one of them interprets a cluster of truths.   The existence of the Church itself is an interpretation of the words: " Thou art Peter, and upon this rock will I build my Church, and the gates of hell shall not prevail against it." The jurisdiction that I have over the world, which the hearts of men recognize and to which their consciences respond, is the interpretation of the words: " Receive ye the Holy Ghost, whosesoever sins ye forgive, they are forgiven unto them; and whosesoever sins ye retain, they are retained."

But lastly there is another appeal which men make in this day.   We are now told that scientific history is the test of truth; and I saw the other day in a document having great pretension from a certain body of men who are troubling Germany and attempting to trouble even England with the name of Old Catholics, that the way to know the pure faith of Jesus Christ is to interpret history by science.   Alas, as I said before, the world is full of pretensions to science; but those who claim to be Catholics, and who yet appeal from the living voice of the Catholic Church to any other tribunal whatsoever, are all of them identical in their principle, and that principle is heresy.   Luther appealed from the voice of the Catholic Church to Scripture, and thereby became a heretic.   There are others who appeal to antiquity, and the appeal is the same—it is an appeal from the living voice, from the divine authority of the Church, to something of their own choice and creation. It matters not to what the appeal is made. That which constitutes both the treason of the act and the heresy of the principle is that they appeal from the living voice, that is from the divine voice. This it is that is being done at this moment by a body of men who profess to be and to intend to live and die Catholics; and what is more, to purify and reform the Church by staying in it. What is their appeal? Their appeal is to history, to scientific history; that is, to history interpreted by themselves. Luther was much more direct and much wiser. He appealed to a book which is certainly written by the Holy Ghost; they appeal to I know not what books, but to books certainly written only by men, and not by the Spirit of God; to human history, the authenticity of which and the purity of the text of which no one can guarantee; and even this they interpret for themselves.

Now bear with me further if I dwell a few moments longer upon this. At the time I speak, in the old Catholic city of Cologne there is assembled together a number of these men —some four or five hundred—with a handful of unhappy priests, perhaps six or eight, of whom the greater part had already the note of unsoundness upon them before they took their deadly step. And what are they? What are these men who are rising up to purify the Church? What do they believe? Some believe all the Council of Trent, but not the Council of the Vatican. Some believe the Church to be infallible, but not its Head; others propose to reject the invocation of saints, and purgatory, and compulsory confession, and I know not what. Others ask for either half or altogether rationalists. And who have they to assist them?

Excommunicated Jansenists from Holland, and members, I grieve to say, of the Established Church from England; and those chosen, as it were, by a happy fatality, one the most extreme of old-fashioned high-church orthodoxy—an estimable and excellent man, whose person I both respect and love; and another whose advanced rationalism is such that even his own brethren can hardly forbear protesting against him. So that we have assembled in this congress, which is to reform and purify the Catholic and Roman Church of all ages, men so irreconcilably in contradiction with themselves that they cannot touch a religious doctrine without discord, and they cannot find anything on which to unite except in opposition to the one immutable truth. There was a day when all the Scribes, and all the Pharisees, and all the Herodians, and all the hypocrites, and all the men who could agree in anything else or at any other time, were united together in one conspiracy, and though their witnesses did not agree together and their discordant voices could not be combined they all had one will and one purpose against the Son of God and against his truth. These men, I bear witness—many of them at least—have no such intention; but we know from the Word of God that neither had they who crucified our Divine Master a knowledge of what they did: "Father, forgive them, for they know not what they do." "Which none of the princes of this world knew; for if they had known it they would never have crucified the Lord of Glory." But they are at this moment fulfilling the very words of the apostles: "And to some the testimony of the Church is life unto life, to others death unto death."

Such, then, is the mission and the work of the Church—to bear its witness, to teach and to judge; and in doing this, whether men will believe or whether men will not believe,

it is accomplishing its triumph in the world. The world for-
gets that there is not only salvation, but there is also judgment; and God, the just judge of all, is putting men on their
trial. The Church is fulfilling its office by proposing the
way of salvation to men, visibly to the eye by its own presence, audibly to the ear by its own teachings, clearly to the
intellect by the evident truth of its doctrines. It is putting
men upon trial and applying the test to their hearts. It
tests their faith to see whether men will believe; it tests their
candor to see whether they will choose God above all things;
it tests their courage to know whether they are ready to take
up their cross and follow their Divine Master. The Church
says to the men of this day: "Whosoever will save his life
shall lose it, and whosoever shall lose his life for my sake
and the Gospel shall save it." And in saying this God is
separating between nation and nation and between man and
man. His " fan is in his hand and he will thoroughly purge
his floor and gather his wheat into the garner, but the chaff
will he burn with unquenchable fire." " He that believeth
and is baptized will be saved; but he that believeth not is
condemned." " We thank God, who always maketh us to
triumph in Christ Jesus and manifesteth the odor of him
by us in every place;" for we now, at this hour, in the midst
of this nineteenth century, in the midst of science and progress, are the odor of life unto life and the odor of death unto
death. For the purpose of God in the world is this—to
gather out, as he did of old, a people for his name. Among
the Gentiles of the old world he chose Israel; so now amongst
the nations of the new world he chooses those that believe.
He knows the number of his elect and he calls them by their
name. He proposes to them the way of salvation and puts
all things necessary—truth and grace—within their reach.

God is putting them on trial, and the Church in this is fulfilling its mission and accomplishing its work.

The world is on its probation now. It has been for generations and generations driving God and Christianity out of its public life. Christianity is cancelled from its public law; Christianity is silent in the legislature; Christianity at this moment lingers in education, but men are endeavoring to close the doors of the schools against it and so to shut Christianity out of the knowledge of the rising generation. Woe to the people the tradition of whose Christian education is cut asunder! Woe to your children and to your posterity if they are brought up without the knowledge of Christianity! The world is laboring with all its might, and all its fraud, and all its riches, and all its public authority, to accomplish this end. I do not say that the men who are doing it know what they do; but I affirm that they are doing what I say. Unbelievers like those who created the infidel revolution of France in the last century knew well what they were doing. " Let us destroy the accursed one," was the language in which they frankly spoke of Jesus Christ. Men are more refined in the present day. They talk only of the religious difficulty. " Let us evade or get around the religious difficulty;" and, under this plea of evading the religious difficulty, Christianity is to be excluded from our schools; that is to say, because grown men choose to controvert and contradict each other as to what is the truth of God, the little ones of Jesus Christ are to be robbed of their faith. Again, the world is separating its civil powers, its public authority from the unity of the faith and of the Church everywhere. It is making it a part of high and perfect legislation, of what we hear called in these days " progress and modern civilization," to separate the Church from the State, and the school from the Church.

Progress has deposed the Head of the Church; it has put in derision a crown of thorns upon his head; and it believes that at last it has the whole world to itself.

This indeed is the triumph of the world. But meanwhile the Church is triumphing, though men know it not. The Church was never more widespread than at this moment; never more luminous in the eyes of men, never more explicitly known in its faith; never more united, vigorous, pure, and confident in its work. Its kingdom is not of this world: that is, it is not derived from it; the foundation of its jurisdiction is in eternity; the source of its truth is in the Holy Ghost, and its imperishable Head is the Son of God at the right hand of the Father. His kingdom is in the world, but not of it. The world may prosper and go its way; it may stop its ears against the voice of the Divine Witness to the truth; nevertheless that witness will be the odor of death unto death.

And England also is on its probation. I bear witness that in England errors are vanishing away, as the snow melts before the sun—passing away, as the hard frosts before the coming of the spring. The errors which were once dominant, lordly, confident, and persecuting—where are they now? At this day men are proclaiming that they are not certain of what their forefathers bequeathed to them; that they cannot precisely tell what was the doctrine which was intended in the Thirty-nine Articles, and was incorporated in statute laws. They are no longer certain of these things; and I bear them witness that a gentler spirit and a kindlier disposition is working in the hearts of many. In the midst of this darkness, truth is rising again, and the old Catholic Church and faith, for which Ireland has stood inflexible as a martyr, with the aureola upon her head, at this day is multiplying the children of faith here and throughout the world. Here too in Lancashire, where the faith of England has never been extinct—where to this day the little children of our flock are the descendants of those who were martyrs and confessors some three hundred years ago—the lingering tradition of faith once more is embodied in the perfect hierarchy of the Church of God, in its perfect order, perfect unity, perfect jurisdiction, perfect authority. And, what is more, the men of England have learned to know it better. They have heard it speak; they have seen it worship; they have even knelt together with us before the same altar, perhaps hardly knowing what they did; and that because the Spirit of God is working for his truth, and multitudes will be saved. We are only in the twilight of the morning; but we can see Jesus standing on the shore, and there is a net in the hands of his apostles let down in the water. But when we are long gone to our rest, who can say what shall be the great draught of souls which shall be miraculously taken in England?

I must bear witness that in England there are tokens full of hope. England never rejected the holy Catholic faith. A tyrannous and guilty king, a corrupt and covetous court, men full of the conceit of false learning, schemers and intriguers, men that hungered to spoil the Church for their own enrichment—these tyrannized over the people of England. The people of England held to their faith and died for it. The people of England never rejected it. They were robbed of it; they were deprived of their inheritance, and their children were born disinherited of their faith; every century from that hour to this they have gone farther and farther from the light of the one truth. Poor English people! Bear with them—I speak as an Englishman—bear with them; they know not what they do in believing that we worship images, that we imbrued our hands in the massacre of St. Bartholomew. Let the men who write these things look at their own hands; there is blood enough upon them. But the English people do not believe these things now; they are passed away. And there has come in the place of these impostures a desire after truth—" Only let me find it;" a craving after unity—" Can we never make an end of these divisions?" a thirsting for the presence of Jesus Christ upon the altar—" Where can I find him?" And what are all these aspirations? They are the evidences of the good odor of life unto life.

And if so, then, dear brethren, you that have the inheritance of faith are on your probation too. You are called to let the light of your faith shine like the day. The silent, penetrating, convincing light of a man who, knowing the faith, speaks it calmly, without controversy, without bickering, without contention, sheds a grace around him. As men that possess the greatest gift of God, and who desire to make everybody else share it to the full, so let your faith shine. And next, as you have faith, so you ought to have the warmth of charity. Where there is light, there is warmth; and where there is greater light there is greater warmth. Where there is perfect truth, there ought to be perfect charity. You who have the whole revelation of God ought to have the whole charity of God in you. Let your neighbors who are round about, even those who are not of the faith, feel that there is something in you—a warmth, a kindness, a sympathy and generosity which they find in no other man. And, lastly, let there be the fragrance of a holy life. This is the good odor of Christ unto God, and this diffuses life unto life wherever you go. You are upon this probation. Be worthy of the great gift which has been given to you. You have it in its fulness. Be, then, worthy of its fulness, in faith and in charity.

And now, dear brethren, in the midst of all the lordly triumph of the world, of all that which no doubt we shall hear to-morrow, be of good heart. As they said to the apostles so they will say to us: " If this be triumph, what can be defeat? We do not quarrel if you are content with these victories." Overhead there is a throne, and round about it are those whom no man can number; the powers and prerogatives of him who sits upon that throne are working mightily in the world. There is one who sits above the water-flood, with all its confusions, whose voice penetrates through all the jangling contradictions of men. He is bringing to its fulfilment the purpose which from all eternity he has predestined. He knows his own by number and by name, and he will gather them out as the shepherd gathers his flock, and he will separate the goats from the sheep. He will reign until the whole of that work is accomplished. When it is done, and when the last of his elect has been gathered in, and the last of his redeemed has been made perfect, then he will manifest himself to all men, and the world shall then know that he has triumphed always and in every place.

HOLMES

OLIVER WENDELL HOLMES, a famous American physician, wit, poet, and novelist, was born in Cambridge, Massachusetts, August 29, 1809. He graduated in the class of 1829, and having decided to study medicine spent two years in Europe. On his return he was appointed professor of anatomy and physiology at Dartmouth College, but resigning in 1841 he engaged in general practice in Boston. In 1847 he became professor of anatomy at Harvard, and was one of the first to prove the contagiousness of puerperal fever. He had written mediocre poetry in college, and published a slender volume in 1836, but his powers were scarcely suspected until in 1857 he began in the pages of the " Atlantic " his " Autocrat of the Breakfast Table," which secured his fame. In 1858 he published " The Professor at the Breakfast Table." In the following year he tried his hand at more formal fiction and issued " Elsie Venner," which was a rather extravagant study of heredity. " The Guardian Angel," the best of his novels, appeared in 1867. " Songs in Many Keys " came in 1862; this and his " Songs of Many Seasons," of 1875, contained many of the poems which he had contributed to the "Atlantic" and to various social occasions. In 1882 he resigned his professorship, and four years later revisited Europe, where he was received with the greatest enthusiasm. On his return he published a vivacious account of his experiences, entitled " Our Hundred Days in Europe." He died at Boston, October 7, 1894. Among his other works are " Currents and Counter-Currents " (1861); " Soundings from the Atlantic " (1864); " Mechanism in Thought and Morals " (1871); " Memoirs of Motley " (1879); " The Iron Gate " (1880); " Emerson " (1885), and " Before the Curfew " (1888). He was a popular lecturer in the days of the Lyceum, and few momentous occasions in Boston passed without Dr. Holmes being invited to participate, either as poet or humorist.

LECTURE ON THE RELIGIOUS POETRY OF THE NINETEENTH CENTURY

DELIVERED NOVEMBER 4, 1853, BEFORE THE MERCANTILE LIBRARY ASSOCIATION, NEW YORK

THERE is one class of poetry which comes home to every human heart in every civilized and Christian land. The song of love and glory grows dull to those who have outlived their passions and earthly aspirations; but the poem for every ear and age, equally in place over the cradle, over the bed of that final slumber which needs no melody to make it deeper, at the foot of the scaffold, in the darkened cathedral, is the holy song which brings everywhere solemn thoughts, peace, and grateful tears.

The author of one truly devotional English hymn has made himself a home in the hearts of both continents. But the real hymn needs true devotional character and simplicity, which I fear the productions of the present century do not always possess; but in their place a strain of affected sentiment and forced ornament.

And so it has been, more or less, since the rough verses of Sternhold and Hopkins; rough, but natural and unaffected, and imbued with a conscious fervor which the critics of later days would have refined away. On the other hand there is the fault, too often chargeable to their school, of turning Scripture into too homely phrases. I will offer a few remarks on the older authors as an introduction to the more recent. Watts, though voluminous and unequal, is still the great centre of English devotional poetry; and for this reason religion must be uppermost in the heart of him who composes hymns that are to seize and keep their hold on the general heart. His hymns have struck deeper into the heart than any ever written by any Protestant. Doddridge has more sentimentality, but less sincere religious solemnity. Cowper is sometimes worthy of his fame, but too often savors of his friend, John Newton. Among the writers of the present century Montgomery is oftenest found in the hymn-books. He has written a number of hymns which do not rank high above the general level of such compositions; but his popularity is chiefly owing to the absence of pretension and display.

The fault of the hymns of this century is that they are overloaded with ornament—somewhat like the favorite tune

of King Charles' organist, of which his Majesty used to think
it ought to make the congregation dance in the aisle. Bow-
ring is obnoxious to this criticism; his verses are too marked
with scene-painting. Yet let us be grateful to him for
" Watchman, tell us of the night."

Henry Kirke White wrote several grand and simple
hymns; and a few of Milman's have found their way into the
collections. His " Brother, thou art gone before us," may
produce a good effect when sung, but is unworthy of him as
it stands in the collection before me. Among the hymn-
writers of this century the first place cannot be denied to
Heber; even Keble owes him a great deal.

Of all the poets of this period there is none that does not
appear pale and wan beside Byron, Moore, and Scott, except
Heber. It is he alone can stand beside such a poem as " The
Assyrian came down like a wolf on the fold." Heber was
in earnest in poetry as in life; and thus it is that we love in
his hymns that imaginative diction which we condemn in
others. None but he could talk in sacred verse of "Afric's
sunny fountains " and " India's coral strand." The richest
diamonds are more frequently worn by sinners than saints;
sanctity is generally lowly; but Heber could aim at gems;
a high-bred Christian scholar, a man with Greek in his head
and a mitre on it, ought to write as he wrote. I have seen
nothing to equal Heber except one piece by an American
clergyman, " Calm on the listening ear of night."

I have been struck with the manner in which sex shows
itself in female hymns; they are always simple and trustful;
their ornaments are humble, flowers and birds, while men
seek the great elements of Nature. Mrs. Hemans's Pilgrim's
song may be called a hymn, and what man has written such
a hymn?

This brief survey shows that a truly beautiful hymn is one of the rarest and most difficult of human compositions. Many seem to consider Scott's " Song of Rebecca " a beautiful hymn as well as a fine poem; but a child would know the difference between such a song and a hymn flowing from a Christian heart. It is an emanation from the fancy more than from the affections. In every Christian body there are hymns which come from and go to the heart, as Scott's splendid rhetoric never can. " The turf shall be my fragrant shrine " is well enough; but to true devotional feeling this idea stands in about the same relation that the embroidered and scented curtain does to the rose of June.

The " Christian Year " of Keble is very Anglican in its character; it is not properly meant for dissenters, and therefore I perhaps should not find fault with it for the character mentioned. Yet a work meant for any class of Christians ought to contain something fit for all. In his material imagery he savors something of Romanism, but in his poem on the gunpowder treason he takes good care to let us know he is not a Papist. It is to be regretted that his verses are not fit for a church without a bishop, or a state without a king.

But in religious, as in other literature, there must be a higher walk; there must be some difference between the music of a camp-meeting and " Te Deum " in " Notre Dame." The religious world stratifies itself in obedience to natural law. Yet there is a great deal through the book which may be read with delight.

Moore and Byron have sometimes come within sight of the sanctuary; but here the high priest himself comes forth. I fancy I can sometimes trace the molds in which some of his productions have been formed; I can now recognize Milton, and again George Herbert; but I don't mention this to detract from Mr. Keble's merit. No doubt he meets the wants of many gentle and contemplative natures better than any other religious poet of the time.

I have so belabored the poetry of the next writer I am about to mention that I might seem to be hostile to his creed; but I find his creed the same as that of Dr. Watts. I should not notice his work, but that it is so often reprinted, which fact shows that it cannot be mere trumpery. " The Course of Time," by Robert Pollok, a young Scottish clergyman, was introduced to the world with extravagant eulogies. Some extracts which appeared in the papers did not seem to justify the claims that had been made for it; it appeared, was widely read, and greatly admired; then it was seen in auction rooms; and finally gravitated from the higher literary circles. Yet it has always had numerous admirers. Pollok is the Scotch Dante, and his poem the Scotch " Inferno." He dwells with a frightful gusto on the torments to which the Creator condemns lost souls; a gusto amounting to a perversity almost incredible in any being that ever hung at a mother's breast. He gloats over unending tortures as an expert of the Inquisition might be expected to gloat over an unfortunate human being tried with the dry pan and the slow fire. Whoever has read the sermon of Jonathan Edwards, a production well suited to produce in the audience untimely births, and supply from it new inmates for the mad-house, can tell what he thinks of the moral effect of such discourses as these. And Pollok was a fellow countryman of Burns, who could not think even on "Auld Nickieben " without some pity! We can read the " Inferno " with an allowance; we know where it was written and when; and the tortures it paints in the next world were not inaptly foreshadowed by the rack and the ecclesiastical tribunal in this. Besides, in Dante's delineations there is something appropriate to his theme and style; the Inferno is the mortal chamber in the Temple of Sin; we receive mysterious glimpses of it, it is wrapt in a fitting gloom and dimness. But the grim Scotchman shows death and torture in daylight and with labored display. The keeper of wild beasts thrusts his hand into their den; we hear the lions growl and see the fierce sparkle in the tiger's eye; but such exhibitions do not please us.

Lucretius himself said, " It is pleasant to stand on the shore and see another struggling with the billows." Rochefoucauld declares there is something agreeable to us in the misfortunes of our best friend. But let us not forget there are men who would jump into the waves to aid their fellows and risk their own safety and even lives to protect a stranger from violence.

Dumas knew well enough how to turn to account portraitures of persons stretched an inch or two beyond their usual length, of human beings, writhing in the *peine forte et dure,* but I am not aware of any moral improvement to be derived from such contemplations; from painting the effects of fire on the human body; from sharing the feelings of Saul when he held the raiment of the ruffians who were beating Stephen to death. Does that poetry make the world wiser or better which shelters itself under the authority of Scripture, to stick its tooth into the souls of men and women who have not yet passed the dread tribunal? Strangely enough the poet's genius seems to forsake him when he comes to speak of happiness. He has a gem leaping in the coronet of love! And again, young love is sparkling cream and silken down! Spencer discourses of love in fitter strains. The humility of the sinner, the tender sentiments, find small expressi⌐

these pages. I have read the book without finding a page
dimmed with the dew which is sure to be shed where the
heart is touched. His Byronic Address to the Deity and his
imitation of Byron's " Ocean," are models of bathos. Here
is a passage :

> " The orphan child laid down his head and died,
>   Nor unamusing was his piteous cry
>   To women, who had now laid tenderness
>   Aside, best pleased with sights of cruelty."

If the man who wrote these lines had ever known a mother,
a sister, or a wife, he never could have spit so venomous a
lie into the face of woman. I have found so many offensive
passages that I feel justified in the severity with which I have
treated his poem; yet there must be something in it, else it
would not maintain so much of popularity as it does. It has
a claim to attention for its mighty plan; the subject is the
grandest ever ventured on by mortal; and the work has a
certain seriousness and solemnity which shows the writer was
in earnest. A great deal that seems to come from a bad
heart may be traced to low breeding, a gloomy faith, and a
diseased bodily condition. A man with one leg, or even a
man in a tight boot, is not what he would be with a full allowance of limbs and an unpinched foot. Pollok labored under
a disease which brought his life to an early close. Had I
known him and seen some passages of his poem, my treatment would not have been critical but professional.

We are jealous of the admission of vice into literature,
but we tolerate all kinds of whinings. If books were properly entitled, some would be called " Dyspeptic Reflections
on the State of Man " or " An Essay by an American Author
of Well-Known Debility." "The Course of Time " is such a
book. It has pleasing passages, which want of time prevents
my alluding to more fully. With the exception of the lines

on Byron, which the subject recommended, none of them have become familiar. Pollok's power of conception of the grand was, I do not doubt, ample, but he rushed in where angels would have feared to tread.

LEAVE NO VERBAL MESSAGE

SPEECH AT DINNER OF MASSACHUSETTS MEDICAL SOCIETY, BOSTON, MAY, 1856

MR. PRESIDENT AND GENTLEMEN,—It is the peculiar privilege of occasions like the present to indulge in such reasonable measure of self-congratulation as the feeling of the hour may inspire. The very theory of the banquet is that it crowns the temples with roses and warms the heart with wine, so that the lips may speak more freely and the ears may listen more lovingly, and our better natures brought into close communion for an hour may carry away the fragrance of friendship mingled with the odor or the blossoms that breathed sweet through the festal circle.

We have suppressed the classical accompaniments of good fellowship, but we claim all its license. Nor are we alone in asserting a title to this indulgence. Of all the multitudinous religious associations that are meeting around us, I have yet to learn that there is one which does not assert or assume its own peculiar soundness in the faith. I have seen a black swan and a white crow in the same collection, but I never heard of a political assembly where all its own crows were not white, and all the swans of all other political aviaries were not blacker than midnight murder or noonday ruffianism.

The few words I have to speak are uttered more freely

because my relations with the medical profession are incidental rather than immediate and intimate. My pleasant task is all performed in the porch of the great temple where you serve daily. I need not blush then to speak the praises of the divine art, even if you should blush to hear them.

I hear it said from time to time that the physician is losing his hold on the public mind. I believe this remark belongs to a class of sayings that repeat themselves over and over, like the Japanese machine-made prayers which our travellers tell us of, and with about as much thought in them. There are country people that are always saying there is a great want of rain—they would have said so in Noah's flood—for the first fortnight, at least; there are city folks for whom business is always dull and money is always tight; there are politicians that always think the country is going to ruin, and there are people enough that will never believe there are any " good old fashioned snow storms " nowadays, until they have passed a night in the cars between a couple of those degenerate snow banks they despise so heartily. There are many things of this sort which are said daily, which always have been said, and always will be said, with more or less of truth, but without any such portentous novelty as need frighten us from our propriety.

We need not go beyond our own limits, Mr. President, to find ample reason for proclaiming boldly that the medical profession was never more truly honored or more liberally rewarded than at this very time and in this very place. There never lived in this community a practitioner held in more love and veneration by all his professional brethren and by the multitude who have profited by his kind and wise counsel than he who, having soothed the last hours of his long cherished friend and associate, still walks among us bearing his burden of years so lightly that he hardly leans upon the staff he holds; himself a staff upon which so many have leaned through fifty faithful years of patient service. Talk about the success of the unworthy pretender as compared with that of the true physician—why, what man could ever have built up such a fame among us, if he had not laid as its corner-stone, truth, fidelity, honor, humanity—all cemented with the courtesy that binds these virtues together in one life-long inseparable union.

Do you complain of the failing revenues of the profession? I question whether from the time when Boylston took his pay in guineas, through the days when John Warren the elder counted his gains in continental currency, looking well in the ledger and telling poorly at the butcher's and the baker's, there was ever a prettier pile made daily than is built up by one of our living brethren who fought his way up stream until the tide turned and wafted him into reputation, which makes his labors too much for one man and something over two horses. The success of one such diligent and faithful practitioner is the truest rebuke to charlatanism. It is a Waterloo triumph, a Perry's victory, not over the squadrons of *Lake* Erie, but the piratical craft of *Quack*-ery.

This world is not so different now from what it always has been. Pliny tells us stories of medical pretenders as good as any modern ones. Dionis has given us in a dozen pages a very pleasant account of the famous charlatans of his own time, which one of our good friends has translated for us into equally pleasant English. The particular shoe that pinches at the moment seems, it is true, the most ill-conditioned bit of leather that was ever cobbled, yet there has always been about the same amount of pinching from the same cause.

You complain for instance of my old friends, the homœo-pathists. I grant you it is provoking to see a former pa-tient smacking his lips over their Barmecide therapeutics. But, after all, they are less exceptionable, personally, and less dangerous than many other wholesale theorists. Then look for a moment at the course which the system follows in almost any community. It appropriates a certain predis-posed fraction of the public, and having made converts of them for a longer or shorter period, its power is mainly ex-hausted in that locality. And what are these predisposed subjects? Many are simple and credulous, some are intel-lectual and cultivated, not a few of eminent social standing; but with rare exceptions they are just exactly the most restless, uncomfortable class of patients the physician has to deal with, poets with bilious fancies, divines whose medi-cal opinions are offered as gratuitously as your advice is ex-pected to be given; philosophical dilettanti who insist on be-ing dissatisfied with the only kind of answer a reasonable patient should expect.

" Opium facit dormire
Quia est in eo
Virtus dormitiva,
Cujus est natura,
Sensus assoupire." [1]

All that class, in short, who, instead of pulling the ropes as they are bid when there is a heavy gale and a lee shore, insist on going aft and breaking the eleventh commandment—

" No conversation with the man at the helm ! "

On the whole, if our friends, who have a perfect right to choose their own names will spare us that little impertinence of calling medical practitioners " allopathists," the profession

---

[1] " Opium makes one sleep because it possesses a soporific virtue, the nature whereof is to allay the senses."

is well off to have no worse antagonists. The next fancy that turns up may not be as harmless. The old brown rat of England was bad enough but by and by the gray Hanover rat came and ate him up. Unfortunately he ate up the cheese and the bacon, too, and a great deal faster than the old practitioner had done before him.

We may be well contented then. If we have one man living among us as much loved and esteemed as ever a physician has been; if we have one man who makes his calling as remunerative as any have ever done in the midst of us, we may be sure there is no lack of respect or reward to all who deserve either. If our most obvious antagonism comes in a comparatively inoffensive shape and with very limited powers of aggression we need not complain of our professional position.

Count in the published lists all that practice the healing art in this great centre of population and who stand outside of your fellowship; all that trade in the fantastic pretences of the many counterfeits that infest the outskirts of medical practice; the eclectics, the mesmerists, the botanics, and the rest; rake all the dark alleys where the advertising sharper lurks behind his half-open door and his alias; count everything, male and female, red, white, and black, clean and unclean, and though the catalogue is freely open to every knave and ignoramus it will be short compared to the list of the names which you enroll among your numbers from the same community. Weigh the amount of character, ability, and knowledge represented in this list against the string of obscurities and more odious notorieties in the other, and you may judge if health or life are anything to your fellow citizens, what place we must hold in their regard.

"*Hi regebant fata*,"—these governed the fates, said the

Natural Historian of ancient Rome speaking of physicians. Governed the fates! Yes, and not only the fates of those that were under their immediate care but often through them the fates of empires and of interests wider and deeper than those of any earthly dynasty. Think of Dubois the elder, when the question was trembling in the balance whether France should be without an empress or her imperial master without an heir! Or go back to that bloody day of Saint Bartholomew and look into the royal assassin's chamber— whom will you find there, hidden from the savage clubs and the crashing guns that were filling the streets with victims, while the bells of St. Germain l'Auxerrois were pealing their death notes to the hunted Huguenots? No brother, guilty of believing the detested creed; no mistress whose blood was tainted with the stain of heresy; no favorite leader in arms, or council who had dared to defend the obnoxious faith— for Coligny's white hairs were the first to be dabbled in their blood; not one of these but the wise old man to whom Charles the Ninth once owed his accursed life; for the divine art sheds its blessings, like the rain, alike on the just and the unjust; the good and great surgeon, too good and too great for such a crowned miscreant, our own old patriarch of chirurgery—Ambrose Paré.

Say, come down to nearer times and places, and look into the chamber where our own fellow citizen struck down without warning by the hand of brutal violence lies prostrate, and think what fearful issues hang on the skill or incompetence of those who have his precious life in charge. One little error, and the *ignis sacer*, the fiery plague of the wounded, spreads its angry blush over the surface and fever and delirium are but the preludes of deadlier symptoms. One slight neglect, and the brain oppressed with the products of disease grows dreamy and then drowsy; its fine energies are palsied and too soon the heart that filled it with generous blood is stilled forever. It took but a little scratch from a glass broken at his daughter's wedding to snatch from life the great anatomist and surgeon, Spigelius, almost at the very age of him for whose recovery we look not without anxious solicitude.

At such an hour as this more than at any other we feel the dignity, the awful responsibility of the healing art. Let but that life be sacrificed and left unavenged, and the wounds of that defenceless head, like the foul witch's blow on her enchanted image, are repeated on the radiant forehead of Liberty herself and flaw the golden circlet we had vainly written with the sacred name of Union!

    " Dii, prohibite minas! Dii, talem avertite casum." [1]

I give you, Mr. President, " The Surgeons of the city of Washington—God grant them wisdom, for they are dressing the wounds of a mighty empire and of uncounted generations."

TRIBUTE TO PAUL MORPHY

DELIVERED AT PUBLIC BANQUET HELD IN BOSTON, MAY 31, 1859

WE have met, gentlemen, some of us as members of a local association, some of us as its invited guests, but all of us as if by a spontaneous, unsolicited impulse to do honor to our young friend who has honored us and all who glory in the name of Americans, as the hero of a long series of bloodless battles won for our common country.

---

[1] " Ye gods forefend from the threats! Ye gods avert such a misfortune! "

His career is known to you all. There are many corners
of our land which the truly royal game of kings and con-
querors has not yet reached, where if an hour is given to pas-
time it is only in an honest match of checkers played with red
and white kernels of corn, probably enough upon the top
of the housewife's bellows. But there is no gap in the
forest, there is no fresh trodden waste in the prairie which
has not heard the name of the New Orleans boy who left the
nursery of his youth like one of those fabulous heroes of whom
our childhood loved to read, and came back bearing with him
the spoils of giants whom he had slain after overthrowing
their castles and appropriating the allegiance of their
queens.

I need not, therefore, tell his story. It is so long that it
takes a volume to tell it.   It is so brief that one sentence may
embrace it all.   Honor went before him and victory followed
after.

You knew the potential significance and the historical
dignity of that remarkable intellectual pursuit, which although it wears the look of an amusement and its student uses
toy-like implements as did the great inventor of logarithms,
Napier of Merchiston, in the well-known ivory bones or rods
by which he performed many calculations, has yet all the
characters of a science, say rather of a science mingled with a
variable human element, so that the perfect chess player would
unite the combining powers of Newton with the audacity of
Leverrier and the shrewd insight of Talleyrand.   You know
who of the world's masters have been chess players; happy
for the world had some of them been nothing worse than chess
players! You know who have celebrated the praises of the
art in prose and verse; among them the classic Italian remembered in those lines of Pope:

"Immortal Vida, on whose honored brow
The poet's bays and critic's ivy grow,—".

who wrote one poem on the Heavenly Teacher, one on the Art of Poetry, and one on the Game of Chess.

That you knew all this may be taken for granted. I need not say that there is something very different from, something far deeper than the pride which belongs to the professed amateurs or the outside admirers of this particular game, noble as it is, famous as it is, which brings us together.

No, gentlemen, this seemingly gracious and pleasing occasion is far more than it seems. Through these lips of ours, as through those which have spoken before us and shall speak after us the words of welcome to our young friend, there flows the warm breath of that true American feeling which makes us all one in the moment of every great triumph achieved by a child of the Great Republic!

We who look upon the sun while the old world sleeps are after all but colonists and provincials in the eye of the ancient civilizations. There are Europeans enough, otherwise intelligent, who, if we may trust the stories of travellers, would be puzzled to say whether a native American of the highest race caught in one of our streets would be white, or black, or red. It cannot be disguised that we have been subject to the presumption of inferiority as a new people, and that nothing has been granted us except what we have taken at the cannon's mouth, at the point of the bayonets, or in that close Indian hug of peaceful but desperate competition in which, sooner or later, must crack the loins of the civilization belonging to one or the other of the two hemispheres.

It would be tedious and ungenial to show in all its details how the American has had to make his way against these obstacles to the position he now holds before the nations. It took the revolutionary war to disprove the assertion that a British officer with a few regiments could march through the length and breadth of our land in the face of its disorderly rebels. Once more we had to argue the question over with our dear obstinate old parent, and it was only after lugging in a dozen of his sea bulldogs by the ears that we succeeded in satisfying him that we could reason yardarm to yardarm as convincingly as we had argued bayonet to bayonet.

You are not old enough, my young friend, to remember the 8th of January, 1815, but you may have heard of a great discussion which took place on that day near your native city of New Orleans. The same question was debated. If the logic of Mr. Andrew Jackson had failed to convince the opposite party, and Mr. Pakenham's syllogism as to provincial inferiority had been followed out in its corollary of sword and fire, your little game of life, sir, might never have been played, which would have been a great misfortune to us and all the world,—except perhaps the late chess champion of England, Mr. Howard Staunton.

We love our British cousins too well to repeat all the sharp things they have said of us. Reviewers, tourists, philosophers like Coleridge and Carlyle, nay some who had lived among us until their flesh and blood had become American, and their very bones were made over again out of our earth, have all had their fling at the colonists and provincials. Such tricks are catching and have reappeared on the other side of the channel. After all the noble words spoken of our land and its institutions by writers like De Tocqueville and Chevallier, M. Jules Janin could not let the queen of tragedy visit us without warning her against the barbarians of the new world, so terrible did we seem to the smooth round coop-fed feuilletoniste of the Parisian cockneys.

Now, gentlemen, there are two ways of meeting this prejudice so natural to the good people of the overripe half of the planet. We can confess the fact of our green immaturity, but argue from the history of the past that we may yet come to something. We can show that all mankind are colonists and provincials with reference to some point or points from which they started; that England herself is but a settlement formed by a band of invading robbers crossed upon a mob of emigrant squatters. We can show that the children of nations have often lived to feed, to teach, and when necessary to chastise their parents. We can remind our old-country friends that Macedonia, the kingdom of the world's conqueror, and the home of the world's philosopher, was but a rough province, speaking a language hardly understood at Athens; and that the great epic, the great poem, the great work of antiquity was written, or spoken, or sung, not in the phrase familiar to Attic ears, but in the liquid dialect of remote provincial Ionia.

That is the first way of arguing the matter. The second course is much shorter and more satisfactory. It consists in administering what in the dialect of our Yankee Ionia is called " a good licking," of course in the most polite and friendly way, to the other party in the discussion whenever we get a chance. And that chance has of late years been afforded us pretty often.

Let us look very briefly at the experiments we have tried in this direction. The first was to take the rod of iron with which we were ruled,—namely, a ramrod with a ball cartridge at the end of it,—and break it over the backs of those who had abused it. This lesson, as we said, had to be repeated, and we trust that costly way of teaching will never have to be tried again with our sturdy old parent.

And thus the great and beneficent era of competition in the arts of peace was at last inaugurated. Now it is not fair to ask everything at once of a young and growing civilization. When our backwoodsmen have just made a clearing we do not expect them to begin rearing Grecian temples, but was not and is not the settler's log cabin good of its kind—better than Irish shanties and English hovels? As larger wants unfolded we have had a fair opportunity of showing what we could do. The first great work of civilized men everywhere is to tame nature. And some of her wild creatures are never yet wholly tamed, though the old world has been at work at them for thousands of years. There is the earth—that huge, dumb servant, out of whose sturdy strength by goading and scourging and scarifying, we wring the slow secret toil that fills his brown arms with food for our necessities. There is the sleepless, restless, complaining monster, that overlaps two thirds of our globe with his imbricated scales, the great ocean—architect and destroyer of continents. There is man's noblest servant among the unreasoning tribes of being, of whom the oldest and grandest of books says that " his neck is clothed with thunder," whose nature the classic fable blended with that of man himself to make the centaur, rival of demigods.

Who has tamed the earth, gentlemen, like the American, whose instruments of husbandry so far surpassed all others in the day of trial that they reaped not only all the grain before them, but all the honors and all the prizes, without leaving anything for the gleaners? Who has tamed the ocean like the American shipbuilder, whose keels have ploughed the furrows in which all the navies of the world may follow at their leisure? Who has so merited that noble Homeric name of horse-subduer—the proud title of heroes—

as the American enchanter, whose triumphs have never been approached before since Bucephalus trembled and stood still at the voice of Alexander.

It is time for the men of the old world to find out that they have to do with a people which, if we may borrow an expression from one of its earliest and greatest friends, "tramples upon impossibilities."

Let me give you proofs from one department of applied science. In the book before me (London, 1852) Mr. Ross, the great English optician, says that 135 degrees is the largest angular pencil of light that can be passed through a microscopic object-glass. On the cover of the object-glass before me, a glass made by Charles A. Spencer, then of Canastota, in the "backwoods" of New York, as they got it in London, is marked 146 degrees, which impossible angle he has since opened, as all the microscopic world knows, to the thrice impossible extent of 170 degrees and upward.

I mention this exceptionally to illustrate the audacity of democratic ingenuity in a department remote from the wants of common life. But it is to supply these common wants that the American brain has been chiefly taxed. Here it has known no equal. One other example is enough. It took a locksmith trained among the guessing Americans to pick the lock of the world's artificers and defy them all to push back the bolts of his own. So much, then, we have made thoroughly and triumphantly ours; the breast of the earth to feed us, the back of the ocean to bear us, the strength of the horse to toil for us, and the lock of the cunning artisan to protect the fruits of our labor from the rogues the old world sends us! We have had first to make life possible, then tolerable, then comfortable, and at last beautiful, with all that intellect can lend it.

And when the old world gets impatient that we will not do everything in the best way at once, when it is not contented with our material triumphs and that greatest of all triumphs—the self-government of thirty empires—not contented that we should move on as the great tide wave moves —one broad-breasted billow, and not a host of special narrow currents; when the old world, filled with those experts, who have often gained their skill for want of nobler objects, like the prisoners who carve cunning devices in their cells, becomes impatient, we must send over sometimes a man and sometimes a boy to try conclusions with its people in some peaceful contest of intelligence. And this young gentleman at my right, looking as tranquil and breathing as calmly as if he were not half smothered in his laurels, is one of the boys we sent. No! I am wrong. The thoughtful mothers of America would have cried out against us with one voice if we had sent this immature youth, his frame not yet knit together in perfect manhood, to task his growing brain in those tremendous conflicts which made the huge Père Morel, the veteran of the Café de la Régence, strike his broad forehead and beg to be released from the very thought of following the frightful complexity of their bewildering combinations. No! the men, with their ambition and proud confidence in his strength, might have been willing to send him, but the women with their tender love as mothers and sisters and—well-wishers, would have said, " He shall not go! "

He went. It was not we that sent him—it was honor! And when we meet to welcome his triumphant return we know what his victories mean. We have had one more squeeze at the great dynamometer which measures the strength of the strongest of the race. There it lies in the central capital of Europe. The boy has squeezed it and it is not now the index that moves, but the very springs that are broken!

The test is as true a one of cerebral powers as if a hundred thousand men lay dead upon the field where the question was decided,—as if a score of line-of-battle ships were swinging, blackened wrecks, upon the water after a game between two mighty admirals. Where there is a given maximum there is always a corresponding average, and there is not one of us who does not think better of the head he carries on his own shoulders since he finds what a battery it is that lies beneath the smooth forehead of this young brother American.

As I stretch my hand above this youthful brow it seems to me that I bear in it the welcome, not of a town or a province, but of a whole people. One smile, one glow of pride and pleasure runs over all the land, from the shore which the sun first greets to that which looks upon the ocean where he lets fall the blazing clasp of his dissolving girdle,—from the realm of our northern sister who looks down from her throne upon the unmelted snows of Katahdin, to hers of the broad river and the still bayou who sits fanning herself among the full-blown roses and listening to the praises of her child as they come wafted to her on every perfumed breeze.

I propose the health of Paul Morphy, the world's chess champion: His peaceful battles have helped to achieve a new revolution; his youthful triumphs have added a new clause to the Declaration of American Independence!

ADDRESS OF WELCOME

DELIVERED AT AN ALUMNI DINNER, CAMBRIDGE, JULY 16, 1863

BROTHERS OF THE ASSOCIATION OF THE ALUMNI,—It is your misfortune and mine that you must accept my services as your presiding officer of the day in the place of your retiring president. I shall not be believed if I say how unwillingly it is that for the second time I find myself in this trying position; called upon to fill, as I best may, the place of one whose presence and bearing, whose courtesy, whose dignity, whose scholarship, whose standing among the distinguished children of the university, fit him alike to guide your councils and to grace your festivals. The name of Winthrop has been so long associated with the State and with the college that to sit under his mild empire is like resting beneath one of these wide-branching elms the breadth of whose shade is only a measure of the hold its roots have taken in the soil.

In the midst of civil strife we, the children of this our common mother, have come together in peace. And surely there never was a time when we more needed a brief respite in some chosen place of refuge, some unviolated sanctuary, from the cares and anxieties of our daily existence than at this very hour. Our life has grown haggard with excitement. The rattle of drums, the march of regiments, the gallop of squadrons, the roar of artillery, seem to have been continually sounding in our ears day and night, sleeping and waking, for two long years and more. How few of us have not trembled and shuddered with fear over and over again for those whom we love. Alas! how many that hear me have mourned over the lost—lost to earthly sight, but immortal in our love and their country's honor! We need a little breathing space to rest from our anxious thoughts, and, as we look back to the tranquil days we passed in this still retreat, to dream of that future when in God's good time, and after his wise purpose is fulfilled, the fair angel who has so long left us shall lay her hand upon the leaping heart of this embattled nation and whisper, peace! be still!

Here of all places in the world we may best hope to find the peace we seek for. It seems as if nothing were left undisturbed in New England except here and there an old graveyard, and these dear old College buildings, with the trees in which they are embowered. The old State House is filled with those that sell oxen and sheep and doves, and the changers of money. The Hancock house, the umbilical scar of the cord that held our city to the past, is vanishing like a dimple from the water.

But Massachusetts, venerable old Massachusetts, stands as firm as ever; Hollis, this very year a centenarian, is waiting, with its honest red face in a glow of cordiality, to welcome its hundredth set of inmates; Holden Chapel, with the skulls of its Doric frieze and the unpunishable cherub over its portal, looks serenely to the sunsets; Harvard, within whose ancient walls we are gathered, and whose morning bell has murdered sleep for so many generations of drowsy adolescents, is at its post, ready to startle the new-fledged freshmen from their first uneasy slumbers. All these venerable edifices stand as they did when we were boys,—when our fathers were boys,—when our grandfathers were boys. Let not the rash hand of innovation violate their sanctities, for the cement that knits their walls is no vulgar mortar, but is tempered with associations and memories which are stronger than the parts they bind together!

We meet on this auspicious morning forgetting all our lesser differences. As we enter these consecrated precincts, the livery of our special tribe in creed and in politics is taken from us at the door, and we put on the court dress of our gracious Queen's own ordering, the academic robe, such as we wore in those bygone years scattered along the seven last decades. We are not forgetful of the honors which our fellow students have won since they received their college "parts,"—their orations, dissertations, disquisitions, colloquies, and Greek dialogues. But to-day we have no rank; we are all first scholars. The hero in his laurels sits next to the divine rustling in the dry garland of his doctorate. The poet, in his crown of bays, the critic, in his wreath of ivy, clasp each other's hands, members of the same happy family. This is the birthday feast for every one of us whose forehead has been sprinkled from the font inscribed " *Christo et Ecclesiæ.*" We have no badges but our diplomas, no distinctions but our years of graduation. This is the republic carried into the university; all of us are born equal into this great fraternity.

Welcome, then, welcome, all of you, dear brothers, to this our joyous meeting! We must, we will call it joyous, though it comes with many saddening thoughts. Our last triennial meeting was a festival in a double sense, for the same day that brought us together at our family gathering gave a new head to our ancient household of the university. As I look to-day in vain for his stately presence and kindly smile, I am reminded of the touching words spoken by an early president of the university in the remembrance of a loss not unlike our own. It was at the commencement exercises of the year 1678 that the Reverend President Urian Oakes thus mourned for his friend Thomas Shepard, the minister of Charlestown, an overseer of the college: "Dici non potest quam me perorantem, in comitiis, conspectus ejus, multo jucundissimus, recrearit et refecerit. At non comparet hodie Shepardus in his comitiis; oculos huc illuc torqueo; quocumque tamen inciderint, Platonem meum in tanta virorum illustrium frequentia requirunt; nusquam amicum et pernecessarium meum in hac solenni panegyri, inter hosce Reverendos Theologos, Academiæ Curatores, reperire aut oculis vestigare possum."[1] Almost two hundred years have gone by since these words were uttered by the fourth president of the college, which I repeat as no unfitting tribute to the memory of the twentieth, the rare and fully ripened scholar who was suddenly ravished from us as some richly freighted argosy that just reaches her harbor and sinks under a cloudless sky with all her precious treasures.

But the great conflict through which we are passing has made sorrow too frequent a guest for us to linger on an occasion like this over every beloved name which the day recalls to our memory. Many of the children whom our Mother had trained to arts have given the freshness of their youth or the strength of their manhood to arms. How strangely frequent in our recent record is the sign interpreted by the words " *E vivis cesserunt stelligeri!* "[2] It seems as if the red war-planet had replaced the peaceful star, and these pages blushed like a rubric with the long list of the martyr-children

---

[1] "I cannot express how much comfort and edification his presence, so delightful, gave me when called upon to speak in our meetings. And to-day our Shepard is not to be seen in our meeting. I turn my eyes hither and thither; wherever they pause, they seek for my Plato in this assemblage of illustrious men. Nowhere can my eyes find him or detect my friend and coadjutor in this solemn throng, among these reverend divines, these guardians of the college."

[2] "Those marked with a star are no longer among the living."

of our university. I cannot speak their eulogy, for there are
no phrases in my vocabulary fit to enshrine the memory of
the Christian warrior,—of him—

> " Who, doomed to go in company with Pain
> And Fear and Bloodshed, miserable train,
> Turns his necessity to glorious gain—"

> " Who, whether praise of him must walk the earth
> Forever, and to noble deeds give birth,
> Or he must fall, to sleep without his fame,
> And leave a dead, unprofitable name,
> Finds comfort in himself and in his cause;
> And while the mortal mist is gathering, draws
> His breath in confidence of Heaven's applause."

Yet again, O brothers! this is not the hour for sorrow.
Month after month until the months became years we have
cried to those who stood upon our walls: "Watchmen, what
of the night?" They have answered again and again: "The
dawn is breaking,— it will soon be day." But the night has
gathered round us darker than before. At last—glory be
to God in the highest!—at last we ask no more tidings of the
watchmen, for over both horizons east and west bursts forth
in one overflowing tide of radiance the ruddy light of victory!

We have no parties here to-day, but is there one breast
that does not throb with joy as the banners of the conquering
Republic follow her retreating foes to the banks of the angry
Potomac? Is there one heart which does not thrill in answer
to the drum-beat that rings all over the world as the army
of the west, on the morning of the nation's birth, swarms
over the silent, sullen earthworks of captured Vicksburg,—
to the reveille that calls up our Northern regiments this
morning *inside* the fatal abatis of Port Hudson? We are
scholars, we are graduates, we are alumni, we are a band of
brothers, but beside all, beyond all, above all, we are
American citizens. And now that hope dawns upon our land
—nay, bursts upon it in a flood of glory,—shall we not feel

its splendors reflected upon our peaceful gathering, peaceful in spite of those disturbances which the strong hand of our citizen-soldiery has already strangled?

Welcome then, thrice welcome, scholarly soldiers who have fought for your and our rights and honor! Welcome, soldierly scholars who are ready to fight whenever your country calls for your services! Welcome, ye who preach courage as well as meekness, remembering that the Prince of Peace came also bringing a sword! Welcome, ye who make and who interpret the statutes which are meant to guard our liberties in peace, but not to aid our foes in war! Welcome, ye whose healing ministry soothes the anguish of the suffering and the dying with every aid of art and the tender accents of compassion! Welcome, ye who are training the generous youths to whom our country looks as its future guardians! Welcome, ye quiet scholars who in your lonely studies are unconsciously shaping the thought which law shall forge into its shield and war shall wield as its thunder-bolt!

And to you, Mr. President, called from one place of trust and honor to rule over the concerns of this our ancient and venerated institution, to you we offer our most cordial welcome with all our hopes and prayers for your long and happy administration.

I give you, brothers, " The association of the Alumni "; the children of our common mother recognize the man of her choice as their new father, and would like to hear him address a few words to his numerous family.

PRENTISS

SARGEANT SMITH PRENTISS, an American orator, was born in Portland, Maine, September 30, 1808, and was educated at Bowdoin College. He studied law for a time, and after an interval spent as private tutor in Natchez, Mississippi, he was admitted to the bar in 1829. He removed to Vicksburg in 1832, entered the Mississippi legislature in 1835, and Congress in 1838. He did not engage frequently in the debates in the House, but on one occasion delivered a strong speech against the sub-treasury bill. He passionately opposed the repudiation of the State debt, and, believing the State of Mississippi dishonored by its course in respect to repudiation, removed to New Orleans in 1845. There the last three years of his life were spent, although his death occurred at Longwood, near Natchez, July 1, 1850. Prentiss's forensic and other orations were greatly praised by his contemporaries, especially by such men as Everett and Webster. One of his most noted speeches was a defence of his friend, Judge Wilkinson, who had been charged with murder. When addressing large numbers of people he spoke with great impetuosity and appeared as if borne away on the stream of his own eloquence. In pleading at the bar he displayed an entire mastery of the subject in hand as well as perfect readiness and command of resource.

THE NEW ENGLAND ADDRESS

DELIVERED BEFORE THE NEW ENGLAND SOCIETY OF NEW ORLEANS, DECEMBER 22, 1845

THIS is a day dear to the sons of New England, and ever held by them in sacred remembrance. On this day from every quarter of the globe they gather in spirit around the Rock of Plymouth and hang upon the urns of their Pilgrim Fathers the garlands of filial gratitude and affection.

We have assembled for the purpose of participating in this honorable duty; of performing this pious pilgrimage. To-day we will visit that memorable spot. We will gaze upon the place where a feeble band of persecuted exiles founded a mighty nation; and our hearts will exult with proud gratification as we remember that on that barren shore our an-

cestors planted not only empire but freedom. We will med-
itate upon their toils, their sufferings, and their virtues, and
to-morrow return to our daily avocations with minds re-
freshed and improved by the contemplation of their high
principles and noble purposes.

The human mind cannot be contented with the present.
It is ever journeying through the trodden regions of the past
or making adventurous excursions into the mysterious realms
of the future. He who lives only in the present is but a
brute, and has not attained the human dignity.

Of the future but little is known; clouds and darkness rest
upon it; we yearn to become acquainted with its hidden
secrets; we stretch out our arms toward its shadowy inhabitants; we invoke our posterity, but they answer us not. We
wander in its dim precincts till reason becomes confused and
at last start back in fear, like mariners who have entered an
unknown ocean, of whose winds, tides, currents, and quick-
sands they are wholly ignorant.

Then it is we turn for relief to the past, that mighty reser-
voir of men and things. There we have something tangible
to which our sympathies can attach; upon which we can lean
for support; from whence we can gather knowledge and learn
wisdom. There we are introduced into nature's vast labora-
tory and witness here elemental labors. We mark with interest the changes in continents and oceans by which she has
notched the centuries.

But our attention is still more deeply aroused by the great
moral events which have controlled the fortunes of those who
have preceded us and still influence our own. With curious
wonder we gaze down the long isles of the past upon the generations that are gone. We behold as in a magic glass men
in form and feature like ourselves, actuated by the same

motives, urged by the same passions, busily engaged in shaping out both their own destinies and ours. We approach them and they refuse not our invocation. We hold converse with the wise philosophers, the sage legislators, and divine poets. We enter the tent of the general and partake of his most secret counsels. We go forth with him to the battlefield and behold him place his glittering squadrons; then we listen with a pleasing fear to the trumpet and the drum, or the still more terrible music of the booming cannon and the clashing arms. But most of all among the innumerable multitudes who peopled the past, we seek our own ancestors, drawn towards them by an irresistible sympathy.

Indeed, they were our other selves. With reverent solicitude we examine into their character and actions, and as we find them worthy or unworthy our hearts swell with pride, or our cheeks glow with shame. We search with avidity for the most trival circumstances in their history and eagerly treasure up every memento of their fortunes. The instincts of our nature bind us indissolubly to them and link our fates with theirs. Men cannot live without a past; it is as essential to them as a future. Into its vast confines we will journey to-day and converse with our Pilgrim Fathers. We will speak to them and they shall answer us.

Two centuries and a quarter ago a little tempest-tossed, weather-beaten bark, barely escaped from the jaws of the wild Atlantic, landed upon the bleakest shore of New England. From her deck disembarked a hundred and one care-worn exiles.

To the casual observer no event could seem more insignificant. The contemptuous eye of the world scarcely deigned to notice it. Yet the famous vessel that bore Cæsar and his fortunes carried but an ignoble freight compared with that of the "Mayflower." Her little band of Pilgrims brought with them neither wealth nor power, but the principles of civil and religious freedom. They planted them for the first time in the western Continent. They cherished, cultivated, and developed them to a full and luxuriant maturity; and then furnished them to their posterity as the only sure and permanent foundations for a free government.

Upon those foundations rests the fabric of our great republic; upon those principles depends the career of human liberty. Little did the miserable pedant and bigot who then wielded the sceptre of Great Britain imagine that from this feeble settlement of persecuted and despised Puritans in a century and a half would arise a nation capable of coping with his own mighty empire in arts and arms.

It is not my purpose to enter into the history of the Pilgrims; to recount the bitter persecutions and ignominious sufferings which drove them from England; to tell of the eleven years of peace and quiet spent in Holland under their beloved and venerated pastor; nor to describe the devoted patriotism which prompted them to plant a colony in some distant land where they could remain citizens of their native country and at the same time be removed from its oppressions; where they could enjoy liberty without violating allegiance. Neither shall I speak of the perils of their adventurous voyage; of the hardships of their early settlement; of the famine which prostrated and the pestilence which consumed them.

With all these things you are familiar, both from the page of history and from the lips of tradition. On occasions similar to this the ablest and most honored sons of New England have been accustomed to tell with touching eloquence 7 the story of their sufferings, their fortitude, their perseverance, and their success. With pious care they have gathered and preserved the scattered memorials of those early days, and the names of Carver, Bradford, Winslow, Standish, and their noble companions, have long since become with us venerated household words.

There were, however, some traits that distinguished the enterprise of the Pilgrims from all others, and which are well worthy of continued remembrance. In founding their colony they sought neither wealth nor conquest, but only peace and freedom. They asked but for a region where they could make their own laws and worship God according to the dictates of their own consciences.

From the moment they touched the shore they labored with orderly, systematic, and persevering industry. They cultivated without a murmur, a poor and ungrateful soil, which even now yields but a stubborn obedience to the dominion of the plough. They made no search for gold nor tortured the miserable savages to wring from them the discovery of imaginary mines. Though landed by a treacherous pilot upon a barren and inhospitable coast, they sought neither richer fields nor a more genial climate. They found liberty and for the rest it mattered little. For more than eleven years they had meditated upon their enterprise, and it was no small matter could turn them from its completion. On the spot where first they rested from their wanderings with stern and high resolve, they built their little city and founded their young republic. There honesty, industry, knowledge and piety grew up together in happy union. There, in patriarchal simplicity and republican equality the Pilgrim fathers and mothers passed their honorable days, leaving to their posterity the invaluable legacy of their principles and example.

How proudly can we compare their conduct with that of the adventures of other nations who preceded them. How did the Spaniard colonize? Let Mexico, Peru, and Hispaniola answer. He followed in the train of the great discoverer like a devouring pestilence. His cry was gold! gold!! gold!!! Never in the history of the world had the *sacra fames auri*[1] exhibited itself with such fearful intensity. His imagination maddened with visions of sudden and boundless wealth, clad in mail, he leaped upon the New World an armed robber. In greedy haste he grasped the sparkling sand, then cast it down with curses when he found the glittering grains were not of gold.

Pitiless as the bloodhound by his side he plunged into the primeval forests, crossed rivers, lakes, and mountains, and penetrated to the very heart of the continent. No region, however rich in soil, delicious in climate, or luxuriant in production could tempt his stay. In vain the soft breeze of the tropics, laden with aromatic fragrance, wooed him to rest; in vain the smiling valleys, covered with spontaneous fruits and flowers, invited him to peaceful quiet. His search was still for gold; the accursed hunger could not be appeased. The simple natives gazed upon him in superstitious wonder and worshipped him as a god; and he proved to them a god, but an infernal one—terrible, cruel, and remorseless. With bloody hands he tore the ornaments from their persons and the shrines from their altars; he tortured them to discover hidden treasure, and slew them that he might search, even in their wretched throats, for concealed gold. Well might the miserable Indians imagine that a race of evil deities had come among them, more bloody and relentless than those who presided over their own sanguinary rites.

---

[1] Cursed thirst for gold.

Now let us turn to the Pilgrims. They too were tempted; and had they yielded to the temptation how different might have been the destinies of this continent—how different must have been our own! Previous to their undertaking the Old World was filled with strange and wonderful accounts of the new. The unbounded wealth, drawn by the Spaniards from Mexico and South America, seemed to afford rational support for the wildest assertions. Each succeeding adventurer returning from his voyage added to the Arabian tales a still more extravagant story.

At length Sir Walter Raleigh, the most accomplished and distinguished of all those bold voyagers, announced to the world his discovery of the province of Guiana and its magnificent capital, the far-famed city of El Dorado. We smile now at his account of the " great and golden city," and " the mighty, rich, and beautiful empire." We can hardly imagine that any one could have believed for a moment in their existence. At that day, however, the whole matter was received with the most implicit faith. Sir Walter professed to have explored the country, and thus glowingly describes it from his own observation :

" I never saw a more beautiful country nor more lively prospects; hills so raised here and there over the valleys—the river winding into divers branches—the plains adjoining, without bush or stubble—all fair green grass—the deer crossing in every path—the birds, towards the evening, singing on every tree with a thousand several tunes—the air fresh, with a gentle easterly wind : and every stone that we stopped to take up promised either gold or silver by its complexion. For health, good air, pleasure, and riches, I am resolved it cannot be equalled by any region either in the east or west."

The Pilgrims were urged in leaving Holland to seek this charming country and plant their colony among its Arcadian bowers. Well might the poor wanderers cast a longing glance towards its happy valleys, which seemed to invite to pious contemplation and peaceful labor. Well might the green grass, the pleasant groves, the tame deer, and the singing birds allure them to that smiling land beneath the equinoctial line. But while they doubted not the existence of this wondrous region they resisted its tempting charms. They had resolved to vindicate at the same time their patriotism and their principles—to add dominion to their native land, and to demonstrate to the world the practicability of civil and religious liberty. After full discussion and mature deliberation they determined that their great objects could be best accomplished by a settlement on some portion of the northern continent, which would hold out no temptation to cupidity—no inducement to persecution. Putting aside, then, all considerations of wealth and ease they addressed themselves with high resolution to the accomplishment of their noble purpose. In the language of the historian, " trusting to God and themselves," they embarked upon their perilous enterprise.

As I said before, I shall not accompany them on their adventurous voyage. On the 22d day of December, 1620, according to our present computation, their footsteps pressed the famous rock which has ever since remained sacred to their venerated memory. Poets, painters, and orators have tasked their powers to do justice to this great scene. Indeed, it is full of moral grandeur; nothing can be more beautiful, more pathetic, or more sublime.

Behold the Pilgrims as they stood on that cold December day—stern men, gentle women, and feeble children—all uniting in singing a hymn of cheerful thanksgiving to the good God who had conducted them safely across the mighty deep, and permitted them to land upon that sterile shore. See how their upturned faces glow with a pious confidence which the sharp winter winds cannot chill, nor the gloomy forest shadows darken:

> " Not as the conqueror comes,
>   They, the true-hearted came;
> Not with the roll of the stirring drums,
>   Or the trumpet that sings of fame;
> Not as the flying come,
>   In silence and in fear—
> They shook the depths of the desert gloom
>   With their hymns of lofty cheer."

Noble and pious band! your holy confidence was not in vain: your " hymns of lofty cheer " find echo still in the hearts of grateful millions. Your descendants, when pressed by adversity, or when addressing themselves to some high action, turn to the " Landing of the Pilgrims," and find heart for any fate——strength for any enterprise.

How simple, yet how instructive, are the annals of this little settlement. In the cabin of the " Mayflower " they settled a general form of government, upon the principles of a pure democracy. In 1636 they published a declaration of rights and established a body of laws. The first fundamental article was in these words : " That no act, imposition, law or ordinance be made, or imposed upon us, at present or to come, but such as has been or shall be enacted by the consent of the body of freemen or associates, or their representatives legally assembled," etc.

Here we find advanced the whole principle of the Revolution—the whole doctrine of our republican institutions. Our fathers, a hundred years before the Revolution, tested successfully, as far as they were concerned, the principle of self-government, and solved the problem whether law and order can co-exist with liberty. But let us not forget that they were wise and good men who made the noble experiment, and that it may yet fail in our hands unless we imitate their patriotism and virtues.

There are some who find fault with the character of the Pilgrims—who love not the simplicity of their manners nor the austerity of their lives. They were men and of course imperfect; but the world may well be challenged to point out in the whole course of history men of purer purpose or braver action—men who have exercised a more beneficial influence upon the destinies of the human race, or left behind them more enduring memorials of their existence.

At all events it is not for the sons of New England to search for the faults of their ancestors. We gaze with profound veneration upon their awful shades; we feel a grateful pride in the country they colonized, in the institutions they founded, in the example they bequeathed. We exult in our birthplace and in our lineage.

Who would not rather be of the Pilgrim stock than claim descent from the proudest Norman that ever planted his robber blood in the halls of the Saxon, or the noblest paladin that quaffed wine at the table of Charlemagne? Well may we be proud of our native land, and turn with fond affection to its rocky shores.

The spirit of the Pilgrims still pervades it, and directs its fortunes. Behold the thousand temples of the Most High that nestle in its happy valleys and crown its swelling hills. See how their glittering spires pierce the blue sky, and seem like so many celestial conductors, ready to avert the lightning of an angry heaven. The piety of the Pilgrim patriarchs is not yet extinct, nor have the sons forgotten the God of their fathers.

Behold yon simple building near the crossing of the village road! It is small and of rude construction, but stands in a pleasant and quiet spot.   A magnificent old elm spreads its broad arms above and seems to lean towards it, as a strong man bends to shelter and protect a child.   A brook runs through the meadow near, and hard by there is an orchard— but the trees have suffered much and bear no fruit except upon the most remote and inaccessible branches.   From within its walls comes a busy hum, such as you may hear in a disturbed bee-hive.

Now peep through yonder window and you will see a hundred children with rosy cheeks, mischievous eyes, and demure faces, all engaged or pretending to be so, in their little lessons.   It is the public school—the free, the common school— provided by law: open to all: claimed from the community as a right, not accepted as a bounty.

Here the children of the rich and poor, high and low, meet upon perfect equality and commence under the same auspices the race of life.   Here the sustenance of the mind is served up to all alike, as the Spartans served their food upon the public table.   Here young Ambition climbs his little ladder, and boyish Genius plumes his half-fledged wing.   From among these laughing children will go forth the men who are to control the destinies of their age and country; the statesman whose wisdom is to guide the Senate—the poet who will take captive the hearts of the people and bind them together with immortal song—the philosopher who, boldly seizing upon the elements themselves, will compel them to his wishes and through new combinations of their primal laws, by some great discovery revolutionize both art and science.

The common village school is New England's fairest boast—the brightest jewel that adorns her brow.   The principle that society is bound to provide for its members' education as well as protection, so that none need be ignorant except from choice, is the most important that belongs to modern philosophy. It is essential to a republican government. Universal education is not only the best and surest, but the only sure foundation for free institutions. True liberty is the child of knowledge; she pines away and dies in the arms of ignorance.

Honor, then, to the early fathers of New England, from whom came the spirit which has built a schoolhouse by every sparkling fountain and bids all come as freely to the one as to the other. All honor, too, to this noble city, who has not disdained to follow the example of her northern sisters, but has wisely determined that the intellectual thirst of her children deserves as much attention as their physical, and that it is as much her duty to provide the means of assuaging the one as of quenching the other.

But the spirit of the Pilgrims survives, not only in the knowledge and piety of their sons, but most of all in their indefatigable enterprise and indomitable perseverance.

They have wrestled with nature till they have prevailed against her and compelled her reluctantly to reverse her own laws. The sterile soil has become productive under their sagacious culture, and the barren rock, astonished, finds itself covered with luxuriant and unaccustomed verdure.

Upon the banks of every river they build temples to industry and stop the squanderings of the spendthrift waters. They bind the naïades of the brawling stream. They drive the dryades from their accustomed haunts and force them to desert each favorite grove; for upon river, creek, and bay they are busy transforming the crude forest into stanch and gallant vessels. From every inlet or indenture along the rocky shore swim forth these ocean birds—born in the wild-wood, fledged upon the wave. Behold how they spread

their white pinions to the favoring breeze, and wing their
flight to every quarter of the globe—the carrier-pigeons of the
world!

It is upon the unstable element the sons of New England
have achieved their greatest triumphs. Their adventurous
prows vex the waters of every sea. Bold and restless as the
old northern vikings, they go forth to seek their fortunes in
the mighty deep. The ocean is their pasture and over its
wide prairies they follow the monstrous herds that feed upon
its azure fields. As the hunter casts his lasso upon the wild
horse, so they throw their lines upon the tumbling whale.
They " draw out Leviathan with a hook." They " fill his
skin with barbed irons," and in spite of his terrible strength
they " part him among the merchants." To them there are
no pillars of Hercules. They seek with avidity new regions,
and fear not to be " the first that ever burst " into unknown
seas. Had they been the companions of Columbus, the great
mariner would not have been urged to return, though he had
sailed westward to his dying day.

Glorious New England! thou art still true to thy ancient
fame and worthy of thy ancestral honors. We, thy children,
have assembled in this far-distant land to celebrate thy birthday. A thousand fond associations throng upon us, roused by
the spirit of the hour. On thy pleasant valleys rest, like
sweet dews of morning, the gentle recollections of our early
life; around thy hills and mountains cling, like gathering
mists, the mighty memories of the Revolution; and far away
in the horizon of thy past gleam, like thine own Northern
Lights, the awful virtues of our Pilgrim sires! But while
we devote this day to the remembrance of our native land,
we forget not that in which our happy lot is cast. We exult
in the reflection that though we count by thousands the miles

which separate us from our birthplace, still our country is the same. We are no exiles meeting upon the banks of a foreign river to swell its waters with our homesick tears, Here floats the same banner which rustled above our boyish heads, except that its mighty folds are wider and its glittering stars increased in number.

The sons of New England are found in every State of the broad Republic. In the East, the South, and the unbounded West, their blood mingles freely with every kindred current. We have but changed our chamber in the paternal mansion; in all its rooms we are at home, and all who inhabit it are our brothers. To us the Union has but one domestic hearth; its household gods are all the same. Upon us then peculiarly devolves the duty of feeding the fires upon that kindly hearth; of guarding with pious care those sacred household gods.

We cannot do with less than the whole Union; to us it admits of no division. In the veins of our children flows northern and southern blood; how shall it be separated; who shall put asunder the best affections of the heart, the noblest instincts of our nature? We love the land of our adoption, so do we that of our birth. Let us ever be true to both; and always exert ourselves in maintaining the unity of our country, the integrity of the Republic.

Accursed, then, be the hand put forth to loosen the golden cord of Union; thrice accursed the traitorous lips, whether of northern fanatic or southern demagogue, which shall propose its severance. But no! the Union cannot be dissolved; its fortunes are too brilliant to be marred; its destinies too powerful to be resisted. Here will be their greatest triumph, their most mighty development. And when, a century hence, this crescent city shall have filled her golden horns;

when, within her broad-armed port shall be gathered the products of the industry of a hundred millions of freemen; when galleries of art and halls of learning shall have made classic this mart of trade; then may the sons of the Pilgrims, still wandering from the bleak hills of the north, stand upon the banks of the great river, and exclaim with mingled pride and wonder, Lo! this is our country; when did the world ever witness so rich and magnificent a city—so great and glorious a Republic!

JOHNSON

A NDREW JOHNSON, the seventeenth President of the United States, was born in Raleigh, North Carolina, December 29, 1808. At an early age he was apprenticed to a tailor, and removing to Greenville, Tennessee, in 1826, worked at his trade there. His education had been of the scantiest description, but he possessed great natural quickness, and upon his marriage a few years later he studied and read under the direction of his wife, who had received an excellent education. After holding several local offices he entered the State legislature as representative in 1835, and was chosen to the State senate in 1841. He sat in Congress in the House of Representatives, 1843-53, and was subsequently governor of Tennessee. He returned to Congress as senator in 1857, at this period actively opposing the Pacific Railroad Bill, and as strenuously advocating retrenchment and the Homestead Bill. At the opening of the Civil War he labored, oftentimes at great personal risk, to keep Tennessee within the Union, and in 1862 was appointed its military governor. He was elected to the vice-presidency in 1864, and on the assassination of Lincoln succeeded him in the presidential chair, April 15, 1865. His stubborn attitude on the reconstruction policy, which he favored, soon resulted in his complete estrangement from the Republican Congress, and its course in opposition was styled by him in a noted speech, "A new rebellion." The struggle between Congress and the President continued until on February 24, 1868, the House of Representatives voted to impeach him for "high crimes and misdemeanors," and, on the 5th of March following, presented eleven articles of impeachment based on his resistance to the acts of Congress. The trial began March 23, and closed on May 26, with the President's acquittal, one vote of the two thirds necessary for conviction being wanting. After the expiration of his presidential term Johnson was twice an unsuccessful aspirant to the Senate, but was elected in 1875 and sat in the extra session in March of that year. He died at Greenville, Tennessee, 1875. Johnson was a man of undoubted ability who triumphed over many obstacles in early life, but he was narrow and obstinate in many of his opinions. He possessed genuine courage, however, and his honesty was unimpeachable.

SPEECH AT ST. LOUIS

OFFERED IN EVIDENCE BY THE PROSECUTION AT HIS TRIAL.
DELIVERED IN ST. LOUIS, SEPTEMBER 9, 1866

F ELLOW CITIZENS OF ST. LOUIS,—In being introduced to you to-night, it is not for the purpose of making a speech. It is true I am proud to meet so many of my fellow citizens here on this occasion and under the favorable circumstances that I do. [Cry: " How about British subjects? "] We will attend to John Bull after a while, so far as that is concerned. [Laughter and loud cheers.] I have just stated that I am not here for the purpose of making a speech, but, after being introduced, simply to tender my cordial thanks for the welcome you have given me in your midst. [A voice: " Ten thousand welcomes!" hurrahs and cheers.]

Thank you, sir; I wish it were in my power to address you under favorable circumstances upon some of the questions that agitate and distract the public mind at this time. Questions that have grown out of a fiery ordeal we have just passed through and which I think as important as those we have just passed by. The time has come when it seems to me that all ought to be prepared for peace—the rebellion being suppressed, and the shedding of blood being stopped, the sacrifice of life being suspended and stayed, it seems that the time has arrived when we should have peace; when the bleeding arteries should be tied up. [A voice: " New Orleans; go on!"]

Perhaps, if you had a word or two on the subject of New Orleans you might understand more about it than you do. [Laughter and cheers.] And if you will go back—[Cries for Seward]—if you will go back and ascertain the cause of the riot at New Orleans, perhaps you would not be so prompt in calling out New Orleans. If you will take up the riot at New Orleans and trace it back to its source, or to its immediate cause, you will find out who was responsible for the blood that was shed there.

If you will take up the riot at New Orleans and trace it back to the Radical Congress [Great cheering and cries of " Bully!"], you will find that the riot at New Orleans was substantially planned—if you will take up the proceedings in their caucuses you will understand that they there knew [Cheers] that a convention was to be called which was extinct by its powers having expired; that it was said and the intention was that a new government was to be organized; and in the organization of that government the intention was to enfranchise one portion of the population called the colored population, who had just been emancipated, and at the same time disfranchise white men. [Great cheering.] When you begin to talk about New Orleans [Confusion] you ought to understand what you are talking about.

When you read the speeches that were made or take up the facts,—on Friday and Saturday before that convention sat,—you will there find that speeches were made incendiary in their character, exciting that portion of the population, the black population, to arm themselves and prepare for the shedding of blood. [A voice: "That's so!" and cheers.] You will also find that that convention did assemble in violation of law, and the intent of that convention was to supersede the recognized authorities in the State government of Louisiana, which had been recognized by the government of the United States, and every man engaged in that rebellion—in that convention, with the intention of superseding and upturning the civil government which had been recognized by the government of the United States—I say that he was a traitor to the constitution of the United States [Cheers], and hence you find that another rebellion was commenced, having its origin in the Radical Congress.

These men were to go there; a government was to be organized, and the one in existence in Louisiana was to be superseded, set aside, and overthrown. You talk to me about New Orleans!

And then the question was to come up, when they had established their government,—a question of political power,—which of the two governments was to be recognized —a new government inaugurated under this defunct convention, set up in violation of law and without the consent of the people. And then when they had established their government, and extended universal or impartial franchise, as they called it, to this colored population, then this Radical Congress was to determine that a government established on negro votes was to be the government of Louisiana. [Voices: " Never," and cheers and " Hurrah for Andy !"]

So much for the New Orleans riot—and there was the cause and the origin of the blood that was shed, and every drop of blood that was shed is upon their skirts, and they are responsible for it. [Cheers.] I could trace this thing a little closer, but I will not do it here to-night. But when you talk about New Orleans and talk about the causes and consequences that resulted from proceedings of that kind, perhaps, as I have been introduced here, and you have provoked questions of this kind, though it doesn't provoke me, I will tell you a few wholesome things that have been done by this Radical Congress. [Cheers.]

In connection with New Orleans and the extension of the elective franchise, I know that I have been traduced and abused. I know it has come in advance of me here as it has elsewhere, that I have attempted to exercise an arbitrary power in resisting laws that were intended to be enforced on the government. [Cheers and cries of " Hear !"]

Yes, that I had exercised the veto power [" Bully for you !"], that I had abandoned the power that elected me, and that I was a t-r-a-i-t-o-r [Cheers] because I exercised the veto power in attempting to, and did arrest for a time, a bill that was called a Freedman's Bureau Bill. [Cheers.] Yes, that I was a t-r-a-i-t-o-r! And I have been traduced, I have been slandered, I have been maligned, I have been called Judas—Judas Iscariot, and all that. Now, my countrymen here to-night, it is very easy to indulge in epithets, it is very easy to call a man Judas and cry out t-r-a-i-t-o-r, but when he is called upon to give arguments and facts he is very often found wanting.

Judas, Judas Iscariot, Judas! There was a Judas once, one of the twelve apostles. Oh, yes! and these twelve apostles had a Christ. [A voice: "And a Moses, too!" Great laughter.] The twelve apostles had a Christ, and he could not have had a Judas unless he had had twelve apostles. If I had played the Judas, who has been my Christ that I have played the Judas with? Was it Thad. Stevens? Was it Wendell Phillips? Was it Charles Sumner? [Hisses and cheers.] Are these the men that set up and compare themselves with the Saviour of Man, and everybody that differs with them in opinion and tries to stay and arrest their diabolical and nefarious policy is to be denounced as a Judas? [" Hurrah for Andy! " and cheers.]

In the days when there were twelve apostles, and when there was a Christ, while there were Judases, there were unbelievers, too. Y-a-s; while there were Judases there were unbelievers. [Voices: " Hear! " "Three groans for Fletcher."] Yes, oh yes! unbelievers in Christ: men who persecuted and slandered and brought him before Pontius Pilate and preferred charges and condemned and put him to death on the cross to satisfy unbelievers. And this same persecuting, diabolical, and nefarious clan to-day would persecute and shed the blood of innocent men to carry out their purposes. [Cheers.]

But let me tell you, let me give you a few words here to-night—and but a short time since I heard some one say in the crowd that we had a Moses. [Laughter and cheers.] Yes, there was a Moses. And I know sometimes it has been said that I would be the Moses of the colored man. ["Never!" and cheers.]

Why, I have labored as much in the cause of emancipation as any other mortal man living. But while I have strived to emancipate the colored man I have felt and now feel that I have a great many white men that want emancipation. [Laughter and cheers.]

There are a set amongst you that have got shackles on their limbs and are as much under the heel and control of their masters as the colored man that was emancipated. [Cheers.]

I call upon you here to-night as freemen—as men who favor the emancipation of the white man as well as the colored ones. I have been in favor of emancipation, I have done nothing to disguise about that—I have tried to do as much and have done as much, and when they talk about Moses and the colored man being led into the promised Land, where is the land that this clan proposes to lead them? [Cheers.]

When we talk about taking them out from among the white population and sending them to other climes, what is it they propose? Why it is to give us a Freedman's Bureau. And after giving us a Freedman's Bureau what then? Why, here in the South it is not necessary for me to talk to you, where I have lived and you have lived, and understand the whole system, and how it operates; we know how the slaves have been worked heretofore.

Their original owners bought the land and raised the ne-groes or purchased them, as the case might be; paid all the expenses of carrying on the farm and in the end, after producing tobacco, cotton, hemp, and flax, and all the various products of the South, bringing them into the market without any profit to them, while these owners put it all into their own pockets. This was their condition before the emancipation. This was their condition before we became their " Moses." [Cheers and laughter.]

Now what is the plan? I ask your attention. Come; as we have got to talking on this subject, give me your attention for a few minutes. I am addressing myself to your brains and not to your prejudices; to your reason and not to your passions. And when reason and argument again resume their empire this mist, this prejudice that has been incrusted upon the public mind must give way and the reason become triumphant. [Cheers.]

Now, my countrymen, let me call your attention to a single fact, the Freedman's Bureau. [Laughter and hisses.]

Yes, slavery was an accursed institution till emancipation took place. It was an accursed institution while one set of men worked them and got the profits. But after emancipation took place they gave us the Freedman's Bureau. They gave us these agents to go into every county, every township, and into every school district throughout the United States, and especially the southern States. They gave us commissioners. They gave us $12,000,000, and placed the power in the hands of the Executive, who was to work this machinery with the army brought to its aid and to sustain it.

Then let us run it on the $12,000,000 as a beginning, and in the end receive $50,000,000 or $60,000,000, as the case may be, and let us work the four millions of slaves. In fine, the Freedman's Bureau was a simple proposition to transfer four millions of slaves in the United States from their original owners to a new set of taskmasters. [Voice: " Never," and cheers.]

I have been laboring four years to emancipate them; and then I was opposed to seeing them transferred to a new set of taskmasters, to be worked with more rigor than they had been heretofore. [Cheers.]

Yes, under this new system they would work the slaves and call on the government to bear all the expense, and if there were any profits left, why they would pocket them [Laughter and cheers], while you, the people, must pay the expense of running the machine out of your pockets, and they get the profits of it. So much for this question.

I simply intended to-night to tender you my sincere thanks; but as I go along, as we are talking about this Congress and these respected gentlemen, who contend that the President is wrong, because he vetoed the Freedman's Bureau Bill, and all this; because he chose to exercise the veto power he committed a high offence, and therefore ought to be impeached. [Voice: " Never!"]

Y-a-s, y-a-s, they are ready to impeach him. [Voice: " Let them try it!"] And if they were satisfied they had the next Congress by as decided a majority as this, upon some pretext or other—violating the constitution, neglect of duty, or omitting to enforce some act of law, some pretext or other —they would vacate the executive department of the United States. [A voice: " Too bad they don't impeach him."] Wha-t? As we talk about this Congress let me call the soldiers' attention to this immaculate Congress. Let me call your attention. Oh! this Congress, that could make war upon the Executive because he stands upon the constitution and vindicates the rights of the people, exercising the veto power in their behalf—because he dared to do this they can clamor and talk about impeachment.

And by way of elevating themselves and increasing confidence with the soldiers throughout the country, they talk about impeachment.

So far as the Fenians are concerned. Upon this subject of Fenians, let me ask you very plainly here to-night to go back into my history of legislation, and even when governor of a State, let me ask if there is a man here to-night who, in the dark days of Know-Nothingism, stood and sacrificed more for their rights? [Voice: "Good!" and cheers.]

It has been my peculiar misfortune always to have fierce opposition because I have always struck my blows direct and fought with right and the constitution on my side. [Cheers.] Yes, I will come back to the soldiers again in a moment. Yes, here was a neutrality law. I was sworn to support the constitution and see that that law was faithfully executed.

And because it was executed, then they raised a clamor and tried to make an appeal to the foreigners, and especially the Fenians. And what did they do? They introduced a bill to tickle and play with the fancy, pretending to repeal the law and at the same time making it worse, and then left the law just where it is. [Voice: "That's so!"]

They knew that whenever a law was presented to me proper in its provisions, ameliorating and softening the rigors of the present law, that it would meet my hearty approbation; but, as they were pretty well broken down and losing public confidence, at the heels of the session they found they must do something. And, hence, what did they do? They pretended to do something for the soldiers. Who has done more for the soldiers than I have? Who has perilled more in this struggle than I have? [Cheers.]

But then, to make them their peculiar friends and favorites of the soldiers, they came forward with a proposition to do what? Why, we will give the soldier fifty dollars bounty —fifty dollars bounty, your attention to this— if he has served two years, and one hundred dollars if he has served three years.

Now, mark you, the colored man that served two years can get his one hundred dollars bounty. But the white man must serve three before he can get his. [Cheers.] But that is not the point. While they were tickling and attempting to please the soldiers by giving them fifty dollars bounty for two years' service, they took it into their heads to vote somebody else a bounty [Laughter], and they voted themselves not fifty dollars for two years' service; your attention—I want to make a lodgment in your minds of the facts, because I want to put the nail in, and having put it in I want to clinch it on the other side. [Cheers.]

The brave boy, the patriotic young man who followed his gallant officers, slept on the tented field, and perilled his life, and shed his blood, and left his limbs behind him, and came home mangled and maimed, can get fifty dollars bounty if he has served two years. But the members of Congress, who never smelt gunpowder, can get four thousand dollars extra pay. [Loud cheering.]

This is a faint picture, my countrymen, of what has transpired. [A voice: "Stick to that question."] Fellow citizens, you are all familiar with the work of restoration. You know since the rebellion collapsed, since the armies were suppressed on the field, that everything that could be done has been done by the executive department of the government for the restoration of the government.

Everything has been done with the exception of one thing; and that is the admission of members from the eleven States that went into the rebellion. And after having accepted the terms of the government, having abolished slavery, having repudiated their debt, and sent loyal representatives, everything has been done excepting the admission of representatives which all the States are constitutionally entitled to. [Cheers.]

When you turn and examine the constitution of the United States you will find that you cannot even amend that constitution so as to deprive any State of its equal suffrage in the Senate. [A voice: "They have never been out."] It is said before me: "They have never been out." I say so too, and they cannot go out. [Cheers.]

That being the fact, under the constitution they are entitled to equal suffrage in the Senate of the United States, and no power has the right to deprive them of it without violating the constitution. [Cheers.] And the same argument applies to the House of Representatives.

How, then, does the matter stand? It used to be one of the arguments, that if the States withdrew their representatives and senators that that was secession—a peaceable breaking up of the government. Now, the radical power in this government turn around and assume that the States are out of the Union, that they are not entitled to representation in Congress. [Cheers.]

That is to say, they are dissolutionists, and their position now is to perpetuate a disruption of the government; and that, too, while they are denying the States the right of representation they impose taxation upon them, a principle upon which, in the Revolution, you resisted the power of Great Britain. We deny the right of taxation without representa-

tion.   That is one of our great principles.   Let the government be restored.   I have labored for it.   Now I deny this
doctrine of secession, come from what quarter it may, whether
from the North or from the South.   I am opposed to it.   I
am for the union of the States.   [Voices: " That's right," and
cheers.]   I am for thirty-six States remaining where they are,
under the constitution as your fathers made it and handed it
down to you.   And if it is altered or amended, let it be done
in the mode and manner pointed by that instrument itself and
in no other.   [Cheers.]

I am for the restoration of peace.   Let me ask this people
here to-night if we have not shed enough blood.   Let me ask:
Are you prepared to go into another civil war?   Let me ask
this people here to-night are they prepared to set man upon
man, and in the name of God, lift his hand against the
throat of his fellow.   [Voice: " Never !"]   Are you prepared
to see our fields laid waste again, our business and commerce
suspended, and all trade stopped?   Are you prepared to see
this land again drenched in our brothers' blood?   Heaven
avert it, is my prayer.   [Cheers.]

I am one of those who believe that man does sin, and,
having sinned, I believe he must repent.   And, sometimes,
having sinned and having repented makes him a better man
than he was before.   [Cheers.]   I know it has been said that
I have exercised the pardoning power.   Y-a-s, I have.
[Cheers and " What about Drake's constitution ?"]   Y-a-s, I
have, and don't you think it is to prevail?   I reckon I have
pardoned more men, turned more men loose and set them at
liberty that were imprisoned, I imagine, than any other man
on God's habitable globe.   [Voice: " Bully iⱼɽ you !" and
cheers.]

Yes, I turned forty-seven thousand of our men who engaged in this struggle, with the arms they captured with them, and who were then in prison, I turned them loose. [Voice: " Bully for you, old fellow!" and laughter.]

Large numbers have applied for pardon and I have granted them pardon. Yet there are some who condemn and hold me responsible for so doing wrong. Yes, there are some who stayed at home, who did not go into the field on the other side, that can talk about others being traitors and being treacherous. There are some who can talk about blood and vengeance and crime and everything to " make treason odious," and all that, who never smelt gunpowder on either side. [Cheers.]

Yes, they can condemn others and recommend hanging and torture, and all that. If I have erred I have erred on the side of mercy. Some of these croakers have dared to assume that they are better than was the Saviour of men himself,— a kind of over-righteousness,—better than everybody else and always wanting to do Deity's work, thinking he cannot do it as well as they can. [Laughter and cheers.]

Yes, the Saviour of men came on the earth and found the human race condemned and sentenced under the law, but when they repented and believed he said: " Let them live." Instead of executing and putting the world to death he went upon the cross and there was painfully nailed by these un- believers that I have spoken of here to-night, and there shed his blood that you and I might live. [Cheers.] Think of it! To execute and hang and put to death eight millions of people. [Voices: " Never!"]

It is an absurdity; and such a thing is impracticable even if it were right. But it is the violation of all law, human and divine. [A voice: " Hang Jeff. Davis!"] You call on Judge Chase to hang Jeff. Davis, will you? [Great cheer-

ing.] I am not the court, I am not the jury, nor the judge.
[Voice: " Nor the Moses!"] Before the case comes to me,
and all other cases, it would have to come on application as a
case for pardon. That is the only way the case can get to
me. Why don't Judge Chase—Judge Chase, the chief justice of the United States, in whose district he is—why don't
he try him? [Loud cheers.]

But perhaps I could answer the question; as sometimes
persons want to be facetious and indulge in repartee, I might
ask you a question: Why don't you hang Thad. Stevens and
Wendell Phillips? [Great cheering.] A traitor at one end
of the line is as bad as a traitor at the other.

I know that there are some who have got their little pieces
and sayings to repeat on public occasions, like parrots, that
have been placed in their mouths by their superiors, who have
not the courage and the manhood to come forward and tell
them themselves, but have their understrappers to do their
work for them. [Cheers.] I know there are some who talk
about this universal elective franchise upon which they
wanted to upturn the government of Louisiana and institute
another; who contended that we must send men there to control, govern, and manage their slave population because they
are incompetent to do it themselves. And yet they turn
round when they get there and say they are competent to go
to Congress and manage the affairs of State. [Cheers.]

Before you commence throwing your stones you ought to be
sure you don't live in a glass house. Then why all this
clamor! Don't you see, my countrymen, it is a question of
power, and being in power as they are, their object is to
perpetuate their power? Hence, when you talk about turning any of them out of office, oh, they talk about " bread and
butter." [Laughter.]

Yes these men are the most perfect and complete " bread-and-butter party " that has ever appeared in this government. [Great cheering.] When you make an effort or struggle to take the nipple out of their mouths how they clamor! They have stayed at home here five or six years, held the offices, grown fat, and enjoyed all the emoluments of position; and now when you talk about turning one of them out, " Oh, it is proscription "; and hence they come forward and propose in Congress to do what? To pass laws to prevent the Executive from turning anybody out. [Voice: " Put 'em out !"] Hence, don't you see what the policy was to be ? I believe in the good old doctrine advocated by Washington, Jefferson, and Madison, of rotation in office.

These people who have been enjoying these offices seem to have lost sight of this doctrine. I believe that when one set of men have enjoyed the emoluments of office long enough they should let another portion of the people have a chance. [Cheers.] How are these men to be got out [Voice: " Kick 'em out!" Cheers and laughter], unless your Executive can put them out, unless you can reach them through the President?

Congress says he shall not turn them out, and they are trying to pass laws to prevent it being done. Well, let me say to you, if you will stand by me in this action [Cheers], if you will stand by me in trying to give the people a fair chance, soldiers and citizens, to participate in those offices, God being willing, I will " kick them out " just as fast as I can. [Great cheering.]

Let me say to you in concluding what I have said, and I intended to say but little, but was provoked into this, rather than otherwise, I care not for the menaces, the taunts, and jeers; I care not for the threats; I do not intend to be bullied by my enemies nor overawed by my friends [cheers], but, God willing, with your help I will veto their measures whenever they come to me. [Cheers.]

I place myself upon the ramparts of the constitution, and when I see the enemy approaching, so long as I have eyes to see or ears to hear, or a tongue to sound the alarm, so help me God, I will do it and call upon the people to be my judges. [Cheers.] I tell you here to-night that the constitution of the country is being encroached upon. I tell you here to-night that the citadel of liberty is being endangered. [A voice: "Go it, Andy!"]

I say to you then, go to work; take the constitution as your palladium of civil and religious liberty; take it as your chief ark of safety. Just let me ask you here to-night to cling to the constitution in this great struggle for freedom, and for its preservation, as the shipwrecked mariner clings to the mast when the midnight tempest closes around him. [Cheers.]

So far as my public life has been advanced, the people of Missouri as well as of other States know that my efforts have been devoted in that direction which would ameliorate and elevate the interests of the great mass of the people. [Voice: "That's so."]

Why, where's the speech, where's the vote to be got of mine, but what has always had a tendency to elevate the great working classes of the people? [Cheers.] When they talk about tyranny and despotism, where's one act of Andrew Johnson that ever encroached upon the rights of a freeman in this land? But because I have stood as a faithful sentinel upon the watch tower of freedom to sound the alarm, hence all this traduction and detraction that has been heaped upon me. ["Bully for Andy Johnson!"]

I now, then, in conclusion, my countrymen, hand over to

you the flag of your country with thirty-six stars upon it. I hand over to you your constitution with the charge and responsibility of preserving it intact. I hand over to you to-night the Union of these States, the great magic circle which embraces them all. I hand them all over to you, the people in whom I have always trusted in all great emergencies,—questions which are of such vital interest,—I hand them over to you as men who can rise above party, who can stand around the altar of a common country with their faces upturned to heaven, swearing by him that lives for ever and ever that the altar and all shall sink in the dust, but that the constitution and the Union shall be preserved. Let us stand by the Union of these States, let us fight enemies of the government, come from what quarter they may. My stand has been taken.

You understand what my position is, and in parting with you now I leave the government in your hands with the confidence I have always had that the people will ultimately redress all wrongs and set the government right. Then, gentlemen, in conclusion, I thank you for the cordial welcome you have given me in this great city of the northwest, whose destiny no one can foretell. Now [Voice: " Three cheers for Johnson! "] then, in bidding you good-night, I leave all in your charge, and thank you for the cordial welcome you have given me in this spontaneous outpouring of the people of your city.

GLADSTONE

WILLIAM EWART GLADSTONE was born in 1809 in Liverpool, where his father, a native of Scotland, had become an opulent merchant, and had also acquired large interests in the British West Indies. The boy William was sent to Eton, and afterward to Christ Church, Oxford, where he took a double first-class. At the same time he so distinguished himself as a ready and forceful speaker in the Oxford Union Debating Society that he received from the Duke of Newcastle, the father of his college friend, Lord Lincoln, the offer of a seat in the House of Commons for the borough of Newark. He entered Parliament as an extreme Conservative, and for a considerable time was known as "the rising hope of the stern and unbending Tories." He supported Sir Robert Peel, however, when the latter determined to renounce the protectionist policy of the Conservative party, and to repeal the Corn Laws. He remained what was known as a Peelite for many years thereafter, and as lately as 1858 accepted from a Conservative administration the appointment of Lord High Commissioner to the Ionian Islands. Subsequently he became a colleague of Lord Palmerston and Lord John Russell, and ultimately became Prime Minister as leader of the Liberal party. When the Liberals were beaten in 1874 he announced his intention of retiring from public life, and during the Beaconsfield Parliament, which lasted until 1880, Lord Hartington was recognized as chief of the Liberal Opposition. When Lord Beaconsfield was beaten at the ballot-box, however, the almost unanimous demand of the Liberal party compelled the return of Mr. Gladstone to power, and he again became Prime Minister, retaining office until the spring of 1885. At the general election held in December of that year the Liberals and Irish Home Rulers between them commanded a large majority of the House of Commons, and Gladstone again was made Prime Minister. He now introduced the project of self-government for Ireland, which is known as the first Home Rule bill, but owing to the secession of the so-called Unionist-Liberals, it was beaten in the House of Commons, and as the Conservatives triumphed in the succeeding general election, Gladstone gave place to Lord Salisbury. He was once more returned to office, nevertheless, in 1892 with a majority of 40 in the House of Commons, and succeeded in carrying through that body his second Home Rule bill, which differed considerably from the first. The measure was beaten, however, in the House of Lords, and Gladstone soon afterward resigned the post of Premier, being succeeded by Lord Rosebery. He died in 1898. We here reproduce the remarkable speeches upon Ireland which he delivered in 1886 and in the years immediately following.

ON DOMESTIC AND FOREIGN AFFAIRS

DELIVERED AT WEST CALDER, NOVEMBER 27, 1879

MR. CHAIRMAN AND GENTLEMEN,—In addressing you to-day, as in addressing like audiences assembled for a like purpose in other places of the county, I am warmed by the enthusiastic welcome which you have been pleased in every quarter and in every form to accord to me. I am, on the other hand, daunted when I recollect, first of all, what large demands I have to make on your patience; and secondly, how inadequate are my powers and how inadequate almost any amount of time you can grant me to set forth worthily the whole of the case which ought to be laid before you in connection with the coming election.

To-day, gentlemen, as I know that many among you are interested in the land and as I feel that what is termed " agricultural distress " is at the present moment a topic too serious to be omitted from our consideration, I shall say some words upon the subject of that agricultural distress and particularly because in connection with it there have arisen in some quarters of the country proposals which have received a countenance far beyond their deserts to reverse or to compromise the work which it took us one whole generation to achieve and to revert to the mischievous, obstructive, and impoverishing system of protection. Gentlemen, I speak of agricultural distress as a matter now undoubtedly serious. Let none of us withhold our sympathy from the farmer, the cultivator of the soil, in the struggle he has to undergo. His struggle is a struggle of competition with the United States. But I do not fully explain the case when I say the United States. It is not with

the entire United States, it is with the western portion of these
States—that portion remote from the seaboard; and I wish in
the first place, gentlemen, to state to you all a fact of very
great interest and importance, as it seems to me, relating to
and defining the point at which the competition of the western States of America is most severely felt. I have in my
hand a letter received recently from one well-known and hon-
orably known in Scotland—Mr. Lyon Playfair, who has recently been a traveller in the United States and who, as you
well know, is as well qualified as any man upon earth for accurate and careful investigation. The point, gentlemen, at
which the competition of the western States of America is
most severely felt is in the eastern States of America. Whatever be agricultural distress in Scotland, whatever it be, where
undoubtedly it is more felt in England, it is greater by much
in the eastern States of America. In the States of New England the soil has been to some extent exhausted by careless
methods of agriculture, and these, gentlemen, are the greatest
of all the enemies with which the farmer has to contend.

But the foundation of the statement I make, that the eastern States of America are those that most feel the competition
of the West is to be found in facts,—in this fact above all,
not only they are not in America, as we are here, talking
about the shortness of the annual returns and in some places
having much said on the subject of rents and of temporary
remission or of permanent reduction. That is not the state
of things; they have actually got to this point that the capital
values of land, as tested by sales in the market, have undergone an enormous diminution. Now I will tell you something that actually happened, on the authority of my friend
Mr. Playfair. I will tell you something that has happened
in one of the New England States,—not, recollect, in a desert

or a remote country,—in an old cultivated country and near one of the towns of these States, a town that has the honorable name of Wellesley.

Mr. Playfair tells me this: Three weeks ago—that is to say about the first of this month, so you will see my information is tolerably recent,—three weeks ago a friend of Mr. Playfair bought a farm near Wellesley for $33 an acre,—for £6 12s. an acre,—agricultural land, remember, in an old settled country. That is the present condition of agricultural property in the old States of New England. I think by the simple recital of that fact I have tolerably well established my case, for you have not come in England and you have not come in Scotland to the point at which agricultural land is to be had—not wild land, but improved and old cultivated land, —is to be had for the price of £6 12s. an acre. He mentions that this is by no means a strange case, an isolated case, that it fairly represented the average transactions that have been going on; and he says that in that region the ordinary price of agricultural land at the present time is from $20 to $50 an acre, or from £4 to £10. In New York the soil is better and the population is greater; but even in the State of New York land ranges for agricultural purposes from $50 to $100, that is to say from £10 to £20 an acre.

I think those of you, gentlemen, who are farmers will perhaps derive some comfort from perceiving that if the pressure here is heavy the pressure elsewhere and the pressure nearer to the seat of this very abundant production is greater and far greater still.

It is most interesting to consider, however, what this pressure is. There has been developed in the astonishing progressive power of the United States—there has been developed a

8   faculty of producing corn for the subsistence of man with a

rapidity and to an extent unknown in the experience of mankind. There is nothing like it in history. Do not let us conceal, gentlemen, from ourselves the fact; I shall not stand the worse with any of you who are farmers if I at once avow that this greater and comparatively immense abundance of the prime article of subsistence for mankind is a great blessing vouchsafed by Providence to mankind. In part I believe that the cheapness has been increased by special causes. The lands from which the great abundance of American wheat comes are very thinly peopled as yet. They will become more thickly peopled and as they become more thickly peopled a larger proportion of their produce will be wanted for home consumption and less of it will come to you, and at a higher price. Again, if we are rightly informed, the price of American wheat has been unnaturally reduced by the extraordinary depression, in recent times, of trade in America, and especially of the mineral trades, upon which many railroads are dependent in America and with which these railroads are connected in America in a degree and manner that in this country we know but little of. With a revival of trade in America it is to be expected that the freights of corn will increase and all other freights, because the employment of the railroads will be a great deal more abundant and they will not be content to carry corn at nominal rates. In some respects therefore you may expect a mitigation of the pressure, but in other respects it is likely to continue.

Nay, the prime minister is reported as having not long ago said,—and he ought to have the best information on this subject, nor am I going to impeach in the main what he stated,— he gave it to be understood that there was about to be a development of corn production in Canada which would entirely throw into the shade this corn production in the United

States. Well, that certainly was very cold comfort as far as the British agriculturist is concerned, because he did not say— he could not say—that the corn production of the United States was to fall off, but there was to be added an enormous corn production from Manitoba, the great Province which forms now a part of the Canada Dominion. There is no doubt, I believe, that it is a correct expectation that vast or very large quantities of corn will proceed from that Province and therefore we have to look forward to a state of things in which, for a considerable time to come, large quantities of wheat will be forthcoming from America, probably larger quantities and perhaps frequently at lower prices than those at which the corn-producing and corn-exporting districts of Europe have commonly been able to supply us. Now that I believe to be, gentlemen, upon the whole, not an unfair representation of the state of things.

How are you to meet that state of things? What are your fair claims? I will tell you. In my opinion your fair claims are, in the main, two. One is to be allowed to purchase every article that you require in the cheapest market and have no needless burden laid upon anything that comes to you and can assist you in the cultivation of your land. But that claim has been conceded and fulfilled.

I do not know whether there is an object, an instrument, a tool of any kind, an auxiliary of any kind, that you want for the business of the farmer which you do not buy at this moment in the cheapest market. But beyond that you want to be relieved from every unjust and unnecessary legislative restraint. I say every unnecessary legislative restraint because taxation, gentlemen, is unfortunately a restraint upon us all, but we cannot say that it is always unnecessary and we cannot say that it is always unjust. Yesterday I ventured to state—and I will therefore not now return to the subject—a number of matters connected with the state of legislation in which it appears to me to be of vital importance both to the agricultural interest and to the entire community, that the occupiers and cultivators of the land of this country should be relieved from restraints under the operation of which they now suffer considerably. Beyond those two great heads, gentlemen, what you have to look to, I believe, is your own energy, your own energy of thought and action, and your care not to undertake to pay rents greater than, in reasonable calculation, you think you can afford. I am by no means sure, though I speak subject to the correction of higher authority, —I am by no means sure that in Scotland within the last fifteen or twenty years something of a speculative character has not entered into rents and particularly, perhaps, into the rents of hill farms. I remember hearing of the augmentations which were taking place I believe all over Scotland—I verified the fact in a number of counties—about twelve or fourteen years ago, in the rents of hill farms, which I confess impressed me with the idea that the high prices that were then ruling, and ruling increasingly from year to year, for meat and wool, were perhaps for once leading the wary and shrewd Scottish agriculturist a little beyond the mark in the rents he undertook to pay. But it is not this only which may press. It is, more broadly, in a serious and manful struggle that you are engaged, in which you will have to exert yourselves to the uttermost, in which you will have a right to claim everything that the legislature can do for you; and I hope it may perhaps possibly be my privilege and honor to assist in procuring for you some of those provisions of necessary liberation from restraint; but beyond that it is your own energies of thought and action to which you will have to trust.

Now, gentlemen, having said thus much my next duty is to warn you against quack remedies, against delusive remedies, against the quack remedies that there are plenty of people found to propose, not so much in Scotland as in England; for, gentlemen, from Midlothian at present we are speaking to England as well as to Scotland.   Let me give a friendly warning from this northern quarter to the agriculturist of England not to be deluded by those who call themselves his friends in a degree of special and superior excellence and who have been too much given to delude him in other times; not to be deluded into hoping relief from sources from which it can never come.   Now, gentlemen, there are three of these remedies.   The first of them, gentlemen, I will not call a quack remedy at all, but I will speak of it notwithstanding in the tone of rational and dispassionate discussion.   I am not now so much upon the controversial portion of the land question— a field which, Heaven knows, is wide enough—as I am upon matters of deep and universal interest to us in our economic and social condition.   There are some gentlemen and there are persons for whom I for one have very great respect, who think that the difficulties of our agriculture may be got over by a fundamental change in the land-holding system of this country.

I do not mean, now pray observe, a change as to the law of entail and settlement and all those restraints which I hope were tolerably well disposed of yesterday at Dalkeith, but I mean those who think that if you can cut up the land, or a large part of it, into a multitude of small properties that of itself will solve the difficulty and start everybody on a career of prosperity.

Now, gentlemen, to a proposal of that kind I for one am not going to object upon the ground that it would be incon-

sistent with the privileges of landed proprietors. In my
opinion, if it is known to be for the welfare of the community at large, the legislature is perfectly entitled to buy out
the landed proprietors. It is not intended probably to con-
fiscate the property of a landed proprietor more than the property of any other man; but the state is perfectly entitled, if it
please, to buy out the landed proprietors as it may think fit
for the purpose of dividing the property into small lots. I
don't wish to recommend it because I will show you the doubts
that to my mind hang about that proposal; but I admit that in
principle no objection can be taken. Those persons who possess large portions of the spaces of the earth are not altogether
in the same position as the possessors of mere personalty; that
personalty does not impose the same limitations upon the action
and industry of man and upon the well-being of the community as does the possession of land; and therefore I freely own
that compulsory expropriation is a thing which for an adequate public object is in itself admissible and so far sound in
principle.

Now, gentlemen, this idea about small proprietors, however,
is one which very large bodies and parties in this country treat
with the utmost contempt; and they are accustomed to point
to France, and say: " Look at France." In France you have
got 5,000,000—I am not quite sure whether it is 5,000,000 or
even more; I do not wish to be beyond the mark in anything—
you have 5,000,000 of small proprietors, and you do not produce in France as many bushels of wheat per acre as you do
in England. Well, now I am going to point out to you a
very remarkable fact with regard to the condition of France.
I will not say that France produces—for I believe it does not
produce—as many bushels of wheat per acre as England does,
but I should like to know whether the wheat of France is pro-

duced mainly upon the small properties of France.   I believe
that the wheat of France is produced mainly upon the large
properties of France, and I have not any doubt that the large
properties of England are upon the whole better cultivated
and more capital is put into the land than in the large
properties of France. But it is fair that justice should be done
to what is called the peasant proprietary. Peasant proprietary
is an excellent thing, if it can be had, in many points of view.
It interests an enormous number of the people in the soil of
the country and in the stability of its institutions and its laws.
But now look at the effect that it has upon the progressive
value of the land—and I am going to give you a very few
figures which I will endeavor to relieve from all complication
lest I should unnecessarily weary you.   But what will you
think when I tell you that the agricultural value of France—
the taxable income derived from the land, and therefore the
income of the proprietors of that land—has advanced during
our lifetime far more rapidly than that of England?   When
I say England I believe the same thing is applicable to Scotland, certainly to Ireland; but I shall take England for my
test because the difference between England and Scotland,
though great, does not touch the principle, and because it so
happens that we have some means of illustration from former
times for England which are not equally applicable for all the
three kingdoms.

Here is the state of the case.   I will not go back any further
than 1851.   I might go back much further; it would only
strengthen my case.   But for 1851 I have a statement made
by French official authority of the agricultural income of
France as well as the income of other real property, namely,
houses.   In 1851 the agricultural income of France was
£76,000,000.   It was greater in 1851 than the whole income

from land and houses together had been in 1821. This is a tolerable evidence of progress, but I will not enter into the detail of it because I have no means of dividing the two—the house income and the land income—for the earlier year, namely, 1821. In 1851 it was £76,000,000—the agricultural income; and in 1864 it had risen from £76,000,000 to £106,000,000. That is to say, in the space of thirteen years the increase of agricultural values in France—annual values—was no less than forty per cent, or three per cent per annum. Now I go to England. Wishing to be quite accurate, I shall limit myself to that with respect to which we have positive figures. In England the agricultural income in 1813-14 was £37,000,000; in 1842 it was £42,000,000, and that year is the one I will take as my starting point. I have given you the years 1851 to 1864 in France. I could only give you those thirteen years with a certainty that I was not misleading you, and I believe I have kept within the mark. I believe I might have put my case more strongly for France.

In 1842, then, the agricultural income of England was £42,000,000; in 1876 it was £52,000,000—that is to say, while the agricultural income of France increased forty per cent in thirteen years the agricultural income of England increased twenty per cent in thirty-four years. The increase in France was three per cent per annum; the increase in England was about one half or three fifths per cent per annum. Now, gentlemen, I wish this justice to be done to a system where peasant proprietary prevails. It is of great importance. And will you allow me, you who are Scotch agriculturists, to assure you that I speak to you not only with the respect which is due from a candidate to a constituency, but with the deference which is due from a man knowing very little of agricultural matters to those who know a great deal?

And there is one point at which the considerations that I have been opening up, and this rapid increase of the value of the soil in France, bear upon our discussions. Let me try to explain it. I believe myself that the operation of economic laws is what in the main dictates the distribution of landed property in this country. I doubt if those economic laws will allow it to remain cut up into a multitude of small properties like the small properties of France. As to small holdings, I am one of those who attach the utmost value to them. I say that in the Lothians—I say that in the portion of the country where almost beyond any other large holdings prevail—in some parts of which large holdings exclusively are to be found—I attach the utmost value to them. But it is not on that point I am going to dwell, for we have no time for what is unnecessary. What I do wish very respectfully to submit to you, gentlemen, is this. When you see this vast increase of the agricultural value of France you know at once it is perfectly certain that it has not been upon the large properties of France, which, if anything, are inferior in cultivation to the large properties of England. It has been upon those very peasant-properties which some people are so ready to decry. What do the peasant-properties mean? They mean what in France is called the small cultivation—that is to say, cultivation of superior articles pursued upon a small scale—cultivation of flowers, cultivation of trees and shrubs, cultivation of fruits of every kind, and all that in fact which rises above the ordinary character of farming produce, and rather approaches the produce of the gardener.

Gentlemen, I cannot help having this belief that, among other means of meeting the difficulties in which we may be placed, our destiny is that a great deal more attention will have to be given than heretofore by the agriculturists of

England, and perhaps even by the agriculturists of Scotland, to the production of fruits, of vegetables, of flowers, of all that variety of objects which are sure to find a market in a rich and wealthy country like this, but which have hitherto been consigned almost exclusively to garden production. You know that in Scotland, in Aberdeenshire—and I am told also in Perthshire—a great example of this kind has been set in the cultivation of strawberries—the cultivation of strawberries is carried on over hundreds of acres at once. I am ashamed, gentlemen, to go further into this matter as if I was attempted to instruct you. I am sure you will take my hint as a respectful hint—I am sure you will take it as a friendly hint. I do not believe that the large properties of this country, generally or universally, can or will be broken up into small ones. I do not believe that the land of this country will be owned as a general rule by those who cultivate it. I believe we shall continue to have, as we have had, a class of landlords and a class of cultivators, but I most earnestly desire to see—not only to see the relations of those classes to one another harmonious and sound, their interests never brought into conflict; but I desire to see both flourishing and prospering, and the soil of my country producing as far as may be under the influence of capital and skill, every variety of product which may give an abundant livelihood to those who live upon it. I say, therefore, gentlemen, and I say it with all respect, I hope for a good deal from the small culture, the culture in use among the small proprietors of France; but I do not look to a fundamental change in the distribution of landed property in this country as a remedy for agricultural distress.

But I go on to another remedy which is proposed, and I do it with a great deal less of respect; nay, I now come to the region of what I have presumed to call quack remedies. There is a quack remedy which is called Reciprocity, and this quack remedy is under the special protection of quack doctors, and among the quack doctors I am sorry to say there appear to be some in very high station indeed, and if I am rightly informed, no less a person than her Majesty's secretary of state for foreign affairs has been moving about the country and indicating a very considerable expectation that possibly by reciprocity agricultural distress will be relieved. Let me test, gentlemen, the efficacy of this quack remedy for your, in some places, agricultural pressure, and generally distress—the pressure that has been upon you, the struggle in which you are engaged. Pray watch its operation; pray note what is said by the advocates of reciprocity. They always say, We are the soundest and best free-traders. We recommend reciprocity because it is the truly effectual method of bringing about free trade. At present America imposes enormous duties upon our cotton goods and upon our iron goods. Put reciprocity into play and America will become a free-trading country. Very well, gentlemen, how would that operate upon you agriculturists in particular? Why, it would operate thus: If your condition is to be regretted in certain particulars and capable of amendment, I beg you to cast an eye of sympathy upon the condition of the American agriculturist. It has been very well said, and very truly said,—though it is a smart antithesis,—the American agriculturist has got to buy everything that he wants at prices which are fixed in Washington by the legislation of America, but he has got to sell everything that he produces at prices which are fixed in Liverpool—fixed by the free competition of the world. How would you like that, gentlemen—to have protective prices to pay for everything that you use—for your

manures, for your animals, for your implements, for all your
farming stock, and at the same time to have to sell what you
produce in the free and open market of the world?　But bring
reciprocity into play, and then if reciprocity doctors are right
the Americans will remove all their protective duties, and the
American farmer, instead of producing as he does now, under
the disadvantage and the heavy disadvantage of having to
pay protective prices for everything that constitutes his farming stock, will have all his tools and implements, and manures,
and everything else purchased in the free, open market of the
world at free-trade prices.　So he will be able to produce his
corn to compete with you even cheaper than he does now.　So
much for reciprocity considered as a cure for distress.　I am
not going to consider it now in any other point of view.

　　But, gentlemen, there are another set of men who are bolder
still, and who are not for reciprocity; who are not content
with that milder form of quackery, but who recommend a
reversion, pure and simple, to what I may fairly call, I think,
the exploded doctrine of protection.　And upon this, gentlemen, I think it necessary, if you will allow me, to say to you a
few words, because it is a very serious matter, and it is all
the more serious because her Majesty's government—I do not
scruple to say—are coquetting with this subject in a way
which is not right.　They are tampering with it; they are
playing with it.　A protective speech was made in the House
of Commons in a debate last year by Mr. Chaplin, on the part
of what is called "the agricultural interest."　Mr. Chaplin
did not use the word protection, but what he did say was this:
He said he demanded that the malt tax should be abolished
and the revenue supplied by a tax upon foreign barley or some
other foreign commodity.　Well, if he has a measure of that
kind in his pocket I don't ask him to affix the word protection

to it. I can do that for myself. Not a word of rebuke, gentlemen, was uttered to the doctrines of Mr. Chaplin. He was complimented upon the ability of his speech and the well-chosen terms of his motion. Some of the members of her Majesty's government— the minor members of her Majesty's government—the humbler luminaries of that great constellation—have been going about the country and telling their farming constituents that they think the time has come when a return to protection might very wisely be tried. But, gentlemen, what delusions have been practised upon the unfortunate British farmer! When we go back for twenty years, what is now called the Tory party was never heard of as the Tory party. It was always heard of as the party of protection. As long as the chiefs of the protective party were not in office, as long as they were irresponsible, they recommended themselves to the good will of the farmer as protectionists, and said they would set him up and put his interests on a firm foundation through protection. We brought them into office in the year 1852. I gave with pleasure a vote that assisted to bring them into office. I thought bringing them into office was the only way of putting their professions to the test. They came into office, and before they had been six months in office they had thrown protection to the winds. And that is the way in which the British farmer's expectations are treated by those who claim for themselves in the special sense the designation of his friends.

It is exactly the same with the malt tax. Gentlemen, what is done with the malt tax? The malt tax is held by them to be a great grievance on the British farmer. Whenever a Liberal government is in office, from time to time they have a great muster from all parts of the country to vote for the abolition of the malt tax. But when a Tory government

comes into office, the abolition of the malt tax is totally forgotten; and we have now had six years of a Tory government
without a word said, as far as I can recollect,—and my friend
in the chair could correct me if I were wrong,—without a
motion made, or a vote taken, on the subject of the malt tax.
The malt tax, great and important as it is, is small in reference to protection. Gentlemen, it is a very serious matter
indeed if we ought to go back to protection, because how did
we come out of protection to free trade? We came out of it
by a struggle which in its crisis threatened to convulse the
country, which occupied Parliaments, upon which elections
turned, which took up twenty years of our legislative life,
which broke up parties. In a word, it effected a change so
serious that if, after the manner in which we effected that
change, it be right that we should go back upon our steps,
then all I can say is, that we must lose that which has ever
been one of the most honorable distinctions of British legislation in the general estimation of the world,—that British
legislation, if it moves slowly, always moves in one direction—that we never go back upon our steps.

But are we such children that, after spending twenty
years—as I may say from 1840 to 1860—in breaking down
the huge fabric of protection, in 1879 we are seriously to set
about building it up again? If that be right, gentlemen,
let it be done, but it will involve on our part a most humiliating confession. In my opinion it is not right. Protection,
however, let me point out, now is asked for in two forms, and
I am next going to quote Lord Beaconsfield for the purpose
of expressing my concurrence with him.

Mostly, I am bound to say, as far as my knowledge goes,
protection has not been asked for by the agricultural interest, certainly not by the farmers of Scotland.

It has been asked for by certain injudicious cliques and classes of persons connected with other industries—connected with some manufacturing industries. They want to have duties laid upon manufactures.

But here Lord Beaconsfield said—and I cordially agree with him—that he would be no party to the institution of a system in which protection was to be given to manufacturers and to be refused to agriculture.

That one-sided protection I deem to be totally intolerable, and I reject it even at the threshold as unworthy of a word of examination or discussion.

But let us go on to two-sided protection and see whether that is any better—that is to say, protection in the shape of duties on manufactures and protection in the shape of duties upon corn, duties upon meat, duties upon butter and cheese and eggs, and every thing that can be produced from the land. Now, gentlemen, in order to see whether we can here find a remedy for our difficulties, I prefer to speculation and mere abstract argument the method of reverting to experience. Experience will give us very distinct lessons upon this matter. We have the power, gentlemen, of going back to the time when protection was in full and unchecked force, and of examining the effect which it produced upon the wealth of the country. How, will you say, do I mean to test that wealth? I mean to test that wealth by the exports of the country and I will tell you why, because your prosperity depends upon the wealth of your customers—that is to say, upon their capacity to buy what you produce. And who are your customers? Your customers are the industrial population of the country who produce what we export and send all over the world. Consequently, when exports increase, your customers are doing a large business, are growing wealthy, are putting money in their pockets, and are able to take that money out of their pockets in order to fill their stomachs with what you produce. When, on the contrary, exports do not increase, your customers are poor, your prices go down, as you have felt within the last few years in the price of meat, for example, and in other things, and your condition is proportionally depressed. Now, gentlemen, down to the year 1842 no profane hand had been laid upon the august fabric of protection. For recollect that the farm-rs' friends always told us that it was a very august fabric, nd that if you pulled it down it would involve the ruin of the ountry. That, you remember, was the commonplace of every Tory speech delivered from a country hustings to a farming constituency. But before 1842 another agency had come into force, which gave new life in a very considerable degree to the industry of the country, and that was the agency of railways, of improved communication, which short-ened distance and cheapened transit, and effected in that way an enormous economical gain and addition to the wealth of the country. Therefore, in order to see what we owe to our friend protection, I won't allow that friend to take credit for what was done by railways in improving the wealth of the country. I will go to the time when I may say there were virtually no railways—that is the time before 1830. Now, gentlemen, here are the official facts which I shall lay before you in the simplest form, and remember, using round numbers. I do that because, although round numbers can-not be absolutely accurate, they are easy for the memory to take in, and they involve no material error, no falsification of the case. In the year 1800, gentlemen, the exports of British produce were £39,500,000 in value. The population at that time,—no, I won't speak of the exact figure of the population, because I have not got it for the three kingdoms. In the years 1826 to 1830,—that is, after a medium period of eight and twenty years,—the average of our exports for those five years, which had been £39,500,000 in 1800, was £37,000,000. It is fair to admit that in 1800 the currency was somewhat less sound, and therefore I am quite willing to admit that the £37,000,000 probably meant as much in value as the £39,500,000, but substantially, gentlemen, the trade of the country was stationary, practically stationary, under protection. The condition of the people grew, if possible, rather worse than better. The wealth of the country was nearly stationary. But now I show you what protection produced; that it made no addition, it gave no onward movement to the profits of those who are your customers. But on these profits you depend; because, under all circumstances, gentlemen, this I think nobody will dispute,—a considerable portion of what the Englishman or the Scotchman produces will some way or other find its way down his throat.

What has been the case, gentlemen, since we cast off the superstition of protection, since we discarded the imposture of protection? I will tell you what happened between 1830, when there were no railways, and 1842, when no change, no important change, had been made as to protection, but when the railway system was in operation, hardly in Scotland, but in England to a very great extent, to a very considerable extent upon the main lines of communication. The exports which in 1830 had been somewhere about £37,000,000, between 1840 and 1842 showed an average amount of £50,000,000. That seems due, gentlemen, to the agency of railways; and I wish you to bear in mind the increasing benefit now derived from that agency, in order that I may not claim any undue credit for freedom of trade. From

1842, gentlemen, onward the successive stages of free trade began; in 1842, in 1845, in 1846, in 1853, and again in 1860, the large measures were carried which have completely re-formed your customs tariff, and reduced it from a taxation of twelve hundred articles to a taxation of, I think, less than twelve.

Now, under the system of protection, the export trade of the country, the wealth and the power of the manufacturing and producing classes to purchase your agricultural products did not increase at all. In the time when railways began to be in operation, but before free trade, the exports of the country increased, as I have shown you, by £13,000,000 in somewhere about thirteen years—that is to say, taking it roughly, at the rate of £1,000,000 a year.

But since 1842 and down to the present time we have had, along with railways, always increasing their benefits,— we have had the successive adoption of free-trade measures; and what has been the state of the export business of the country? It has risen in this degree, that that which from 1840 to 1842 averaged £50,000,000 from 1873 to 1878 averaged £218,000,000. Instead of increasing, as it has done between 1830 and 1842, when railways only were at work, at the rate of £1,000,000 a year—instead of remaining stagnant as it did when the country was under protection pure and simple, with no augmentation of the export trade to enlarge the means of those who buy your products, the total growth in a period of thirty-five years was no less than £168,000,000, or, taking it roughly, a growth in the export trade of the country to the extent of between £4,000,000 and £5,000,000 a year. But, gentlemen, you know the fact. You know very well that while restriction was in force you did not get the prices that you have been getting for the last twenty years. The price of wheat has been much the same as it had been before. The price of oats is a better price than was to be had on the average of protective times. But the price, with the exception of wheat, of almost every agricultural commodity, the price of wool, the price of meat, the price of cheese, the price of every thing that the soil produces, has been largely increased in a market free and open to the world; because, while the artificial advantage which you got through protection, as it was supposed to be an advantage, was removed, you were brought into that free and open market, and the energy of free trade so enlarged the buying capacity of your customers that they were willing and able to give you and did give you a great deal more for your meat, your wool, and your products in general, than you would ever have got under the system of protection. Gentlemen, if that be true—and it cannot, I believe, be impeached or impugned—if that be true, I don't think I need further discuss the matter, especially when so many other matters have to be discussed.

I will therefore ask you again to cross the seas with me. I see that the time is flying onward, and, gentlemen, it is very hard upon you to be so much vexed upon the subject of policy abroad. You think generally, and I think, that your domestic affairs are quite enough to call for all your attention. There was a saying of an ancient Greek orator, who unfortunately very much undervalued what we generally call the better portion of the community—namely, women; he made a very disrespectful observation which I am going to quote, not for the purpose of concurring with it, but for the purpose of an illustration.

Pericles, the great Athenian statesman, said with regard to women, their greatest merit was to be never heard of.

Now, what Pericles untruly said of women, I am very much disposed to say of foreign affairs—their great merit would be to be never heard of. Unfortunately, instead of being never heard of, they are always heard of, and you hear almost of nothing else; and I can't promise you, gentlemen, that you will be relieved from this everlasting din, because the consequences of an unwise meddling with foreign affairs are consequences that will for some time necessarily continue to trouble you, and that will find their way to your pockets in the shape of increased taxation.

Gentlemen, with that apology I ask you again to go with me beyond the seas. And as I wish to do full justice I will tell you what I think to be the right principles of foreign policy; and then, as far as your patience and my strength will permit, I will, at any rate for a short time, illustrate those right principles by some of the departures from them that have taken place of late years. I first give you, gentlemen, what I think the right principles of foreign policy.

The first thing is to foster the strength of the empire by just legislation and economy at home, thereby producing two of the great elements of national power—namely, wealth, which is a physical element, and union and contentment, which are the moral elements,—and to reserve the strength of the empire, to reserve the expenditure of that strength, for great and worthy occasion abroad. Here is my first principle of foreign policy: good government at home.

My second principle of foreign policy is this: that its aim ought to be to preserve to the nations of the world—and especially, were it but for shame, when we recollect the sacred name we bear as Christians, especially to the Christian nations of the world—the blessings of peace. That is my second principle.

My third principle is this: Even, gentlemen, when you do a good thing you may do it in so bad a way that you may entirely spoil the beneficial effect; and if we were to make ourselves the apostles of peace in the sense of conveying to the minds of other nations that we thought ourselves more entitled to an opinion on that subject than they are, or to deny their rights—well, very likely we should destroy the whole value of our doctrines. In my opinion the third sound principle is this: to strive to cultivate and maintain, aye, to the very uttermost, what is called the concert of Europe; to keep the powers of Europe in union together. And why? Because by keeping all in union together you neutralize and fetter and bind up the selfish aims of each. I am not here to flatter either England or any of them. They have selfish aims as unfortunately we in late years have too sadly shown that we too have had selfish aims; but their common action is fatal to selfish aims. Common action means common objects; and the only objects for which you can unite together the powers of Europe are objects connected with the common good of them all. That gentlemen is my third principle of foreign policy.

My fourth principle is: that you should avoid needless and entangling engagements. You may boast about them, you may brag about them, you may say you are procuring consideration for the country. You may say that an Englishman can now hold up his head among the nations. You may say that he is now not in the hands of a Liberal ministry, who thought of nothing but pounds, shillings, and pence. But what does all this come to, gentlemen? It comes to this, that you are increasing your engagements without increasing your strength; and if you increase engagements without increasing strength you diminish strength, you abolish strength; you really reduce the empire and do not increase it. You render it less capable of performing its duties; you render it an inheritance less precious to hand on to future generations.

My fifth principle is this, gentlemen: to acknowledge the equal rights of all nations. You may sympathize with one nation more than another. Nay, you must sympathize in certain circumstances with one nation more than another. You sympathize most with those nations as a rule with which you have the closest connection in language, in blood, and in religion, or whose circumstances at the time seem to give the strongest claim to sympathy. But in point of right all are equal, and you have no right to set up a system under which one of them is to be placed under moral suspicion or espionage, or to be made the constant subject of invective. If you do that, but especially if you claim for yourself a superiority, a pharisaical superiority over the whole of them, then I say you may talk about your patriotism if you please, but you are a misjudging friend of your country, and in undermining the basis of the esteem and respect of other people for your country you are in reality inflicting the severest injury upon it. I have now given you, gentlemen, five principles of foreign policy. Let me give you a sixth and then I have done.

And that sixth is: that in my opinion foreign policy, subject to all the limitations that I have described, the foreign policy of England should always be inspired by the love of freedom. There should be a sympathy with freedom, a desire to give it scope, founded not upon visionary ideas, but upon the long experience of many generations within the shores of this happy isle, that in freedom you lay the firmest foundations both of loyalty and order; the firmest foundations for the development of individual character and the best provision for the happiness of the nation at large.

In the foreign policy of this country the name of Canning ever will be honored. The name of Russell ever will be honored. The name of Palmerston ever will be honored by those who recollect the erection of the kingdom of Belgium and the union of the disjoined provinces of Italy. It is that sympathy, not a sympathy with disorder, but on the contrary founded upon the deepest and most profound love of order,— it is that sympathy which in my opinion ought to be the very atmosphere in which a foreign secretary of England ought to live and to move.

Gentlemen, it is impossible for me to do more to-day than to attempt very slight illustrations of those principles. But in uttering those principles I have put myself in a position in which no one is entitled to tell me—you will hear me out in what I say—that I simply object to the acts of others and lay down no rules of action myself. I am not only prepared to show what are the rules of action which in my judgment are the right rules, but I am prepared to apply them nor will I shrink from their application. I will take, gentlemen, the name which most of all others is associated with suspicion and with alarm and with hatred in the minds of many Englishmen. I will take the name of Russia, and at once I will tell you what I think about Russia, and how I am prepared as a member of Parliament to proceed in anything that respects Russia. You have heard me, gentlemen, denounced sometimes I believe as a Russian spy, sometimes as a Russian agent, sometimes as perhaps a Russian fool, which is not so bad, but still not very desirable. But, gentlemen, when you come to evidence the worst thing that I have ever seen quoted out of any speech or writing of mine about Russia is that I did one day say, or I believe I wrote, these terrible words: I recommended Englishmen to imitate Russia in her good deeds. Was not that a terrible proposition? I cannot recede from it. I think we ought to imitate Russia in her good deeds, and if the good deeds be few I am sorry for it, but I am not the less disposed on that account to imitate them when they come. I will now tell you what I think just about Russia.

I make it one of my charges against the foreign policy of her Majesty's government that, while they have completely estranged from this country—let us not conceal the fact—the feelings of a nation of eighty millions, for that is the number of the subjects of the Russian empire,—while they have contrived completely to estrange the feelings of that nation they have aggrandized the power of Russia. They have aggrandized the power of Russia in two ways which I will state with perfect distinctness. They have augmented her territory. Before the European powers met at Berlin Lord Salisbury met with Count Schouvaloff, and Lord Salisbury agreed that, unless he could convince Russia by his arguments in the open Congress of Berlin, he would support the restoration to the despotic power of Russia of that country north of the Danube which at the moment constituted a portion of the free state of Roumania. Why, gentlemen, what had been done by the Liberal government which forsooth attended to nothing but pounds, shillings, and pence? The Liberal government had driven Russia back from the Danube. Russia, which was a Danubian power before the Crimean war, lost this position on the Danube by the Crimean war; and the Tory government, which has been incensing and inflaming you against Russia, yet nevertheless by binding itself beforehand to support, when the judgment was taken, the restoration of that country to Russia, has aggrandized the power of Russia.

It further aggrandized the power of Russia in Armenia; but I would not dwell upon that matter if it were not for a very strange circumstance. You know that an Armenian province was given to Russia after the war, but about that I own to you I have very much less feeling of objection. I have objected from the first vehemently and in every form to the granting of territory on the Danube to Russia, and carrying back the population of a certain country from a free state to a despotic state; but with regard to the transfer of a certain portion of the Armenian people from the government of Turkey to the government of Russia I must own that I contemplate that transfer with much greater equanimity. I have no fear myself of the territorial extensions of Russia in Asia, no fear of them whatever. I think the fears are no better than old women's fears. And I don't wish to encourage her aggressive tendencies in Asia or anywhere else. But I admit it may be and probably is the case that there is some benefit attending upon the transfer of a portion of Armenia from Turkey to Russia.

But here is a very strange fact. You know that that portion of Armenia includes the port of Batoum. Lord Salisbury has lately stated to the country that, by the treaty of Berlin the port of Batoum is to be only a commercial port. If the treaty of Berlin stated that it was to be only a commercial port, which of course could not be made an arsenal, that fact would be very important. But happily, gentlemen, although treaties are concealed from us nowadays as long and as often as is possible, the treaty of Berlin is an open instrument. We can consult it for ourselves; and when we consult the treaty of Berlin we find it states that Batoum shall be essentially a commercial port, but not that it shall be only a commercial port. Why, gentlemen, Leith is essentially a

commercial port, but there is nothing to prevent the people
of this country if in their wisdom or their folly they should
think fit from constituting Leith as a great naval arsenal or
fortification; and there is nothing to prevent the Emperor of
Russia, while leaving to Batoum a character that shall be
essentially commercial, from joining with that another character that is not in the slightest degree excluded by the treaty,
and making it as much as he pleases a port of military defence.   Therefore I challenge the assertion of Lord Salisbury; and as Lord Salisbury is fond of writing letters to the
" Times " to bring the Duke of Argyll to book, he perhaps
will be kind enough to write another letter to the " Times "
and tell in what clause of the treaty of Berlin he finds it
written that the port of Batoum shall be only a commercial
port.   For the present I simply leave it on record that he has
misrepresented the treaty of Berlin.

With respect to Russia I take two views of the position
of Russia.   The position of Russia in Central Asia I believe
to be one that has in the main been forced upon her against
her will.   She has been compelled—and this is the impartial
opinion of the world,—she has been compelled to extend her
frontier southward in Central Asia by causes in some degree
analogous to, but certainly more stringent and imperative
than, the causes which have commonly led us to extend in a
far more important manner our frontier in India; and I think
it, gentlemen, much to the credit of the late government, much
to the honor of Lord Clarendon and Lord Granville that
when we were in office we made a covenant with Russia in
which Russia bound herself to exercise no influence or interference whatever in Afghanistan, we on the other hand making known our desire that Afghanistan should continue free
and independent.   Both the powers acted with uniform strict-

ness and fidelity upon this engagement until the day when we were removed from office. But Russia, gentlemen, has another position—her position in respect to Turkey; and here it is that I have complained of the government for aggrandizing the power of Russia; it is on this point that I most complain.

The policy of her Majesty's government was a policy of repelling and repudiating the Slavonic populations of Turkey in Europe and of declining to make England the advocate for their interests. Nay, more; she became in their view the advocate of the interests opposed to theirs. Indeed she was rather the decided advocate of Turkey; and now Turkey is full of loud complaints—and complaints I must say not unjust—that we allured her on to her ruin; that we gave the Turks a right to believe that we should support them; that our ambassadors, Sir Henry Elliot and Sir Austin Layard, both of them said we had most vital interests in maintaining Turkey as it was, and consequently the Turks thought if we had vital interests we should certainly defend them; and they were thereby lured on into that ruinous, cruel, and destructive war with Russia. But by our conduct to the Slavonic populations we alienated those populations from us. We made our name odious among them. They had every disposition to sympathize with us, every disposition to confide in us. They are as a people desirous of freedom, desirous of self-government, with no aggressive views, but hating the idea of being absorbed in a huge despotic empire like Russia. But when they found that we and the other powers of Europe under our unfortunate guidance declined to become in any manner their champions in defence of the rights of life, of property, and of female honor,—when they found that there was no call which could find its way to the heart of England through its government or to the hearts of other powers, and that Russia alone was disposed to fight for them, why naturally they said Russia is our friend. We have done everything, gentlemen, in our power to drive these populations into the arms of Russia. If Russia has aggressive dispositions in the direction of Turkey— and I think it probable that she may have them,—it is we who have laid the ground upon which Russia may make her march to the south,—we who have taught the Bulgarians, the Servians, the Roumanians, the Montenegrins, that there is one power in Europe and only one which is ready to support in act and by the sword her professions of sympathy with the oppressed populations of Turkey. That power is Russia, and how can you blame these people if in such circumstances they are disposed to say Russia is our friend? But why did we make them say it? Simply because of the policy of the government, not because of the wishes of the people of this country. Gentlemen, this is the most dangerous form of aggrandizing Russia. If Russia is aggressive anywhere, if Russia is formidable anywhere, it is by movements toward the south, it is by schemes for acquiring command of the straits or of Constantinople; and there is no way by which you can possibly so much assist her in giving reality to these designs as by inducing and disposing the populations of these provinces who are now in virtual possession of them, to look upon Russia as their champion and their friend, to look upon England as their disguised perhaps but yet real and effective enemy.

Why, now, gentlemen, I have said that I think it not unreasonable either to believe or at any rate to admit it to be possible that Russia has aggressive designs in the east of Europe. I do not mean immediate aggressive designs. I do not believe that the Emperor of Russia is a man of aggressive schemes or policy. It is that, looking to that question in the long run, looking at what has happened and what may happen in ten or twenty years, in one generation, in two generations, it is highly probable that in some circumstances Russia may develop aggressive tendencies toward the south.

Perhaps you will say I am here guilty of the same injustice to Russia that I have been deprecating because I say that we ought not to adopt the method of condemning anybody without cause and setting up exceptional principles in proscription of a particular nation. Gentlemen, I will explain to you in a moment the principle upon which I act and the grounds upon which I form my judgment. They are simply these grounds: I look at the position of Russia, the geographical position of Russia relatively to Turkey. I look at the comparative strength of the two empires; I look at the importance of the Dardanelles and the Bosphorus as an exit and a channel for the military and commercial marine of Russia to the Mediterranean; and what I say to myself is this: If the United Kingdom were in the same position relatively to Turkey which Russia holds upon the map of the globe I feel quite sure that we should be very apt indeed both to entertain and to execute aggressive designs upon Turkey. Gentlemen, I will go further and will frankly own to you that I believe if we, instead of happily inhabiting this island, had been in the possession of the Russian territory and in the circumstances of the Russian people we should most likely have eaten up Turkey long ago. And consequently in saying that Russia ought to be vigilantly watched in that quarter I am only applying to her the rule which in parallel circumstances I feel convinced ought to be applied and would be justly applied to judgments upon our own country.

Gentlemen, there is only one other point on which I must still say a few words to you, although there are a great many upon which I have a great many words yet to say somewhere or other.

Of all the principles, gentlemen, of foreign policy which I have enumerated that to which I attach the greatest value is the principle of the equality of nations; because without recognizing that principle there is no such thing as public right and without public international right there is no instrument available for settling the transactions of mankind except material force. Consequently the principle of equality among nations lies in my opinion at the very basis and root of a Christian civilization, and when that principle is compromised or abandoned with it must depart our hopes of tranquillity and of progress for mankind.

I am sorry to say, gentlemen, that I feel it my absolute duty to make this charge against the foreign policy under which we have lived for the last two years, since the resignation of Lord Derby. It has been a foreign policy in my opinion wholly, or to a perilous extent, unregardful of public right and it has been founded upon the basis of a false, I think an arrogant and a dangerous, assumption, although I do not question its being made conscientiously and for what was believed the advantage of the country,—an untrue, arrogant, and dangerous assumption that we are entitled to assume for ourselves some dignity which we should also be entitled to withhold from others and to claim on our own part authority to do things which we would not permit to be done by others. For example when Russia was going to the Congress at Berlin we said: "Your treaty of San Stefano is of no value. It is an act between you and Turkey; but the concerns of Turkey by the treaty of Paris are the concerns of Europe at large. We insist upon it that the whole of your treaty of San Stefano shall be submitted to the Congress at

Berlin that they may judge how far to open it in each and every one of its points, because the concerns of Turkey are the common concerns of the powers of Europe acting in concert."

Having asserted that principle to the world what did we do? These two things, gentlemen: secretly, without the knowledge of Parliament, without even the forms of official procedure, Lord Salisbury met Count Schouvaloff in London and agreed with him upon the terms on which the two powers together should be bound in honor to one another to act upon all the most important points when they came before the Congress at Berlin. Having alleged against Russia that she should not be allowed to settle Turkish affairs with Turkey because they were but two powers and these affairs were the common affairs of Europe and of European interest, we then got Count Schouvaloff into a private room, and on the part of England and Russia, they being but two powers, we settled a large number of the most important of these affairs in utter contempt and derogation of the very principle for which the government had been contending for months before, for which they had asked Parliament to grant a sum of £6,000,000, for which they had spent that £6,000,000 in needless and mischievous armaments. That which we would not allow Russia to do with Turkey, because we pleaded the rights of Europe, we ourselves did with Russia, in contempt of the rights of Europe. Nor was that all, gentlemen. That act was done, I think, on one of the last days of May, in the year 1878, and the document was published, made known to the world, made known to the Congress at Berlin, to its infinite astonishment unless I am very greatly misinformed.

But that was not all. Nearly at the same time we performed the same operation in another quarter. We objected to a treaty between Russia and Turkey as having no authority, though that treaty was made in the light of day—namely, to the treaty of San Stefano; and what did we do? We went not in the light of day but in the darkness of the night,—not in the knowledge and cognizance of other powers, all of whom would have had the faculty and means of watching all along and of preparing and taking their own objections and shaping their own policy,—not in the light of day, but in the darkness of the night, we sent the ambassador of England in Constantinople to the minister of Turkey and there he framed, even while the Congress of Berlin was sitting to determine these matters of common interest, he framed that which is too famous, shall I say, or rather too notorious, as the Anglo-Turkish convention.

Gentlemen, it is said and said truly that truth beats fiction; that what happens in fact from time to time is of a character so daring, so strange, that if the novelist were to imagine it and put it upon his pages the whole world would reject it from its improbability. And that is the case of the Anglo-Turkish convention. For who would have believed it possible that we should assert before the world the principle that Europe only could deal with the affairs of the Turkish empire and should ask Parliament for six millions to support us in asserting that principle, should send ministers to Berlin who declared that unless that principle was acted upon they would go to war with the material that Parliament had placed in their hands and should at the same time be concluded a separate agreement with Turkey, under which those matters of European jurisdiction were coolly transferred to English jurisdiction; and the whole matter was sealed with the worthless bribe of the possession and administration of the island of Cyprus! I said, gentlemen, the worthless bribe of the island of Cyprus, and that is the truth. It is worthless for our purposes—not worthless in itself; an island of resources, an island of natural capabilities, provided they are allowed to develop themselves in the course of circumstances without violent and unprincipled methods of action. But Cyprus was not thought to be worthless by those who accepted it as a bribe. On the contrary you were told that it was to secure the road to India; you were told that it was to be the site of an arsenal very cheaply made and more valuable than Malta; you were told that it was to revive trade. And a multitude of companies were formed and sent agents and capital to Cyprus and some of them, I fear, grievously burned their fingers there. I am not going to dwell upon that now. What I have in view is not the particular merits of Cyprus, but the illustration that I have given you in the case of the agreement of Lord Salisbury with Count Schouvaloff and in the case of the Anglo-Turkish convention, of the manner in which we have asserted for ourselves a principle that we had denied to others— namely, the principle of overriding the European authority of the treaty of Paris and taking the matters which that treaty gave to Europe into our own separate jurisdiction.

Now, gentlemen, I am sorry to find that that which I call the pharisaical assertion of our own superiority has found its way alike into the practice and seemingly into the theories of the government. I am not going to assert anything which is not known, but the prime minister has said that there is one day in the year—namely, the 9th of November, Lord Mayor's day—on which the language of sense and truth is to be heard amidst the surrounding din of idle rumors generated and fledged in the brains of irresponsible scribes. I do not agree, gentlemen, in that panegyric upon the 9th of November. I am much more apt to compare the 9th of November—certainly a well-known day in the year—but as to some of the

speeches that have lately been made upon it I am very much
disposed to compare it with another day in the year well
known to British tradition and that other day in the year is
the 1st of April. But, gentlemen, on that day the prime
minister, speaking out,—I do not question for a moment his
own sincere opinion,—made what I think one of the most
unhappy and ominous allusions ever made by a minister of
this country. He quoted certain words easily rendered as
" Empire and Liberty "—words (he said) of a Roman statesman, words descriptive of the state of Rome—and he quoted
them as words which were capable of legitimate application to
the position and circumstances of England. I join issue with
the prime minister upon that subject and I affirm that nothing
can be more fundamentally unsound, more practically ruinous, than the establishment of Roman analogies for the
guidance of British policy. What, gentlemen, was Rome?
Rome was indeed an imperial state, you may tell me,—I
know not, I cannot read the counsels of Providence,—a state
having a mission to subdue the world, but a state whose very
basis it was to deny the equal rights, to proscribe the independent existence of other nations. That, gentlemen, was
the Roman idea. It has been partially and not ill described
in three lines of a translation from Virgil by our great poet
Dryden, which runs as follows:

> " O Rome! 'tis thine alone with awful sway
> To rule mankind, and make the world obey,
> Disposing peace and war thine own majestic way."

We are told to fall back upon this example. No doubt the
word " empire " was qualified with the word " liberty." But
what did the two words " liberty " and " empire " mean in
a Roman mouth? They meant simply this: " Liberty for
ourselves, empire over the rest of mankind."

I do not think, gentlemen, that this ministry or any other ministry is going to place us in the position of Rome. What I object to is the revival of the idea. I care not how feebly, I care not even how, from a philosophic or historical point of view, how ridiculous the attempt at this revival may be. I say it indicates an intention—I say it indicates a frame of mind, and the frame of mind unfortunately I find has been consistent with the policy of which I have given you some illustrations—the policy of denying to others the rights that we claim ourselves. No doubt, gentlemen, Rome may have had its work to do and Rome did its work. But modern times have brought a different state of things. Modern times have established a sisterhood of nations, equal, independent, each of them built up under that legitimate defence which public law affords to every nation, living within its own borders and seeking to perform its own affairs; but if one thing more than another has been detestable to Europe it has been the appearance upon the stage from time to time of men who, even in the times of Christian civilization, have been thought to aim at universal dominion. It was this aggressive disposition on the part of Louis XIV, King of France, that led your forefathers, gentlemen, freely to spend their blood and treasure in a cause not immediately their own and to struggle against the method of policy which, having Paris for its centre, seemed to aim at an universal monarchy.

It was the very same thing a century and a half later which was the charge launched and justly launched against Napoleon, that under his dominion France was not content even with her extended limits, but Germany, and Italy, and Spain, apparently without any limit to this pestilent and pernicious process, were to be brought under the dominion or influence of France and national equality was to be trampled under foot and national rights denied. For that reason England in the struggle almost exhausted herself, greatly impoverished her people, brought upon herself and Scotland too the consequences of a debt that nearly crushed their energies, and poured forth their best blood without limit in order to resist and put down these intolerable pretensions.

Gentlemen, it is but in a pale and weak and almost despicable miniature that such ideas are now set up, but you will observe that the poison lies—that the poison and the mischief lie—in the principle and not the scale.

It is the opposite principle which I say has been compromised by the action of the ministry and which I call upon you and upon any who choose to hear my views to vindicate when the day of our election comes; I mean the sound and the sacred principle that Christendom is formed of a band of nations who are united to one another in the bonds of right; that they are without distinction of great and small; there is an absolute equality between them,—the same sacredness defends the narrow limits of Belgium as attaches to the extended frontiers of Russia or Germany or France. I hold that he who by act or word brings that principle into peril or disparagement, however honest his intentions may be, places himself in the position of one inflicting—I won't say intending to inflict—I ascribe nothing of the sort—but inflicting injury upon his own country and endangering the peace and all the most fundamental interests of Christian society.

ON THE BEACONSFIELD MINISTRY

DELIVERED IN EDINBURGH, MARCH 17, 1880

GENTLEMEN,—When I last had the honor of addressing you in this hall I endeavored in some degree to open the great case which I was in hopes would, in conformity with what I may call constitutional usage, then have been brought at once before you. The arguments which we made for a dissolution were received with the usual contempt, and the Parliament was summoned to attempt for the first time in our history the regular business of a seventh session. I am not going now to argue on the propriety of this course, because, meeting you here in the capital of the county and of Scotland, I am anxious to go straight to the very heart of the matter, and amidst the crowd of topics that rush upon the mind to touch upon some of those which you will judge to be most closely and most intimately connected with the true merits of the great issue that is before us.

At last the dissolution has come, and I postpone the consideration of the question why it has come, the question how it has come, on which there are many things to be said. It has come, and you are about to give your votes upon an occasion which, allow me to tell you, entails not only upon me, but upon you, a responsibility greater than you ever had to undergo. I believe that I have the honor of addressing a mixed meeting, a meeting principally and very largely composed of freeholders of the county, but in which warm and decided friends are freely mingled with those who have not declared in our favor, or even with those who may intend to vote against us.

Now, gentlemen, let me say a word in the first place to those whom I must for the moment call opponents. I am not going to address them in the language of flattery. I am not going to supplicate them for the conferring of a favor. I am not going to appeal to them on any secondary or any social ground. I am going to speak to them as Scotchmen and as citizens; I am going to speak to them of the duty that they owe to the empire at this moment; I am going to speak to them of the condition of the empire, of the strength of the empire, and of the honor of the empire; and it is upon these isssues that I respectfully ask for their support. I am glad that, notwithstanding my Scotch blood, and notwith-standing the association of my father and my grandfather with this country, it is open to our opponents if they like to describe me as a stranger; because I am free to admit that I stand here in consequence of an invitation, and in conse-quence of treatment the most generous and the most gratify-ing that ever was accorded to man. And I venture to assure every one of my opponents that if I beg respectfully to have some credit for upright motives, that credit I at once accord to them. I know very well they are not accustomed to hear it given me; I know very well that in the newspapers which they read they will find that violent passion, that outrageous hatred, that sordid greed for office, are the motives and the only motives by which I am governed. Many of these papers constitute in some sense their daily food; but I have such faith in their intelligence, and in the healthiness of their constitution as Scotchmen, that I believe that many of them will by the inherent vigor of that constitution correct and neutralize the poison thus administered; will consent to meet me upon equal grounds, and will listen to the appeal which I make.

The appeal which I make to them is this: If my position here is a serious one, their position is serious too. My allegations have been before you for a length of time. I will not now again read to a Midlothian audience the letter in which I first accepted this candidature. By every word of that letter I abide; in support of every allegation which that letter contains, I am ready to bring detailed and conclusive proof. These allegations—I say to you, gentlemen, to that portion of my audience—these allegations are of the most serious character. I admit as freely as you can urge that if they be unfounded, then my responsibility—nay, my culpability—before my country cannot be exaggerated. But, on the other hand, if these allegations be true—if it be true that the resources of Great Britain have been misused; if it be true that the international law of Europe has been broken; if it be true that the law of this country has been broken; if it be true that the good name of this land has been tarnished and defaced; if it be true that its condition has been needlessly aggravated by measures both useless, and wanton, and mischievous in themselves—then your responsibility is as great as mine. For I fully admit that in 1874 you incurred no great or special responsibility. You were tired of the Liberal government; you were dissatisfied with them. [Cries of " No, no! "] Oh, I beg pardon; I am addressing my opponents. Scotchmen, I believe, as much as Englishmen, like plain speaking, and I hope I have given you some proof that if that be your taste I endeavor to meet it as well as I can; and I thank you heartily for the manner in which, by your kindly attention, you have enabled me to say what I think is the truth, whether it be palatable or whether it be not.

Now the great question which we have been debating for the last three or four years—for I do not carry back the pith of what I have principally to say to the six years of the government—is the question of the policy which has been pursued during that time; most especially by far the policy of the last two years, and the effect of that policy upon the condition of the country, upon the legislation of the country, upon the strength of the empire, and above all upon the honor of the empire. I am now going to compare the conduct of the present government, which is commended to you as masterly in forethought and sagacity and truly English in spirit—I am going to compare it with the conduct of the last government and to lay before you the proceedings of the results. It so happens that their histories are a not inconvenient means of comparison. England, as you are aware, has been involved in many guarantees. I said England—do not be shocked; it is the shortest word—Great Britain or the United Kingdom is what one ought to say. The United Kingdom—the British empire—has been and is involved in many guarantees for the condition of other countries. Among others, we were involved, especially since the Peace of Paris, but also before the Peace of Paris, in a guarantee for Turkey, aiming to maintain its integrity and its independence; and we were involved in another guarantee for Belgium, aiming to maintain its integrity and its independence. In the time of the present government the integrity and the independence of Turkey were menaced — menaced by the consequences of rank, festering corruption from within. In the time of the late government the integrity and independence of Belgium were not less seriously menaced. We had been living in perfect harmony and friendship with two great military states of Europe—with

Prussia and with France. France and Prussia came into conflict, and at the moment of their coming into conflict a document was revealed to us which the ministers of those two states had had in their hands. Whoever was its author, whoever was its promoter, that is no affair of mine—it is due to Prince Bismarck to say that he was the person who brought it to light—but they had in their hands an instrument of a formal character, touching a subject that was considered and entertained. And that bad instrument was an instrument for the destruction of the freedom, independence, and integrity of Belgium. Could there be a graver danger to Europe than that?

Here was a State—not like Turkey, the scandal of the world, and the danger of the world from misgovernment, and from the horrible degradation it inflicted upon its subject races—but a country which was a marvel to all Europe for the peaceful exercise of the rights of freedom, and for progress in all the arts and all pursuits that tend to make mankind good and happy. And this country, having nothing but its weakness that could be urged against it, with its four or five millions of people, was deliberately pointed out by somebody and indicated to be destroyed, to be offered up as a sacrifice to territorial lust by one or other of those ministers of powers with whom we were living in close friendship and affection. We felt called upon to enlist ourselves on the part of the British nation as advocates and as champions of the integrity and independence of Belgium. And if we had gone to war we should have gone to war for freedom, we should have gone to war for public right, we should have gone to war to save human happiness from being invaded by tyrannous and lawless power. This is what I call a good cause, gentlemen. And though I detest war, and there are no epithets too strong, if you could supply me with them, that I will not endeavor to heap upon its head—in such a war as that, while the breath in my body is continued to me, I am ready to engage. I am ready to support it, I am ready to give all the help and aid I can to those who carry this country into it. Well, gentlemen, pledged to support the integrity and independence of Belgium, what did we do? We proposed to Prussia to enter into a new and solemn treaty with us to resist the French empire, if the French empire attempted to violate the sanctity of freedom in Belgium; and we proposed to France to enter into a similar treaty with us to pursue exactly the same measures against Prussia, if Prussia should make the like nefarious attempt. And we undertook that, in concert with the one, or in concert with the other, whichever the case might be, we would pledge all the resources of this empire, and carry it into war for the purpose of resisting mischief and maintaining the principles of European law and peace.

I ask you whether it is not ridiculous to apply the doctrine or the imputation, if it be an imputation, that we belong to the "Manchester School," or to a Peace Party—we who made these engagements to go to war with France if necessary, or to go to war with Prussia if necessary, for the sake of the independence of Belgium? But now I want you to observe the upshot. I must say that in one respect we were very inferior to the present government—very inferior indeed. Our ciphers, our figures, were perfectly contemptible. We took nothing except two millions of money. We knew perfectly well that what was required was an indication, and that that indication would be quite intelligible when it was read in the light of the new treaty engagement which we were contracting; and consequently we asked Parliament to

give us two millions of money for the sake of somewhat enlarging the numbers of available soldiers, and we were quite
prepared to meet that contingency had it arrived. The great
man who directs the councils of the German empire [Bis-
marck] acted with his usual promptitude. Our proposal
went to him by telegraph and he answered by telegraph,
" Yes," the same afternoon. We were not quite so fortunate
with France, for at that time the councils of France were
under the domination of some evil genius which it is difficult
to trace and needless to attempt to trace. There was some
delay in France—a little unnecessary haggling—but after
two or three days France also came into this engagement,
and from that moment the peace of Belgium was perfectly
secured. When we had our integrity and our independence
to protect we took the measures which we believed to be
necessary and sufficient for that protection; and in every
year since those measures, Belgium, not unharmed only, but
strengthened by having been carried safely and unhurt
through a terrible danger, has pursued her peaceful career,
rising continually in her prosperity and happiness, and still
holding out an example before all Europe to teach the nations
how to live.

Well, gentlemen, as that occasion came to us with respect
to Belgium so it came to our successors with respect to
Turkey. How did they manage it? They thought themselves bound to maintain the integrity and independence of
Turkey, and they were undoubtedly bound conditionally to
maintain it. I am not now going into the question of right,
but into the question of the adaptation of the means to an end.
These are the gentlemen who are set before you as the people
whose continuance in office it is necessary to maintain to
attract the confidence of Europe; these are the gentlemen

whom patriotic associations laud to the skies as if they had a monopoly of human intelligence; these are the gentlemen who bring you " Peace with Honor "; these are the gentlemen who go in special trains to attend august assemblies and receive the compliments of august statesmen; these are the gentlemen who for all these years have been calling upon you to pay any number of millions that might be required as a very cheap and insignificant consideration for the immense advantages that you derive from their administration.

Therefore I want you to know, and I have shown you, how we set about to maintain integrity and independence, and how it was maintained then. I ask how they have set about it. But, gentlemen, on their own showing they have done wrong. We have it out of their own mouths. I won't go to Lord Derby; I will go to the only man whose authority is higher for this purpose than Lord Derby's, namely, Lord Beaconsfield. He tells you plainly that what the government ought to have done was to have said to Russia, " You shall not invade Turkey." Gentlemen, that course is intelligible. It is a guilty course, in my opinion, to have taken up arms for maintaining the integrity of Turkey against her subject races, or to take up arms against what the Emperor of Russia believed to be a great honor to humanity in going to apply a remedy to these mischiefs. But Lord Beaconsfield has confessed in a public speech that the proper course for the government to have taken was to have planted their foot and to have said to the Emperor of Russia : " Cross not the Danube; if you cross the Danube, expect to confront the power of England on the southern shore." Now, gentlemen, that course is intelligible, perfectly intelligible; and if you are prepared for the responsibility of maintaining such an integrity and such an independence irrespectively of other considerations against the Christian races in Turkey, that was the course for you to pursue. It was not pursued, because the agitation, which is called the Bulgarian agitation, was too inconvenient to allow the government to pursue it, because they saw that if they did that which Lord Beaconsfield now tells us it would have been right to do, the sentiment of the country would not have permitted them to continue to hold their office; and hence came that vacillation, hence came that ineptitude of policy which they now endeavor to cover by hectoring and by boasting, and which, within the last year or two, they have striven, and not quite unsuccessfully, to hide from the eyes of many by carrying measures of violence into other lands, if not against Russia, if not against the strong, yet against the weak, and endeavoring to attract to themselves the credit and glory of maintaining the power and influence of England.

Well, gentlemen, they were to maintain the integrity and independence of Turkey. How did they set about it? They were not satisfied with asking for our humble two millions; they asked for six millions. What did they do, first of all? First of all they encouraged Turkey to go to war. They did not counsel Turkey's submission to superior force; they neither would advise her to submit, nor would they assist her to resist. They were the great causes of her plunging into that deplorable and ruinous war, from the consequences of which, her Majesty's speech states this year, Turkey has not yet recovered, and there is not the smallest appearance of hope that she will ever recover. But afterwards, and when the war had taken place, they came and asked you for a vote of six millions. What did they do with the six millions? They flourished it in the face of the world. What did they gain for Turkey? In the first place, they sent a fleet to the

Dardanelles and the Bosphorus. Are you aware that in sending that fleet they broke the law of Europe? They applied for a firman to the Sultan. The Sultan refused, and they had no right to send that fleet. But, however that may be, what was the use of sending that fleet? The consequence was that the Russian army, which had been at a considerable distance from Constantinople, marched close up to Constantinople. Is it possible to conceive an idea more absurd than that which I really believe was entertained by many of our friends—I do not say our friends in Midlothian, but in places where the intelligence is high—that the presence of certain British ironclads in the Sea of Marmora prevented the victorious Russian armies from entering Constantinople? What could these ironclads do? They could have battered down Constantinople no doubt; but what consolation would that have been to Turkey, or how would it have prevented Russian armies from entering? That part of the pretext set is too thin and threadbare to require any confutation. But they may say that that vote of six millions was an indication of the intention of England to act in case of need; and when it was first proposed it was to strengthen the hands of England at the Congress. But did it strengthen the hands of England; and if so, to what purpose was that strength used? The treaty of San Stefano had been signed between Russia and Turkey; the treaty of Berlin was substituted for it. What was the grand difference between the treaty of Berlin and the treaty of San Stefano? There was a portion of Bessarabia which, down to the time of the treaty of Berlin, enjoyed free institutions, and by the treaty of Berlin, and mainly through the agency of the British government, which had pledged itself beforehand by what is called the Salisbury-Schouvaloff Memorandum, to support Russia in her demand for that territory if Russia adhered to that demand, England, with the vote of six millions given to strengthen her influence, made herself specially responsible for handing back that territory, which enjoyed free institutions, to be governed despotically by the Russian empire.

That is the first purpose for which, as I have shown you, your vote of six millions was available. What was the second? It was to draw a line along the Balkan Mountains, by means of which northern Bulgaria was separated from southern Bulgaria, and southern Bulgaria was re-named eastern Roumelia. The Sultan has not marched and cannot march a man into eastern Roumelia. If he did the consequences would be that the whole of that population, who are determined to fight for their rights, would rise against him and his troops, and would be supported by other forces that could be drawn to it under the resistless influences of sympathy with freedom. You may remember that three or four years ago utter scorn was poured upon what was called the " bag-and-baggage policy." Are you aware that that policy is at this moment the basis upon which are regulated the whole of the civil state of things in Bulgaria and eastern Roumelia? What that policy asked was that every Turkish authority should be marched out of Bulgaria, and every Turkish authority has gone out of Bulgaria. There is not a Turk at this moment who, as a Turk, holds office under the Sultan either in Bulgaria or in southern Bulgaria, which is called eastern Roumelia—no, not one. The despised " bag-and-baggage policy " is at this moment the law of Europe, and that is the result of it; and it is for that, gentlemen, that the humble individual who stands before you was held up and reviled as a visionary enthusiast and a verbose—I forget what— rhetorician, although I believe myself there was not much

verbosity in that particular phrase. It appeared to me the
people of England understood it pretty well—nay, more, the
Congress of Berlin seemed to have understood it, and the state
of things which I recommended was irresistible, and now,
I thank God, is irreversibly established in those once unhappy
provinces. Gentlemen, we have got one more thing to do in
regard to these provinces and that is this—I urged it at the
same time when I produced this monstrous conception of the
" bag-and-baggage policy "—it is this, to take great care that
the majority of the inhabitants of these provinces, who are
Christians, do not oppress either the Mohammedans, or the
Jewish, or any other minority. That is a sacred duty; I
don't believe it to be a difficult duty; it is a sacred duty. I
stated to you just now that there was not a Turk holding
office as a Turk in these provinces. I believe there are Turks
holding office—and I rejoice to hear it—holding office through
the free suffrage of their countrymen, and by degrees I hope
that they, when they are once rid of all the pestilent and
poisonous associations, and the recollections of the old ascendency, will become good and peaceful citizens like other people.
I believe the people of Turkey have in them many fine qualities, whatever the governors may be, capable under proper
education, gentlemen, of bringing them to a state of capacity
and competency for every civil duty.

Gentlemen, it still remains for me to ask you how this
great and powerful government has performed its duty of
maintaining the integrity and independence of Turkey. It
has had great and extraordinary advantages. It has had the
advantage of disciplined support from its majority in the
House of Commons. Though I am not making any complaint, as my friend in the chair knows, it was not exactly the
same as happened in the days of recent Liberal govern-

ments. It had had unflinching and incessant support from the large majority of the Lords. That was very far from being our case in our day. There is no reason why I should not say so. I say freely—it is an historical fact—that the House of Lords, when the people's representatives are backed by a strong national feeling, when it would be dangerous to oppose, confront, or resist, then the House of Lords pass our measures. So they passed the Disestablishment of the Irish Church, and so they passed the Irish Land Act; and I have no doubt that, if it pleases the Almighty, they will pass many more good measures. But the moment the people go to sleep—and they cannot be always awake—when public opinion flags and ceases to take a strong and decided interest in public questions, that moment the majority of the House of Lords grows. They mangle, they postpone, they reject the good measures that go up to them.

I will show you another advantage which the present administration possesses. They are supported by several foreign governments. Did you read in the London papers within the last few weeks an account of the energetic support they derived from the Emperor of Austria? Did you see that the Emperor of Austria sent for the British Ambassador, Sir Henry Elliot, and told him that a pestilent person, a certain individual named Mr. Gladstone, was a man who did not approve the foreign policy of Austria, and how anxious he was —so the Emperor of Austria was pleased complacently to say—for the guidance of the British people and of the electors of Midlothian—how anxious he was that you should, all of you, give your votes in a way to maintain the Ministry of Lord Beaconsfield.[1] Well, gentlemen, if you approve the

[1] Subsequent disclosures proved that this was not strictly correct, and Mr. Gladstone apologetically withdrew the statement.

foreign policy of Austria, the foreign policy that Austria has usually pursued, I advise you to do that very thing; if you want to have an Austrian foreign policy dominant in the councils of this country, give your votes as the Emperor of Austria recommends. What has that foreign policy of Austria been? I do not say that Austria is incurable. I hope it will yet be cured, because it has got better institutions at home, and I heartily wish it well if it makes honest attempts to confront its difficulties. Yet I must look to what that policy has been. Austria has ever been the unflinching foe of freedom in every country of Europe. Austria trampled under foot, Austria resisted the unity of Germany. Russia, I am sorry to say, has been the foe of freedom too; but in Russia there is an exception—Russia has been the friend of Slavonic freedom; but Austria has never been the friend even of Slavonic freedom. Austria did all she could to prevent the creation of Belgium. Austria never lifted a finger for the regeneration and constitution of Greece. There is not an instance—there is not a spot upon the whole map where you can lay your finger and say, " There Austria did good." I speak of its general policy; I speak of its general tendency. I do not abandon the hope of improvement in the future, but we must look to the past and to the present for the guidance of our judgments at this moment. And in the Congress of Berlin Austria resisted the extension of freedom and did not promote it; and therefore I say, if you want the spirit of Austria to inspire the councils of this country in Heaven's name take the Emperor's counsel; and I advise you to lift the Austrian flag when you go about your purposes of canvass or of public meetings. It will best express the purpose you have in view, and I for one cannot complain of your consistency, whatever in that case I might think of the tendency of your views in respect of principle, of justice, of the happiness of mankind, or of the greatness, the dignity, and the honor of this great empire.

But, gentlemen, still one word more, because I have not spoken of what has been the upshot of all this. There are a great many persons in this country, I am afraid, as well as in other countries, who are what is called Worshippers of Success, and at the time of the famous " Peace with Honor " demonstration there was a very great appearance of success. I was not myself at that time particularly safe when I walked in the streets of London.[1] I have walked with my wife from my own house, I have walked owing my protection to the police; but that was the time, gentlemen, when all those curious methods of maintaining British honor and British dignity were supposed to have been wonderfully successful. And now I want to ask you, as I have shown you the way we went about maintaining the independence and integrity of Belgium—what has become of the independence and integrity of Turkey? I have shown that they neither knew in the first instance the ends toward which they should first have directed their efforts, nor, when they have chosen ends, have they been able rationally to adapt their means to the attainment of those ends. I am not speaking of the moral character of the means, but how they are adapted to the end. And what did the vote of six millions achieve for Turkey? I will tell you what it achieved. It did achieve one result, and I want you well to consider whether you are satisfied with it or not, especially those of you who are Conservatives. It undoubtedly cut down largely the division of Bulgaria, established by the treaty of

[1]At the time of the " Jingo " excitement Mr. and Mrs. Gladstone were hustled by a gang of rowdies in Cavendish Square, and were saved only from violence by taking refuge in the house of Dr., afterwards Sir Andrew, Clark.

San Stefano. Now, I am not going to maintain that that division was a right one, for that depends on a knowledge more minute than I possess; but the effect of it was to cut it down, as is perfectly well known—that is, put back under the direct rule of the Sultan of Turkey, and in the exact condition in which all European Turkey, except the Principalities, had been before the war, the population inhabiting the country of Macedonia, and about a million of people, the vast majority of them Christians. Two substantive and definite results, the two most definite results, produced were these—first of all that Bessarabia, that had been a country with free institutions, was handed back to despotism; and secondly a million and a half of people inhabiting Macedonia, to whom free institutions had been promised by the treaty of San Stefano, are now again placed under the Turkish pashas and have not received one grain of benefit of importance as compared with their condition before the war.

But how as regards Turkey? I have shown results bad enough in regard to freedom. What did the British plenipotentiaries say at Berlin? They said that some people seemed to suppose we had come to cut and carve Turkey. That is quite a mistake, said the plenipotentiaries; we have come to consolidate Turkey. Some of the scribes of the foreign office coined a new word, and said it was to " rejuvenate " Turkey. How did they rejuvenate this unfortunate empire, this miserable empire, this unhappy government which they have lured into war and allowed and encouraged to pass into war because they allowed their ambassadors at Constantinople, Sir Henry Elliot and Sir Austen Layard, to whisper into the ear of the Turk that British interests would compel us to interfere and help her? What has been the result to Turkey? Now, I will say, much as the Christian populations have the right to complain, the Sultan of Turkey has a right to complain very little less. How has the Sultan been treated? We condescended to obtain from him the island of Cyprus, at a time when Austria was pulling at him on one side and freedom on the other. We condescended to take from him that miserable paltry share of the spoil. That is not all. What is the condition of Turkey in Europe? It is neither integrity nor independence. The Sultan is liable to interference at any moment, at every point of his territory, from every one that signed the treaty of Berlin. He has lost ten millions of subjects altogether, ten millions more are in some kind of dependence or other—in a condition that the Sultan does not know whether they will be his subjects to-morrow or the next day. Albania is possessed by a league. Macedonia, as you read in the papers, is traversed by brigands. Thessaly and Epirus, according to the treaty of Berlin, should be given to Greece. The treasury of Turkey is perfectly empty, disturbances have spread through Turkey in Asia, and the condition of that government whose integrity and independence you were told that " Peace with Honor " had secured, is more miserable than at any previous period of its history; and wise and merciful indeed would be the man that would devise some method of improving it.

To those gentlemen who talk of the great vigor and determination and success of the Tory government, I ask you to compare the case of Belgium and Turkey. Try them by principles, or try them by results, I care not which, we knew what we were about and what was to be done when we had integrity and independence to support. When they had integrity and independence to protect they talked indeed loud enough about supporting Turkey, and you would suppose they were prepared to spend their whole resources upon it; but all

their measures have ended in nothing except that they have
reduced Turkey to a state of greater weakness than at any portion of her history, whereas, on the other hand, in regard to
the twelve or thirteen millions of Slavs and Roumanian population, they have made the name of England odious throughout the whole population, and done everything in their power
to throw that population into the arms of Russia, to be the tool
of Russia in its plans and schemes, unless indeed, as I hope
and am inclined to believe, the virtue of free institutions they
have obtained will make them too wise to become the tools of
any foreign power whatever, will make them intent upon
maintaining their own liberties, as becomes a free people playing a noble part in the history of Europe.

I have detained you too long, and I will not, though I
would, pursue this subject further. I have shown you what I
think the miserable failure of the policy of the government.
Remember we have a fixed point from which to draw our
measurements. Remember what in 1876 the proposal of
those who approved of the Bulgarian agitation and who were
denounced as the enemies of Turkey, remember what that proposal would have done. It would have given autonomy to
Bulgaria, which has now got autonomy; but it would have
saved all the remainder at less detriment to the rest of the
Turkish Empire. Turkey would have had a fair chance.
Turkey would not have suffered the territorial losses which
she has elsewhere suffered, and which she has suffered, I must
say, in consequence of her being betrayed into the false and
mischievous, the tempting and seductive, but unreal and unwise policy of the present administration.

There are other matters which must be reserved for other
times. We are told about the Crimean War. Sir Stafford
Northcote tells us the Crimean War, made by the Liberal

government, cost the country forty millions of debt, and an income tax of one shilling and four pence per pound. Now what is the use of telling us that? I will discuss the Crimean War on some future occasion, but not now. If the Liberal government were so clever that they contrived to burden the country with forty millions of debt for this Crimean War, why does he not go back to the war before that and tell us what the Tory government did with the Revolutionary War, when they left a debt on the country of some nine hundred millions, of which six hundred and fifty millions they had made in the Revolutionary War, and not only so, but left the blessing and legacy of the corn laws, and of a high protective system, an impoverished country, and a discontented population—so much so that for years that followed that great Revolutionary War, no man could say whether the constitution of this country was or was not worth five years' purchase. They might even go further back than the Revolutionary War. They have been talking loudly of the colonies, and say that, forsooth, the Liberal party do nothing for the colonies. What did the Tory party do for the colonies? I can tell you. Go to the war that preceded the Revolutionary War. They made war against the American continent. They added to the debt of the country two hundred millions in order to destroy freedom in America. They alienated it and drove it from this country. They were compelled to bring this country to make an ignominious peace; and, as far as I know, that attempt to put down freedom in America, with its results to this country, is the only one great fact which has ever distinguished the relations between a Tory government and the colonies.

But, gentlemen, these must be matters postponed for another occasion. I thank you very cordially, both friends and opponents, if opponents you be, for the extreme kindness with which you have heard me. I have spoken, and I must speak in very strong terms of the acts done by my opponents. I will never say that they did it from vindictiveness, I will never say that they did it from passion, I will never say that they did it from a sordid love of office; I have no right to use such words; I have no right to entertain such sentiments; I repudiate and abjure them. I give them credit for patriotic motives—I give them credit for those patriotic motives which are incessantly and gratuitously denied to us. I believe we are all united in a fond attachment to the great country to which we belong, to the great empire which has committed to it a trust and function from Providence, as special and remarkable as was ever entrusted to any portion of the family of man. When I speak of that trust and that function I feel that words fail. I cannot tell you what I think of the nobleness of the inheritance which has descended upon us, of the sacredness of the duty of maintaining it. I will not condescend to make it a part of controversial politics. It is a part of my being, of my flesh and blood, of my heart and soul. For those ends I have labored through my youth and manhood, and, more than that, till my hairs are gray. In that faith and practice I have lived, and in that faith and practice I shall die.

THE GOVERNMENT OF IRELAND BILL[1]

HOUSE OF COMMONS, APRIL 8, 1886

I COULD have wished, Mr. Speaker, on several grounds, that it had been possible for me on this single occasion to open to the House the whole of the policy and intentions of the government with respect to Ireland. The two questions of land and of Irish government are, in our view, closely and inseparably connected, for they are the two channels through which we hope to find access, and effectual access, to that question which is the most vital of all—namely, the question of social order in Ireland. As I have said, those two questions are, in our view—whatever they may be in that of any one else—they are in our view, for reasons which I cannot now explain, inseparable the one from the other. But it is impossible for me to attempt such a task. Even as it is, the mass of materials that I have before me I may, without exaggeration, call enormous. I do not know that at any period a task has been laid upon me involving so large and so diversified an exposition, and it would be in vain to attempt more than human strength can, I think, suffice to achieve. I may say that, when contemplating the magnitude of that task, I have been filled with a painful mistrust; but that mistrust, I can assure the House, is absorbed in the yet deeper feeling of the responsibility that would lie upon me, and of the mischief that I should inflict upon the public interest, if I should fail to bring home to the minds of members, as

---

[1] The Government of Ireland Bill, generally known as the "Home Rule" Bill, passed its first reading on April 13th without a division after four nights' debate.

I seem to perceive in my own mind, the magnitude of all the varied aspects of this question. What I wish is that we should no longer fence and skirmish with this question, but that we should come to close quarters with it; that we should get if we can at the root; that we should take measures not merely intended for the wants of to-day and of to-morrow, but if possible that we should look into a more distant future; that we should endeavor to anticipate and realize the future by the force of reflection; that we should if possible unroll it in anticipation before our eyes, and make provision now, while there is yet time, for all the results that may await upon a right or wrong decision of to-day.

Mr. Speaker, on one point I rejoice to think that we have a material, I would say a vital, agreement. It is felt on both sides of the House, unless I am much mistaken, that we have arrived at a stage in our political transactions with Ireland, where two roads part one from the other, not soon probably to meet again. The late government—I am not now referring to this as a matter of praise or blame, but simply as a matter of fact—the late government felt that they had reached the moment for decisive resolution when they made the announcement, on the last day [January 26] of their ministerial existence, that their duty compelled them to submit to Parliament proposals for further repressive criminal legislation. We concur entirely in that conclusion, and we think that the time is come when it is the duty of Parliament, when the honor of Parliament and its duty alike require, that it should endeavor to come to some decisive resolution in this matter; and our intention is, sir, to propose to the House of Commons that which, as we think, if happily accepted, will liberate Parliament from the restraints under which of late years it has ineffectually struggled to perform the business of the country; will restore legislation to its natural, ancient, unimpeded course; and will, above all, obtain an answer—a clear, we hope, and definite answer—to the question whether it is or is not possible to establish good and harmonious relations between Great Britain and Ireland on the footing of those free institutions to which Englishmen, Scotchmen, and Irishmen are alike unalterably attached.

Now, when I say that we are imperatively called upon to deal with the great subject of social order in Ireland, do not let me for a moment either be led myself or lead others into the dangerous fault of exaggeration. The crime of Ireland, the agrarian crime of Ireland, I rejoice to say, is not what it was in other days—days now comparatively distant, days within my own earliest recollection as a member of Parliament. In 1833 the government of Lord Grey proposed to Parliament a strong Coercion Act. At that time the information at their command did not distinguish between agrarian and ordinary crime as the distinction is now made. As to the present time, it is easy to tell the House that the serious agrarian crimes of Ireland, which in 1881 were 994, in 1885 were 239. But I go back to the period of 1832. The contrast is, perhaps, still more striking. In 1832 the homicides in Ireland were 248, in 1885 they were 65. The cases of attempts to kill, happily unfulfilled, in the first of those years were 209, in 1885 were 37. The serious offences of all other kinds in Ireland in 1832 were 6,014, in 1885 they were 1,057. The whole criminal offences in Ireland in the former years were 14,000, and in the latter year 2,683.

So far, therefore, sir, we are not to suppose that the case with which we have now to deal is one of those cases of extreme disorder which threaten the general peace of society. Notwithstanding that, sir, in order to lay the ground for the important measure we are asking leave to introduce—and well I am aware that it does require broad and solid grounds to be laid in order to justify the introduction of such a measure—in order to lay that ground, I must ask the House to enter with me into a brief review of the general features of what has been our course with regard to what is termed coercion, or repressive criminal legislation. And sir, the first point to which I would call your attention is this, that whereas exceptional legislation— legislation which introduces exceptional provisions into the law—ought itself to be in its own nature essentially and absolutely exceptional, it has become for us not exceptional but habitual. We are like a man who, knowing that medicine may be the means of his restoration to health, endeavors to live upon medicine. Nations, no more than individuals, can find a subsistence in what was meant to be a cure. But has it been a cure? Have we attained the object which we desired, and honestly desired, to attain? No, sir, agrarian crime has become, sometimes upon a larger and sometimes upon a smaller scale, as habitual in Ireland as the legislation which has been intended to repress it, and that agrarian crime, although at the present time it is almost at the low water-mark, yet has a fatal capacity of expansion under stimulating circumstances, and rises from time to time, as it rose in 1885, to dimensions and to an exasperation which becomes threatening to general social order, and to the peace of private and domestic life. I ought, perhaps, to supply an element which I forgot at the moment in comparing 1832 and 1885, that is to remind the House that the decrease of crime is not so great as it looks, because the population of Ireland at that time was nearly 8,000,000, whereas it may be taken at present at 5,000,000. But the exact proportion, I believe, is fairly represented by the figure I will now give. The population of Ireland now, compared with that time, is under two-thirds; the crime of Ireland now, as compared with that period, is under one-fifth.

But the agrarian crime in Ireland is not so much a cause as it is a symptom. It is a symptom of a yet deeper mischief of which it is only the external manifestation. That manifestation is mainly threefold. In the first place, with certain exceptions for the case of winter juries, it is impossible to depend in Ireland upon the finding of a jury in a case of agrarian crimes according to the facts as they are viewed by the government, by the judges, and by the public, I think, at large. That is a most serious mischief, passing down deep into the very groundwork of civil society. It is also, sir, undoubtedly a mischief that the cases where the extreme remedy of eviction is resorted to by the landlord—possibly in some instances unnecessarily resorted to, but in other instances resorted to after long patience has been exhausted—these cases of eviction, good, bad, and indifferent as to their justification, stand pretty much in one and the same discredit with the rural population of Ireland, and become, as we know, the occasion of transactions that we all deeply lament. Finally, sir, it is not to be denied that there is great interference in Ireland with individual liberty, in the shape of intimidation. Now, sir, I am not about to assume the tone of the Pharisee on this occasion. There is a great deal of intimidation in England, too, when people find occasion for it; and if we, the English and the Scotch, were under the conviction that we had such grave cause to warrant irregular action, as is the conviction entertained by a very large part of the population in Ireland, I am not at all sure that we should not, like that part of the population in Ireland, resort to the rude and unjustifiable remedy of intimidation. I am very ambitious on this important and critical occasion to gain one object—that is, not to treat this question controversially. I have this object in view, and I do not despair of attaining it; and in order that I may do nothing to cause me to fail of attaining it, I will not enter into the question, if you like, whether there is ever intimidation in England or not. But I will simply record the fact, which I thought it but just to accompany with a confession with regard to ourselves—I will simply record the fact that intimidation does prevail, not to the extent that is supposed, yet to a material and painful extent, in Ireland. The consequence of that is to weaken generally the respect for law, and the respect for contract, and that among a people who, I believe, are as capable of attaining to the very highest moral and social standard as any people on the face of the earth. So much for coercion—if I use the phrase it is for brevity for repressive legislation generally—but there is one circumstance to which I cannot help drawing the special attention of the House.

Nothing has been more painful to me than to observe that in this matter we are not improving, but, on the contrary, we are losing ground. Since the last half century dawned, we have been steadily engaged in extending, as well as in consolidating, free institutions. I divide the period since the Act of Union with Ireland into two— the first from 1800 to 1832, the epoch of what is still justly called the great Reform Act, and, secondly, from 1833 to 1885. I do not know whether it has been as widely observed as I think it deserves to be that in the first of those periods—thirty-two years—there were no less than eleven years—it may seem not much to say, but wait for what is coming—there were no less than eleven of those thirty-two years in which our statute book was free throughout the whole year from repressive legislation of an exceptional kind against Ireland. But in the fifty-three years since we advanced far in the career of Liberal principles and actions —in those fifty-three years, from 1833 to 1885—there were but two years which were entirely free from the action of this special legislation for Ireland. Is not that of itself almost enough to prove that we have arrived at the point where it is necessary that we should take a careful and searching survey of our position? For, sir, I would almost venture, trusting to the indulgent interpretation of the House, to say that the coercion we have heretofore employed has been spurious and ineffectual coercion, and that if there is to be coercion—which God forbid—it ought to be adequate to attain its end. If it is to attain its end it must be different, differently maintained, and maintained with a different spirit, courage, and consistency compared with the coercion with which we have been heretofore familiar.

Well, sir, what are the results that have been produced? This result above all—and now I come to what I consider to be the basis of the whole mischief—that rightly or wrongly, yet in point of fact, law is discredited in Ireland, and discredited in Ireland upon this ground especially—that it comes to the people of that country with a foreign aspect, and in a foreign garb. These coercion bills of ours, of course; for it has become a matter of course—I am speaking of the facts and not of the merits—these coercion bills are stiffly resisted by the members who represent Ireland in Parliament. The English mind, by cases of this kind and by the tone of the press toward them, is estranged from the Irish people, and the Irish mind is estranged from the people of England and Scotland. I will not speak of other circumstances attending the present state of Ireland, but I do think that I am not assuming too much when I say that I have shown enough in this comparatively brief review—and I wish it could have been briefer still—to prove that if coercion is to be the basis for legislation we must no longer be seeking as we are always laudably seeking, to whittle it down almost to nothing at the very first moment we begin, but we must, like men, adopt it, hold by it, sternly enforce it till its end has been completely attained, with what results to peace, goodwill, and freedom I do not now stop to inquire. Our ineffectual and spurious coercion is morally worn out. I give credit to the late government for their conception of the fact. They must have realized it when they came to the conclusion in 1885 that they would not propose the renewal or continuance of repressive legislation. They were in a position in which it would have been comparatively easy for them to have proposed it, as a Conservative government following in the footsteps of a Liberal administration. But they determined not to propose it. I wish I could be assured that they and the party by whom they are supported were fully aware of the immense historic weight of that determination.

I have sometimes heard language used which appears to be-
token an idea on the part of those who use it that this is a
very simple matter—that, in one state of facts, they judged
one way in July,[1] and that, in another state of facts, they
judged another way in January;[2] and that consequently
the whole ought to be effaced from the minds and memories of men. Depend upon it the effect of that decision
of July never can be effaced—it will weigh, it will tell
upon the fortunes and circumstances both of England and
of Ireland. The return to the ordinary law, I am afraid,
cannot be said to have succeeded.

Almost immediately after the lapse of the Crimes Act
boycotting increased fourfold. Since that time it has been
about stationary; but in October it had increased fourfold
compared with what it was in the month of May. Well,
now, if it be true that resolute coercion ought to take the
place of irresolute coercion—if it be true that our system,
such as I have exhibited it, has been—we may hide it from
ourselves, we cannot hide it from the world—a failure in regard to repressive legislation, will that other coercion, which
it is possible to conceive, be more successful? I can indeed
conceive, and in history we may point to circumstances in
which coercion of that kind, stern, resolute, consistent,
might be, and has been, successful. But it requires, in
my judgment, two essential conditions, and these are—the
autocracy of government and the secrecy of public transactions. With those conditions that kind of coercion to
which I am referring might possibly succeed. But will it
succeed in the light of day, and can it be administered by

---

[1] When Lord Salisbury's administration which had just been formed decided
not to propose the renewal of the "Crimes" Act.
[2] Soon after the general election.

the people of England and Scotland against the people of
Ireland—by the two nations which, perhaps, above all
others upon earth—I need hardly except America—best
understand and are most fondly attached to the essential
principles of liberty?

Now I enter upon another proposition to which I hardly
expect broad exception can be taken. I will not assume—
I will not beg—the question, whether the people of England
and Scotland will ever administer that sort of effectual coercion which I have placed in contrast with our timid and
hesitating repressive measures; but this I will say, that
the people of England and Scotland will never resort to
that alternative until they have tried every other. Have
they tried every other? Well, some we have tried, to
which I will refer. I have been concerned with some of
them myself. But we have not yet tried every alternative,
because there is one—not unknown to human experience—
on the contrary, widely known to various countries in the
world, where this dark and difficult problem has been solved
by the comparatively natural and simple, though not always
easy, expedient of stripping law of its foreign garb and in-
vesting it with a domestic character. I am not saying that
this will succeed; I by no means beg the question at this
moment; but this I will say—that Ireland, as far as I
know, and speaking of the great majority of the people
of Ireland, believes it will succeed, and that experience
elsewhere supports that conclusion. The case of Ireland,
though she is represented here not less fully than England
or Scotland, is not the same as that of England or Scotland.
England, by her own strength and by her vast majority in
this House, makes her own laws just as independently as

if she were not combined with two other countries. Scotland—a small country, smaller than Ireland, but a country endowed with a spirit so masculine that never in the long course of history, excepting for two brief periods, each of a few years, was the superior strength of England such as to enable her to put down the national freedom beyond the border—Scotland, wisely recognized by England, has been allowed and encouraged in this House to make her own laws as freely and as effectually as if she had a representation six times as strong. The consequence is that the mainspring of law in England is felt by the people to be English, the mainspring of law in Scotland is felt by the people to be Scotch; but the mainspring of law in Ireland is not felt by the people to be Irish, and I am bound to say—truth extorts from me the avowal—that it cannot be felt to be Irish in the same sense as it is English and Scotch. The net results of this statement which I have laid before the House, because it was necessary as the groundwork of my argument, are these—In the first place, I admit it to be little less than a mockery to hold that the state of law and of facts conjointly which I have endeavored to describe conduces to the real unity of this great, noble, and world-wide empire. In the second place, something must be done, something is imperatively demanded from us, to restore to Ireland the first conditions of civil life—the free course of law, the liberty of every individual in the exercise of every legal right, the confidence of the people in the law and their sympathy with the law—apart from which no country can be called, in the full sense of the word, a civilized country, nor can there be given to that country the blessings which it is the object of civilized society to attain. Well, this is my introduction to the task I have to perform; and now I ask attention to the problem we have before us.

It is a problem not unknown in the history of the world; it is really this—there can be no secret about it as far as we are concerned—how to reconcile Imperial unity with diversity of legislation. Mr. Grattan not only held these purposes to be reconcilable, but he did not scruple to go the length of saying this—"I demand the continued severance of the Parliaments with a view to the continued and everlasting unity of the empire." Was that a flight of rhetoric, an audacious paradox? No, it was the statement of a problem which other countries have solved, and under circumstances much more difficult than ours. We ourselves may be said to have solved it, for I do not think that any one will question the fact that, out of the last six centuries, for five centuries at least Ireland has had a Parliament separate from ours. That is a fact undeniable. Did that separation of Parliament destroy the unity of the British Empire? Did it destroy it in the eighteenth century? Do not suppose that I mean that harmony always prevailed between Ireland and England. We know very well there were causes quite sufficient to account for a recurrence of discord. But I take the eighteenth century alone. Can I be told that there was no unity of empire in the eighteenth century? Why, sir, it was the century which saw our navy come to its supremacy. It was the century which witnessed the foundation of that great gigantic manufacturing industry which now overshadows the whole world. It was, in a pre-eminent sense, the century of empire, and it was in a sense but too conspicuous the century of wars. Those wars were carried on, that empire was maintained and enormously enlarged, that trade was established, that navy was brought to supremacy when England and Ireland had separate parliaments. Am I to be told that there was no unity of empire in that state of things? Well, sir, what has happened elsewhere? Have any other countries had to look this problem in the face? The last half century—the last sixty or seventy years since the great war—has been particularly rich in its experience of this subject and in the lessons which it has afforded to us. There are many cases to which I might refer to show how practicable it is, or how practicable it has been found by others whom we are not accustomed to look upon as our political superiors—how practicable it has been found by others to bring into existence what is termed local autonomy, and yet not to sacrifice but to confirm Imperial unity.

Let us look to those two countries, neither of them very large, but yet countries which every Englishman and every Scotchman must rejoice to claim as his kin—I mean the Scandinavian countries of Sweden and Norway. Immediately after the great war in 1814 the Norwegians were ready to take sword in hand to prevent their coming under the domination of Sweden. But the Powers of Europe undertook the settlement of that question, and they united those countries upon a footing of strict legislative independence and co-equality. Now, I am not quoting this as an exact precedent for us, but I am quoting it as a precedent, and as an argument *à fortiori*, because I say they confronted much greater difficulties, and they had to put a far greater strain upon the unity of their country, than we can ever be called upon to put upon the unity of ours. The legislatures of Sweden and of Norway are absolutely independent. The law even forbids what I hope never will happen between England and Ireland—that a Swede, if I am correct in my impression, should bear office of any kind in the Norwegian Ministry. There is no sort of supremacy or superiority in the legislature of Sweden over the legislature of Norway. The legislature of Norway has had serious controversies, not with Sweden, but with the King of Sweden, and it has fought out those controversies successfully upon the strictest constitutional and parliamentary grounds. And yet with two countries so united, what has been the effect? Not discord, not convulsions, not danger to peace, not hatred, not aversion, but a constantly growing sympathy; and every man who knows their condition knows that I speak the truth when I say that in every year that passes the Norwegians and the Swedes are more and more feeling themselves to be the children of a common country, united by a tie which never is to be broken.

I will take another case—the case of Austria and Hungary. In Austria and Hungary there is a complete duality of power. I will not enter upon the general condition of the Austrian Empire, or upon the other divisions and diversities which it includes, but I will take simply this case. At Vienna sits the Parliament of the Austrian monarchy; at Buda-Pesth sits the Parliament of the Hungarian crown; and that is the state of things which was established, I think, nearly twenty years ago. I ask all those who hear me whether there is one among them who doubts? Whether or not the condition of Austria be at this moment, or be not, perfectly solid, secure, and harmonious, after the enormous difficulties she has had to confront on account of the boundless diversity of race, whether or not that condition be perfectly normal in every minute

particular, this, at least, cannot be questioned, that it is a
condition of solidity and of safety compared with the time
when Hungary made war on her—war which she was unable
to quell, when she owed the cohesion of the body politic to
the interference of Russian arms; or in the interval that followed when there existed a perfect legislative union and a
supreme imperial council sat in Vienna.

Now, I have quoted these illustrations as illustrations
which show, not that what we are called upon to consider
can be done, but that infinitely more can be done—has been
done—under circumstances far less favorable. What was
the state of Sweden and Norway—two small countries, Norway undoubtedly inferior in population, but still unassail-
able in her mountain fastnesses—what was the case of Sweden and Norway for bringing about a union by physical
and material means? There were no means to be used
but moral means, and those moral means have been completely successful. What again, was the case of Austria,
where the seat of empire in the archduchy was associated
not with the majority, but with the minority of the population, and where she had to face Hungary with numbers far
greater than her own? Even there, while having to attempt what was infinitely more complex and more dangerous than even prejudice can suppose to be that which I am
about to suggest, it is not to be denied that a great relative
good and relative success have been attained. Our advantages are immense in a question of this kind. I do not
know how many gentlemen who hear me have read the
valuable work of Professor Dicey on the Law of the Constitution. No work that I have ever read brings out in a
more distinct and emphatic manner the peculiarity of the
British Constitution in one point, to which, perhaps, we

seldom have occasion to refer—namely, the absolute supremacy of Parliament. We have a Parliament to the
power of which there are no limits whatever, except such
as human nature, in a divinely ordained condition of things,
imposes. We are faced by no co-ordinate legislatures, and
are bound by no statutory conditions. There is nothing
that controls us, and nothing that compels us, except our
convictions of law, of right, and of justice. Surely that is
a favorable point of departure in considering a question
such as this.

I have referred to the eighteenth century. During that
century you had beside you a co-ordinate legislature. The
legislature of Ireland before the Union had the same title
as that of Great Britain. There was no juridical distinction
to be drawn between them. Even in point of antiquity
they were as nearly as possible on a par, for the Parliament
of Ireland had subsisted for 500 years. It had asserted its
exclusive right to make laws for the people of Ireland.
That right was never denied, for gentlemen ought to recollect, but all do not, perhaps, remember, that Poynings'
law[1] was an Irish law imposed by Ireland on herself. That
claim of the Parliament of Ireland never was denied until
the reign of George I.;[2] and that claim denied in the reign
of George I. was admitted in the reign of George III.[3] The
Parliament—the great Parliament of Great Britain—had to
retract its words and to withdraw its claim, and the legislature which goes by the name of Grattan's Parliament was
as independent in point of authority as any legislature over
the wide world. We are not called upon to constitute another co-ordinate legislature. While I think it is right to

---

[1] 1494.   [2] 1719.   [3] 1782.

modify the Union in some particulars, we are not about
to propose its repeal.

What is the essence of the Union? That is the question. It is impossible to determine what is and what is not
the repeal of the Union, until you settle what is the essence
of the Union. Well, I define the essence of the Union to
be this—that before the Act of Union there were two independent, separate, co-ordinate Parliaments; after the Act of
Union there was but one. A supreme statutory authority
of the Imperial Parliament over Great Britain, Scotland and
Ireland, as one United Kingdom was established by the Act
of Union. That supreme statutory authority it is not asked,
so far as I am aware, and certainly it is not intended, in the
slightest degree to impair. When I heard the honorable
member for Cork,[1] in a very striking speech at the commencement of the session, ask for what I think he termed
local autonomy or Irish autonomy, I felt that something
was gained in the conduct of this great question. If he
speaks, as I believe he speaks, the mind of the vast majority of the representatives of Ireland, I feel that we have
no right to question for a moment, in this free country,
under a representative system, that the vast majority of
the representatives speak the mind of a decided majority
of the people. I felt, sir, that something had been gained.
Ireland had come a great way to meet us, and it was more
than ever our duty to consider whether we could not go
some way to meet her. The term dismemberment of the
empire, as applied to anything that is now before us, is, in
my judgment—I will not argue it at any length now—simply a misnomer. To speak, in connection with any medi-

[1] Mr. Parnell.

tated or possible plan, of the dismemberment of the empire or the disintegration of the empire is, in the face of the history of the eighteenth century, not merely a misnomer, but an absurdity. Some phrases have been used which I will not refer to, simply because I do not think that they quite accurately describe the case, and because they might open a door to new debate. We hear of national independence, we hear of legislative independence, we hear of an independent Parliament, and we hear of federal arrangements. These are not descriptions which I adopt or which I find it necessary to discuss.

Then again, under a sense of the real necessities of the case, there are gentlemen who have their own philanthropic, well-intended plans for meeting this emergency. There are those who say, "let us abolish the Castle"; and I think that gentlemen of very high authority, who are strongly opposed to giving Ireland a domestic legislature, have said, nevertheless, that they think there ought to be a general reconstruction of the administrative government in Ireland. Well, sir, I have considered that question much, and what I want to know is this—how, without a change in the legislature, without giving to Ireland a domestic legislature, there is to be, or there even can possibly be, a reconstruction of the administration. We have sent to Ireland to administer the actual system the best men we could find. When Lord Spencer undertook that office, he represented, not in our belief, merely, but in our knowledge —for we had known him long—the flower of the British aristocracy, that portion of the British aristocracy which to high birth and great influence of station unites a love of liberty and of the people as genuine as that which breathes within any cottage in the land. And yet, sir, what is the result? The result is that, after a life of almost unexampled devotion to the public service in Ireland, Lord Spencer's administration not only does not command, which is easily understood, the adhesion and the commendation of the honorable member for Cork and his colleagues, but it is made the subject of cavil and of censure in this House of Parliament, and from the spot where I now stand, by members of the late Conservative government. I want to know—for we have not come to our conclusions without making careful examination of the conclusions of other people—I want to know how it is possible to construct an administrative system in Ireland without legislative change, and what gentlemen mean when they speak of the administrative system of Ireland. The fault of the administrative system of Ireland, if it has a fault, is simply this—that its spring and source of action, or, if I can use an anatomical illustration without a blunder, what is called the motor muscle is English and not Irish. Without providing a domestic legislature for Ireland, without having an Irish Parliament, I want to know how you will bring about this wonderful, superhuman, and, I believe, in this condition, impossible result, that your administrative system shall be Irish and not English.

There have been several plans liberally advised for granting to Ireland the management of her education, the management of her public works, and the management of one subject and another—boons very important in themselves—under a central elective body; boons any of which I do not hesitate to say I should have been glad to see them accepted, or I should have been glad to see a trial given to a system which might have been constructed under them, had it been the desire and the demand of Ireland. I do not think such a scheme would have possessed the advantage of finality. If it had been accepted, and especially if it had been freely suggested from that quarter—by the Irish representatives—it might have furnished a useful *modus vivendi*. But it is absurd, in my opinion, to talk of the adoption of such a scheme in the face of two obstacles—first of all, that those whom it is intended to benefit do not want it, do not ask it, and refuse it; and, secondly, the obstacle, not less important, that all those who are fearful of giving a domestic legislature to Ireland would naturally and emphatically, and rather justly, say: "We will not create your central board and palter with this question, because we feel certain that it will afford nothing in this world except a stage from which to agitate for a further concession, and because we see that by the proposal you make you will not even attain the advantage of settling the question that is raised."

Well, sir, what we seek is the settlement of that question; and we think that we find that settlement in the establishment, by the authority of Parliament, of a legislative body sitting in Dublin for the conduct of both legislation and administration under the conditions which may be prescribed by the act defining Irish, as distinct from imperial, affairs. There is the head and front of our offending. Let us proceed to examine the matter a little further. The essential conditions of any plan that Parliament can be asked or could be expected to entertain are, in my opinion, these —The unity of the empire must not be placed in jeopardy; the safety and welfare of the whole—if there is an unfortunate conflict, which I do not believe—the welfare and security of the whole must be preferred to the security and

advantage of the part. The political equality of the three
countries must be maintained. They stand by statute on a
footing of absolute equality, and that footing ought not to
be altered or brought into question. There should be what
I will at present term an equitable distribution of imperial
burdens.

Next I introduce a provision which may seem to be
exceptional, but which, in the peculiar circumstances of
Ireland, whose history unhappily has been one long chain
of internal controversies as well as of external difficulties,
is necessary in order that there may be reasonable safeguards for the minority. I am asked why there should
be safeguards for the minority. Will not the minority in
Ireland, as in other countries, be able to take care of itself? Are not free institutions, with absolute publicity,
the best security that can be given to any minority? I
know, sir, that in the long run our experience shows they
are. After we have passed through the present critical
period, and obviated and disarmed, if we can, the jealousies with which any change is attended, I believe, as
most gentlemen in this House may probably believe, that
there is nothing comparable to the healthy action of free
discussion, and that a minority asserting in the face of day
its natural rights is the best security and guarantee for its
retaining them. We have not reached that state of things.
I may say, not entering into detail, there are three classes
to whom we must look in this case. We must consider—
I will not say more on that subject to-day—the class immediately connected with the land. A second question, not,
I think, offering any great difficulty, relates to the civil
service and the offices of the executive government in

Ireland. The third question relates to what is commonly called the Protestant minority, and especially that important part of the community which inhabits the province of Ulster, or which predominates in a considerable portion of the province of Ulster.

I will deviate from my path for a moment to say a word upon the state of opinion in that wealthy, intelligent, and energetic portion of the Irish community, which, as I have said, predominates in a certain portion of Ulster. Our duty is to adhere to sound general principles, and to give the utmost consideration we can to the opinions of that energetic minority. The first thing of all, I should say, is that if, upon any occasion, by any individual or section, violent measures have been threatened in certain emergencies, I think the best compliment I can pay to those who have threatened us is to take no notice whatever of the threats, but to treat them as momentary ebullitions, which will pass away with the fears from which they spring, and at the same time to adopt on our part every reasonable measure for disarming those fears. I cannot conceal the conviction that the voice of Ireland, as a whole, is at this moment clearly and constitutionally spoken. I cannot say it is otherwise when five-sixths of its lawfully-chosen representatives are of one mind in this matter. There is a counter voice; and I wish to know what is the claim of those by whom that counter voice is spoken, and how much is the scope and allowance we can give them. Certainly, sir, I cannot allow it to be said that a Protestant minority in Ulster, or elsewhere, is to rule the question at large for Ireland. I am aware of no constitutional doctrine tolerable on which such a conclusion could be adopted or justified. But I think that the Protestant minority should have its wishes considered to the utmost practicable extent in any form which they may assume.

Various schemes, short of refusing the demand of Ireland at large, have been proposed on behalf of Ulster. One scheme is that Ulster itself, or, perhaps with more appearance of reason, a portion of Ulster, should be excluded from the operation of the bill we are about to introduce. Another scheme is that a separate autonomy should be provided for Ulster, or for a portion of Ulster. Another scheme is that certain rights with regard to certain subjects —such, for example, as education and some other subjects —should be reserved and should be placed to a certain extent under the control of provincial councils. These, I think, are the suggestions which have reached me in different shapes; there may be others. But what I wish to say of them is this—there is no one of them which has appeared to us to be so completely justified, either upon its merits or by the weight of opinion supporting and recommending it, as to warrant our including it in the bill and proposing it to Parliament upon our responsibility. What we think is that such suggestions deserve careful and unprejudiced consideration. It may be that that free discussion, which I have no doubt will largely take place after a bill such as we propose shall have been laid on the table of the House, may give to one of these proposals, or to some other proposals, a practicable form, and that some such plan may be found to be recommended by a general or predominating approval. If it should be so, it will, at our hands, have the most favorable consideration, with every disposition to do what equity may appear to recommend. That is what I have to say on the subject of Ulster.

I have spoken now of the essential conditions of a good plan for Ireland, and I add only this—that in order to be a good plan it must be a plan promising to be a real settlement of Ireland. To show that without a good plan you can have no real settlement, I may point to the fact that the great settlement of 1782 was not a real settlement. Most unhappily, sir, it was not a real settlement; and why was it not a real settlement? Was it Ireland that prevented it from being a real settlement? No, sir, it was the mistaken policy of England, listening to the pernicious voice and claims of ascendency. It is impossible, however, not to say this word for the Protestant Parliament of Ireland. Founded as it was upon narrow suffrage, exclusive in religion, crowded with pensioners and place-holders holding every advantage, it yet had in it the spark, at least, and the spirit of true patriotism. It emancipated the Roman Catholics of Ireland when the Roman Catholics of England were not yet emancipated. It received Lord Fitzwilliam with open arms; and when Lord Fitzwilliam promoted to the best of his ability the introduction of Roman Catholics into Parliament, and when his brief career was unhappily intercepted by a peremptory recall from England, what happened? Why, sir, in both Houses of the Irish Parliament votes were at once passed by those Protestants, by those men, mixed as they were with so large an infusion of pensioners and of placemen, registering their confidence in that nobleman and desiring that he should still be left to administer the government of Ireland. What the Irish Parliament did when Lord Fitzwilliam was promoting the admission of Roman Catholics into Parliament justifies me in saying there was a spirit there which, if free scope had been left to it, would in all probability have been enabled to work out a happy solution for every Irish problem and difficulty, and would have saved to the coming generation an infinity of controversy and trouble.

I pass on to ask how are we to set about the giving effect to the proposition I have made, to the purpose I have defined, of establishing in Ireland a domestic legislature to deal with Irish as contradistinguished from Imperial affairs? And here, sir, I am confronted at the outset by what we have felt to be a formidable dilemma. I will endeavor to state and to explain it to the House as well as I can. Ireland is to have a domestic legislature for Irish affairs. That is my postulate from which I set out. Are Irish members in this House, are Irish representative peers in the other House, still to continue to form part of the respective assemblies? That is the first question which meets us in consideration of the ground I have opened. Now I think it will be perfectly clear that if Ireland is to have a domestic legislature, Irish peers and Irish representatives cannot come here to control English and Scotch affairs. That I understand to be admitted freely. I never heard of their urging the contrary, and I am inclined to believe that it would be universally admitted. The one thing follows from the other. There cannot be a domestic legislature in Ireland dealing with Irish affairs, and Irish peers and Irish representatives sitting in Parliament at Westminster to take part in English and Scotch affairs. My next question is, Is it practicable for Irish representatives to come here for the settlement, not of English and Scotch, but of Imperial affairs? In principle it would be very difficult, I think, to object to that proposition. But then its acceptance depends entirely upon our arriving at the conclusion

6422 THE GOVERNMENT OF IRELAND BILL

that in this House we can draw for practical purposes a distinction between affairs which are Imperial and affairs which are not Imperial. It would not be difficult to say in principle that as the Irish legislature will have nothing to do with Imperial concerns let Irish members come here and vote on Imperial concerns. All depends on the practicability of the distinction. Well, sir, I have thought much, reasoned much, and inquired much, with regard to that distinction. I had hoped it might be possible to draw a distinction, and I have arrived at the conclusion that it cannot be drawn. I believe it passes the wit of man; at any rate it passes not my wit alone but the wit of many with whom I have communicated. It would be easy to exhibit a case; but the difficulty, I may say, in my opinion, arises from this. If this were a merely legislative House, or if the House of Lords were merely a legislative House— this House, of course, affords the best illustration—I do not think it would be difficult to draw a distinction. We are going to draw the distinction—we have drawn the distinction—in the Bill which I ask leave to lay on the table for legislative purposes with reference to what I hope will be the domestic legislature of Ireland. But this House is not merely a legislative House; it is a House controlling the Executive; and when you come to the control of the Executive, then your distinction between Imperial subjects and non-Imperial subjects totally breaks down—they are totally insufficient to cover the whole case.

For example, suppose it to be a question of foreign policy. Suppose the Irish members in this House coming here to vote on a question of foreign policy. Is it possible to deny that they would be entitled to take part in discussing an address to the crown for the dismissal of the foreign minister? It is totally impossible to deny—it is totally impossible to separate—the right of impugning the policy of and the right of action against the minister. Well, sir, if on that account members might take part in an address dismissing the foreign minister, I want to know, considering the collective responsibility of government—a principle, I hope, which will always be maintained at the very highest level that circumstances will permit, for I am satisfied that the public honor and the public welfare are closely associated with it—if that be so, what will be the effect of the dismissal of the foreign minister on the existence and action of the government to which he belongs? Why, sir, the government in nineteen cases out of twenty will break down with the foreign minister; and when these gentlemen, coming here for the purpose of discussing Imperial questions alone, could dislodge the government which is charged with the entire interests of England and Scotland, I ask you what becomes of the distinction between Imperial and non-Imperial affairs? I believe the distinction to be impossible, and therefore I arrive at the next conclusion— that Irish members and Irish peers cannot, if a domestic legislature be given to Ireland, justly retain a seat in the Parliament at Westminster.

If Irish members do not sit in this House and Irish peers do not sit in the other House, how is Ireland to be taxed? I shall assume, as a matter of course, that we should propose that a general power of taxation should pass to the domestic legislature of Ireland. But there is one very important branch of taxation, involving, indeed, a second branch, which is susceptible of being viewed in a very different aspect from the taxes of Ireland generally.

I mean the duties of customs and duties of excise relatively to customs. One thing I take to be absolutely certain. Great Britain will never force upon Ireland taxation without representation. Well, sir, if we are never to force upon Ireland taxation without representation, then comes another question of the deepest practical interest—are we to give up the fiscal unity of the empire? I sometimes see it argued that, in giving up the fiscal unity of the empire, we should give up the unity of the empire. To that argument I do not subscribe. The unity of the empire rests upon the supremacy of Parliament and on considerations much higher than considerations merely fiscal. But I must admit that, while I cannot stand on the high ground of principle, yet on the very substantial ground of practice to give up the fiscal unity of the empire would be a very great public inconvenience and a very great public misfortune—a very great public misfortune for Great Britain; and I believe it would be a still greater misfortune for Ireland were the fiscal unity of the empire to be put to hazard and practically abandoned. I may say also, looking as I do with hope to the success of the measure I now propose, I, at any rate, feel the highest obligation not to do anything, not to propose anything, without necessity, that would greatly endanger the right comprehension of this subject by the people of England and Scotland, which might be the case were the fiscal unity of the empire to be broken.

There is the dilemma. I conceive that there is but one escape from it, and that is, if there were conditions upon which Ireland consented to such arrangements as would leave the authority of levying customs duties, and such excise duties as are immediately connected with customs, in the hands of Parliament here, and would by her will consent to set our hands free to take the course that the general exigencies of the case appear to require. These conditions I take to be three—In the first place, that a general power of taxation over and above these particular duties should pass unequivocally into the hands of the domestic legislature of Ireland. In the second place, that the entire proceeds of the customs and excise should be held for the benefit of Ireland, for the discharge of the obligations of Ireland, and for the payment of the balance, after discharging those obligations, into an Irish exchequer, to remain at the free disposal of the Irish legislative body.

But there is another point which I think ought to engage, and may justly engage, the anxious attention in particular of the representatives of Ireland; and it is this:— The proposal which I have now sketched is that we should pass an act giving to Ireland what she considers an enormous boon, under the name of a Statutory Parliament for the control of Irish affairs, both legislative and administrative. But one of the provisions of that act is the withdrawal of Irish representative peers from the House of Lords, and Irish members from the House of Commons. Well, then, I think it will naturally occur to the Irish, as it would in parallel circumstances to the Scotch or the English—and more especially to the Scotch—mind, what would become of the privileges conveyed by the act after the Scotch members, who were their natural guardians, were withdrawn from Parliament? I was speaking of the Scotch members in order to bring it very distinctly to the minds of honorable members, supposing that Scotland had entertained—what she never had reason to entertain—the desire for a domestic legislature. I must confess I think that Ireland ought to have security on that subject—security that advantage would not be taken, so far as we can preclude the possibility of it, of the absence of Irish representatives from Parliament for the purpose of tampering with any portion of the boon which we propose to confer on Ireland by this act. I think we have found a method for dealing with that difficulty. I may be very sanguine, but I hope that the day may come when Ireland will have reason to look on this act, if adopted by Parliament, as for practical purposes her Magna Charta. A Magna Charta for Ireland ought to be most jealously and effectively assured, and it will be assured, against unhallowed and unlawful interference.

Two cases at once occur to the mind. There might be alterations of detail in a law of this kind on which everybody might be agreed. We think it would be very absurd to require either the construction or reconstruction of a cumbrous and difficult machinery for the purpose of disposing of cases of this kind, and therefore we propose that the provisions of this act might be modified with the concurrence of the Irish legislature, or in conformity with an address from the Irish legislature. That is intended for cases where there is a general agreement. I hope it will not happen, but I admit it might happen, that in some point or other the foresight and sagacity now brought to bear on this subject might prove insufficient. It is possible, though I trust it is not probable, that material alterations might be found requisite, that on these amendments there might be differences of opinion; and yet, however improbable the case may be, it is a case which it might be proper to provide for beforehand. What we then should propose is that the provisions of this act should not be altered, except either on an address from the Irish legislature to the crown such as I have described, or else, after replacing and recalling into action the full machinery under which Irish representatives now sit here, and Irish peers sit in the House of Lords, so that when their case again came to be tried they might have the very same means of defending their constitutional rights as they have now. Now, we believe that is one of those cases which are often best averted by making a good provision against them.

Now, upon the footing which I have endeavored to describe, we propose to relieve Irish peers and representatives from attendance at Westminster, and at the same time to preserve absolutely the fiscal unity of the empire. Let me say that there are several reasons that occur to me which might well incline the prudence of Irishmen to adopt an arrangement of this kind. If there were Irish representatives in this House at the same time that a domestic legislature sat in Ireland, I think that the presence of those Irish representatives would have some tendency to disparage the domestic legislature. I think there would be serious difficulties that would arise besides the insurmountable difficulty that I have pointed out as to the division of subjects. Even if it were possible to divide the subjects, what an anomaly it would be, what a mutilation of all our elementary ideas about the absolute equality of members in this House, were we to have ordinarily among us two classes of members, one of them qualified to vote on all kinds of business and another qualified only to vote here and there on particular kinds of business, and obliged to submit to some criterion or other—say the authority of the chair—novel for such a purpose and difficult to exercise—in order to determine what kinds of business they could vote upon, and what kinds of business they must abstain from voting on! There would, I think, be another difficulty in determining what the number of those members should be. My opinion is that there would be great jealousy of the habitual presence of 103 Irish members in this House, even for limited purposes, after a legislative body had been constructed in Ireland; and on the other hand I can very well conceive that Ireland would exceedingly object to the reduction—the material reduction—of those members. I am sorry to have to mention another difficulty, which is this—Ireland has not had the practice in local self-government that has been given to England and Scotland. We have unfortunately shut her out from that experience. In some respects we have been jealous, in others niggardly toward Ireland. It might be very difficult to Ireland in the present state of things to man a legislative chamber in Dublin, and at the same time to present in this House an array of so much distinguished ability as I think all parties will admit has been exhibited on the part of Ireland during recent Parliaments on the benches of this House.

But I pass on from this portion of the question, having referred to these two initiatory propositions as principal parts of the foundation of the bill—namely, first, that it is proposed that the Irish representation in Parliament at Westminster should cease unless in the contingent and I hope hardly possible case to which I have alluded, and next that the fiscal unity of the empire shall be absolutely maintained. My next duty is to state what the powers of the proposed legislative body will be.

The capital article of that legislative body will be that it should have the control of the executive government of Ireland as well as of legislative business. Evidently, I think, it was a flaw in the system of 1782 that adequate provision was not made for that purpose, and we should not like to leave a flaw of such a nature in the work we are now undertaking. In 1782 there were difficulties that we have not now before us. At that time it might have been very fairly said that no one could tell how a separate legislature would work unless it had under its control what is termed a responsible government. We have no such difficulty and no such excuse now. The problem of responsible government has been solved for us in our colonies. It works very well there; and in perhaps a dozen cases in different quarters of the globe it works to our perfect satisfaction. It may be interesting to the House if I recount the fact that that responsible government in the colonies was, I think, first established by one of our most distinguished statesmen, Earl Russell, when he held the office of Colonial Secretary in the government of Lord Melbourne. But it was a complete departure from established tradition, and if I remember right, not more than two or three years before that generous and wise experiment was tried Lord Russell had himself written a most able despatch to show that it could not be done; that with responsible government in the colonies you would have two centres of gravity and two sources of motion in the empire; while a united empire absolutely required that there should be but one, and that consequently the proposition could not be entertained. Such was the view of the question while it was yet at a distance, and such perhaps may have been our view on the subject I am now discussing while it was yet at a distance. But it has been brought near to us by the circumstances of the late election, and I believe that if we look closely at its particulars we should find that many of the fears with which we may have regarded it are perfectly unreal, and especially so that great panic, that great apprehension of all, the fear lest it should prove injurious to what it is our first duty to maintain—namely, the absolute unity and integrity of the empire.

There is another point in regard to the powers of the legislative body of which I wish to make specific mention. Two courses might have been followed. One would be to endow this legislative body with particular legislative powers. The other is to except from the sphere of its action those subjects which we think ought to be excepted, and to leave it everything else which is the consequence of the plans before us. There will be an enumeration of disabilities, and everything not included in that enumeration will be left open to the domestic legislature. As I have already said, the administrative power by a responsible government would pass under our proposals with the legislative power. Then, sir, the legislative body would be subject to the provisions of the act in the first place as to its own composition. But we propose to introduce into it what I would generally explain as two orders, though not two Houses; and we suggest that with regard to the popular order, which will be the more numerous, the provisions of the act may be altered at any period after the first dissolution; but with regard to the other and less numerous order, the provisions of the act can only be altered after the assent of the crown to an address from the legislative body for that purpose. We should provide generally—and on that I conceive there would be no difference of opinion—that this body should be subject to all the prerogatives of the crown, but only should insert a particular provision to the effect that its *maximum* duration, without dissolution, should not exceed five years.

I will now tell the House—and I would beg particular attention to this—what are the functions that we propose to withdraw from the cognizance of this legislative body. The three grand and principal functions are, first, everything that relates to the crown—succession, prerogatives, and the mode of administering powers during incapacity, regency, and, in fact, all that belongs to the crown. The next would be all that belongs to defence—the army, the navy, the entire organization of armed force. I do not say the police force, which I will touch upon by and by, but everything belonging to defence. And the third would be the entire subject of foreign and colonial relations. Those are the subjects most properly Imperial, and I will say belonging as a principle to the legislature established under the Act of Union and sitting at Westminster. There are some other subjects which I will briefly touch upon. In the first place, it would not be competent to the domestic legislature in Ireland to alter the provisions of the act which we are now about to pass, as I hope, and which I ask that we should pass with the consent of the three countries —it would not be competent to the Irish legislative body to alter those provisions, excepting in points where they are designedly left open as part of the original contract and settlement. We do not propose universal disability as to contracts, but there are certain contracts made in Ireland under circumstances so peculiar that we think we ought to except them from the action of the legislative body. There are also some analogous provisions made in respect to

charters anterior to the act which in our opinion ought
only to be alterable after the assent of the crown to an
address from the legislative body for that purpose. There
is another disability that we propose to lay upon the legislative body; and it is one of those with respect to which
I am bound to say in my belief there is no real apprehension that the thing would be done, but at the same time,
though there may not be a warranted apprehension, there
are many honest apprehensions which it is our duty to
consider as far as we can. We propose to provide that the
legislative body should not be competent to pass a law for
the establishment or the endowment of any particular religion. Those I may call exceptions of principle. Then
there are exceptions of what I may call practical necessity
for ordinary purposes. The first of these is the law of trade
and navigation. I assume that as to trade and navigation
at large, it would be a great calamity to Ireland to be
separated from Great Britain. The question of taxation in
relation to trade and navigation I have already mentioned.
The same observation applies to the subject of coinage and
legal tender, but we do not propose to use the term "currency," simply because there is an ambiguity about it.
Ireland might think fit to pass a law providing for the
extinction of private issues in Ireland, and that no bank-
notes should be issued in Ireland except under the authority and for the advantage of the state. I own it is my
opinion that Ireland would do an extremely sensible thing
if she passed such a law. It is my most strong and decided
opinion that we ought to have the same law ourselves, but
the block of business has prevented that and many other
good things toward the attainment of which I hope we are
now going to open and clear the way. I only use that as

an illustration to show that I should be very sorry if we were needlessly to limit the free action of the Irish legislature upon Irish matters. There are other subjects on which I will not dwell. One of them is the subject of weights and measures; another is the subject of copyright. These are not matters for discussion at the present moment.

There is, however, one other important subject with regard to which we propose to leave it entirely open to the judgment of Ireland—that subject is the Post-Office. Our opinion is that it would be for the convenience of both countries if the post-office were to remain under the control of the Postmaster-General; but the post-office requires an army of servants, and I think that Ireland might not wish to see all the regulations connected with that unarmed army left to an English authority. We have, therefore, placed the post-office in the bill under circumstances which would enable the legislative body in Ireland to claim for itself authority on this subject if it should see fit. There are some other matters, such as the quarantine laws, and one or two others which stand in the same category. Now, sir, that I believe I may give as a sufficient description of the exceptions from the legislative action of the proposed Irish legislature, bearing in mind the proposition that everything which is not excepted is conferred.

I have dealt with the powers of the legislative body.

I come next to the composition of the legislative body. We propose to provide for it as follows. I have referred to the protection of minorities. We might constitute a legislative body in Ireland by a very brief enactment if we were to say that the 103 members now representing Ireland and 103 more members, perhaps elected by the same constituencies, should constitute the one and only legislative House in Ireland without the introduction of what I may call the dual element. But, sir, we are of opinion that if a proposition of that kind were made, in the first place, it would be stated that it did not afford legitimate protection for minorities. And, in the second place, it might be thought by many of those who would be less sensitive on the subject of minorities that some greater provision was required for stability and consistency in the conduct of the complex work of legislation than could possibly be supplied by a single set of men elected under an absolutely single influence. Upon that account, sir, we propose to introduce into this legislative body what we have termed two orders. These orders would sit and deliberate together. There would be a power on the demand of either order for separate voting. The effect of that separate voting would be that while the veto was in force, while it sufficed to bar the enactment of a bill, there would be an absolute veto of one order upon the other. Such veto, in our view, might be salutary and useful for the purpose of insuring deliberation and consistency with adequate consideration in the business of making laws. But it ought not to be perpetual. If it were perpetual, a block would arise, as it might arise conceivably, and as really, we may almost say, we have seen it arise in certain cases in the colonies, particularly in one [1] where there were two perfectly independent orders. What we, therefore, propose is that this veto can only be operative for a limited time, say until a dissolution, or for a period of three years, whichever might be the longer of the two.

---

[1] In 1832 the House of Assembly in Lower Canada stopped the supplies.

So much, sir, for the relation of these two orders, the one to the other. I may observe that that distinction of orders would be available and is almost necessary with a view to maintaining the only form of control over the judicial body known to us in this country—viz., the concurrence of two authorities chosen under somewhat different influences in one common conclusion with regard to the propriety of removing a judge from his office.

Now, sir, I will just describe very briefly the composition of these orders. It may not have occurred to many gentlemen that, if we succeed in the path we are now opening, with respect to the twenty-eight distinguished individuals who now occupy the place of representative peers of Ireland, it will not be possible, we think, for them to continue to hold their places in the House of Lords after the Irish representatives have been removed from attending the House of Commons. I do not say that the precedent is an exact one, but the House may remember that in the case of the disestablishment of the Irish Church we did disable the bishops who were entitled to sit for life from continuing—I mean disable them personally from continuing—to sit in the House of Lords after the disestablishment of the Irish Church. We do not wish, sir, to entail this personal disability. We propose that these twenty-eight peers shall have the option of sitting, if they think fit, as a portion of the first order in the Irish legislative assembly. And that they shall have the power—that they shall personally have the power—of sitting there, as they sit in the House of Lords, for life. There may, sir, be those who think this option will not be largely used. I am not one of that number. I believe that the Irish peers have an

Irish as well as an imperial patriotism. In the eighteenth
century Irish peers were not ashamed of the part they
played in the Irish Parliament. It was, I think, the Duke
of Leinster who moved the address in the Irish House of
Peers, which he carried, expressing the confidence of that
House in Lord Fitzwilliam. I may be too sanguine, but
I say boldly that if this measure pass under happy circumstances, especially if it pass without political exasperation,
one of its effects will be a great revival of the local as well
as a great confirmation and extension of imperial patriotism.
At any rate it is our duty, I think, to provide that the Irish
peers, the twenty-eight representative Irish peers, may form
part of the Irish legislative body. There will be no disability entailed upon any Irish peer from being at once a
member of the Irish legislative body and likewise of the
House of Lords. In the last century many distinguished
men sat in both, and in the circumstances we certainly see
no cause for putting an end to the double qualification
which was thus enjoyed, and which, I think, worked bene-
ficially. There is a difficulty, however, to which I will
just advert for one moment in combining the connection
or place of these twenty-eight peers who are to sit for life
with the rest of the first order of the chamber. We propose
as to the remainder of the first order that it shall consist
of seventy-five members, to be elected by the Irish people
under conditions which we propose to specify in the
schedule to the act, not yet filled up as to its details.
But I mention at once the two provisions which would
apply to the election of seventy-five members. First of all,
the constituency would be a constituency composed of persons occupying to the value of £25 and upward, and secondly, they would be elected for a period, as a general rule,

of ten years, with a little exception I need not now refer to. Thirdly, they will be elected subject to a property qualification of realty to the extent of £200 a year, or of personalty to the extent of £200 a year, or a capital value of £4,000. The peers would ultimately be replaced by twenty-eight members, elected under the above conditions. We cannot insure that all these twenty-eight peers shall die at the same time: it would, consequently, be extremely difficult to devise an electoral machinery for the purpose of supplying their places by election. We therefore propose to grant to the crown power, limited to a term which we think may fairly well exhaust the present generation, of filling their places by nomination, not for life, but down to the date to be fixed by the act. After the system had ceased to operate, and the representative peers had ceased to be in that first order, the first order of the legislative body would be elected entirely upon the basis I have described.

With regard to the second order, its composition would be simple. Of course, it would be proposed to the 103 gentlemen who now represent Ireland in this House from county districts, from citizen towns, and from the University of Dublin, that they should take their places in the Irish Legislative Chamber in Dublin. We should likewise propose as nearly as possible to duplicate that body. Another 101 members, not 103, we propose should be elected by the county districts and the citizen towns in exactly the same manner as that in which the present 101 members for counties and towns have been elected. We shall also propose that in the event of any refusal to sit, refusals to accept 11 the option given, the place shall be filled up by election under the machinery now existing. I ought to say a word about Dublin University. We do not propose to interfere by any action of ours with the existing arrangements of Dublin University in one way or another. But certainly we could not ask the House to adopt a plan at our suggestion which would double the representation of Dublin University. We propose to leave it as it is, but at the same time to empower the legislative body, if it should think fit, to appoint a corresponding representation by two members in favor of the Royal University of Ireland. There would be no compulsion to exercise that power, but it would be left to the discretion of the legislative body. The effect of that would be to give to the first order of the proposed Legislative Chamber, or body, a number making 103; to give to the second order the number of 206 at the outside, or 204 if the power with regard to the Royal University were not exercised, and to leave the relations of the two orders upon the footing which I have described.

I must now say a few words upon the subject of the Executive, and what we think most requisite with regard to the executive is that our act should be as elastic as possible. It is quite evident that though the legislative transition can be made, and ought to be made, *per saltum*, by a single stroke, the executive transition must necessarily be gradual. We propose, therefore, sir, to leave everything as it is until it is altered in the regular course; so that there shall be no breach of continuity in the government of the country, but that by degrees, as may be arranged by persons whom we feel convinced will meet together in a spirit of coöperation, and will find no great, much less insurmountable, difficulty in their way, the old state of things shall be adjusted to the new. On the one hand, the representatives of the old system will remain on the ground; on the other hand, the principle of responsible government is freely and fully conceded. That principle of responsible government will work itself out in every necessary detail. It has often, sir, been proposed to abolish the viceroyalty, and some gentlemen have even been sanguine enough to believe that to abolish the viceroyalty was to solve the whole Irish problem. I must say that I think that that involves a faculty of belief far beyond any power either of the understanding or imagination to which I have ever been able to aspire. We propose to leave the viceroyalty without interference by the act, except in the particulars which I am about to name. The office of the viceroyalty will only be altered by statute. He would not be the representative of a party. He would not quit office with the outgoing government. He would have round him, as he has now, in a certain form, a privy council, to aid and to advise him. Within that privy council the executive body would form itself under the action of the principle of responsible government for the purpose of administering the various offices of the State. The Queen would be empowered to delegate to him in case his office should be permanently continued—which I am far from believing to be unlikely—any of the prerogatives which she now enjoys, or which she would exercise under this act: and, finally, we have not forgotten that his office almost alone is still affected by one solitary outstanding religious disability—a kind of Lot's wife when everything else has been destroyed—and that religious disability we propose by our bill to remove.

The next point is with regard to the judges of the superior courts, and here I draw a partial distinction between the present and the future judges. As regards the judges of the superior courts, now holding office, we desire to secure to them their position and their emoluments in the same absolute form as that in which they now exist. Although they would become chargeable upon the Consolidated Fund of Ireland, which we propose to constitute by the act, still they would retain their lien—so to call it—on the Consolidated Fund of Great Britain. Under the peculiar circumstances of Ireland, we cannot forget that some of these judges, by no fault of their own, have been placed in relations more or less uneasy with popular influences, and with what under the new Constitution will in all probability be the dominating influence in that country. We cannot overlook the peculiarities of Irish history in framing the provisions of this bill, and we therefore propose, both with regard to the judges now holding office and with regard to other persons who in what they deemed loyal service to the empire have been concerned in the administration and conduct of the criminal law in Ireland, that her Majesty may, not lightly or wholesale, but if she should see cause on any particular occasion, by order in council, antedate the pensions of these particular persons. With regard to the future judges we hold the matter to be more simple. We propose to provide that they should hold office during good behavior, that their salaries—these are the superior judges alone—should be charged on the Irish Consolidated Fund, that they shall be removable only on a joint address from the two orders of the legislative body, and that they should be appointed under the influence, as a general rule, of the responsible Irish government. There is an exception which we propose to make in regard to the Court of Exchequer, which is a Court of Revenue Pleas. I will not enter into any details now, but the enormous financial relations which will subsist between Great Britain and Ireland if our measure be carried made us feel, for reasons which I shall perhaps on another occasion more fully explain, that it is necessary for us to keep a certain amount of hold on the Court of Exchequer, or, at least, on two of its members; but the general rule of our measure will be that the action of the judges will pass under the new Irish executive, and will rest with them, just as it rested in former times with the old Irish executive.

I must now say a few words on the important subject of the Irish Constabulary. The substance of those words really amounts to this—that I think there remains much for consideration in order to devise the details of a good and prudent system; but we think it our first duty to give a distinct assurance to the present members of that distinguished and admirable force that their condition will not be put to prejudice by this act, either in respect of their terms of office, their terms of service, or with regard to the authority under which they are employed. The case of the Dublin police is not quite the same, but we propose the same conditions with regard to the Dublin police, as far, at least, as the terms of service are concerned. With regard to the local police I will say nothing, because I do not want at present to anticipate what may be matter hereafter for free consideration or discussion, or for the action of the Irish legislative body. There will be no breach of continuity in the administration with regard to the police.

One thing I cannot omit to say. The constabulary, as I have said, is an admirable force, and I do not intend to qualify in the smallest degree what I have already said, but the constabulary on its present footing exhibits one of the most remarkable instances of waste of treasure and of enormous expense, not with good results, but with unhappy results, with which and under which the civil government and the general government of Ireland have hitherto been carried on. The total charge of the constabulary amounts to a million and a half, including the Dublin police. Now, Ireland is a cheaper country than England, and if the service were founded on the same principle and organized in the same manner, it ought, per thousand of the population, to be cheaper in Ireland than in England, assuming Ireland to be in a normal condition; and our object is to bring it into a normal condition.

Now the House will perhaps be surprised when I tell them this. The present constabulary of Ireland costs £1,500,000 a year, every penny of it now paid out of the British Exchequer. If the police of Ireland were organized upon the same principles and on the same terms as the police in England, instead of costing £1,500,000, it would cost £600,000 a year. That will convey to the House an idea, first, of the enormous charge at which we have been governing Ireland under our present system, and, secondly, of the vast field for judicious reductions which the system I am now proposing ought to offer to the Irish people. I anticipate a vast reduction, both in the force and in the expenditure. The charge is now a million and a half. We propose that the Consolidated Fund of Great Britain—this subject I shall revert to in the financial statement which I shall have to put before the House—shall for a time relieve the Irish legislative body of all expenditure in excess of a million. I am bound to say that I do not look upon a million as the proper charge to be imposed on Ireland. I am perfectly convinced, however, that the charge will be reduced to a much smaller sum, of which Ireland, of course, will reap the benefit. After two years the legislative body may fix the charge for the whole police and for the constabulary of Ireland, with a saving of existing rights. One thing I must say. We have no desire to exempt the police of Ireland in its final form from the ultimate control of the legislative body. We have no jealousies on the subject; and I own I have a strong personal opinion that when once the recollection of the old antipathies has been effectually abated, the care of providing for the ordinary security of life and property of the citizens will be regarded as the very first duty of any good local government in Ireland. I think it will be understood from what I have stated that the constabulary would remain under the present terms of service and under the present authority, although I do not say that this is to be so forever. Assuming control over the constabulary, that control will be prospective, and will not import any injury to existing rights.

With respect to the civil service, of course the future civil service of the country generally will be absolutely under the legislative body. With respect to the present civil service, we have not thought that their case was exactly analogous either to the constabulary or the judicial offices, and yet it is a great transition, and moreover it will without doubt be the desire of the legislative body of Ireland forthwith, or very early, to effect a great economy in its establishment. We have, therefore, considered to some extent in what way we can at once provide what is just for the civil servants of Ireland, and at the same time set free the hands of the legislative body to proceed with the salutary work of economy and retrenchment. Our opinion is that, upon the whole, it will be wise in the joint interests of both to authorize the civil servants now serving to claim the gratuity or pension which would be due to them upon the abolition of their offices, provided they shall serve not less than two years to prevent an inconvenient lapse in the practical business of the country, and at the close of those two years both parties would be free to negotiate afresh, the civil servants not being bound to remain and the legislative body not being in any way bound to continue to employ them. That is all I have to say upon the subject of the new Irish Constitution.

I am afraid I have still many subjects on which I have some details to show, and I fear I have already detained the House too long. I have now, sir, to give a practical exposition of the phrase which I have used that we looked upon it as an essential condition of our plan that there should be an equitable distribution of imperial charges. The meaning of that is, what proportion shall Ireland pay? I must remind gentlemen before I enter upon the next explanation that the proportion to be paid is not the only thing to be considered; you have to consider the basis upon which that proportionate payment is to be applied. Looking upon the proportionate payment, we now stand thus. At the time of the Union, it was intended that Ireland should pay two-seventeenths, or in the relation of 1 to 7½, out of the total charge of the United Kingdom. The actual true payment now made by the Irish taxpayer is not 1 to 7½, but something under 1 to 12, or about 1 to 11½—that is the total expenditure. The proposal I make is that the proportion chargeable to Ireland shall be 1 to 14, or one-fifteenth, but that will not be understood until I come to join it with other particulars. I will look, however, sir, a little to the question, what are the best tests of capacity to pay ? Many of these tests have been suggested—one of them is the income tax, which I conceive to be a very imperfect indication. The income tax, I believe, would give a proportion, not of 1 to 14, but of 1 to 19. This is to be borne in mind if you have regard to the income tax, that while, on the one hand, it is paid in Ireland upon a lower valuation than in England or in Scotland—because, as we all know, in England Schedule A is levied on the full rent—it is also unquestionable that many Irishmen also hold securities upon which dividends are received in London and pay income tax, I hope, before the dividends come into the hands of the persons entitled to them. Therefore it is almost a certainty that a considerable sum ought to be added to the Irish income tax, which would raise it from the proportion of 1 to 19 to perhaps 1 to 17. But there are two other tests which I consider far superior to the income tax. One is the test afforded us by the death duties, not by the amount levied, because the amounts levied vary capriciously according to the consanguinity scale, but by the property passing under the death duties. The amount of property on which, on an average of three years, the death duties fell was for Great Britain £170,000,000, and for Ireland £12,908,000, or 1 to 13. I have taken three years, because they represent the period since we entered upon a somewhat new administration of the death duties, and that is by far the best basis of comparison. When we come to the valuation, inasmuch as

Ireland is valued much lower in proportion to the real value than England and Scotland, the valuation in the latest year for which we have returns is in Great Britain £166,000,000, and for Ireland £13,833,000, giving a proportion of 1 to 12, or one-thirteenth.

Under these circumstances, what ought we to do? In my opinion, we ought to make for Ireland an equitable arrangement, and I think that when I propose to assume the proportion of one-fifteenth, it will be seen that that is an equitable or even generous arrangement, after I have mentioned three considerations. The first of these considerations is that if we start an Irish legislative body, we must start it with some balance to its credit. But if we are to start it with a balance to its credit, I know of no way except the solitary £20,000 a year which still remains to be worked out of the Church surplus after all the demands made upon it. I know of no way of honestly manufacturing that balance except by carving it out of the budget for the coming year, and providing for the sum at the expense, as it will then be, not of the Irish exchequer exclusively, but at the expense of the English and Scotch taxpayers. That is one consideration; the second consideration is this. I take this one to fourteen or one-fifteenth for the purpose of ascertaining what share Ireland is to pay to the imperial expenditure. But when I said that Ireland now pays 1 to 11½ or 1 to 12½ of the imperial expenditure, I meant the amount of the whole gross imperial expenditure; and when I say that we shall ask her to pay one-fifteenth of the imperial expenditure in the future, that is an imperial expenditure very materially cut down. For, upon consideration, it has been thought right in computing the military expenditure to exclude from it altogether what

ought strictly to be called war charges. We do not propose
to assume, in fixing the future imperial contribution of Ireland, to base that calculation on the supposition of her sharing in charges analogous, for example, to the vote of credit
for eleven millions last year. Therefore this proportion of
one-fifteenth is to be applied to a scale of imperial expenditure materially reduced.

But, sir, there is another consideration which I think it
right to mention. It is this—that this imperial contribution would be paid by Ireland out of a fund composed, in
the first instance, of the entire receipts paid into the Irish
exchequer; but that, sir, is not a true test of the amount of
taxation paid by Ireland. There are goods which pay duty
in England, and which are exported, duty paid, to Ireland,
which are consumed in Ireland, and upon which, therefore,
the duty is really paid by Irishmen, while the receipts go
into the imperial exchequer. But there is not only a corresponding movement the other way, but there is a movement
very much larger and more important. More than one million of duty, I think £1,030,000, is paid upon spirits in Ireland that are exported to Great Britain. Every shilling of
that duty is really paid by the Englishman and the Scotchman; but at the same time the whole receipts go into the
Irish exchequer. The same thing holds with respect to
the porter brewed in Ireland. The same thing holds with
regard to the very considerable manufacture of tobacco
carried on in Ireland. We have made it the object of
our best efforts to ascertain how much money Ireland loses
to England by the process which I have described—and
which I have no doubt is accurately understood by all
members of the House—how much money Ireland loses to

Great Britain by the flow of duty-paid commodities from Great Britain to Ireland; and how much Great Britain loses to Ireland from the flow of such commodities from Ireland to Great Britain. The result of this investigation is—I state it with confidence, not actually as if it were to be demonstrated in every point by parliamentary returns, but I state it as a matter of certainty with regard to a far greater portion of the sum, and as a matter certainly subject to very little doubt—that the Irish receipt gains from Great Britain by the process I have described more than Great Britain gains from Ireland, and more to no less an amount than £1,400,000, paid by the British taxpayer, and forming part of the Irish receipt. If you maintain the fiscal unity of the empire, if you do not erect—which I trust you will not erect —custom-houses between Great Britain and Ireland, if you let things take their natural course, according to the ordinary and natural movement of trade, £1,400,000 will be paid to the benefit of Ireland as a charge upon the English and Scotch taxpayer, and will form a portion of the fund out of which Ireland will defray the imperial contribution which we propose to levy upon her.

If this amount of imperial contribution to be paid by Ireland, which I have described as one-fourteenth, comes to be reduced by subtracting this sum of £1,400,000, the portion which Ireland will have to pay will be, not one-fourteenth, but a fraction under one-twenty-sixth. That is a very great change. It is a benefit she gets not only in the state of the law, but owing to the course of trade. We cannot take it away without breaking up the present absolute freedom between the two countries. I hope this will be borne in mind by those who think this charge of one-fifteenth is a heavy charge to be thrown upon Ireland;

and by those who think, as I certainly do, that in a case of this kind, after all that has occurred when two countries are very strong and very rich, compared with a third of far more restricted means, the pecuniary arrangements ought to be equitable and even bountiful in some moderate degree. It will be interesting to the House to know what payment *per capita* the plan I have described will allot to the Irishman and to the Briton respectively. I use the word "Briton" because I know that it will gratify my friends from Scotland. The incidents of this plan *per capita* I will state as follows. In the first place, if I were to take the present contribution of Ireland to the entire expenditure of the country according to the receipts of the two exchequers, the inhabitant of Great Britain pays £2 10s. *per capita*, and the inhabitant in Ireland £1 13s. 7d. That is obviously and inequitably high for Ireland. But if I take the real payment of the Irish taxpayer, and compare that with the real payment of the English taxpayer, it will follow that the English payment is £2 10s. 11d. as against £1 7s. 10d. of Ireland, which is certainly a more equitable proportion.

Now I pass to the basis of one-fourteenth or one-fifteenth. This is not founded upon the total expenditure of the country, but upon what we are about to reckon as imperial expenditure and the respective contribution to the imperial exchequer. The respective contribution *per capita* will be for Great Britain £1 10s. 11d., and for Ireland 13s. 5d., and I do not think that that is an inequitable arrangement. I wish to exhibit exactly what alterations we propose to make. Under the proportion now proposed, Ireland will pay 13s. 5d., while, if the present proportion were maintained, she would pay 16s. 10d., which will be a very considerable diminution in the amount of her contribution *per capita*.

I will state only one other striking fact with regard to the Irish expenditure. The House would like to know what an amount has been going on—and which at this moment is going on—of what I must call not only a waste of public money, but a demoralizing waste of public money, demoralizing in its influence upon both countries. The civil charges *per capita* at this moment are in Great Britain 8s. 2d. and in Ireland 16s. They have increased in Ireland in the last fifteen years by sixty-three per cent, and my belief is that if the present legislative and administrative systems be maintained you must make up your minds to a continued never-ending and never-to-be-limited augmentation. The amount of the Irish contribution upon the basis I have described would be as follows—One-fifteenth of the annual debt charge of £22,000,000 would be £1,466,-000, one-fifteenth of the army and navy charge, after excluding what we call war votes, and also excluding the charges for volunteers and yeomanry, would be £1,666,000, and the amount of the civil charges, which are properly considered imperial, would entail upon Ireland £110,000, or a total charge properly imperial of £3,242,000. I am now ready to present what I may call an Irish budget, a debtor and creditor account for the Irish exchequer. The customs produce in Ireland a gross sum of £1,880,000, the excise £4,300,000, the stamps £600,000, the income tax £550,000, and non-tax revenue, including the post-office, £1,020,000. And, perhaps, here again I ought to mention as an instance of the demoralizing waste which now attends Irish administration, that which will perhaps surprise the House to know—namely, that while in England and Scotland we levy from the post-office and telegraph system a large surplus income, in Ireland the post-office and the telegraphs just pay their expenses, or leave a surplus so small as not to be worth mentioning. I call that a very demoralizing way of spending money. Although I believe that there is no purer department in the country than the post-office, yet the practical effect of our method of administering Ireland by influences known to be English and not Irish leads to a vast amount of unnecessary expenditure.

The total receipts of the Irish exchequer are thus shown to amount to £8,350,000, and against that I have to place an imperial contribution which I may call permanent, because it will last for a great number of years, of £3,242,000. I put down £1,000,000 for the constabulary, because that would be a first charge, although I hope that it will soon come under very effective reduction. I put down £2,510,-000 for the other civil charges in Ireland, and there again I have not the smallest doubt that that charge will likewise be very effectually reduced by an Irish government. Finally, the collection of revenue is £834,000, making a total charge thus far of £7,586,000. Then we have thought it essential to include in this arrangement, not only for our own sakes, but for the sake of Ireland also, a payment on account of the Sinking Fund against the Irish portion of the national debt. The Sinking Fund is now paid for the whole national debt. We have now got to allot a certain portion of that debt to Ireland. We think it necessary to maintain that Sinking Fund, and especially for the interest of Ireland. When Ireland gets the management of her own affairs, I venture to prophecy that she will want, for useful purposes, to borrow money. But the difficulty of that operation will be enormously higher or lower according to the condition of her public credit. Her public credit is not yet born. It has yet to lie like an infant in the cradle, and it may require a good deal of nursing, but no nursing would be effectual unless it were plain and palpable to the eye of the whole world that Ireland had provision in actual working order for discharging her old obligations so as to make it safe for her to contract new obligations more nearly allied to her own immediate wants. I therefore put down three-quarters of a million for Sinking Fund. That makes the total charge £7,946,000, against a total income of £8,350,000, or a surplus of £404,000. But I can state to the House that that £404,000 is a part only of the fund, which, under the present state of things, it would be the duty of the Chancellor of the Exchequer of the three countries to present to you for the discharge of our collective expenditure.

Sir, the House has heard me with astonishing patience while I have endeavored to perform what I knew must prove an almost interminable task. There is only one subject more on which I feel it still necessary to detain the House. It is commonly said in England and Scotland—and in the main it is, I think, truly said—that we have for a great number of years been struggling to pass good laws for Ireland. We have sacrificed our time, we have neglected our own business, we have advanced our money, which I do not think at all a great favor conferred on her, and all this in the endeavor to give Ireland good laws. That is quite true in regard to the general course of legis-

lation since 1829. But many of those laws have been
passed under influences which can hardly be described
otherwise than as influences of fear. Some of our laws
have been passed in a spirit of grudging and of jealousy.
It is most painful for me to consider that after four or five
years' parliamentary battle, when a Municipal Corporation
Act [1840] was passed for Ireland, it was a very different
measure to that which in England and Scotland created
complete and absolute municipal life. Were I to come to
the history of the land question I could tell a still sadder
tale. Let no man assume that he fully knows that history
until he has followed it from year to year, beginning with
the Devon Commission [appointed 1843] or with the efforts
of Mr. Sharman Crawford.[1] The appointment of the Devon
Commission does, in my opinion, the highest honor to the
memory of Sir Robert Peel. Then notice the mode in
which the whole labors of that commission were frustrated
by the domination of selfish interests in the British Parliament. Our first effort at land legislation was delayed until
so late a period as the year 1870. I take this opportunity
of remarking that sound views on the land question were
not always confined to Irish members, nor to the Liberal
side of this House. The late Mr. Napier, who became Lord
Chancellor of Ireland, when he sat [1848-58] in this House
for the academical constituency of Dublin, developed with
great earnestness truly liberal views on the subject of Irish
land, and made generous efforts in that direction—efforts
which were, however, intercepted.

But, sir, I do not deny the general good intentions of
Parliament on a variety of great and conspicuous occasions,

---

[1] Member for Rochdale, 1841-52, and founder of the Tenant Right Association.

and its desire to pass good laws for Ireland. But let me say that in order to work out the purposes of government there is something more in this world occasionally required than even the passing of good laws. It is sometimes requisite not only that good laws should be passed, but also that they should be passed by the proper persons. The passing of many good laws is not enough in cases where the strong permanent instincts of the people, their distinctive marks of character, the situation and history of the country, require not only that these laws should be good, but that they should proceed from a congenial and native source, and besides being good laws, should be their own laws. In former times it might have been doubted—I have myself doubted—whether this instinct had been thus developed in Ireland. If such doubts could be entertained before the last general election they can be entertained no longer.

The principle that I am laying down I am not laying down exceptionally for Ireland. It is the very principle upon which, within my recollection, to the immense advantage of the country, we have not only altered but revolutionized our method of governing the colonies. I had the honor to hold office in the Colonial Department—perhaps I ought to be ashamed to confess it—fifty-one years ago. At that time the colonies were governed from Downing Street. It is true that some of them had legislative assemblies, but with these we were always in conflict. We were always fed with information by what was termed the British party in those colonies. A clique of gentlemen constituted themselves the British party; and the non-British party, which was sometimes called the "disloyal party," was com-

posed of the enormous majority of the population. We had
continual shocks, continual debates, and continual conflicts. All that has changed. England tried to pass good
laws for the colonies at that period, but the colonies said,
"We do not want your good laws; we want our own."
We admitted the reasonableness of that principle, and it is
now coming home to us from across the seas. We have to
consider whether it is applicable to the case of Ireland.
Do not let us disguise this from ourselves. We stand face
to face with what is termed Irish nationality. Irish nationality vents itself in the demand for local autonomy or separate and complete self-government in Irish, not in imperial
affairs. Is this an evil in itself? Is it a thing that we
should view with horror or apprehension? Is it a thing
which we ought to reject or accept only with a wry face,
or ought we to wait until some painful and sad necessity
is incumbent upon the country, like the necessity of 1780
or the necessity of 1793? Sir, I hold that it is not. There
is a saying of Mr. Grattan—who was indeed a fiery and
fervid orator, but he was more than that, he was a statesman, his aphorisms are in my opinion weighty, and even
profound, and I commend them to the careful reflection
and examination of the country—when he was deprecating
the surrender of the Irish Parliament, and pointing out
that its existence did not prevent the perfect union of the
two countries, he remarked, "The channel forbids union,
the ocean forbids separation." Is that channel nothing?
Do what you will with your steamers and your telegraphs,
can you make that channel cease to exist, or to be as if it
were not? These sixty miles may appear a little thing, but
I ask you what are the twenty miles between England and
France? These few miles of water have exercised a vital

influence upon the whole history, the whole development, and the whole national character of our people.

These, sir, are great facts. I hold that there is such a thing as local patriotism, which in itself is not bad, but good. The Welshman is full of local patriotism—the Scotchman is full of local patriotism; the Scotch nationality is as strong as it ever was, and should the occasion arise—which I believe it never can—it will be as ready to assert itself as in the days of Bannockburn. I do not believe that that local patriotism is an evil. I believe it is stronger in Ireland even than in Scotland. Englishmen are eminently English, Scotchmen are profoundly Scotch, and, if I read Irish history aright, misfortune and calamity have wedded her sons to her soil. The Irishman is more profoundly Irish, but it does not follow that because his local patriotism is keen he is incapable of imperial patriotism. There are two modes of presenting the subject. The one is to present what we now recommend as good, and the other to recommend it as a choice of evils. Well, sir, I have argued the matter as if it were a choice of evils; I have recognized as facts entitled to attention the jealousies which I do not share or feel, and I have argued it on that ground as the only ground on which it can be argued, not only in a mixed auditory, but in the public mind and to the country, which cannot give a minute investigation to the operations of that complicated question. But in my own heart I cherish the hope that this is not merely the choice of the lesser evil, but may prove to be rather a good in itself. What is the answer to this? It is only to be found in the view which rests upon the basis of despair and of absolute condemnation of Ireland and Irishmen as exceptions to the beneficent provisions which enable men in general, and Europeans in particular, and Americans, to be capable of performing civil duties, and which considers an Irishman either as a *lusus naturæ* or one for whom justice, common-sense, moderation, and national prosperity have no meaning, and who can only understand and appreciate perpetual strife and dissension. Well, sir, I am not going to argue that view, which to my mind is founded on a monstrous misconception. I say that the Irishman is as capable of loyalty as another man—I say that if his loyalty has been checked in its development, why is it? Because the laws by which he is governed do not present themselves to him, as they do to us in England and Scotland, with a native and congenial aspect, and I think I can refer to two illustrations which go strongly to support the doctrine I have advanced. Take the case of the Irish soldier, and of the Irish constabulary. Have you a braver or a more loyal man in your army than the Irishman, who has shared every danger with his Scotch and English comrades, and who has never been behind them when confronted by peril, for the sake of the honor and safety of his empire? Compare this case with that of an ordinary Irishman in Ireland. The Irish soldier has voluntarily placed himself under military law, which is to him a self-chosen law, and he is exempted from that difficulty which works upon the population in Ireland—namely, that they are governed by a law which they do not feel has sprung from the soil. Consider how common it is to hear the observation, in discussing the circumstances of Ireland, that while the constabulary are largely taken from the Roman Catholic population and from the very class most open to disaffection, where disaffection exists, they form a splendid model of obedience, discipline, and devotion such as the world can hardly match. How is this? It is because they have undertaken a voluntary service which takes them completely out of the category of the ordinary Irishman. They are placed under an authority which is to them congenial because freely accepted. Their loyalty is not checked by the causes that operate on the agricultural population of Ireland. It has grown as freely in the constabulary and in the army as if every man in the constabulary and every Irish soldier had been an Englishman or a Scotchman.

However this may be, we are sensible that we have taken an important decision—our choice has been made. It has not been made without thought; it has been made in the full knowledge that trial and difficulty may confront us on our path. We have no right to say that Ireland through her constitutionally-chosen representatives will accept the plan I offer. Whether it will be so I do not know —I have no title to assume it—but if Ireland does not cheerfully accept it, it is impossible for us to attempt to force upon her what is intended to be a boon; nor can we possibly press England and Scotland to accord to Ireland what she does not heartily welcome and embrace. There are difficulties, but I rely upon the patriotism and sagacity of this House; I rely on the effects of free and full discussion; and I rely more than all upon the just and generous sentiments of the two British nations. Looking forward, I ask the House to assist us in the work which we have undertaken, and to believe that no trivial motive can have driven us to it—to assist us in this work which we believe will restore Parliament to its dignity, and legislation to its free and unimpeded course. I ask you to stay that waste of public treasure which is involved in the present system of

government and legislation in Ireland; and which is not a
waste only, but which demoralizes while it exhausts. I
ask you to show to Europe and to America that we too
can face political problems which America twenty years
ago faced, and which many countries in Europe have been
called upon to face, and have not feared to deal with. I
ask that in our own case we should practice with firm and
fearless hand what we have so often preached—the doctrine which we have so often inculcated upon others—
namely, that the concession of local self-government is
not the way to sap or impair, but the way to strengthen
and consolidate unity. I ask that we should learn to rely
less upon merely written stipulations, and more upon those
better stipulations which are written on the heart and mind
of man. I ask that we should apply to Ireland that happy
experience which we have gained in England and in Scotland, where the course of generations has now taught us
not as a dream or a theory, but as practice and as life,
that the best and surest foundation we can find to build
upon is the foundation afforded by the affections, the convictions, and the will of the nation; and it is thus, by the
decree of the Almighty, that we may be enabled to secure
at once the social peace, the fame, the power, and the per-
manence of the empire.

HOME RULE

HOUSE OF COMMONS, APRIL 13, 1886

I WILL make at the outset one or two very brief remarks upon the speech of the right honorable gentleman.[1] He has quoted words from me with an extension given to them that they do not carry in the original document. The argument which I made upon the proposal[2] of 1871 was this —that no case had at that time been made to justify any radical change in any of the institutions of the country generally, or any interference with the Constitution of the Imperial Parliament, and I own that at that time, after the Church Act of 1869 and after the Land Act of 1870, I did cherish the hope that we might be able, by legislation from this House, to meet the wants and the wishes of Ireland. I cherished that hope at that time; but at that time, if the right honorable gentleman has done me the justice to make himself completely acquainted with my sentiments expressed in that speech, he will find that it contains none of the apprehensions with which the minds of honorable members opposite are filled, and that, on the contrary, I then stated in the most explicit manner that I had heard with joy, and I accepted with the utmost satisfaction, the assurance that the demand which was beginning to be made by Mr. Butt for Home Rule did not involve in any way the

---

[1] Sir Michael Hicks-Beach.
[2] The Home Government Association, afterward the Home Rule League, was founded in 1870. In 1871 Mr. Isaac Butt, Member for the City of Limerick, was elected leader of the Irish party. He is said to have invented the phrase "Home Rule."

disintegration of the empire. But I certainly will not enter
into a discussion on the Transvaal Convention, with regard
to which I may make the observation that I think that the
topics we have to deal with relevant to the matter are sufficient, and I do not consider that any observation from me
is wanted on an act which I believe has been recognized by
this country as a great act of justice, and as the undoing—
perhaps that is the more accurate description of it—of the
great act of injustice which stains the memory of our legislation on this subject.

The right honorable gentleman says that I have shown
mistrust of the Irish legislature by providing safeguards for
minorities. I have already stated in the most distinct terms
that the safeguards provided, so far as I am concerned, are
not in consequence of mistrust entertained by me, but they
are in consequence of mistrust entertained by others. They
are reasonable precautions by way of contribution on our
part to disarm honest though unfounded jealousy; and however little it may appear that they are likely to attain their
end, yet I cannot regret that we have made them. One
more observation with respect to the foreign garb of English laws. The right honorable gentleman must understand that I have used those words not with respect to the
beneficial acts which have been passed on many occasions
by this Parliament for the purpose of meeting the wants of
Ireland, but with regard to the ordinary operations of the
criminal law in that country, especially in association, as
it has constantly been, with the provisions of special repressive or coercive legislation.

Lastly, I must express the astonishment with which I
heard the right honorable gentleman refer to the Roman
Catholic Association. He spoke of the disappearance of

that association from the scene as a great triumph obtained by the vigor and firmness of the government and the Parliament over unruly elements in Ireland. Why, sir, on the contrary, the disappearance of the Roman Catholic Association was due entirely to the introduction of the Roman Catholic Relief Bill,[1] as unhappily the introduction of that Relief Bill was due, as the Duke of Wellington himself declared, to his apprehension of civil war, and as the alternative to it. The right honorable gentleman could not have afforded a more unhappy instance of that which has been a too common feature of the relations of this House to Ireland, and of those combinations the recurrence of which we are striving to avoid. I was told by my noble friend the member for the Rossendale division [2] that I had not a formulated demand from Ireland. No, sir; but the Duke of Wellington had a pretty well formulated demand; and we now know—and I am glad that the observations of the right honorable gentleman gave the Irish members below the gangway an opportunity of bearing testimony—we now know in substance what is demanded by Ireland through her constitutionally chosen representatives; and therefore I say, if it be a just and reasonable demand, we cannot hasten too soon to meet it; and we will not wait until the day of disaster, the day of difficulty, and I will add the day of dishonor, to yield, as we have so often yielded, to necessity that which we were unwilling to yield to justice.

Sir, I desire to avoid details in this stage of the debate and at this hour of the night, and I will endeavor to make this sacrifice at any rate, that I will neither defend myself nor censure anybody else; but I will deal as far as I can

---

[1] In 1829.   [2] Lord Hartington, now Duke of Devonshire.

with some of the arguments that have recently been laid
before us.

One detail I must notice which has been largely introduced into this debate, and in so striking a manner by many
members of the House—it is that which relates to the presence of Irish members, or the cessation of that presence, at
Westminster. When I spoke on Thursday last I laid down
—and now I am going to answer an appeal of the right
honorable gentleman who asked me what were the essential
conditions of this bill—I laid down, I say, five essential conditions, from which it appeared to me we could under no circumstances depart, and under which the grant of a domestic
legislature to Ireland would be justifiable and wise. These
were the essential conditions under which, in our opinion,
the granting of a domestic legislature to Ireland would be
justifiable and wise—first, that it must be consistent with
imperial unity; secondly, that it must be founded upon the
political equality of the three nations; thirdly, that there
must be an equitable distribution of imperial burdens;
fourthly, that there should be safeguards for the minority; and fifthly, that it should be in the nature of a settlement, and not of a mere provocation for the revival of fresh
demands. I stated that these were the only conditions.

I find I have been reported as having stated that the
retention of customs and excise by this country, and the
absence of Irish members from this House, were likewise
vital and essential conditions. I do not think I used those
epithets. If I did, it was probably an inadvertence, for
which I apologize, and unquestionably it was in entire contradiction to what I had just stated before, when I laid
down the only essential conditions. Sir, what I think with
regard to the Irish members—although the question is much

too large for me to attempt to enter fully into it at present—what I thought clear with regard to the Irish members was, in the first place, this—that the 103 Irish members could not possibly continue as now to come here and vote upon all matters—English, Scotch, Irish, and Imperial alike. That I conceived to be wholly indisputable. I stated that I had hoped—that I had long tried to find—some practicable means of distinction between Imperial and British matters, and that my efforts had entirely failed, nor could I see my way to such a distinction. I also stated that in my opinion it was impossible for England, and that no doubt England would never desire or dream of inflicting or forcing upon Ireland taxation without representation; that if Irish members were to disappear either permanently or for a time —I do not say I used these epithets—were to disappear from this House, it must be by the consent of Ireland herself.

Since that time a variety of suggestions have been made in many speeches, which have shown how much interest is felt in this question. It has been suggested that Irish members might come here with limited powers. But I have certainly failed to discover means of drawing the line. It has been stated that they might come in limited numbers, and it has been suggested in a wise and weighty speech delivered by my honorable friend the member for Bedford [1] last night, that an interval of absence from this House was eminently desirable, and perhaps almost of vital necessity for Ireland herself with a view to her own purposes. Then, says my honorable friend, if I understood him right, after such an interval of years has passed, during which, God knows, there will be enough to do for any Parliament—any repre-

---

[1] Mr. Whitbread.

sentative body that Ireland can be supplied with—after
such an interval, if it is desired that Irish members in
any number or any proportion, or under any conditions
should reappear in this House, that is a problem which,
however difficult, British statesmanship may be found adequate to solve. There was great force in what my honorable friend said. I cannot, however, bind myself with regard to these observations or to any of the propositions
which I have just cited. I cannot bind myself, still less
any of my colleagues, but I think, bearing in mind the importance of the subject, and the vast and immeasurable importance of the purposes we have in view, I do not think
we should be right—it would be even presumptuous—were
we to take upon ourselves, in the face of the House, at this
early stage of the discussion on the bill, entirely to close the
doors against any consideration of this kind.

The position, therefore, remains exactly as it was; but
I have thought that that reference which I have made to
the speech of my honorable friend is no more than that,
and other portions of that speech, eminently deserve.

Now, sir, my right honorable friend, the member for
East Edinburgh,[1] has addressed the House very fully to-
night, and has raised a great number of questions connected with this bill. My right honorable friend is ter-
ribly alarmed at the argument drawn from the presence of
86 Nationalist members, 85 of them from Ireland, in this
Parliament. He is perfectly alarmed at this argument. I
do not know whether he did me the honor to refer to my
view of it. If he did, he is entirely mistaken. He treated
it as if a statement had been made by me to the effect that

---

[1] Mr. Goschen.

because there are 85 Nationalist members in this House, you must do whatever they demand; and, treating it in that way and having created this phantom, it is easy enough to show that it is a most formidable proposition. He spent a long time in showing the most portentous consequences to which it would lead. Yes, sir, but that is not the argument so far as I used it; it was not the argument so far as I have heard it. What I ventured to say was this—that the deliberate and constitutional expression of the wishes of Ireland through the vast majority of her members entails upon this House the duty and the obligation of a respectful and a favorable consideration of every wish that Ireland may entertain consistently with the interests and the integrity of the empire. My right honorable friend said there was a parity in principle between Ireland and Scotland. I entirely agree with him. His experience as a Scotch member is short. If the vast majority of Scotchmen demand something on the ground that Scotch feeling and opinion show that it is essentially required in order to satisfy the just wishes of Scotland, I would advise my right honorable friend, if he wishes to be consistent with regard to the integrity of the empire, not to put himself in conflict with those expressions of opinion.

Then, sir, my right honorable friend said that no analogy could be drawn—and so said my noble friend the member for Rossendale—from the proceedings of the Protestant Parliament of Grattan. What was the meaning of all this? I have been arguing and others have argued that Grattan's Parliament showed no tendency and no disposition toward a separation of the kingdoms, and that Grattan himself looked upon the separation of the Parliaments as a means of uniting the hearts of the people.

That has been met by the statement now that that was a Protestant Parliament and a landlords' Parliament. Sir, if that is the way to make a Parliament safe and sound, if to re-introduce religious disabilities, if to narrow the franchise, if to centre power in the hands of the landlords, or if you are to go further and fill more than half the benches of Parliament with pensioners and placemen, then, if these are the elements of safety in a Parliament, in what gross and woful error have we been in this Parliament for half a century. We have been breaking down the exclusive power of class; we have been widening the franchise over the whole kingdom and effacing from the statute book one by one—until the very last perhaps is contained in this bill—every vestige of religious disability. There is no faith in the people with those who make these declarations. Their faith seems to be in shutting out the people, and in regarding popular influence as a source of danger. In this happy country we have found it a source of strength; and the enterprise we are now engaged in is to see whether we cannot also find security for it in Ireland that it shall be to her a similar source of strength under circumstances happier than those of her history heretofore.

My right honorable friend seems to sum up the misdeeds of the Irish people in an emphatic question—"In what country except Ireland would a no rent manifesto have been produced?" That is the inquiry which he puts. My first observation upon it is this—in what country except Ireland can you show so lamentable, so deplorable a history—a history so disgraceful to those who had any hand in bringing it about—and relations so deplorable between those who owned the land and those

who occupied it? The speech of my right honorable
friend appeared to proceed upon the assumption that
there were ineradicable and incurable vices in Irishmen
which placed them in a category different from the
people of other nations—that they had a sort of double
dose of original sin. Is it to be wondered at that the
notions of Irishmen should to some extent be gone awry
upon the subject of land and the relations connected with
it when you bear in mind that the Devon Commission, appointed by a Tory government, reported that the agricultural population of Ireland were called upon to bear, and
that they did bear, with admirable and exemplary patience,
sufferings greater than those which fell to the lot of any
other people in Europe? Are you so ignorant as to suppose, when these sufferings had been borne for generations, I may say for centuries, as disclosed to the world
on the highest authority, and when attempt after attempt
to apply something like a remedy to the miseries that
existed from the operation of the land laws in Ireland
had failed through the narrow jealousy and selfishness of
a class—that these things could pass without leaving a
mark in history? Does my right honorable friend think
that these things can pass and set their mark upon history,
and yet leave no mark in the nature and disposition and
habits of men who have been sufferers under such abomi-
nations?

My right honorable friend thinks my analogy with foreign countries is bad; that Austria and Hungary, Norway
and Sweden, have nothing to do with these things. But
my statement has been entirely misapprehended. I will
recall the terms of it for the benefit of the right honorable
gentleman. I never said that the analogy was exact, that

the circumstances were exactly parallel. What I said was that the circumstances were such as would show that we are called upon in this country to do, with infinitely greater advantages, what they have done in the face of infinitely greater difficulties. My right honorable friend appears to think it a difficulty in our way that we have got an Imperial Parliament and a greater number of subordinate local parliaments related to the British Empire. My point is that there is not in Sweden a supremacy of the Swedish Parliament over Norway; that there is not in Austria a supremacy of the Austrian Parliament over Hungary, and that, even without the advantage of such supremacy, the problem has in those countries been solved in substance, and that, in the case of Norway and Sweden particularly, by the adoption of the simple expedient of granting a domestic legislature and practical local independence, the union of the two countries, which at one time seemed hopeless and impossible, has become close, and is growing closer from day to day. Then how is it that these illustrations have no bearing upon the great problem that we have before us?

Again, my right honorable friend states as a difficulty that our interests are so interlaced with Ireland. I am astonished to hear that observation called upon to pass muster and do duty among the arguments against this bill. Why, if our interests are so interlaced—and I thank God it is true that they are so interlaced—is not that in itself a strong presumption of the extreme unlikelihood that Irishmen will overlook that interlacing and proceed as if we were perfectly independent, as if they had nothing to do with us, no benefit to derive from us, and no injury to suffer from injury to us? No! the truth

is this. It is assumed—and this is the basis of the speech
of my right honorable friend—that the Irishman will do
wrong, and that there is no way of making him listen to
the dictates of prudence, of kindness, of justice, of good
sense, except by taking into your own hands the reins by
which you can govern him and teaching him how he shall
walk. On that principle it is that my right honorable
friend went over all the different classes of subjects, and
desc.ibed the dreadful changes that everything was to undergo; legislation was to be changed, administration was
to be changed, the civil service was to be changed, the
face of nature itself was to be changed. Such is the terrible picture. And why? Is there no common-sense
among that portion of our fellow-countrymen?

The speech of my right honorable friend recalled to
my memory a striking sentence of Lord Russell's fifty
years ago, which implanted itself deeply on my memory
at the time, and which I have never forgotten, and I hope
never shall forget. It was at the time when, under the
administration of the Melbourne government, Mr. Thomas
Drummond was Under-Secretary for Ireland, and when
with singular success he was endeavoring to conduct the
Irish administration, so far as he could, in sympathy with
the feelings of the people. His misdeeds, as I suppose I
must call them, found their climax in the utterance of
the portentous doctrine which shocked Conservatism from
Land's End to John o' Groats—he had the audacity to
say that "property had its duties as well as its rights."
The corresponding misdeeds of Mr. Drummond, and in
some sense of the Lord Lieutenant, caused many debates
in this House, in which I am thankful to say I took no
part, but to which I was an attentive listener. Every sort

of objection and accusation was brought forward against the proceedings of the Irish Government of that day; and Lord Russell, in his quiet way, rising to take part in a debate, said—"It appears to me that all these objections, all these difficulties, and all these accusations"—I may not be quoting every word accurately, but I am very near the mark—"may be summed up in one single sentence. It comes, sir, to this—that as England is inhabited by Englishmen, and Scotland by Scotchmen, so Ireland is inhabited by Irishmen." Lord Russell knew very well that Irishmen did not come here to conquer us 700 years ago, but that we went to Ireland to conquer—we favored Irishmen with our company, we have been all along the stronger party of the two, and it is one of the uniform and unfailing rules that guide human judgment, if not of the moment yet of history, that when a long relation has existed between a nation of superior strength and one of inferior strength, and when that relation has gone wrong, the responsibility and the guilt rests in the main upon the strong rather than upon the weak.

My right honorable friend asked me questions as to the provisions of this bill, and I must confess my surprise at some of them, coming as they do from one who is an old official hand. They were questions most proper to be asked—perhaps on the second reading of a bill—certainly in committee, but I have never heard of such questions upon the motion for leave to introduce a bill. If questions of that kind are to be asked, why, sir, this House ought to alter its rules and give an honorable member applying for leave to introduce a bill the power of laying it upon the table of the House before it is read a first time. For example, my right honorable friend asked a question about the veto. Well, sir, we have stated with regard to that point that there is no limitation to the veto in the bill, and, if the right honorable gentleman asks my opinion, my opinion is that the principle upon which the veto is now worked—if the right honorable gentleman will take the trouble to read the valuable work ("The Law of the Constitution") of Professor Dicey, to which I have before referred, he will find a most careful and interesting elucidation of the subject—the principle upon which the veto is now worked in the great colonial dependencies of this country—though I do not admit that Ireland will be reduced to the *status* of a colony—I believe that principle to be applicable for all practical purposes to Ireland with a domestic legislature.

Then my right honorable friend asked a question about the levying of the income tax. He did not seem to have even a very elementary idea of what the Irish income tax would be, and he asked where the dividends would be payable, whether the dividends would be payable in London or in Dublin. Why, sir, no such questions can possibly arise under this bill as the bill stands. The Irish income tax will be just as distinct from the income tax of England and Scotland as if it were a French income tax. Well, I will give you another illustration, as if it were an Indian income tax. From time to time they have in India the blessing of an income tax; but in India the whole machinery, the incidence of the tax, the liability to pay it, are all as totally distinct from the tax in this country as if the income tax there were laid in another planet.

My right honorable friend finally laid very much stress on the case of the United States of America. He pointed out that insidious advisers recommended the Northern

States not to insist upon the maintenance of the Union, but that they did insist on the maintenance of the Union, and carried their point. Why, true, sir; but having carried their point, what did they do? Having the Southern States at their feet, being in a position in which they were entitled to treat them as conquered countries, they invested every one of them with that full autonomy, a measure of which we are now asking for Ireland. I say a measure of which autonomy, because I believe that their autonomy is much fuller than that which we are now asking for Ireland.

Well, sir, I may say some words more. My right honorable friend said—I am not quite sure whether my right honorable friend said so, but certainly my noble friend, the member for Rossendale did—that these enactments if carried would lead to further demands from Ireland. That is a favorable objection. The right honorable gentleman [Sir Michael Hicks-Beach, the leader of the Opposition] who has just sat down has been extremely cautious in this matter, and he has promised Ireland—I hope I am not misrepresenting him—almost nothing except a reasonable allowance of repressive criminal legislation. The phantom of local government and a little control over education and public works, and such things, find no place whatever in the speech of the leader of the Opposition, but they find a place in the speech of my right honorable friend behind me, and of my noble friend the member for Rossendale. Well, sir, we are going to give to the Irish people— if we are permitted—that which we believe to be in substantial accordance with their full, possible, and reasonable demands. In our opinion that is the way to stop further demands.

I should like to quote Mr. Burke—and I hope we shall hear much of Mr. Burke in the course of this discussion—for the writings of Mr. Burke upon Ireland, and still more upon America, are a mine of gold for the political wisdom with which they are charged, applicable to the circumstances of to-day, full of the deepest and most valuable lessons to guide the policy of a country. He was speaking for conciliation with America, and those to whom he was preaching in vain met him with this idle cavil that his conciliation would tend to further demands. They refused this conciliation, but further demands came, and they were granted—with hands dyed in blood, and after hundreds of millions had been added to our national debt, and when disparagement, at the very least, of England's fame went through the length and breadth of the world in connection with that wretched consummation—were granted, leaving behind them in America an inheritance, not of goodwill or affection such as now prevails, but of rancor and resentment which for generations were not effaced, and which were the happy consequences of a courageous resistance. I am not afraid, sir, of the same consequences in the same form. There is no question of war with Ireland, but it is a question of what I care for more than anything else—the character, the honor, and the fair fame of my country; it is a question of humanity, of justice, and of a desire to make atonement for a long—a too long—series of former, and not yet wholly forgotten, wrongs. Now, sir, what did Mr. Burke say on that occasion when he was advocating conciliation with America? He said that the more and the better state of liberty any people possessed, the less would they hazard in the vain attempt to make it more.

What are the proposals of my noble friend? They are:

First a little dose of coercion, and next a grudging gift to Ireland of such self-government as England and Scotland may be pleased to choose for themselves. Now I deny the justice of the principle that self-government in Ireland is necessarily to be limited by the wishes of England and Scotland for themselves. Upon what basis of justice does that argument rest? Why may not Ireland have specialities in her case which England and Scotland may not have? We have no right to say that what England wants and Scotland wants Ireland may have, but nothing else. You must show that what Ireland wants is mischievous before you are justified in refusing her. I am speaking now of the favorite topic of "further demands." Was there ever a device more certain to prolong all the troubles of Parliament? Was there ever a system of policy less hopeful of attaining any solid standing-ground than this proposal to dole out to Ireland from year to year with grudging and misgiving, and with a frank statement that it is a dangerous business, that which she does not want, and which, if she accepts at all, she will only accept for the purpose of making further demands? It was denied in very clear language by the Irish representatives that they sought to press forward from this measure to other measures. They claim, and very fairly and reasonably claim— because no member of Parliament could divest himself of the right—to examine in committee the provisions of the bill, and to demand this or that amendment. But they have expressly disclaimed the intention to make what my noble friend calls further demands. Let him put to them the same question, and ask them for the same assurances, as to the proposals made in this debate by a most distinguished person [Sir M. Hicks-Beach]—one who, unfortunately, I know only three years ago declared that there should be no extension of local government until the Irish members made a total change in their methods of speech and action. No doubt measures doled out in the shape of municipal corporations here and there would be certain to be used for the purpose of making further demands. I commend the consistency and caution of the right honorable gentleman, the leader of the Opposition, because he fairly told us at the commencement of the session [January 21], when he was asked what boons would be given to Ireland in the way of local government, that no enlargement of the powers of local government should be given which might be used as a lever to weaken and destroy the legislative union, or (as he went on to say) enable the political majority to tyrannize over the minority. A very sensible, a very consistent course. If you grant some small modicum of local government, it would simply be a device for securing perpetual disturbance of this Parliament from year to year by Irish members, and they would strengthen the leverage with which they would use those demands and advance them to their natural consummation.

My noble friend complains that this was a question which had not been referred to the people. I should like to know what is the upshot of that observation. What does it mean? I think it can hardly mean anything else than this—that the government had committed a fault in bringing forward this question at the present time because it had not brought the matter under public consideration at the general election. It seems to me that that is an extraordinary doctrine. I want to know where it is to be found laid down by any constitutional authority. My honorable friend the Attorney-General [Sir Charles Russell] asked whether there was any mandate for coercion. No, sir, there was no mandate for coercion, and you cannot want a mandate for any measures necessary to maintain the law. Very well, sir; but if you do not want a mandate for the measures of force and repression, intended to maintain the law, much less do you want a mandate for measures intended to maintain and strengthen the law by laying hold of the hearts of the people, and which aim at no force and no repression, but at a union far closer and more durable than that which now exists on the statute book.

I do not know whether my noble friend has given much attention to the case of the Reform Act, but it is a rather curious one from this point of view. The election of 1830 was conducted almost entirely without reference to the subject of reform. At that time the election extended over very many weeks, and it was only just before it had quite finished—and the Yorkshire election, if I recollect rightly, was about the last—that those great events occurred in Paris which produced a sympathetic effect here and roused a cry for reform in England, but in the main the Parliament was elected without the least reference to reform. Yes, sir; but when that Parliament met, and when it was found that the wants of the country required reform, although it was denounced as revolution—and I can assure honorable gentlemen opposite that all their invectives are weak and ineffective in comparison—Parliament set about its work manfully; the government proposed to Parliament, and Parliament entertained, the great proposal then laid before it. It would be a very different thing, indeed, if my colleagues who have spoken in the debate had evaded the real issue, or had declared that the question was unfit to come before us. I never uttered an opinion, nor shall I utter an opinion, that it is a subject unfit to come before the people; I think we who propose this bill should be the last persons who should be jealous of any reference to the people.

Coming now to the proposals of my right honorable friend the member for West Birmingham, in the first place, let me say that I at once accord to him—what, however, he cannot want according from me—that is, his perfect and entire good faith in the representations that he made, upon which a misapprehension prevailed between us, as to his title to enter upon certain matters. If anything further is required upon that point, it certainly can keep until Friday next, when the bill on the land question is brought forward. Quite irrespective of the land law, my right honorable friend stated four points, any one of which was an ample justification of the step which he felt himself called upon to take. But he, at any rate, gave no countenance to coercive legislation. He looks into the future, and he sees how light and trivial is the talk about coercive legislation. But my right honorable friend went a great deal further, and suggested a commission or committee, to be formed of all parties, to deal with this subject. I will not criticise that proposal. I venture the opinion that no solution of the question will ever proceed from a royal commission or a committee composed of all parties, much less pass through Parliament. Then my right honorable friend spoke of federation. If you are to have federation there must be somebody to federate, and there will be nobody, except a legislative body is entitled to act for the people. It appears to me that my right honorable friend goes further than we do, because he is in favor of not only giving a domestic legislature, but of appending to it that rather formidable post-

script of some arrangement under which this Parliament is
to part with some of its powers and throw them into the
common stock along with powers coming from other portions of the empire. I cannot, therefore, say that he has
remained behind us in this matter.

What is really material to observe is the mutual relations of harmony and concord subsisting between the plans
of those who think they ought to sink differences and unite
together for the purpose of finding a solution for the Irish
problem. The Chancellor of the Exchequer, in his masterly statement, exhibited in full detail the relations actually subsisting among those most distinguished gentlemen
and great parliamentary authorities. He has shown that the
Border Burghs does not agree with Birmingham, and that
Birmingham does not agree with Rossendale, and that Rossendale does not agree with Paddington, and, again, Edinburgh is distinct in shade from them all. There is a decided
want of common feature, common action, common purpose,
common principle; there is no united basis of action except
the basis of hostility to this bill.

When I speak of this plan, I speak of it as a plan in its
essence and not in its detail. It may derive much advantage from the wisdom of Parliament. It has been produced
and brought to light under a degree of pressure such as I
believe never was applied by circumstances to any government, such at least, I will venture to say, as there is no case
of in the half-century to which my recollection extends. It
may be improved by the wisdom of this House, but speaking of it as a plan, I say it holds the field. It has many
enemies; it has not a single rival. No one has been bold
enough to propose an intelligible system of what, in my
opening statement, I called effectual coercion—the only

kind of coercion that can be adequate to the end you have in view. And, sir, as the plan holds the field, the subject holds the field. Never, I think, have I witnessed such signs of public absorption in this House and out of this House. And, sir, it is safe to prophecy that the subject will continue to hold the field. Many who are here advocate important reforms; many think, and I am one of them, that legislation is in arrear. The demands upon your time and thought are beyond your capacity, even with your best exertions, to meet. But, sir, you may dismiss all these subjects from your mind until this matter is disposed of, until the Irish problem is solved. I am not speaking of what gentlemen opposite may threaten or say; I am looking at the nature of the case; I am looking at the profound interest of the whole English and Scotch people, ay, and of the whole civilized world. Until this problem is solved it is idle to think of making real progress with the business of this country, in respect to the important subjects which are perfectly ripe for the handling of Parliament. We have come to the time for decisive action; we have come to the time for throwing aside not only private interests and partial affections, but private devices and partial remedies. We have come to the time for looking at the whole breadth of this subject and endeavoring to compass it in our minds. We have come to the time when we must answer this question—whether we will make one bold attempt to free Parliament for its great and necessary work, and to establish harmony by Irish laws for Ireland, or whether we will continue, on the other hand, to struggle on as we have done before, living from hand to mouth, leaving England and Scotland to a famine of needful and useful legislation, and Ireland to a continuance of social disease, the depth of which we have never understated, of social disease that you do not know how to deal with, and of angry discord with Great Britain, which you make no attempt to cure.

HOME RULE

HOUSE OF COMMONS, MAY 10, 1886

SIR—I was the latest of the members of this House who had an opportunity of addressing the House in the debate on the introduction of this bill; yet I think no one will be surprised at my desiring to submit some observations in moving the second reading. And this on the double ground—First of all, because unquestionably the discussion has been carried on since the introduction of the bill throughout the country with remarkable liveliness and activity; and, secondly, because so many criticisms have turned on an important particular of the bill with respect to which the government feel it to be an absolute duty on our part that we should, without any delay whatever, render to the House the advantage of such explanations as, consistently with our public duty, it may be in our power to make.

I am very sorry to say that I am obliged to introduce into this speech—but only I hope to the extent of a very few sentences—a statement of my own personal position in regard to this question, which I refrained from mentioning to the House at the time when I asked for leave to bring in the bill. But I read speeches which some gentlemen opposite apparently think it important to make to their constituencies, and which contain statements so entirely erroneous and baseless that, although I do not think it myself to be a subject of great importance and relevancy to the question, yet as they do think it to be so, I am bound to set them right, and to provide them with the means of avoiding similar errors on future occasions. Although it is not a very safe thing for a man who has been for a long time in public life—and sometimes not very safe even for those who have been for a short time in public life—to assert a negative, still I will venture to assert that I have never in any period of my life declared what is now familiarly known as Home Rule in Ireland to be incompatible with imperial unity. ["Oh, oh!"] Yes; exactly so. My sight is bad, and I am not going to make personal references; but I dare say the interruption comes from some member who has been down to his constituents and has made one of those speeches stuffed full of totally untrue and worthless matter.

I will go on to say what is true in this matter. In 1871 the question of Home Rule was an extremely young question. In fact, Irish history on these matters in my time has divided itself into three great periods. The first was the Repeal period under Mr. O'Connell, which began about the time of the Reform Act and lasted until the death of that distinguished man. On that period I am not aware of ever having given an opinion; but that is not the question which I consider is now before us. The second period was that between the death of Mr. O'Connell and the emergence, so to say, of the subject of Home Rule. That was the period in which physical force and organizations with that object were conceived and matured, taking effect under the name generally of what is known as Fenianism. In 1870 or 1871 came up the question of Home Rule. In a speech

which I made in Aberdeen at that period I stated the great
satisfaction with which I heard and with which I accepted
the statements of the proposers of Home Rule, that under
that name they contemplated nothing that was at variance
with the unity of the empire.

But while I say this, do not let it be supposed that I
have ever regarded the introduction of Home Rule as a
small matter, or as entailing a slight responsibility. I admit, on the contrary, that I have regarded it as a subject
of the gravest responsibility, and so I still regard it. I
have cherished, as long as I was able to cherish, the hope
that Parliament might, by passing—by the steady and the
continuous passing of—good measures for Ireland, be able
to encounter and dispose of the demand for Home Rule in
that manner which obviously can alone be satisfactory. In
that hope undoubtedly I was disappointed. I found that
we could not reach that desired point. But two conditions
have been always absolute and indispensable with me in regard to Home Rule. In the first place, it was absolutely
necessary that it should be shown, by marks at once unequivocal and perfectly constitutional, to be the desire of the
great mass of the population of Ireland; and I do not hesitate to say that that condition has never been absolutely
and unequivocally fulfilled, in a manner to make its fulfilment undeniable, until the occasion of the recent election.[1] It was open for any one to discuss whether the
honorable member for Cork—acting as he acted in the last
Parliament, with some forty-five members—it was open to
any one to question how far he spoke the sentiments of
the mass of the Irish population. At any rate, it is quite

---

[1] When, out of 103 members, 85 Home Rulers were returned.

evident that any responsible man in this country, taking
up the question of Home Rule at that time, and urging
the belief that it was the desire of the mass of the Irish
population, would have been encountered in every quarter
of the House with an incredulity that it would have been
totally impossible for him to overcome. Well, I own that
to me that question is a settled question. I live in a country of representative institutions; I have faith in representative institutions; and I will follow them out to their
legitimate consequences; and I believe it to be dangerous
in the highest degree, dangerous to the Constitution of this
country and to the unity of the empire, to show the smallest hesitation about the adoption of that principle. Therefore that principle for me is settled.

The second question—and it is equally an indispensable
condition with the first—is this, Is Home Rule a thing compatible or incompatible with the unity of the empire?
Again and again, as may be in the recollection of Irish members, I have challenged, in this House and elsewhere, explanations upon the subject, in order that we might have
clear knowledge of what it was they so veiled under the
phrase, not exceptionable in itself, but still open to a multitude of interpretations. Well, that question was settled in
my mind on the first night of this session, when the honorable gentleman, the leader of what is termed the Nationalist
party from Ireland, declared unequivocally that what he
sought under the name of Home Rule was autonomy for
Ireland. Autonomy is a name well known to European
law and practice, as importing, under a historical signifi-
cation sufficiently definite for every practical purpose, the
management and control of the affairs of the territory to
which the word is applied, and as being perfectly com-

patible with the full maintenance of imperial unity. If
any part of what I have said is open to challenge, it can
be challenged by those who read my speeches, and I find
that there are many readers of my speeches when there is
anything to be got out of them and turned to account. I
am quite willing to stand that test, and I believe that what
I have said now is the exact and literal and absolute truth
as to the state of the case.

I shall not dwell at any great length on the general argument in favor of the bill; but I will notice one or two
points that have been taken, and which, if they do not
express any very definite argument, yet give expression to
feelings which are entitled on my part to deference and respect. A great objection which is felt by some honorable
gentlemen is much to this effect—"Do not, in these great
matters, experiment in politics; do not let us have this
kind of legislation, uncertain as to its effect, involving
great issues, and therefore liable to be marked—I may say
stigmatized—by the name of experiment." Because, although in one sense every law is an experiment, yet I
perfectly understand, and I am the first to admit, that
experimenting in politics is a bad and dangerous practice.
Now, what is experimenting in politics? If I understand
it, it is the practice of proposing grave changes without
grave causes. Is this a case in which there is no grave
cause with which we have to deal? Why, sir, we have
to deal with the gravest of all causes that can solicit the
attention of a legislature—namely, the fact that we have
to treat the case of a country where the radical sentiment
of the people is not in sympathy with the law. I defy
any man, be he an opponent or not, to deny that we have
to deal with the case of a country where the radical senti-

ment of the people is not in sympathy with the law. Of course, I am making general assertions. I do not say that an action on a bill of exchange between debtor and creditor in Ireland could not be settled without reference to any international prejudice. I speak of the most important parts of the law—of those parts which touch agricultural relations, the one great standing, pervading employment and occupation of the country—I speak above all of the criminal law, of the very first exigencies of political society; and I will not argue the question whether the criminal law of Ireland, especially when it concerns agricultural relations, has or has not the sympathy of the people until I find some one who is ready to say, after all he knows about evictions, about the operations of the Land League, and about the verdicts of juries, that the criminal law in Ireland has the sympathy of the people. Not only is this a matter of fact, but it is a matter of fact with which we are constantly dealing, which has run through three generations of men, and that almost without intermission.

We have tried expedients. What has been our great expedient? Our great expedient has been that to which I admit *prima facie* a government will first and justifiably resort. Our first expedient has been that which is known as repression or coercion. Has that class of experiment, has that class of expedient, been successful? I argued this point at full length in introducing the bill, and I will not argue it now at any detail whatsoever. I will only make this one assertion, which I believe to be absolutely undeniable—namely, that this medicine of coercion, if it be a medicine, is a medicine which we have been continually applying in increasing doses with diminishing results. When a physician has before him such a phenomenon as that he should direct his attention and his efforts to some other quarter and to some other method. We have—and I am glad to admit it—tried remedies. I see it stated sometimes that nothing has been so miserable a failure as the course of remedial legislation with respect to Ireland with which the members of the present government, and I myself for a long time, have been associated. I refer now to the removal of religious disabilities, to the disestablishment of the Church, to the reform of the Land Laws, and to the removal—or, if not the absolute removal, to the enormous mitigation—of the intolerable grievances, perhaps the worst of all after the land grievance, under which Ireland used to labor with respect to education.

If I am asked what I think of all these measures, I deny that they have failed. We have not failed, but we have not finished. They have had this effect—that the disease of Ireland has taken a different and a milder form. I am sorry to arouse scepticism whichever way I go. When I said just now that social order in Ireland was disturbed there were signs of dissent from honorable members opposite—and now when I say that the disease of Ireland has taken a milder form there are also signs of dissent, and it seems to me impossible that anything said by me can be true. My meaning is this—the disease of Ireland is in a milder form; but, in my opinion, it is in a form still extremely serious, and yet in a milder form than it took in 1832, when murders, excesses, and outrages were manifold to what they are now, so as to indicate a different state of things at the present time from what existed then and an undoubted growth of what are known as law-abiding habits—or I might go further back to the dreadful rebellion of 1798, which took a great effort on the part of this country

to put down. No, sir, that legislation has not failed. I
admit that it is incomplete, that it has not reached, that
it has not touched the goal, the terminating point of the
race we had to run, and something yet remains to be
done.

But there is another notion which has gone abroad.
I have spoken of former expedients and remedies, but
there is now a notion that something might be done by
judicious mixtures of coercion and concessions. These
judicious mixtures are precisely the very thing that we
have tried. Go back to the Roman Catholic emancipation
(1829). The Duke of Wellington made a judicious mixture
upon that occasion. He proposed that we should open the
doors of Parliament—and I am thankful he did so—to
the Roman Catholics of Ireland, but he at the same time
disfranchised the 40s. freeholder on the principle of judicious mixture. When Sir R. Peel in 1843–44 put Mr.
O'Connell on his trial, and succeeded in obtaining in Ireland a conviction which was afterward quashed on a point
of form that was a strong step in the direction of coercion—
but he followed it up immediately by the important act
(1845) for enlarging the endowment of Maynooth, by an
act for facilitating the granting of charitable bequests to the
Roman Catholic Church, and I must also say—although it
may shock some honorable gentlemen opposite—by a third
act, which was then viewed as a great boon to the Roman
Catholic interest—namely, the act for the foundation of
undenominational colleges. There was another case of
judicious mixture. It happened when we were disestab-
lishing the Church there was great disorder in Westmeath,
and in the middle, I think, of the Land Bill, we arrested
the progress of that measure and introduced a very strong

measure[1] of coercion for Westmeath, all on the principle
of judicious mixture. The government which came into
office in 1880 and which was put out of office in 1885—the
whole course of that government was nothing but one of
rigid and incessant effort of judicious mixtures. Therefore
do not let us suppose that the merit of novelty attaches to
that recommendation.

But I have seen another recommendation made, and
made, I think, by a person of very great authority, I believe in my hearing, to the effect that if we could only cast
away party spirit in dealing with Ireland we should do
well. Then, I think, a good many honorable members
opposite cheered, indicating that they were ready to cast
away party spirit. What is meant by this? Is it meant
that party spirit is to be expelled generally from the circuit
of English politics? Is that so? Is there a dreamer who,
in the wildness of his dreams, has imagined that you can
really work the free institutions of this country upon any
other principles than those in the main which your fathers
have handed down to you and which have made the country
what it is? Those cheers may be meant in sarcasm. I accept them in good faith. I believe that in uttering the
words that I have just used I have quite as strong a meaning, and I am ready to act upon the principle which I have
laid down quite as much, and perhaps a little more, than
a great many honorable members opposite who cheered. It
may be said, "We do not think you can get on altogether
without party spirit, but do at any rate cast out party spirit
from Irish affairs." Is that a more hopeful recommendation?

---

[1] The Peace Preservation (Ireland) Act, 1870.

It will be convenient to take the case of the two sides of the House separately, and first I ask is it desirable that the Tory party should cast out party spirit? I should say —undoubtedly. But if I should press it upon the right honorable gentleman opposite he would be entitled to make an answer to me which I should feel to be a crushing answer, because he would say, "Before you talk of casting away party spirit from the handling of Irish affairs you must show that it has been applied to those affairs in some sense different from, and in a more guilty and more mischievous manner than that in which it has been applied to other affairs." I will not speak of the last year or two, during which there may have been strong prejudices. I will go back half a century to the time when great resistance was offered, and I, as a humble and as a silent follower, had my share of responsibility for that resistance. I mean the resistance (1836–40) to the extension of the franchise in Ireland, especially of the municipal franchise. I deeply lament that opposition was ever offered; I may say *quorum pars exigua fui*. The conduct of the Tory party of that day, under Sir Robert Peel and the Duke of Wellington, Lord Stanley, and Sir James Graham, although very mistaken, was perfectly honest. I am not prepared to say that Irish affairs have been handled in this House, speaking generally, by either party with a larger admixture of party feeling or with a smaller flavor of true patriotic tone than other affairs of the country. It is idle to set up as remedies, as alternatives and as policies to adopt in great crises these suggestions which are totally visionary and unreal, and which never could become the basis of human action in a legislative assembly.

So much for experiment. Here I stand upon the ground

that a great necessity is before us, that a growing and urgent evil requires to be dealt with, that some strong and adequate application to the case is requisite, and that the whole and the only question is whether the application we propose is the right one. Let me say this upon this particular question of a legislature for Ireland, that it appears to be a very popular topic with our opponents, who say, "Why do you depart from the course taken by all the statesmen of the nineteenth century?" Now, let us see what has been done and said by all "the statesmen of the nineteenth century." The great case produced is the famous Repeal debate in 1834, in which I myself was one of the majority who voted against the repeal of the Union. A very remarkable passage from a very remarkable speech of Sir Robert Peel, well deserving to be kept fresh in the memory of posterity, from its terseness and power, has again become familiar to the people of this day, as I myself heard it with my own ears that day, with admiration. What was Sir Robert Peel then doing? In the first place, he was opposing the repeal of the Union. You call this repeal of the Union. You must at least allow us to have an opinion on that subject. For my part, I am not prepared at this moment to say that the question of the repeal of the Union should be reopened. I may be right or wrong in that matter, but my opinion is that Ireland has done much, by wisdom and moderation, by bringing her essential demands within certain limits, to facilitate the task set before us. But even if this were repeal of the Union, I admit, without the least question, that up to a certain point the Union is upon its trial. I admit, without the least question, that in my opinion this bill constitutes a most important modification of that act. But was Sir

Robert Peel in the same circumstances in 1834 as we found
ourselves in 1884? He had had one generation of experience; we have had nearly three. In the days when he
spoke, the statute book of England was loaded with a mass
of acts inflicting the most cruel grievances upon Ireland,
and it was a perfectly rational opinion for a man like Lord
Macaulay, who was deeply interested in Ireland, and other
politicians of his character, to think that by the removal
of those grievances you might save the Union. What was
then a matter of reasoning and speculation has now become
a matter of knowledge.

So Lord Macaulay is one who is quoted like Sir Robert
Peel. I remember well a passage of splendid eloquence delivered by Lord Macaulay against the repeal of the Union,
a Union of which I will not say anything more now than
that I do not desire to rake up the history of that movement—a horrible and shameful history, for no epithets
weaker than these can in the slightest degree describe or
indicate ever so faintly the means by which, in defiance of
the national sentiment of Ireland, consent to the Union was
attained. I think in 1834, or not very distant from that
date, Lord Macaulay, in words of burning eloquence, denounced the repeal of the Union. Macaulay, I think in
1859, or certainly many years later in his life, if not so late
as that, in his Life of Pitt, declared that the Union without
the measures which Mr. Pitt finally hoped to procure from
it—and to which in fact it became the greatest impediment—
without those measures the Union was union only in name,
and being a union only in name, it was in rank opposition
to all the national and patriotic sentiment of Ireland. How
was it possible that its authority could commend itself to the
people of that country? I do not admit that the question of

the Union, so far as it is now on its trial, has been decided, or has been touched, by statesmen of the nineteenth century. Those of whom I spoke never had before them what we have before us, the bitter fact, the rich though painful story of the experience which the rolling years of the last half century have afforded us.

Well, then, sir, we are told again with extraordinary boldness, "Why do you depart from the old Whig traditions?" If there is one thing more than another which my honorable friend the member for Bedford was doing in his admirable speech which he delivered on this subject, it was in showing that he was acting in strict consonance and conformity with the old Whig traditions. What were the old Whig traditions? The organs of that tradition were Mr. Sheridan and Lord Grey—the Lord Grey of that day—or rather the Mr. Grey of that day, afterward still more famous as Lord Grey. Then there were Lord Fitzwilliam, and, above all, Mr. Fox, and even above Mr. Fox himself there was Mr. Burke. Upon this great subject of the relations with Ireland Mr. Burke never modified by one hair-breadth the generous and wise declaration of his youth and of his maturer manhood. Mr. Burke did not live to the date of the Union, but he placed on record in the first place his political adhesion to the opinions of Mr. Grattan, and in the second place he placed upon record his full satisfaction with the state of things that prevailed in Ireland—the political state of things, especially the acts of 1782 and 1783,[1] and in a letter written not long before his lamented death, he said that he trusted that Ireland had seen the last of her revolutions. By that he meant that the act of 1782 did

---

[1] Whereby legislative independence was granted to Ireland.

amount to a revolution—a blessed and peaceful revolution, but still a revolution—a revolution effected by those peaceful means, by that bold and wise British statesmanship, such as in 1844, and again at a later period, was commended by Lord Beaconsfield.

It may be said with perfect truth that Lord Grey declined at a later date to be a party to the repeal of the Union. In that respect, in my opinion, he was perfectly consistent. For my own part, if I may refer to myself, I do not at all regret the vote which I gave fifty-two years ago against the repeal of the Union, considering what that repeal involved, and considering the amount of information we had with regard to its working. The Union, whatever may be our opinion with regard to the means by which it was obtained, was a statute of vast importance, for it modified and in many respects transformed the relations between Great Britain and Ireland. Such a statute as that cuts deep tracks in history; those tracks cannot be effaced in later times. But we are acting in most complete conformity with Whig traditions and the principles upon which Whig statesmen founded their action. They did not say that the principle of the Union between Great Britain and Ireland was abstractly bad; they did not say, "We in our minds are opposed to it, and therefore Ireland and Great Britain shall not have it"; but they said it was opposed to the sentiment of the Irish people. They said it was in opposition to all that was most honorable and upright, most respected, and most disinterested in Ireland, and nothing but mischief, nothing but disorder, nothing but dishonor, could come from a policy founded upon the overriding of all those noble qualities, and by means which would not bear the face of day, imposing the arbitrary will of the legislature upon the nation, in spite of its almost unanimous opposition.

Now, sir, it should be borne in mind that there was at that time in existence the greatest difference of sentiment from what we now witness in Ireland. The north was more opposed to the Union probably than the south. I remember that the town of Cork used to be quoted as a spot on which love of the Union might be detected by the careful observer. Unquestionably the promises held out by Mr. Pitt did induce a division of sentiment among the Roman Catholic clergy of that time. I believe that the Irish national patriotic sentiment which I have mentioned with sympathy was more vivid in the north of Ireland than in any other quarter.

Well, sir, honorable gentlemen say, "Do not talk to us about foreign countries; do not talk to us about British colonies; do not mention Canada—it has nothing whatever to do with the case. Canada is loyal and content; Ireland is disloyal and disaffected." But Sir Charles Gavan Duffy in an able paper[1] admits the charge. He says: "When it was determined to confer Home Rule on Canada, Canada was in the precise temper attributed to Ireland. She did not get Home Rule because she was loyal and friendly, but she is loyal and friendly because she got Home Rule." Now, sir, I am on this subject able to speak as a witness. I sat in Parliament during the whole of the Canadian controversy [1834–40], and I even took, what was for me as a young member, an active part in the discussions upon the subject. And what was that Canadian controversy? The case of Canada is not parallel to the case of Ireland. It

---

[1] "Mr. Gladstone's Irish Constitution," in the "Contemporary Review," May, 1886.

does not agree in every particular, and the bill which we offer to Ireland is different in many important particulars from the acts which have disposed of the case of Canada. But although it is not parallel, it is analogous. It is strictly and substantially analogous. What, sir, was the issue in the case of Canada? Government from Downing Street. These few words embrace the whole controversy—government from Downing Street being, of course, under the government of St. Stephen's.

What was the cry of those who resisted the concession of autonomy to Canada? It was the cry which has slept for a long time, and which has acquired vigor from sleeping—it was the cry with which we are now becoming familiar—the cry of the unity of the empire. Well, sir, in my opinion the relation with Canada was one of very great danger to the unity of the empire at that time, but it was the remedy for the mischief, and not the mischief itself, which was regarded as dangerous to the unity of the empire. Here I contend that the cases are precisely parallel, and that there is danger to the unity of the empire in your relations with Ireland; but unfortunately, while you are perfectly right in raising the cry, you are applying the cry and the denunciation to the remedy, whereas you ought to apply it to the mischief.

In those days what happened? In those days habitually in this House the mass of the people of Canada were denounced as rebels. Some of them were Protestants, and of English and Scotch birth. The majority of them were Roman Catholic, and of French extraction. The French rebelled. Was that because they were of French extraction and because they were Roman Catholics? No, sir; for the English of Upper Canada did exactly the same thing.

They both of them rebelled, and perhaps I may mention—
if I may enliven the strain of the discussion for a moment—
that I remember Mr. O'Connell, who often mingled wit and
humor with his eloquence in those days when the discussion
was going on with regard to Canada, and when Canada
was the one dangerous question—the one question which
absorbed interest in this country as the great question of
the hour—when we were engaged in that debate, Mr. O'Connell intervened, and referred to the well-known fact that a
French orator and statesman named Papineau had been the
promoter and the leader of the agitation in Canada; and
what said Mr. O'Connell? He said: "The case is exactly
the case of Ireland, with this difference, that in Canada the
agitator had got the 'O' at the end of his name instead of
at the beginning." Well, these subjects of her Majesty
rebelled—were driven to rebellion and were put down.
We were perfectly victorious over them, and what then
happened? Directly the military victory was assured—as
Mr. Burke told the men of the day of the American war
—the moment the military victory was assured the political
difficulty began. Did they feel it? They felt it; they gave
way to it. The victors were the vanquished, for if we were
victors in the field we were vanquished in the arena of
reason. We acknowledged that we were vanquished, and
within two years we gave complete autonomy to Canada.
And now gentlemen have forgotten that great lesson of
history. By saying that the case of Canada has no relation
to the case of Ireland, I refer to that little sentence written
by Sir Charles Duffy, who himself exhibits in his own person as vividly as anybody the transition from a discontented to a loyal subject. "Canada did not get Home
Rule because she was loyal and friendly, but she has

become loyal and friendly because she has got Home
Rule.''

Now I come to another topic, and I wish to remind you
as well as I can of the definition of the precise issue which
is at the present moment placed before us. In the introduction of this bill I ventured to say that its object was to establish, by the authority of Parliament, a legislative body
to sit in Dublin for the conduct of both legislation and administration under the conditions which may be prescribed
by the act defining Irish as distinctive from imperial affairs.
I laid down five, and five only, essential conditions which
we deemed it to be necessary to observe. The first was the
maintenance of the unity of the empire. The second was
political equality. The third was the equitable distribution
of imperial burdens. The fourth was the protection of minorities. And the fifth was that the measure which we proposed to Parliament—I admit that we must stand or fall by
this definition quite as much as by any of the others—that
the measure should present the essential character and char-
acteristics of a settlement of the question.

Well, sir, that has been more briefly defined in a resolution[1] of the Dominion Parliament of Canada, with which,
although the definition was simpler than my own, I am
perfectly satisfied. In their view there are three vital
points which they hope will be obtained, and which they
believe to be paramount, and theirs is one of the most
remarkable and significant utterances which have passed
across the Atlantic to us on this grave political question.

---

[1] "That . . . . this House earnestly hopes that such measures will be
adopted by the Imperial Parliament as will, while preserving the integrity
and well-being of the empire, and the rights and status of the minority, be
satisfactory to the people of Ireland, and as will permanently remove the
discontent so long unhappily prevailing in that country."

["Oh! oh!"] I just venture to put to the test the question of the equity of those gentlemen. You seem to consider that these manifestations are worthless. Had these manifestations taken place in condemnation of the bills and policy of the government, would they have been so worthless?

A question so defined—for the establishment of a legislative body to have effective control of legislation and administration in Ireland for Irish affairs, and subject to those conditions about which, after all, there does not appear in principle to be much difference of opinion among us—that is the question on which the House is called upon to give a vote, as solemn and as important as almost, perhaps, any in the long and illustrious records of its history.

Sir, in the interval which has taken place since the introduction of the bill much discussion has arisen upon a variety of its particulars, which I am very far from grumbling at or complaining of. One of them, however, is exciting so much feeling that it is quite necessary that it should receive the notice of my colleagues and of myself in the present debate. I mean that which relates to the exclusion or disappearance—for it really can hardly be called an exclusion when it is rather desired and sought for by the parties themselves—of the Irish members from the benches of this House.

Now, sir, in this explanation which I am about to give, I do not address myself to those who are hostile to the principle of this bill. I wish with all my heart I could say something without vitally prejudicing the public interests involved in this measure, that would tend to reconcile or to abridge the differences between her Majesty's Government and a body of gentlemen with whom hitherto they

have had the happiness of acting in as perfect concord—
allowing for the necessary freedom of human opinion and
the occasional differences that may arise—as ever consolidated together the different sections of the Liberal party.
Unhappily, sir, while I have the most cordial respect for
those gentlemen, I am not able to promise myself that they
will listen with much interest to what I have got to say.
There are others who, as I believe, accept not less cordially
than her Majesty's Government themselves what I have
declared to be the principle of this bill, and who at the
same time see greater difficulties than we do—though we
have seen great difficulties all along, and I never represented this measure as one in which all the points were
clearly indisputable. The case bristles with difficulties of
detail throughout, which only require good will and patient
intelligence to deal with, and different men feel them in
different modes and different degrees.

What has happened, sir, is this. I do not deny the fact
that many friends of this measure, whom we should be loth
indeed to alienate, have taken strong objection to the provisions with respect to the future absence of Irish members
from this House under two heads. In the first place, they
recall a proposition which I myself stated very strongly in
introducing the bill—namely, the great political principle
that there ought not to be taxation without representation.
In that I stated what was an obvious truth. It is quite
evident that we never would enforce upon Ireland taxation
without representation, and nothing but the consent of Ireland could have induced her Majesty's Government to
contemplate such a thing for a single moment. But many
gentlemen—and I do not find fault with them—are not
satisfied even with the consent of Ireland. Gentlemen will

recollect that though we now hear sometimes of persons
being more popish than the Pope, and many phrases of that
kind, the original phrase was *Hibernis ipsis Hiberniores*.
The meaning of that phrase was this—that those English
families, those portions of the English race, who went and
planted themselves among the Irishry, after a moderate time
became more Irish than the Irish themselves. We have
had that illustrated wholesale on the present occasion. I
must own that this is a difficulty which I regard with respect and with sympathy, and I trust that in any attempt
to meet it I shall have the sympathy of the House in general—at all events, of those who can on any terms tolerate
the principle of this bill. Besides that objection—which is
an objection strictly upon argumentative and constitutional
grounds as respects taxation—there is undoubtedly another
sentiment more vague, less definite, in a different region of
the human mind; there is a sentiment of regret that there
should cease to be a symbolical manifestation of the common concern of Ireland with ourselves in the unity of the
empire, and in the transaction of imperial affairs.

Well, now, sir, how do we stand with regard to this
case? First of all, let me say, however much it may appear
to be a paradox to English members, yet history undoubtedly teaches us that, to whatever cause it may be due,
foreign affairs, what I may call over-sea affairs, do not
stand in exactly the same relations to Ireland as they do
to England and Scotland. This is what I mean—I am not
raising any disputable proposition—I mean the feeling of
the people; and it appears to me perfectly natural that the
inhabitants of a country like Ireland, whose difficulties have
been so great, whose woes have been innumerable, whose
13 hopes have been intermittent and continually disappointed

—the history of a country like that must throw back the mind of the people upon itself and its own concerns, and in that way it is that I can understand why it is that Irish gentlemen do now—what we all do if we are men of common-sense in the common affairs of life—that is, we look to the principle, and do not think so much about objects which in our view are secondary as that which is central and essential, that which is central and essential being the management of Irish affairs. What I am now going to say has not had so much notice as it deserves. Ireland is not so entirely excluded by the bill as it stands from imperial affairs as gentlemen may be disposed to think. I refer, and I by no means refer alone, to the principle which is contained in the 39th clause of the bill—the clause which provides for the recall of Irish representatives of both Houses before this House can proceed to any alteration of the statute upon which the two legislatures are not in accord. I hope that is a provision which there will be little, if any, occasion for putting into action. But the principle involved is an important principle.

Besides that, there is another clause which provides that in certain circumstances the Irish Assembly may vote sums of money in relation to subjects which are excluded from its ordinary cognizance. This provision has been misunderstood to mean that the Irish legislative body might in certain circumstances vote money for the establishment of a Church.

Well, sir, I have really not examined whether the words of the statute will bear such a construction as has been put upon them. But if they bear such a construction, undoubtedly an effectual remedy ought to be applied. The meaning of the words is simply this—our belief in drawing

the act was this—that it might be felt right in the event—
as I trust the improbable—event of a great war, wherein
this country and Ireland were engaged with a common feeling and common interest, for the crown to send a message
to the Irish legislative body to ask them freely to testify
their participation in our interests and privileges by voting
money and supplies. [Laughter.] Some gentlemen differ
from me as to the measure by which they estimate the
ludicrous and the serious. My own estimates are sometimes in an inverse relation to theirs. What they think
ludicrous seems to me to be serious, and possibly *vice
versa*. It is supposed to be ridiculous that a practically
independent body in Ireland—yes, practically independent
in the regular exercise of its statutory functions—should
entertain such a proposal. But it was not ridiculous when
Ireland had an independent Parliament.

I said just now that it was a wonderful thing to see how
little in other days Ireland had interposed in foreign affairs.
I have had the debates looked up during the whole period
of Grattan's Parliament, and if I except certain discussions
relating to foreign treaties of commerce—I will speak of
that matter by and by—there are only two occasions upon
which that Parliament debated foreign affairs, so far as I
can discover. Both of those occasions are occasions on
which by message from the crown they were invited to
vote sums of money for purposes of war. One of them
was in 1790, when there was a seizure of British vessels
by Spanish men-of-war. A vote of money was then asked
and was given. The second was in 1795, when a contribution was asked toward the expenses of the French War.
On the first occasion the Irish Parliament granted the
money without question. I do not believe myself that

pecuniary illiberality has ever been a vice of Ireland. On the second occasion they granted it, but moved an amendment, full, I think, of good sense, hoping for a speedy conclusion of hostilities. For my part, I heartily wish that prayer of the Irish Parliament had been complied with. I take blame to myself for not having explained to the House the provision to which I have just referred—namely, the provision for the voting of money by the Irish legislative body in answer to the message from the crown. But my right honorable friend the Chief Secretary—Mr. John Morley—will bear me out when I say that after I had spoken I remarked to him that I regretted the omission of which I had been guilty.

Moreover, sir, although the statute will limit the legislative powers of the Irish legislative body, there are other moral powers of influence which it will possess, and which we do not and cannot limit. The privilege of free speech is not going to be taken away from Ireland—that privilege of free speech will attach to the members of this legislative body and to the legislative body collectively, and a considerable influence may be exercised upon proceedings at Westminster through resolution and by address from the legislative body.

However, sir, while I wish these provisions to be understood, I do not mean to limit what I have to say by reference to them. I wish to say what her Majesty's Government have thought to be their duty with regard to the feeling which has been copiously expressed in many portions of the country by gentlemen friendly to the principle of the bill. Undoubtedly it is our plain duty to consider how far we can go without prejudice to the main purpose of the bill to meet that desire. We shall do that upon grounds of policy, and upon grounds of principle. We shall make willing steps in that direction as far as duty will permit us to go. There are three things which I had better at once say we cannot do, and are unwilling to entertain in any shape. We are not willing to break up the parliamentary traditions of this House, or to introduce a principle of confusion into the working of the House. That is the first. The second is, we are not willing to fetter against its will the action of the Irish legislative body in any case except where cardinal and imperial interests require it. We will do nothing that shall have the effect of placing our measure in such a condition that Ireland, through her representatives, can only offer to it a qualified and a grudging, instead of a free, cordial assent and acceptance. And, third, we can do nothing that will have the effect of placing the committee of the bill before the second reading. That may be a phrase mysterious to some, but the meaning of it is this—that to determine in detail, even if upon points of importance, everything which is of great interest touching this bill, before you obtain assent to the principle of the bill, is not practicable; and if it be practicable, the rules of this House are based upon folly, for undoubtedly it would be much more convenient in many respects, before you are called upon to assent to the principle of a bill, to have it in the exact form in which it is to be finally adopted.

There is another thing to be considered, and it is this. It has very often happened to me in the course of a great experience in parliamentary legislation, that you hold communications with one class of gentlemen—you happen to be good-tempered or bad-tempered as the case may be—you feel a great desire to meet the views of that class of gentlemen, and you unwarily pledge yourself to propose the thing they desire. It is settled within the four walls of a private room. Then you come into this House, which happily—I thank God for it—is the place of the most thorough publicity in the whole world, and you find other sets of persons, quite as much entitled to be heard, who are at daggers drawn with the first. But the government has unwarily committed itself; and a quarrel ensues, while it is perfectly possible that if they had been allowed to reserve their discretion, and freely to consider the particulars in the committee, they might have been able to find means to conciliate those of opposite views, so as to bring about general satisfaction. What I mean is this, and I think the House will agree with me—I admit that when a thing is right, and when you see it to be practicable, you may promise before the second reading of a bill that if agreeable to the House you will do it. But we cannot do more than promise a fair consideration hereafter to a fair proposal, unless it is such a proposal as we can see our way to embodying in a workable shape. I do not think that is an unfair proposal. In violation of these three conditions we can do nothing. But we are ready and willing to do everything that they will allow.

Then I take the first objection that has been made to the proposed exclusion of the Irish representatives from this Parliament. It is that the principle that representation should accompany taxation would thereby be violated. Now what I am about to say involves a considerable responsibility; but the question whether and how far the difficulty may be met has been considered, and I am prepared to say that we can give full satisfaction to those who advance this objection. If agreeable to the

House, we will meet it in committee by providing that
when a proposal is made to alter the taxation in respect
of customs and excise, Irish members shall have an opportunity of appearing in this House to take a share in
the transaction of that business. It will then be impossible to urge against the bill that it is proposed by the
government that representation should not accompany
taxation.

In regard to such matters of common interest between
Great Britain and Ireland as those which form the subject
of foreign treaties, no doubt the objections urged from some
quarters may be met in some considerable degree by the
adoption of a system of executive communications, which
is the system adopted in certain foreign countries. There
are cases in which two countries are disunited in their
legislatures, but united in national action and feeling.
They find themselves able, by executive communications,
to provide for the common handling of common subjects.
But we do not feel that the plan of executive communications need of necessity be the only one. There are various plans which have been proposed in order to indicate
and maintain common action on imperial subjects, and
which are well worthy of consideration. For example,
it has been proposed that a joint commission should be
appointed representing the Houses of Parliament on this
side of the water, and representing the Irish legislative
body in due proportion of members, and that that commission should meet from time to time as occasion might
arise during the session of Parliament to consider common
questions and report their opinions to both legislative
bodies upon many, at any rate, of the imperial matters
that are reserved by the bill as it stands. I hesitate to

say upon "any" of those questions, for I incline to the belief, for example, that the question relating to the succession of the crown—in all the different branches of the subject—ought not to go to any secondary authority. But I can conceive that many subjects, such, for example, as treaties of commerce, might well be considered by a commission of this kind. I do not say of this plan as absolutely as I do of the plan as to taxation, that we are quite ready to propose it if it be the wish of Parliament, for it has been little canvassed, and objections may be raised to it which we have failed to anticipate: but I can say that we look at the proposal as one which might satisfy jealousies, might have other advantages, and is not open, so far as we know, to serious objection.

Another proposal is that a joint committee of the kind which I have described could be appointed to consider how far and upon what conditions other than those provided in the statute Irish members should come here. There is yet another suggestion, that Irish members might be entitled to come to Parliament—I assume generally that corresponding opportunity would be given to Irish peers—upon occasions when the legislative body should, by an address to the crown, have expressed a desire that they should do so. I do not say that that is open to objection on principle. At the same time, I see considerable difficulties as to the particular way of making it a practicable plan. I will, however, state broadly that it is our duty to give an unprejudiced ear to proposals which others may make for the purpose of insuring the continued manifestation of common interest between Great Britain and Ireland in imperial concerns. That end, we say distinctly, is a good end; means for attaining it we regard with favor, subject to the condi-

tion that they shall not be so handled as to introduce into
this House the principle of confusion, nor so handled as
to impose on the Irish legislative body limitations of its
liberty in any matters except such as affect high imperial
policy. (Lord R. Churchill asked whether the Irish members would reappear in their full numbers.) I am much
obliged to the noble lord. The clause now in the bill
contemplating the recall of the Irish representatives in a
certain contingency makes no difference from the present
arrangements as to the numbers in which they would
come. We do not feel that the subject involves a vital
principle, nor have we arrived at any binding decision;
but my own personal opinion is that if we were to bring
back the Irish members in any other numbers than the
present we should first have to devise a new system of
election, and I am not sure that it would be wise to com-
plicate the matter in that way. I should be inclined to
hope that, so far as it is desirable that Irish members should
reappear in Parliament, the Irish people would be liberally
and amply, rather than scantily and jealously, represented.

There is only one other subject to which I must advert.
We propose a change of which, if viewed as an abstract and
speculative change, the postponement for a year or even
longer would not have been a matter of vital consequence.
But this concession, if you like to call it so—in my view it
is something much higher than a concession, it is a great
reformation and improvement—this change is not proposed
upon grounds of general expediency alone, or in the view
of abstract improvement alone; it is proposed in order to
meet the first necessity of civilized society. Social order
is not broken up in Ireland, it is undermined, it is sapped,
and by general and universal confession it imperatively re-

quires to be dealt with. It is because this measure is one for the restoration of social order by the removal, not merely of the symptoms but of the cause of the mischief, that we recommend it to the consideration of Parliament. We are all agreed up to a certain point—(An honorable member: "No")—all except a solitary gentleman opposite. We all agree upon this, that social order in Ireland imperatively requires to be dealt with, but when we come to the method, then, unfortunately, our differences come into view. Were I to take all the individual opinions that have been expressed as to the mode of dealing with Irish questions, I should simply bewilder the House. I will only look at the main and leading divisions of power and influence in this assembly.

There are in the House two great parties, independently of the Irish party, and there is a third body, whom I will not call a party, because I am happy to think that as a party we are not yet divided from them, and I trust may never be. But we are vitally divided on this great and significant question from those whom I will not call a party, but whom I must call a body, but who are so important that they may possibly hold the balance and decide the question between the two great British parties in this House. The mass of the Irish representatives have committed in the eyes of many gentlemen opposite a new, a mortal offence—an offence more deadly than any former offence. They have committed the offence of agreeing with us in this matter. As long as their favors were bestowed in another quarter [1] great toleration was to be expected, and was

---

[1] The Council of Irish Nationalists called upon their fellow-countrymen in Great Britain to vote against the Liberals at the general election of November, 1885.

happily experienced, by them from those who are now very
much shocked in their highest moral qualities at our alliance
with the Irish party, which alliance amounts simply to a coincidence of views on a great vital and determining public
question.

Of the two political parties in the House both have
spoken and spoken plainly. I do, indeed I must, admire
the tact, the caution, I will not say the astuteness, with
which most of the leaders of the Tory party have abstained
from overmuch hurrying themselves with forecasts of the
future, or pledges as to the mode of meeting it, with regard to the Irish question. Finding that they had on this
side of the House allies—I do not use the word in an invidious sense, it is the same kind of alliance that there is
with gentlemen from Ireland—that is to say, it is an honorable and conscientious coincidence of opinion—finding that
they had allies of that kind ready to do their work, with
equal politeness and wisdom, they have left the doing of
that work to them. But notwithstanding that, they have
spoken and spoken plainly for themselves. When the
noble lord the member for Paddington [Lord Randolph
Churchill] was brought to the point, and when it was said
he had not declared a policy, he pointed—and he was justified in pointing—not even to a phrase, but to a date, and
he said: "Our policy is the 26th of January." [1] I accept
that reply from the noble lord. It is true and it is just,
and that was, and that is, the declaration of policy for
Ireland from the Tory party.

---

[1] On that day the late government gave notice that a bill would be introduced "for the purpose of suppressing the National League and other dangerous associations, for the prevention of intimidation and for the protection of life,
property, and public order in Ireland."

I remember, and many others may recollect, the fervid and almost endless cheering with which the gentlemen then sitting on this side of the House accepted the announcement of the 26th of January. That is a plain, manly, and straightforward announcement. What was it? The notice did not convey, and we could not expect that it should convey, a full description of the proposals that were to be made; but it so far described them that it indicated one point with perfect clearness, and that was the suppression of the National League. I may say, in parenthesis, that I trust that we shall be suppressors of the National League. That, if it comes about, will certainly be by a different process. The suppression of the National League —what does it mean and what does it come to?

A noble friend of mine [Earl Cowper], to whom I refer with the greatest respect, when he held office in Ireland, said: "We want to drive discontent under the ground." I own I thought at the time that that expression was what is called a slip of the tongue and I suppose there is no man among us who does not occasionally slip into that form of error. But if, instead of its being a slip of the tongue, it is exalted into a policy, then what is the meaning of the suppression of the National League? It is the conversion of the proceedings of that body—which I am not now called upon to discuss or characterize—it is the conversion of the proceedings of that body, taken daringly but openly in the face of day, into the proceedings of secret societies—the last resort in this and other countries of the extreme and hopeless difficulties of political problems; and, in my opinion, nothing is to be gained by procuring and bringing about the substitution of the secret communities for the open action of a body like the National League.

It is sought apparently to take away discontent from the surface. We are not contented with so limited an ambition. We desire to take away discontent neck and crop. We desire to abolish it root and branch, or, if I may once more put into requisition a phrase which had its day, we desire to abolish Irish discontent "bag and baggage." I do not believe that Parliament would pass a proposal for the abolition, in the present circumstances, of the National League. If it did pass such a proposal, in my opinion it is doubtful whether it would have made any contribution whatever to a real solution of the Irish difficulty; whether, on the contrary, it would not have administered a new aggravation to it. However that may be, I own that that party has spoken plainly, and their policy is summed up in the words "repression or coercion."

When this government was formed it was formed on the principle of looking for some method of dealing with Ireland other than by the method of coercion; and that policy has now taken definite form and shape in the proposal of autonomy for Ireland. You have spoken plainly and we have spoken plainly. Has the third power in the House spoken plainly? Has that power which is to hold the scales, and which may decide the issue, told the country in what manner, when it is forced to face this tremendous problem, it intends to deal with it?

There are few men in this House, I am sure there is no man outside of it, who does not admire the temper and the courage with which my noble friend the member for Rossendale has behaved on this question. In obedience to his conscience, and to his conscience alone, he has rent asunder with pain, and perhaps with agony, party ties to which he has been among the most faithful of all adherents. And

speaking generally of those who act with him, I believe
that in their several spheres the same may be said of them.
Nor do I feel, although I may lament that they have come
under what I think are narrow and blind influences, that
their titles to my respect are one whit diminished by what
they have said or done. I make these admissions freely
and without stint. My noble friend has assumed an immense responsibility. It is not for me to find fault with
those who assume immense responsibility. My responsibility in this matter is perhaps even greater than his. Next
to mine, and you will never find me here to extenuate it, I
know no subject of her Majesty that has a greater load of
responsibility upon him than my noble friend. I do not
blame, I have no title to blame, him. All honor and praise
to him for his undertaking the task which I know to be of
enormous difficulty. But it may be a task of leading the
determining and superior forces of parliamentary opinion
toward a conclusion on the Irish question. If that is so,
I ask what does he mean to do? Has not the time arrived
when we ought to know what his policy is to be?

I have endeavored to search it out by such means as I
could. Is it to be the policy announced to the Loyalist
minority at Belfast in November last? (A Home Rule
Member: "So-called 'Loyalist minority.'") I assume the
phrase. In politics I like to give to every class of men
the name by which they like to be called. Well, sir, in
Belfast my noble friend made very considerable promises
on the 5th of last November, and he said an extremely
bold thing—"I should not shrink," he said, "from a great
and bold reconstruction of the Irish government." Well,
all I can say is this, that we who are now the government
are exceedingly daring; but our daring is nothing like

yours. The man who will undertake to reconstruct the Irish government without touching the legislative principle from which administrative government derives its life, if he is not "a traitor or a fool"—these are words not ours, but are reserved for gentlemen quite different from us—he is either a magician or a man not much accustomed to the practical transaction of public affairs.

That is not all, sir. My noble friend did not stop by promising, in the exuberance of his zeal, that which I am convinced is absolutely impossible—namely, to reconstruct the Irish government for any practical purpose without providing a new spring of action, which can only be provided on the principle of the policy we propose. But my noble friend did not promise absolutely the principle of the policy we propose, because he said that nothing could be done in the direction of giving Ireland anything like complete control over her own affairs, either in a day or a session or perhaps a parliament. But he pointed to the means by which it was to be done—namely, by the work of time, by the growth of small beginnings the superstructure was to be raised on a wise and sound foundation. Yes, but what is the principle really at issue between us? It is this, not whether we are right in proposing at one step to give to Ireland complete control of her own affairs, but whether it is a thing right to be done at all. At Belfast in November my noble friend in this passage implied that it might be a thing right to be done. To-night he is to move that it is a thing wrong to be done. What, then, is his policy? I am sorry to think that since November the movement of my noble friend has not been forward, but rather, as it appears to me, backward. We have heard nothing since November of this complete reconstruction of the Irish government, and the gradual progress on a sound foundation of a well-built structure. But I rejoice in that declaration on one ground—namely, that it implies that the complete control by Ireland of her own affairs is a thing which may be contemplated, and that, in the view of my noble friend, it is a thing compatible with the unity of the empire. Therefore I am convinced that it is not a thing to be renounced *ab initio*—to be renounced and proscribed as a something tending to disintegrate and break up the unity of the empire.

I confess that I do not believe in this gradual superstructure. I believe the meaning of it would be, if practicable, that a series of boons would be offered to Ireland, every one of which would, with an enormous loss of parliamentary time and temper, and with an immense obstruction of public business, be either entirely repudiated by Ireland, or be received in a grudging temper and with the fullest notification that whatever power of that kind you gave her would be used simply as an instrument for acquiring more power. I am very disinterested upon that subject. I should have disappeared from the scene while my noble friend's process was in a very early stage indeed. But I own I do not believe that that is the wisest method of dealing with the great Irish question. I believe we have reached one of those crises in the history of nations where the path of boldness is the path, and the only path, of safety. At least we have come to a time when there is one thing we ought to know, and that is our own minds. We ought to know and we ought to tell our minds. There is another thing which I hold to be essential—we ought not to take this great Irish question, and cast the fate of Ireland into the lottery of politics. I think it is obvious that I am not open to the reproach of casting the fate of Ireland into the lottery of politics, because what you tell me is that I am steering Ireland to utter destruction and certain ruin. If we are proposing to drive Ireland down the cataract, point out to us the way of escape. Is it really to be supposed that the last declaration of my noble friend, which was the keeping alive of two or three clauses of the Crimes Act, which we intended to have kept in existence had we remained in office last year—is that really the policy for Ireland? To that no assent, no approval has been given from the important party opposite.

Sir, Parliament is entitled to know at this time of day the alternatives that are open to its choice. You say that we offer the alternative of ruin. At any rate, in our view it is of a very different character. But even in your view, it is a definite proposal, which is our justification on its behalf, and is the only contribution which we can make to the solution of the question. Parliament is entitled to have before it the alternatives proposed—the alternatives of policy, not of plan, proposed by those who are taking steps which may in certain contingencies with high probability bring into their hands the supreme direction of affairs. The Tory party have announced their policy. Repression—the 26th of January. That is a policy I understand. Here I know with whom, and with what, I have to deal. But as regards my noble friend, I must say that I am totally ignorant with whom, and with what, I am dealing, so far as policy is concerned. I hope that the notice he has given for to-night has been given with the intention of tracing out for us a palpable and visible road into the darkness, and that he will tell us on what principle it is that he proposes to make provision for the government of Ireland. Let us know these alternatives. The more they are examined the better I believe it will be for us all. It will become reasonably clear—I won't say to demonstration—that we have before us a great opportunity of putting an end to the controversy of 700 years—ay, and of knitting together, by bonds firmer and higher in their character than those which heretofore we have mainly used, the hearts and affections of this people and the noble fabric of the British Empire.

HOME RULE

HOUSE OF COMMONS, JUNE 7, 1886

MR. SPEAKER—I shall venture to make, sir, a few remarks on the speech of the right honorable gentleman,[1] but I will first allow myself the satisfaction of expressing what I believe to be a very widespread sentiment, and saying with what pleasure I listened to two speeches this evening—the singularly eloquent speech of the senior member for Newcastle and the masterly exposition—for I cannot call it less—of the honorable member for Cork. Sir, I feel a strong conviction that speeches couched in that tone, marked alike by sound statesmanship and farseeing moderation, will never fail to produce a lasting effect upon the minds and convictions of the people of England and Scotland. Sir, with respect to the personal question which has arisen between the honorable member for Cork and the right honorable gentleman opposite, I think it no part of my duty to interfere. I have avoided, and I shall avoid, in the discussion of this

---

[1] Sir Michael Hicks-Beach, in the course of whose speech Mr. Parnell had referred to his communication with Lord Carnarvon.

question, so far as I can, all matters which are of a purely polemical character between party and party. I presume that this subject will be carried further. I understand a distinct allegation to be made by the honorable member for Cork with regard to some person, whose name he does not give, but who is one of a limited body. In that limited body it will not be difficult, I conclude, to procure it if it can be given. Upon that I pass no judgment. I simply make this comment upon a subject which is of considerable public interest. The right honorable gentleman opposite will do me the justice to say that I have not sought, before taking office or since taking it, to make the conduct which right honorable gentlemen opposite pursued on their accession to power, matter of reproach against them. If they do not like to do me that justice I shall not ask it.

On the speech of the right honorable gentleman I need not dwell at great length. He began by stating a series of what he succinctly described as simple facts. I will not say his simple facts are pure fictions, because that would hardly, perhaps, be courteous. But they are as devoid of foundation as if they had been pure fiction. The right honorable gentleman declared—though I do not see that it has much to do with the matter—that this is the bill of one man. Well, I am amazed that the right honorable gentleman speaks as if he had been at my elbow all day and every day through the autumn and winter of last year. How can any man know that this is the bill of one man? (A laugh.) How can the honorable member who laughs know that this is the bill of one man? Reference is made to the allegations of my right honorable friend the member for West Birmingham. My right honorable friend could only speak within the compass of his knowledge, and if he said that it was the bill of one man he would know no more about it than the honorable member opposite. What my right honorable friend said, and said truly, was to state the time at which the bill came before the Cabinet. But, sir, long before that time the subject of the bill and its leading details had been matter of anxious consideration between me and my nearest political friends. (Cries of "Name!") I never heard a more extraordinary demand in my life, not to say gross impropriety. I refer to those of my colleagues who were most likely to give the most valuable aid, and with whom from the first I was in communication. Then, sir, the right honorable gentleman says we were installed in office by the help of the honorable member for Cork. The right honorable gentleman appears to have forgotten the elementary lessons of arithmetic. It is perfectly true that the energetic assistance of the honorable member for Cork might have kept the right honorable gentleman in office. The right honorable gentleman speaks of the party behind him and the Liberal party, as it then was on this side of the House, as if they had been two equal parties, and only required the honorable member for Cork and his friends to turn the scale. (Lord Randolph Churchill: "They were.") They were, says the noble lord! The noble lord's arithmetic is still more defective—335 is by 85 votes a larger party than 250. Then the right honorable gentleman says that, with the exception of the customs and excise duties, no change was made in the bill after it was first submitted to the Cabinet. He has no means of knowing that, even if it were true, but it happens to be entirely untrue. Provisions of great importance had never been seen by my right honorable friend the member for West Birmingham. My right honorable friend took ex-

ception to certain provisions of the bill without being
acquainted with the whole *corpus* of the bill. That is the
fact; so that the right honorable gentleman is entirely
wrong also upon this as well as upon his other "simple
facts." Then the right honorable gentleman says that I
had announced that this bill was not to be reconstructed.
I announced that I did not promise that it should be reconstructed. (A laugh.) There are actually gentlemen opposite—members of Parliament chosen to represent the country—who think this a matter of laughter, and can see no
distinction between promises that a bill shall not be reconstructed, and not having promised that it shall be. I conceive that a person who has promised that a bill shall be
reconstructed is bound to reconstruct it. Is that true?
A person who has not promised that a bill shall be reconstructed is free to reconstruct it, but is not bound to do
so. I hope I have made a clear distinction; and I am glad
to see that the laughter opposite has ceased as light has
flowed in upon the minds of those honorable gentlemen.
I was struck with another observation of the right honorable gentleman. He says that this bill, whatever else may
happen, will at any rate be rejected by the votes of a majority of English and Scotch members—(Opposition cheers)
—and he is cheered by those who teach us that they are,
above all things, anxious for the maintenance of an absolutely united kingdom, and an absolutely united parliament, in which Irish members are in all respects to be
assimilated to, and identical with, those representing English and Scotch constituencies. The right honorable gentleman talks about a dissolution, and I am glad to find that
upon that point he and we are much more nearly associated
in our views and expectations than upon almost any other

point. After what the right honorable gentleman has said,
and the want of acquaintance which he has shown with the
history of this bill, on which he dwelt so long, and after
what was said by my right honorable friend behind me
[Mr. Goschen], I must again remind the House, at any
rate, in the clearest terms I can use, of the exact position
in which we stand with reference to the bill. In the first
place, I take it to be absolutely beyond dispute, on broad
and high parliamentary grounds, that that which is voted
upon to-night is the principle of the bill as distinguished
from the particulars of the bill. What may be the principle of the bill, I grant you freely I have no authority to
determine. (A laugh.) The honorable member laughs; I
am much obliged for his running commentary, which is not
usual, on my observations, but it is our duty to give our
own sense of the construction of the principle of the bill,
and I think I drew a confirmation of that construction from
the speech of the right honorable gentleman, because he
himself said this was a bill for the purpose of establishing
a legislative body in Ireland for the management of Irish
affairs. Well, sir, that—if we have any power or any title
to give our view on the subject—is the principle of the
bill. As respects the principle of the bill, I apprehend it
to be beyond all question that members voting for the
principle of the bill are in this sense entirely and absolutely free—that if they consider that there is another set
of provisions by means of which better and fuller effect
may be given to the principle of the bill, they are at liberty
to displace all the particulars they find in it which hinder
that better and fuller effect being given to the principle.
(A laugh.) That does not admit of doubt. I am quite
certain the honorable member who laughs will not rise in

his place at any time and say that a member is not at
liberty to remove each and all, if he thinks fit, of the particulars of the bill, if in good faith he believes that the
principle of the bill can be better and more adequately
promoted by a different set of provisions. But the government have taken certain engagements. They have taken
an engagement as to taxation for the intervention of Irish
members, to the terms of which I need not refer. They
have also taken an engagement on the claim of Ireland to
a continued concern through her members in the treatment
of imperial subjects generally. And that has entailed a
positive pledge to reconstruct the 24th clause, and to adopt
certain consequential amendments connected with it. One
more question has been raised, and has excited a deep
interest—and that is with respect to other amendments to
the bill. Of course as to the freedom of honorable members
to suggest other amendments, I have spoken in terms which,
I think, are abundantly large. As respects our duty, there
can be no question at all that our duty, if an interval is
granted to us, and the circumstances of the present session
require the withdrawal of the bill, and it is to be re-intro-
duced with amendments at an early date in the autumn—of
course it is our duty to amend our bill with every real
amendment and improvement, and with whatever is calculated to make it more effective and more acceptable for the
attainment of its end. It is, as a matter of course, and
without any specific assurance, our duty to consider all
such amendments. We are perfectly free to deal with
them; but it would be the meanest and basest act on the
part of the government to pretend that they have a plan
of reconstruction ready beforehand, cut and dry in their
minds, at a time when, from the very nature of the case, it

must be obvious that they can have no such thing. So much then for the situation, for the freedom of members to propose amendments, for the duty of the government to consider amendments and improve their bill, if they can, with the view of a fuller and better application of the principle; but subject, let me add, to conditions—five in number—which have been clearly enumerated on a former occasion, and from which there is no intention on our part to recede. The right honorable gentleman speaks of Ulster as a question of principle. The question of Ulster, or whatever the common name of the question may be, may be one of great importance; but I must say that while I in no respect recede from the statement made in regard to it at the opening of these debates, yet I cannot see that any certain plan for Ulster has made any serious or effective progress.

The honorable and gallant gentleman, the member for North Armagh, emphatically disclaims the severance of Ulster from the rest of Ireland, and the honorable member for Cork has laid before us a reasoned and elaborate argument on that subject to-day, which, as it appears to me, requires the careful attention of those who propose such a plan for our acceptance. We retain, however, perfect freedom to judge the case upon its merits. Now, sir, I want to say a word upon the subject of Irish loyalism, because we are obliged to use phrases in debates of this kind which cannot be explained from time to time when using them, and it is well that there should be a little understanding beforehand. When I hear the speeches of the honorable member for South Belfast and of some other gentlemen it always appears to me that he is under the pious conviction that loyalty is innate in the Irish Protestants, and disloyalty innate in—some other persons. I do believe that he is under the impression that at all times, in all the long generations of Irish history, that has been the distinction to be drawn between Protestants and persons who are not Protestants. Is Protestant loyalism a thing that has a date and origin, or is it not? Has the honorable member, or the honorable and gallant member for North Armagh, inquired what was the state of Ireland in the eighteenth century with respect to loyalty? As far as regarded the great mass of the population—the Roman Catholic population—they were hardly born into political life until the close of the century; and for a long period, in the time of Dean Swift, who describes their incapacity for political action as something beyond belief, it would have been absurd to speak of them as loyal or disloyal. But at the close of the century the Protestants and Roman Catholics of Ireland were described in a short passage by Mr. Burke, which I shall now read to the House. The date of it is 1797, and it is taken from a letter to Mr. Windham. He speaks of the subject of disaffection. "It"—that is to say disaffection—"has cast deep roots in the principles and habits of the majority among the lower and middle classes of the whole Protestant part of Ireland. The Catholics who are intermingled with them are more or less tainted. In the other parts of Ireland (some in Dublin only excepted) the Catholics, who are in a manner the whole people, are as yet sound; but they may be provoked, as all men easily may be, out of their principles."

What does that show? That the Protestants, not having grievances to complain of, have become loyal; but in many cases the Roman Catholics have been provoked, as Mr. Burke says all men easily may be, out of their principles of loyalty. And these are words, and these are ideas, which show us what is the way in which to promote loyalty, and what is the way in which we can destroy it.

Another subject on which I shall dwell only for a moment is that of federation. Many gentlemen in this House are greatly enamored of this idea, and the object they have in view is a noble object. I will not admit the justice of the disparagement cast by the right honorable gentlemen on the British empire. I do not consider that this is a "loosely connected empire." But I admit that, if means can be devised of establishing a more active connection with our distant colonies, the idea is well worthy the attention of every loyal man. The idea of federation is a popular one. I will give no opinion upon it now; but I suspect that it is beset with more difficulties than have as yet been examined or brought to light. But this bill, whatever be its rights or wrongs in any other respect, is unquestionably a step—an important step—in that direction. Federation rests essentially upon two things, and upon two things alone, as preconditioned. One is the division of legislature, and the other is the division of subjects, and both those divisions are among the vital objects of this bill. The right honorable gentleman has referred to the question of supremacy. My own opinion is that this debate has, in a considerable degree, cleared the ground upon that subject. It is most satisfactory to me to hear the statements of the honorable member for Cork. I own I have heard some astounding doctrines—astounding to an ignorant layman—from learned lawyers; but still, upon the whole, the balance of authority seems to me to have established, as a clear and elementary proposition that cannot be denied that this Parliament, be it the imperial Par-

liament or not, as long as it continues in its legal identity,
is possessed now, as it was possessed before the Union and
before the time of Grattan's Parliament, of a supremacy
which is absolutely, and in the nature of things inalienable, which it could not part with if it would, and which
it would not part with if it could. There is no doubt a
practical question, because it is quite true that in constituting a legislature in Ireland we do what we did when
we constituted a legislature for Canada and for Australia.
We devolve an important portion of power—we did it in
Canada, and I hope we shall do it in Ireland—and we devolve it with a view to not a partial, not a nominal, but a
real and practical independent management of their own
affairs. That is what the right honorable gentleman objects to doing. That is the thing which we desire and
hope and mean to do. It is obvious that the question
may be raised, How are you to deal with the possible
cases where the imperial government, notwithstanding this
general division of affairs, may be compelled by obligations of imperial interest and honor to interfere? My answer is that this question has received a far better solution
from practical politics, and from the experience of the last
forty or fifty years, than could ever have been given to it
by the definition of lawyers, however eminent they may
be. When the legislature of Canada was founded this
difficulty arose. We had the case of the Canadian Rebellion, where I myself, for one, was of opinion, and Lord
Brougham was also of opinion—I know not now whether
rightly or wrongly—that the honor of the crown had been
invaded by the proposition to grant compensation for losses
in the rebellion to those who had been rebels, and who had
incurred those losses as rebels. I say nothing now about

our being right or wrong; but in 1849 Lord Brougham brought forward a motion on the subject in the House of Lords, and I myself did the same in the House of Commons. The important part was the declaration which was drawn from Ministers of the crown. Lord John Russell then, in answer to me, laid down what I conceive to be a true and sound doctrine, in terms which, I think, may be described as classical and authoritative in their manner of dealing with this question. Lord Russell, speaking on the 14th of June, 1849, said—"I entirely concur with the right honorable gentleman—and it is, indeed, in conformity with the sentiments I expressed in a despatch written, I think, some ten years ago—that there are cases which must be left to the decision of the responsible Ministers of the crown. There are cases where the honor of the crown and the safety of this country are concerned, and in such cases it requires the utmost temper in the colonies, and the utmost temper and firmness in this country, in order to prevent differences from being pushed to a collision which might be fatal to the connections between the mother country and the colonies. I fully admit that there are such cases; but when the right honorable gentleman goes on to say that he considers the Earl of Elgin has received some instructions from the government of this country by which he is debarred from asking the advice and direction of the crown upon questions which affect imperial policy and the national honor, he is totally mistaken in that unwarranted assumption."

That passage, as I believe, contains, very justly and clearly set forth, the practical mode by which this question, difficult in the abstract, will be settled now as it has been settled before; and we shall find that as it has been perfectly easy to reconcile the rights of Canada with the supremacy of the imperial Parliament, it will not be less easy in practice to reconcile the rights and the autonomy of Ireland with the same supremacy.

I wish now to refer to another matter. I hear constantly used the terms Unionists and Separatists. But what I want to know is, Who are the Unionists? I want to know who are the Separatists? I see this bill described in newspapers of great circulation and elsewhere, as a Separation Bill. Several gentlemen opposite adopt and make that style of description their own. Speaking of that description, I say that it is the merest slang of vulgar controversy. Do you think this bill will tend to separation? Well, your arguments, and even your prejudices, are worthy of all consideration and respect; but is it a fair and rational mode of conducting a controversy to attach these hard names to measures on which you wish to argue, and on which I suppose you desire to convince by argument? Let me illustrate. I go back to the Reform Act of Lord Grey. When that Reform Bill was introduced, it was conscientiously and honestly believed by great masses of men, and intelligent men, too, that the bill absolutely involved the destruction of the monarchy. The Duke of Wellington propounded a doctrine very much to this effect; but I do not think that any of those gentlemen, nor the newspapers that supported them, ever descended so low in their choice of weapons as to call the measure "The Monarchy Destruction Bill." Such language is a mere begging of the question. Now, I must make a large demand on your patience and your indulgence—we conscientiously believe that there are Unionists and Disunionists; but that it is our policy that leads to union and yours to separation. This involves a very large and deep historical question. Let us try for a few moments to look at it historically. The arguments used on the other side of the House appear to me to rest in principle and in the main upon one of two suppositions. One of them, which 1 will not now discuss, is the profound incompetency of the Irish people; but there is another, and it is this. It is, I believe, the conscientious conviction of the honorable gentlemen opposite, that when two or more countries, associated, but not incorporated together, are in disturbed relations with each other, the remedy is to create an absolute legislative incorporation. On the other hand, they believe that the dissolution of such an incorporation is clearly the mode to bring about the dissolution of the political relations of those countries. I do not deny that there may be cases in which legislative incorporation may have been the means of constituting a great country, as in the case of France. But we believe, as proved by history, that where there are those disturbed relations between countries associated, but not incorporated, the true principle is to make ample provision for local independence, subject to imperial unity. These are propositions of the greatest interest and importance. Gentlemen speak of tightening the ties between England and Ireland as if tightening the ties were always the means to be adopted. Tightening the tie is frequently the means of making it burst, while relaxing the tie is very frequently the way to provide for its durability, and enable it to stand a stronger strain; so that it is true, as was said by the honorable member for Newcastle, that the separation of legislatures is often the union of countries, and the union of legislatures is often the severance of countries.

Can you give me a single instance from all your historical inquiries where the acknowledgment of local independence has been followed by the severance of countries? [Cries of "Turkey!" "Servia!"] I was just going to refer to those countries, and to make the admission—that what I have said does not apply where a third power has intervened, and has given liberty, in defiance of the sovereign power, to the subject state. But do you propose to wait until some third power shall intervene in the case of Ireland, as it intervened in the case of America? [An honorable member: "We are not afraid."] I never asked the honorable gentleman whether he was afraid. It does not matter much whether he is afraid or not; but I would inculcate in him that early and provident fear which, in the language of Mr. Burke, is the mother of safety. I admit that where some third power interferes, as France interfered in the case of America, you can expect nothing to result but severance, with hostile feeling on both sides. But I am not speaking of such cases. That is not the case before us. But I ask you to give me a single instance where, apart from the intervention of a third power, the independence of the legislatures was followed by the severance of the nations. I can give several instances where total severance of countries has been the consequence of an attempt to tighten the bond—in the case of England and America, in the case of Belgium and Holland. The attempt to make Belgians conform to the ways and ideas and institutions of Holland led to the severance of the two countries. In the case of Denmark and the Duchies, they long attempted to do what, perhaps, gentlemen would wish much to do in Ireland—namely, to force Danish institutions and ideas on the Duchies.

Those long attempts ended, as we all know, together with the insufficient acknowledgment of the ancient institutions of those Duchies, in the total loss of those Duchies to Denmark, and their incorporation in another political connection. But let us not look simply to the negative side. Where local independence has been acknowledged and legislative severance has been given, there, in a number of cases, it has been made practicable to hold countries together that otherwise could not have been held together, and the difficulties which existed either have been lessened or altogether removed. The world is full of such cases. (An honorable member: "Turkey.") An honorable gentleman imprudently interrupted me by calling out "Turkey." I am going to tell him that in Turkey, with its imperfect organization, in cases where there has not been violent interference, where the matter has not been driven to a point to provoke armed interference by a foreign power, local autonomy has been tried, and tried with the best effect. In the island of Crete, which twenty years ago appeared to be almost lost to Turkey, loosening the ties to Constantinople has immensely improved the relations between the Sultan and that island. (Lord Randolph Churchill—"Chronic revolution.") Chronic revolution! What are the tests of chronic revolution? Has it paid its tribute? Has it called for the armed force of Turkey to put down revolt? Then I will take another case, the case of the Lebanon. That was the subject of international arrangement twenty-three or twenty-four years ago. The Lebanon was in chronic revolution, and was under the absolute sway of Constantinople. The Lebanon was placed under a system of practical local independence, and from that day to this it has never been a trouble

to Turkey. In a case more remarkable, the case of the island of Samos, which has enjoyed for a length of time, I believe, a complete autonomy, and in which, singular as it may seem, it has never been possible to create disorder, a real attachment to the Turkish empire, or, at any rate, a contentment with the political tie, subsists and holds that country in tranquillity, so that even Turkey bears testimony to the principle of which I speak. There are numbers of other cases. The case of Norway and Sweden is most remarkable, because of these two countries the stronger and more populous can hardly hope to have power to coerce the weaker—two countries completely separate, having absolutely no connection of legislative or executive government, and united together recently—only sixty years ago. That union has been found practicable, and practicable only, by means of granting a just autonomy and independence. Take the case of Denmark and Iceland. (Laughter.) Laughter is, with honorable gentlemen opposite, a very common weapon now, and it is very difficult for me to contend with it at this period of my life. Perhaps twenty, thirty, or forty years ago I could have defended myself against it with more ease. It has been said that the Parliament of Iceland has been dissolved, and that there have been difficulties. Well, there have been difficulties between the Parliament of Iceland and the crown of Denmark. The crown of Denmark is, unhappily, in difficulties with the legislative body of Denmark, but between the legislative body of Denmark and the legislative body of Iceland there have been, I believe, no difficulties. When my honorable friend, the Under Secretary of State for Foreign Affairs [Mr. Bryce], in his
14 admirable speech, quoted the case of Iceland, honorable

gentlemen opposite, with their usual method of rebuke, laughed; and some one, endeavoring to dignify, adorn, and decorate that laughter with an idea, called out, "Distance; Iceland is so distant." Well, if it is so distant, I apprehend that that makes it a great deal more difficult for Denmark to hold her down by force, and therefore more necessary for her to choose the methods which are most likely to secure contentment and tranquillity. But if you object to the case of Iceland on account of distance, what do you say to the case of Finland? Is that country distant from Russia? Are you aware that the social and political difficulties, which have so often threatened the peace of Russia, and which were fatal not many years ago to the life of one of the best and worthiest of her sovereigns, have no place in Finland? Why? Because Finland has perfect legislative autonomy, the management of her own affairs, the preservation of her own institutions. That state of things has given contentment to Finland, and might be envied by many better known and more famous parts of the world. But the case of Austria is, perhaps, the most remarkable of all. I will not refer now to Austria and Hungary further than to say that I believe my right honorable friend, the member for East Edinburgh [Mr. Goschen], is entirely wrong, for all practical purposes, in what he said as to the mixture of executive governments as far as local affairs are concerned. As far as joint affairs are concerned, it is a different matter; but there is a perfect independence between Austria and Hungary so far as local affairs are concerned. The case there, I should state, was surrounded with difficulties infinitely transcending any before us. But it is not Austria and Hungary alone. It is not too much to say of Austria that that great empire, with the multitude of states of which it is composed, is held together by local autonomy and nothing else, and that the man who should attempt to banish local autonomy from Austria, and to gather together the representatives of her states in Vienna to deal with the local affairs of the provinces, would seal the death-warrant of the empire. Long may she flourish, as having based herself upon so just and so enlightened a principle. The most striking instance in the wide circuit of her empire is Galicia. Galicia is inhabited by Poles. Austria has one of the fragments of that unhappy and dissevered country under her charge. Well, I need not speak of Russia and Poland, while even in Prussia the relations of Prussian Poland are, at this moment, the subject of the most serious difficulty. There are no difficulties between Galicia and Austria. Why? Because Austria has treated Galicia upon the principle of placing trust and confidence in her, and has invested her with full practical power over the management of her own affairs. Now, I do not think that I have thrown out any unfair challenges. I have asked for instances from the other side, in which the granting of Home Rule has been attended with evil consequences, but none has been given—whereas I have given a multitude of instances in support of my proposition, which is that the severance which we propose to make for local purposes between the Irish legislative body and Parliament meeting in these walls, is not a mode of disunion, but is a mode of closer union, and is not a mode of separation, but is a mode preventing separation.

Before I leave this point, I must refer to the case of Canada, because it is so remarkable, and because, notwithstanding the multitude of circumstantial differences between Canada and Great Britain, yet still the resemblances in prin-

ciple are so profound and so significant. My right honorable friend, the member for West Birmingham, said, as I
understood him the other day, that he had been investigat-
ing the case of Canada. I own I thought I knew something
about it, because in the early years of my parliamentary life
I took great interest in it, and some part in the great discussions on the disposal of Canada some fifty years ago. My
reading of the history of Canada sustains my original propositions. My right honorable friend announced to the House
that he had found that the legislative councils in Canada
had been established for the purpose of protecting the minority. Where did he find that? I read not long ago the
very lengthened and detailed debates in Parliament on the
subject of the establishment of those legislative councils,
and from the beginning to the end of those debates, while
the character of the legislative councils was abundantly discussed, there is not a word about their being appointed for
the protection of minorities. But I will not rest the case of
Canada upon that ground. What does the case of Canada
show? It shows two things—first, that between 1830 and
1840 there were most formidable differences between Great
Britain and Canada, and that those differences were completely cured and healed by the establishment of a responsible government with a free executive—that is to say, that
those differences were absolutely cured by the very remedy
which we now propose to apply in the case of Ireland.
But, as I have shown, supremacy was not relinquished, it
remained as was stated in the citation from Lord Russell.
But after that, what happened? The two provinces changed
most fundamentally in their relative importance, and the
stereotyped arrangements of the union of 1840 were found
to be totally inadequate to deal with the altered conditions.

of the provinces among themselves. Recollect that these provinces were united provinces, with one legislature. Discord arose between them. What was the mode adopted of curing that discord? The mode which we now propose of the severance of the legislatures—the establishment of an extended union under which, at this moment, with the multiplied legislatures of those provinces, a substantial and perfect political harmony exists. I can understand, then, the disinclination which honorable gentlemen opposite have to go into history as to these cases, but it will be unfolded more and more as these debates proceed, if the controversy be prolonged—it will more and more appear how strong is the foundation upon which we stand now, and upon which Mr. Grattan stood over eighty-six years ago, when he contended that a union of the legislatures was the way to a moral and a real separation between the two countries.

It has been asked in this debate, Why have we put aside all the other business of Parliament, and why have we thrown the country into all this agitation for the sake of the Irish question? ("Hear, hear!") That cheer is the echo that I wanted. Well, sir, the first reason is this—because in Ireland the primary purposes of government are not attained. What said the honorable member for Newcastle in his eloquent speech? That in a considerable part of Ireland distress was chronic, disaffection was perpetual, and insurrection was smouldering. What is implied by those who speak of the dreadful murder that lately took place in Kerry? And I must quote the Belfast outrage along with it—not as being precisely of the same character, but as a significant proof of the weakness of the tie which binds the people to the law. Sir, it is that you have not got that respect for the law, that sympathy with the law on the part of the people, without which real civilization cannot exist. That is our first reason. I will not go back at this time on the dreadful story of the Union; but that, too, must be unfolded in all its hideous features if this controversy is to be prolonged—that Union of which I ought to say that, without qualifying in the least any epithet I have used, I do not believe that that Union can or ought to be repealed, for it has made marks upon history that cannot be effaced. But I go on to another pious belief which prevails on the other side of the House, or which is often professed in controversies on the Irish question. It is supposed that all the abuses of English power in Ireland relate to a remote period of history, and that from the year 1800 onward, from the time of the Union, there has been a period of steady redress of grievances. Sir, I am sorry to say there has been nothing of the kind. There has been a period when grievances have been redressed under compulsion, as in 1829, when Catholic emancipation was granted to avoid civil war. There have been grievances, mixed up with the most terrible evidence of the general failure of government, as was exhibited by the Devon Commission in the year 1843. On a former night I made a quotation from the report which spoke of the laborer. Now I have a corresponding quotation, which is more important, and which speaks of the cotter. What was the proportion of the population which, more than forty years after the Union, was described by the Devon report as being in a condition worse and more disgraceful than any population in Europe? Mr. O'Connell has estimated it in this House at 5,000,000 out of 7,000,000; and Sir James Graham, in debate with him, declined to admit that it was

5,000,000, but did admit that it was 3,500,000. Well, sir,
in 1816 Parliament passed an act of Irish legislation. What
was the purpose of that act? The act declared that, from
the state of the law in Ireland, the old intertangled usages,
which had replaced in an imperfect manner tribal usages on
which the tenure of land in Ireland was founded—Parliament swept them away, and did everything to expose the
tenant to the action of the landlord, but nothing to relieve
or to deal with, by any amendment of the law, the terrible
distress which was finally disclosed by the Devon Commission. Again, what was the state of Ireland with regard to
freedom? In the year 1820 the sheriff of Dublin and the
other gentry of that county and capital determined to have
a county meeting to make compliments to George IV.—the
trial of Queen Caroline being just over. They held their
county meeting, the people went to the county meeting,
and a counter address was moved, warm in professions of
loyalty, but setting out the grievances of the country, and
condemning the trial and proceedings against the queen.
The sheriff refused to hear it. He put his own motion,
but refused to put the other motion; he left the meeting,
which continued the debate, and he sent in the military to
the meeting, which was broken up by force. That was the
state of Ireland as to freedom of petition and remonstrance
twenty years after the Union. Do you suppose that would
have been the case if Ireland had retained her own Parliament? No, sir.

Other cases I will not dwell upon at this late hour, simply on account of the lateness of the hour. From 1849,
when we passed an act which enabled the landlords of Ireland to sell improvements on their tenants' holdings over
their heads, down to 1880, when a most limited and care-

fully framed bill, the product of Mr. Forster's benevolence, was passed by this House, and rejected by an enormous majority in the House of Lords, thereby precipitating the Land Act of 1881, it is impossible to stand by the legislation of this House as a whole since the Union. I have sometimes heard it said, You have had all kinds of remedial Legislation. The two chief items are the Disestablishment of the Church and the reform of the Land laws. But what did you say of these? Why, you said the change in the land laws was confiscation, and the disestablishment of the Church was sacrilege. You cannot at one and the same time condemn these measures as confiscation and sacrilege, and at the same time quote them as proofs of the justice with which you have acted to Ireland. I must further say that we have proposed this measure because Ireland wants to make her own laws. It is not enough to say that you are prepared to make good laws. You were prepared to make good laws for the colonies. You did make good laws for the colonies, according to the best of your light. The colonists were totally dissatisfied with them. You accepted their claim to make their own laws. Ireland, in our opinion, has a claim not less urgent.

Now, sir, what is before us? What is before us in the event of the rejection of this bill? What alternatives have been proposed? There I must for a moment comment on the fertile imagination of my right honorable friend, the member for West Birmingham. He has proposed alternatives, and plenty of them. My right honorable friend says that a dissolution has no terrors for him. I do not wonder at it. I do not see how a dissolution can have any terrors for him. He has trimmed his vessel and he has touched his rudder in such a masterly way, that in whichever direction the winds of heaven may blow they must fill his sails. Let me illustrate my meaning. I will suppose different cases. Supposing at the election—I mean that an election is a thing like Christmas, it is always coming—suppose that at an election public opinion should be very strong in favor of the bill. My right honorable friend would then be perfectly prepared to meet that public opinion, and tell it—"I declared strongly that I adopted the principle of the bill." On the other hand, if public opinion was very adverse to the bill, my right honorable friend again is in complete armor, because he says—"Yes, I voted against the bill." Supposing, again, public opinion is in favor of a very large plan for Ireland, my right honorable friend is perfectly provided for that case also. The government plan was not large enough for him, and he proposed in his speech on the introduction of the bill that we should have a measure on the basis of federation, which goes beyond this bill. Lastly—and now I have very nearly boxed the compass— supposing that public opinion should take quite a different turn, and, instead of wanting very large measures for Ireland, should demand very small measures for Ireland, still the resources of my honorable friend are not exhausted, because then he is able to point out that the last of his plans was four provincial councils controlled from London. Under other circumstances I should perhaps have been tempted to ask the secret of my right honorable friend's recipe; as it is, I am afraid I am too old to learn it. But I do not wonder that a dissolution has no terrors for him, because he is prepared in such a way and with such a series of expedients to meet all the possible contingencies of the case.

Well, sir, when I come to look at these practical alterna-

tives and provisions, I find that they are visibly creations
of the vivid imagination, born of the hour, and perishing
with the hour, totally and absolutely unavailable for the
solution of a great and difficult problem, the weight of
which and the urgency of which my right honorable friend
himself in other days has seemed to feel. But I should not
say now that our plan has possession of the field without
a rival. Lord Salisbury has given us a rival plan. My
first remark is that Lord Salisbury's policy has not been
disavowed. It is therefore adopted. What is it? (A
laugh.) Another laugh? It has not been disavowed; what
is it? Great complaints are made because it has been called
a policy of coercion, and Lord Salisbury is stated to have
explained in "another place" that he is not favorable to
coercion, but only to legislative provisions for preventing
interference by one man with the liberty of another, and
for insuring the regular execution of the law. And that,
you say, is not coercion? Was that your view six months
ago? What did the Liberal Government propose when they
went out of office? They proposed to enact clauses against
the — (Cries of "No, No," from the Opposition.) (Lord
Randolph Churchill—"They never made any proposal.")
Perhaps not; but it was publicly stated. It was stated by
me in a letter to the right honorable gentleman. (Sir
Michael Hicks-Beach—"In October.") Certainly; but it
was stated in order to correct a rather gross error of the
right honorable gentleman. It was stated as what we had
intended when we were going out of office; unless I am
greatly mistaken, it was publicly stated in this House long
before. However, it is not very important. What were
the proposals that we were about to make, or that we were
supposed to be about to make? Well, a proposal about

"Boycotting"—to prevent one man interfering with the liberty of another; and a proposal about a change of venue to insure the execution of the ordinary law. And how were these proposals viewed? Did not the Tories go to the elections putting upon their placards, "Vote for the Tories, and no Coercion"? (Sir Walter B. Barttelot—"No, no!") I do not say that every Tory did it. The honorable and gallant baronet cries "No." No doubt he did not do it: but he had no Irish voters. (Sir W. B. Barttelot—"If I had I would have done it.") Then it means this—that these proposals which we were about to make were defined as coercion by the Tories at the election, and Lord Salisbury now denies them to be coercion; and it is resented with the loudest manifestations of displeasure when any one on this side of the House states that Lord Salisbury has recommended twenty years of coercion. Lord Salisbury recommended, as he says himself, twenty years of those measures which last year were denounced by the Tories. But what did Lord Salisbury call them himself? What were his own words? His words were—"My alternative policy is that Parliament should enable the government of England to govern Ireland." What is the meaning of those words? Their meaning, in the first instance, is this: The government does not want the aid of Parliament to exercise their executive power; it wants the aid of Parliament for fresh legislation. The demand that the Parliament should enable the government of England to govern Ireland is a demand for fresh legislative power. This fresh legislative power, how are they to use? "Apply that recipe honestly, consistently, and resolutely for twenty years, and at the end of that time you will find Ireland will be fit to accept any gift in the way of local government or repeal of coercion laws that you may wish to give." And yet objections and complaints of misrepresentations teem from that side of the House when any one on this side says that Lord Salisbury recommended coercion, when he himself applies that same term in his own words.

A question was put to me by my honorable friend the member for Bermondsey, in the course of his most instructive speech. My honorable friend had a serious misgiving as to the point of time. Were we right in introducing this measure now? He did not object to the principle; he intimated a doubt as to the moment. I may ask my honorable friend to consider what would have happened had we hesitated as to the duty before us, had we used the constant efforts that would have been necessary to keep the late government in office, and allowed them to persevere in their intentions. On the 26th of January they proposed what we termed a measure of coercion, and I think we were justified in so terming it, because anything attempting to put down a political association can hardly have another name. Can it be denied that that legislation must have been accompanied by legislation against the press, legislation against public meetings, and other legislation without which it would have been totally ineffective? Would it have been better, if a great controversy cannot be avoided —and I am sensible of the evil of this great controversy— I say it is better that parties should be matched in conflict upon a question of giving a great boon to Ireland, rather than—as we should have been if the policy of January 26 had proceeded—that we should have been matched and brought into conflict, and the whole country torn with dispute and discussion upon the policy of a great measure of coercion. That is my first reason. My second reason is this. Let my honoraole friend recollect that this is the earliest moment in our parliamentary history when we have the voice of Ireland authentically expressed in our hearing. Majorities of Home Rulers there may have been upon other occasions; a practical majority of Irish members never has been brought together for such a purpose. Now, first, we can understand her; we are able to learn authentically what she wants and wishes, what she offers and will do; and as we ourselves enter into the strongest moral and honorable obligations by the steps which we have taken in this House, so we have before us practically an Ireland under the representative system, able to give us equally authentic information, able morally to convey to us an assurance, the breach and rupture of which would cover Ireland with disgrace. There is another reason, but not a very important one. It is this—I feel that any attempt to palter with the demands of Ireland so conveyed in forms known to the Constitution, and any rejection of the conciliatory policy might have an effect that none of us could wish in strengthening that party of disorder which is behind the back of the Irish representatives, which skulks in America, which skulks in Ireland, which, I trust, is losing ground and is losing force, and will lose ground and will lose force in proportion as our policy is carried out, and which I cannot altogether dismiss from consideration when I take into view the consequences that might follow upon its rejection. What is the case of Ireland at this moment? Have honorable gentlemen considered that they are coming into conflict with a nation? Can anything stop a nation's demand, except its being proved to be immoderate and unsafe? But here are multitudes, and I believe millions upon millions, out of doors, who feel this demand to be

neither immoderate nor unsafe. In our opinion there is
but one question before us about this demand. It is as to
the time and circumstance of granting it. There is no question in our minds that it will be granted. We wish it to be
granted in the mode prescribed by Mr. Burke. Mr. Burke
said, in his first speech at Bristol—"I was true to my old-
standing invariable principle, that all things which came
from Great Britain should issue as a gift of her bounty and
beneficence rather than as claims recovered against struggling litigants, or at least, if your beneficence obtained no
credit in your concessions, yet that they should appear the
salutary provisions of your wisdom and foresight—not as
things wrung from you with your blood by the cruel grip
of a rigid necessity."

The difference between giving with freedom and dignity
on the one side, with acknowledgment and gratitude on the
other, and giving under compulsion—giving with disgrace,
giving with resentment dogging you at every step of your
path—this difference is, in our eyes, fundamental, and this
is the main reason, not only why we have acted, but why
we have acted now. This, if I understand it, is one of the
golden moments of our history—one of those opportunities
which may come and may go, but which rarely return, or,
if they return, return at long intervals, and under circumstances which no man can forecast. There have been such
golden moments even in the tragic history of Ireland, as
her poet says:

> "One time the harp of Innisfail
> Was tuned to notes of gladness."

And then he goes on to say:

> "But yet did oftener tell a tale
> Of more prevailing sadness."

But there was such a golden moment—it was in 1795—
it was on the mission of Lord Fitzwilliam. At that moment it is historically clear that the Parliament of Grattan
was on the point of solving the Irish problem. The two
great knots of that problem were, in the first place, Roman
Catholic emancipation; and, in the second place, the reform
of Parliament. The cup was at her lips, and she was ready
to drink it, when the hand of England rudely and ruthlessly
dashed it to the ground, in obedience to the wild and
dangerous intimations of an Irish faction—

> "Ex illo fluere ac retro sublapsa referri,
> Spes Danaum."—Verg. Æn. ii. 169.

There has been no great day of hope for Ireland, no
day when you might hope completely and definitely to end
the controversy till now—more than ninety years. The
long periodic time has at last run out, and the star has
again mounted into the heavens. What Ireland was doing
for herself in 1795 we at length have done. The Roman
Catholics have been emancipated—emancipated after a
woful disregard of solemn promises through twenty-nine
years, emancipated slowly, sullenly, not from goodwill, but
from abject terror, with all the fruits and consequences
which will always follow that method of legislation. The
second problem has been also solved, and the representation
of Ireland has been thoroughly reformed; and I am thankful to say that the franchise was given to Ireland on the re-
adjustment of last year with a free heart, with an open
hand, and the gift of that franchise was the last act required to make the success of Ireland in her final effort
absolutely sure. We have given Ireland a voice; we must
all listen for a moment to what she says. We must all

listen, both sides, both parties—I mean as they are divided on this question—divided, I am afraid, by an almost immeasurable gap. We do not undervalue or despise the forces opposed to us. I have described them as the forces of class and its dependants; and that as a general description—as a slight and rude outline of a description—is, I believe, perfectly true. I do not deny that many are against us whom we should have expected to be for us. I do not deny that some whom we see against us have caused us by their conscientious action the bitterest disappointment. You have power, you have wealth, you have rank, you have station, you have organization. What have we? We think that we have the people's heart; we believe and we know we have the promise of the harvest of the future. As to the people's heart, you may dispute it, and dispute it with perfect sincerity. Let that matter make its own proof. As to the harvest of the future, I doubt if you have so much confidence, and I believe that there is in the breast of many a man who means to vote against us to-night a profound misgiving, approaching even to a deep conviction, that the end will be as we foresee, and not as you do—that the ebbing tide is with you, and the flowing tide is with us.

Ireland stands at your bar, expectant, hopeful, almost suppliant. Her words are the words of truth and soberness. She asks a blessed oblivion of the past, and in that oblivion our interest is deeper than even hers. My right honorable friend, the member for East Edinburgh, asks us to-night to abide by the traditions of which we are the heirs. What traditions? By the Irish traditions? Go into the length and breadth of the world, ransack the literature of all countries, find, if you can, a single voice, a single book—find, I would almost say, as much as a single newspaper article, unless the product of the day, in which the conduct of England toward Ireland is anywhere treated except with profound and bitter condemnation. Are these the traditions by which we are exhorted to stand? No; they are a sad exception to the glory of our country. They are a broad and black blot upon the pages of its history; and what we want to do is to stand by the traditions of which we are the heirs in all matters except our relations with Ireland, and to make our relations with Ireland to conform to the other traditions of our country. So we treat our traditions—so we hail the demand of Ireland for what I call a blessed oblivion of the past. She asks also a boon for the future; and that boon for the future, unless we are much mistaken, will be a boon to us in respect of honor, no less than a boon to her in respect of happiness, prosperity, and peace. Such, sir, is her prayer. Think, I beseech you, think well, think wisely, think, not for the moment, but for the years that are to come, before you reject this bill.

FAVRE

JULES CLAUDE GABRIEL FAVRE, a noted French statesman, was born at Lyons, France, March 21, 1809. While a law student in Paris he entered with enthusiasm into the revolution of 1830, and he subsequently came into notice at the Lyons bar as a defender of political prisoners. He was called to the Paris bar in 1846, and in the revolution of 1848 was especially prominent. He strenuously opposed the acts of Louis Napoleon as president, but after the *coup d'état* of December, 1851, he confined his energies for several years entirely to his profession. In 1858, however, his defence of Orsini, the would-be assassin of the Emperor Louis Napoleon, brought him again before the public eye and secured his election to the Corps Législatif as member for Paris. In that body he eloquently opposed the emperor's policy on leading public questions, his speeches on the Mexican expedition making a profound impression. In the closing months of the empire he vehemently opposed the measures which ultimately led to the Franco-Prussian war and was among the few who opposed the declaration of war. After the fall of Sédan, Favre became vice-president of the provisional government and its minister of foreign affairs, subsequently conducting with Bismarck the preliminaries of peace. In 1871 he published his political apology, " Le Gouvernement du 4 Septembre," and soon after withdrew from politics for a time and devoted himself to law and literature. In 1876 he was returned to the Senate for the Department of the Rhône. His death took place at Versailles, January 19, 1880. As an eloquent opposition leader Favre appeared to best advantage, but as a diplomatist he was a signal failure. In 1867 he was elected to the Academy on the death of Victor Cousin, and while a pure Theist at that time he became a Protestant in his later years. His published works include " Rome et la République Française " (1871); " Conférences et Discours Littéraires " (1873); " De la Reforme Judiciare " (1877); " Conférences et Mélanges " (1880); " Discours Parlementaires " (1881); " Plaidoyers Politiques et Judiciaries " (1882).

SPEECH BEFORE THE CORPS LEGISLATIF

DELIVERED APRIL 12, 1860, AFTER THE PEACE OF VILLA FRANCA

GENTLEMEN,—The speakers to whom you listened during yesterday's session have apparently forborne to state definitely the questions raised by the debate now before the Chamber. It appears nevertheless that we are not able to evade them, so forcibly do they bear upon the situation to which France is brought by an undertaking in which her honor, and perhaps also her fate, is involved. We should be lacking in our duty if we did not endeavor to indicate, according to our light, the solutions that the dignity and the interest of the country alike require.

I know that such language may seem over-bold in the face of a constitution which gives us so insignificant a part, reserving meanwhile one so vast for one all-powerful will; of a constitution that does not permit our words to go forth from this place without undergoing the humiliation of revision, and oftentimes the insult of mutilation. Nevertheless, since the opportunity to express an opinion is given, permit me to do it with the utmost frankness.

We have to discover what have been the fruits—what must be the consequences—of the glorious campaign so suddenly ended on the banks of the Mincio by a peace so unexpected.

You have not forgotten it: when a year ago at this time we had to point out the political purpose of this war we did not hesitate to affirm that it was the enfranchisement of Italy.

The official organs of the government maintained silence before you; but the only voice in this country which was and is permitted to make itself heard with authority as well as power made known to the world that we were not deceived in our apprehension of the causes and import of the great event which disquieted all Europe. To drive Austria back behind the Alps and to leave Italy free, such was the programme proposed to France, aroused and in arms, ready to pour out her treasure and her blood.

It must be admitted that this programme, despite its grandeur, was then little understood and not well received. The partisans of Italy were rare and little credited; general opinion judged them severely; it accepted too readily the ac-

cusations of frivolity and of inconsistency lavished upon this
-generous and devoted nation, and it appeared to many minds
that in giving herself to it France would undertake labor
both adventurous and unprofitable. I hasten to add, gentlemen, that the Italians responded nobly to their detractors.
They have shown, as we were reminded yesterday, of what
self-denial patriotism is the source: they have known how to
silence old rivalries that have until now divided them, to control individual ambitions, to calm the passions, to re-establish
order in the midst of the fermentation of popular victory; in
short, to control factions which have always been represented
as ready to rend each other.

This work of pacific assimilation, the real seal of Italian
regeneration, is not only a moral conquest which is an honor
to France, to whose intervention it is due, it is also for our
own greatness, present and to come, a result immense and
fruitful and which enables one to say that it has been an
effort not alone for the success of a generous idea, but for
the defence and consolidation of a great national interest.

Turn to the annals of history and you will see that since
the fall of the Roman empire two rival interests have never
ceased disputing the supremacy of Europe; this excessive hostility is that of two races personified, the one by Germany,
the other by France. Italy has been their battlefield and
their stake, as if God had reserved for her this chastisement
as expiation for that servitude under whose weight she had
during eight centuries crushed the entire world.

Then, in the Middle Ages, France was powerful enough
to impose her rule upon the peninsula, to make of it a high-
way to the north, and it was toward this end that the efforts
of the most glorious representatives of our monarchy tended;
to-day if the interests are the same the means have changed;

that which is the best guarantee of the greatness and security of France is the independence and the unity of Italy.

If I had not heard yesterday expressions of distrust that astonished me I should not hesitate to characterize as pusillanimous a policy that is affrighted at beholding in that beautiful country a free and powerful nation. As for myself, when I cast my eyes over the map of Europe and see that vast triangle of which the centre is the Mediterranean, of which the sides are Italy and Spain, and of which France is the apex, with their twelve hundred leagues of coast, commanding from the ocean to the Adriatic, it appears that these three countries, united not by bonds of sovereignty but by an intelligent federation, developing by their unity the infinite riches of their wonderful soil, combining the treasures of their genius—artistic, industrial, military, scientific, and naval—are destined not to bring all Europe under their yoke, but to cause the shining upon her of an era of civilization and of prosperity, whose brilliancy one may not even imagine.

France in marching to the deliverance of Italy did not seek the realization of a sentimental Utopia; she carried out a wise policy; she remained faithful to the traditions of her past and to the law of her future. It was this that sober minds perceived clearly in the midst of these great events. As to the nation at large, it comprehended that the end being indicated honor made it a law to attain it. To drive Austria back behind the Alps, to make of Italy a nation free and independent, such was the promise made in the face of the world! You know, gentlemen, how these splendid hopes have been shattered!

Thanks to the impetuous courage of our legions and to the bravery of the Piedmontese troops Austria has not been able to stand upon a single battlefield. Utterly routed by three great victories and a series of brilliant engagements, she retired precipitately within her fortresses; but with the army of debarkation carried by our fleet in the rear, on the right the Tuscan reinforcements burning with the desire to show themselves worthy of their glorious competitors, on the left the gallant monarch of Piedmont, and in the centre the great mass of our forces, she was not able to resist. Without doubt she might have allowed herself to be besieged behind her walls, but that was a measure fraught with peril in the face of an army inflamed by success, in the midst of a population thoroughly aroused and waiting only a favorable hour to rise in revolt.

With a final effort the war was gloriously finished and the word of France was maintained. I have no hesitation in affirming that no one then doubted of success; men the most opposed to the principle of war understood that the honor of France was engaged until the enterprise undertaken should be accomplished; that it was impossible to withdraw (the word does not belong to our nation), even to delay; and that the soldiers of our army gone down into Italy with the banner of liberators should not sheathe their swords until that banner should float in all parts of her territory occupied by Austria.

Nevertheless it was of no avail! In the same way that the decree for war had depended upon the will of one man, it depended also upon the same will to enchain victory and to leave unaccomplished the work with which the dignity and interest of the country were associated.

I do not say this, gentlemen, to criticise what is beyond my right, but I consider it a duty to allow no occasion to escape without pointing out the fate which has befallen my country and to make her understand that she has placed herself in the hands of a master.

I say it boldly, the peace of Villa Franca gives the lie to the proclamation of the 3d of May! Therefore Italy has not consented to the re-establishment of Austria's power that it has been determined to impose upon her. Despite the injunctions of our diplomacy, despite the menaces of our official communications, she has marched with a firm and resolute step toward that great work of unity to which our government no longer accords its aid; she has placed her independence under the protection of the military loyalty of Victor Emmanuel, and also to-day under the safeguard of French honor, and to-day one can consider this important transformation as an accomplished fact.

Italy free from the Alps to the Adriatic—there you have the promise! It was not enough to make it at the beginning of the war at the head of the troops full of warlike enthusiasm, but later after victory. On the 8th of June, 1859, a proclamation was made to the Italians at Milan which remains famous. It said, "Providence sometimes vouchsafes to nations, as to individuals, the opportunity for sudden development, but only on condition that they know how to profit by it. Take advantage then of the chance which presents itself to you; your hopes for independence so long expressed, so often shattered, will be realized if you show yourselves worthy. League yourselves together with but one end in view—the enfranchisement of your country. Organize yourselves as a military force! Be to-day but soldiers; to-morrow you shall be the citizens of a great and free country."

The Italians, gentlemen, believed in these words. The noble city of Venice, so grand by reason of her traditions and her misfortunes, demonstrated by her heroic defence in

1848, saw on the horizon the ensigns of our ships, and even then saluted with enthusiasm the arrival of the cohorts of liberators. Suddenly the French flags disappeared and the glorious captive has fallen back yet more heavily under the weight of her chains! Listen to her groans, open your hearts to the recital of her woes, count the number of fugitives heartbroken for their country in its death-agony, and you will have no need to ask yourself if France can deny her responsibility or intrench herself in indifference.

Just here, gentlemen, is a dilemma from which we cannot escape: if the war of 1859 were legitimate it was only because Austrian domination was not; if the rule of Austria in Italy were legitimate then the war entered into by France was impious and contrary to the law of nations; if Austria wrought deeds of violence in Italy we should drive her out:— she is still there.

With the question put in this way, what do you make of it? A condition unsettled and consequently intolerable, an incertitude that paralyzes everything. This uncertainty must cease unless the honor of France is to be compromised,—since France cannot rest under the imputation of non-performance of her promises.

There are moreover, gentlemen, two logical sequences from which it is impossible to escape. That which is accomplished in northern Italy as a necessary consequence is repeated in its centre. These are the reasons which have dictated the policy of France toward the Holy See.

I feel the more authorized, gentlemen, to explain with frankness my position upon this Roman question brought forward yesterday, because the facts appear to me to have especial significance. It suffices only to inquire into them to comprehend our real situation! There has been much comment upon the fluctuations in policy of the French government toward the Holy See; I believe myself that these variations are only seeming.

I do not deny that since the peace of Villa Franca, the cabinet of the Tuileries may not have made or appeared to make efforts to re-establish the Romans under the paternal yoke of the papacy, as an honorable speaker has yesterday said; but all the world will agree with me that it has been most easily resigned to the non-success of its negotiations, and that it has been but slightly surprised thereat. And just here I go straight to the truth! I pass over all the ambiguities, all the subterfuges, all the ruses of diplomacy and I arrive at this conclusion: The cabinet of the Tuileries has pronounced the condemnation of the temporal power of the papacy! In order to prove it it is not necessary to go back in memory to 1831 and to talk of the blood of a Bonaparte shed by pontifical hands! I prefer to confine myself to general facts whose tendency can escape no one.

To the great surprise of the entire world there appeared at the end of the year 1859 a pamphlet,—whose author I do not seek,—which was widely circulated, and for which the government allowed itself to be considered responsible. It is there then that its opinion is to be sought. Now that opinion is not doubtful, and I admired yesterday the chivalrous confidence of those who still assert that the government desires to maintain the temporal power of the papacy. Why should we delude ourselves? By a combination of divers circumstances, by a series of causes dating far back, the temporal power of the Pope is seriously menaced under the conditions in which it is exercised to-day. The Papal throne is to-day established upon a volcano, and the pontiff who is charged by God with the maintenance of order upon the earth is himself constantly threatened by a revolution. He, the representative of the highest moral authority upon earth, maintains it only under the protection of foreign armies. These military occupations protect only to compromise him; they excite against him all the susceptibilities of the national sentiment, they demonstrate that he cannot confide himself to the love and respect of his people.

The policy of the government is herein so clearly explained that I have nothing to add to it. Considering its origin it would be easy for me to show by history that the temporal power is a fact analogous to numberless others of the same nature, that the establishment of feudalism explains. Entirely separate from dogma it in no way merits the reverence lavished upon it by those who believe it necessary to the exercise of spiritual authority.

Established during the twelfth century it has filled history by turns with the brilliancy of its services, the story of its intrigues, and the scandal of its crimes. Always too feeble to defend itself, constantly reduced to depend upon aid from without, it has also become a permanent cause of the divisions, the agitations, and the wars of Italy. Here you have the proof written upon every page of history; a fact of great value to recall in this discussion is that the temporal power of the Pope claimed as a guarantee of his spiritual independence has been on the contrary a cause of long servitude. Besides, what does it avail to talk of the past? Does not the spectacle that we have under our eyes suffice? Is it not shown that the temporal authority of the Holy See subsists only on condition that it is supported, sometimes by Austria, sometimes by France, and those who exert it are so thoroughly conscious of their unpopularity that abandoned to themselves they do not even wait for an uprising, but hasten to screen themselves by flight as soon as foreign occupation ceases to protect their tyranny.

Why this ceaseless talk of temporal independence which is but a fiction? And if it were permitted me to further explain my idea I could prove without difficulty that the Church herself, severed from the cares and perils of her temporary power, would be the greater in the eyes of the people, and her authority increased as it was purified.

But these great questions are not within our province. The domain within which I must restrict myself is that of policy, and there inevitable consequences obtrude themselves.

Well, then, if it be true that Italian unity is for France a question alike of interest and honor; if at the same time the temporal power is a permanent obstacle to this union, this power must be abolished. I do not say that it is necessary to employ the force of our arms, but that at least they shall not assist in its maintenance. It is time to put an end to this double game that is being played upon the banks of the Po and upon the Tiber.

Emancipators in the north, we cannot become subservient in the south; if it is objected that our soldiers protect the Holy Father at Rome, I respond that protection without obedience is either ridiculous, or it is oppression in disguise; if we are the defenders of the temporal power let us march upon Bologna already in insurrection, let us invade Romagna, establish the power of the Pope upon its ruins, and stifle liberty in Italian blood, that is the complement of the expedition to Rome. But if we recognize the rights of the people of Bologna by the same token we proclaim that of the Romans, and the presence of our troops that keep them in subjection is an insult to our policy.

Gentlemen, it is with genuine regret that I have heard extolled in this place the action of a French general who has placed his sword at the service of the pontifical power. I have no fear in saying that this decision will find little response from without, and that most of the old friends of this officer will experience as much sorrow as surprise at his extraordinary intention, but that which crowned the general astonishment and which caused me the utmost surprise was the affirmative sign by which the President of the Council of State made known yesterday that an authorization apparently asked for had been favorably received by the French government, and that it was permitted this officer to serve in the Pontifical army without losing his authority; therefore the statement is official; but there are moral effects greater than all administrative acts. Either the commission of this officer is absurd or it obliges him to take command of that army of mercenaries, Swiss, Germans, and Croatians, who sell their blood for the Papacy, to march at their head for the conquest of Romagna and to gather from the smoking walls of Bologna the bloody laurels of Colonel Schmidt. But on that day he will have facing him the allies of France, and perhaps behind the Piedmontese lines he will find the valiant legions whom he has so often led to victory, and there he will be reduced to the alternative of resigning his command or of drawing his sword against his country.

As for myself, I demand of the government that it cease those many equivocations unworthy of a nation like France, and that it put an end to the misunderstandings which are the direct consequence of a policy of liars and turncoats unacceptable to the country.

[Special translation by Mary Emerson Adams.]